# THE MASS MEDIA AND LATINO POLITICS

This timely volume illuminates the current body of research at the convergence of media, US Latinos, and politics. Building on historical assessments and contemporary social science-based research, the chapters herein document the evolution of political communication in the United States in response to the influence of Latino constituencies.

Demonstrating that studying the mass media can enhance the understanding of Latino politics in the United States, volume editor Federico A. Subervi-Vélez and his contributors

- study theoretical foundations, establishing what is currently known and how study of the media promotes understanding of Latino politics;
- assess how Spanish-language media have covered elections, and how English-language media have covered Latino-related issues and candidates during elections;
- examine campaign strategies, political advertisements, and surveys to determine how the main political parties have used the media to gain Latino votes;
- provide answers to the question regarding whether evidence exists that exposure to the media influences Latino politics.

The volume concludes with a discussion of the steps that should be taken in the next generation of political communication research related to Latinos, and proposes an agenda with theoretical and methodological guidelines pertaining to content analyses, studies of campaign strategies and advertisements, and survey research.

With relevance to political communication, political science, and Latino studies, *The Mass Media and Latino Politics* establishes the benchmark for the current state of scholarship in this arena. It is required reading for scholars and researchers in these areas, and will be useful as a text for advanced courses on politics, media, and minority populations in the United States.

**Federico A. Subervi-Vélez** is a media researcher and consultant specializing in Latino issues. He is a professor at the School of Journalism and Mass Communication, Texas State University–San Marcos, where he directs the Center for the Study of Latino Media and Markets, and the Latinos and Media Project (LaMP). His previous academic positions include UC Santa Barbara and the University of Texas at Austin.

## LEA's COMMUNICATION SERIES
Edited by Jennings Bryant and Dolf Zillmann

Selected titles include:

MAKING MEDIA CONTENT
The influence of constituency groups on mass media
*J. A. Fortunato*

MASS MEDIA, AN AGING POPULATION,
AND THE BABY BOOMERS
*J. H. Lipschultz and M. L. Hilt*

HANDBOOK OF POLITICAL COMMUNICATION
RESEARCH
*L. L. Kaid*

LAW FOR ADVERTISING, BROADCASTING,
JOURNALISM,
AND PUBLIC RELATIONS
A comprehensive primer for students and practitioners
*M. G. Parkinson and L. M. Parkinson*

THE DYNAMICS OF PERSUASION (Third Edition)
*R. M. Perloff*

POLITICAL COMMUNICATION
Politics, Press, and Public in America
*R. M. Perloff*

DEFENDING THE FIRST
Commentary on First Amendment issues and cases
*J. Russomanno*

# THE MASS MEDIA AND LATINO POLITICS

Studies of U.S. Media Content, Campaign Strategies and Survey Research: 1984–2004

*Edited by*
*Federico A. Subervi-Vélez*

Routledge
Taylor & Francis Group

NEW YORK AND LONDON

First published 2008
by Routledge
270 Madison Ave, New York, NY 10016

Simultaneously published in the UK
by Routledge
2 Park Square, Milton Park, Abingdon, Oxon OX14 4RN

*Routledge is an imprint of the Taylor & Francis Group, an informa business*

Typeset in Goudy by
RefineCatch Limited, Bungay, Suffolk
Printed and bound in the United States of America on acid-free paper by
Edwards Brothers, Inc.

*Library of Congress Cataloging in Publication Data*
The mass media and Latino politics: studies of U.S. media content,
campaign strategies, and survey research: 1984–2004 / [edited by
Federico A. Subervi-Vélez].
    p. cm. – (LEA's communication series)
Includes bibliographical references and index.
ISBN 978–0–805–85704–7 – ISBN 978–0–805–85705–4 – ISBN 978–1–
4106–1870–2 1. Hispanic Americans—Politics and government.
2. Hispanic Americans and mass media. 3. Hispanic Americans—
Statistics. 4. Mass media—Political aspects—United States. 5. Political
participation—United States. 6. Political campaigns—United States.
7. Communication in politics—United States. 8. United States—
Ethnic relations—Political aspects. 9. United States—Politics and
government—2001– I. Subervi-Vélez, Federico A.
    E184.S75M386 2008
    323.11968073—dc22
    2007020166

ISBN10: 0–805–85704–4 (hbk)
ISBN10: 0–805–85705–2 (pbk)
ISBN10: 1–4106–1870–6 (ebk)

ISBN13: 978–0–805–85704–7 (hbk)
ISBN13: 978–0–805–85705–4 (pbk)
ISBN13: 978–1–4106–1870–2 (ebk)

DEDICATED TO THE MEMORY OF
MY MOTHER,
SANTA VÉLEZ

# CONTENTS

# CONTENTS

# FOREWORD

Politicians, media commentators and community activists have been trumpeting the growing Latino population wave and its potential impact on politics since at least the "Decade of the Hispanic" predictions of the late 1970s. But, despite all the hype and attendant publicity, the growth of Latinos and their media in the United States over the past three decades has been portrayed more as a political possibility than something to be systematically studied and analyzed by dispassionate scholars grounded in both political science and communication.

While the numerical growth of Latinos in the United States and the media that address them are undeniable realities and have been key factors in some political campaigns, too little attention has been paid beyond these individual campaigns to examining the interrelationship between Latino media and Latino political awareness, attitudes and action. Scholars and political professionals recognize that the increase in the number of Latinos and their media means that political times are changing and they understand something about how they are changing. But, too often they have had relatively little evidence and analysis beyond case studies of specific campaigns to build a more comprehensive understanding of the depth of these changes and their impact on both politics and the media.

Fortunately, for those of us interested in the growing importance of Latinos and their media on politics and other aspects of U.S. society, the chapters in this volume by political scientists and communication researchers offer both scholarly evidence and insightful analyses of the roles members of this ethnic group and the media directed toward them have played, are playing and will continue to play in influencing the U.S. electoral process.

This book also comes at a time when the pervasiveness of media in American society is both at an all time high and so is its diversity. More people are spending more time with media and they are spending it with an increasingly complex set of different media technologies, focused on different content and often in different languages. U.S. media continue to move steadily from a dominance of mass media outlets aimed at attracting a broad cross section of the potential audience (such as prime time network television) to class media outlets targeted to specific audience segments (such as most magazines, radio stations and cable television channels) and continue to grow in both numbers and influence. These changes in media strategies and behavior come at a time when both the Latino media and the audiences they reach are rapidly growing and are projected to continue growing for the foreseeable future.

The chapters in this book describe and analyze the critical role of these media in socializing and mobilizing political opinion and action in a growing set of communities that contain many newcomers to the United States and its political system. In these studies the authors go far beyond cursory examinations of obvious campaign strategies that have been part of some political outreach since the 1970s: playing ethnic music, using token Spanish phrases at press conferences, and buying advertising on Spanish-language media that have typified political campaigns. Instead the authors take a more systematic approach in examining the ways in which political campaign strategies, core messages and targeted campaigns have been shaped by the growing political power of Latinos and the influence of the media that reach them, especially in key battleground states during national elections. This multidimensional approach in examining campaigns across several decades represents a significant contribution to the body of knowledge and analysis that is available to shape our understanding of the influence of media on the political attitudes and behaviors of Latinos in the United States.

Another important contribution of this volume is the multidisciplinary background of the authors of the studies presented. In the past, scholars looking at this phenomenon have largely been true to their disciplines. Political scientists have generally treated targeted media outreach campaigns as a subdivision of the larger political strategic planning. By the same token, communication scholars have examined political campaigns as a subset of a larger communication media process. This book brings both together in chapters by insightful scholars from both fields that incorporate the appropriate theoretical foundations and research methods of their respective fields and other disciplines. As a result, readers of this book will gain a comprehensive appreciation of the importance of the issues presented and discussed in the chapters and conclusion.

The logical order of the book begins with opening chapters establishing the theoretical foundations for the book and examining some of the knowledge that has already been established regarding the influence of newspapers and other media on Latino political behavior. Subsequent chapters examine English and Spanish-language media coverage in specific elections over two decades beginning in 1984. The set of chapters then examines the lessons learned in these campaigns and analyzes how they have been, or have not been, applied in campaign communication strategies dating back as far as the 1950s, using studies of election campaigns over those years.

All of this is tied together in a final chapter that summarizes the studies and their key conclusions, questions some commonly-held assertions and assumptions about the political activity of Latinos and their media, and makes recommendations for the future, including future research in this area of growing importance. The editor helps set the stage for future studies by warning against drawing broad conclusions about all Latino media from individual studies and by citing differences in coverage strategies by different types of media and owners.

A volume on such a complex topic of importance deserves a deep and thoughtful reading. Those who take Latino political campaigning and communicating seriously will do themselves a service by setting aside enough time to read and comprehend the meaning of what the book contains, preferably in a quiet setting next to a warm and illuminating fire that can nurture further thought and understanding.

Félix F. Gutiérrez
University of Southern California

# ACKNOWLEDGMENTS

During the many years dedicated to compile, analyze and report the data and chapters presented in this book, numerous people from Puerto Rico to New York and California, and from Illinois to Florida and Texas have helped in ways that cannot be fully acknowledged here. A first word of appreciation goes to Dr. Diana Vélez (not related to my family heritage), who in 1987 was a program officer at the Tinker Foundation. Her belief in my research proposal and guidance were instrumental in obtaining $73,000 from that foundation to launch the national studies on Latino political communication. In the same year, Dr. William (Bill) Díaz, who at the time was a program officer at the Ford Foundation, also believed in my quest and helped secure $35,000 from his foundation.

Other very outstanding supporters of my academic pursuits dating back to my years as a doctoral student at the University of Wisconsin have been Drs. Steve Chaffee, Félix Gutiérrez, Jorge Schement, Ilya Adler, Gonzalo Soruco, Klaus Schönbach, and Michael Salwen. All served at some point of my life as guiding lights and were among the first scholars to value my ventures into Latinos and media issues, and more specifically into political communication. Diana, Bill, Steve, Félix, Jorge, Ilya, Gonzalo, Klaus, and Michael: I agree with all of you now; indeed, I should have studied and written about only a couple of newspapers in one or two cities during one election period instead of so many media in five cities over a long period of time. Had I done that, years ago I would have finished a book on my own, certainly with fewer pages and chapters. Delayed as it was, the purpose for which I started this line of research has now been met: to provide, with the collaboration of many other scholars, a multifaceted analysis of the role of the mass media in the dynamics of Latino politics in the United States.

The Ford Foundation's Fellowship Program, administered by the National Research Council, is another agency that merits my sincerest appreciation: first, because in 1988 it awarded me a postdoctoral fellowship that allowed me the freedom from teaching duties and thus be able to travel numerous times across the country to engage in the first round of research related to this project; second, because that postdoctorate fellowship, and all the benefits stemming from being a Ford Fellow since then, have been invaluable for my professional and personal growth. Thank you kindly, Ford Fellows and administrative staff at the Fellowship Office of the National Research Council, for all you do for us.

My appreciation is also extended to colleagues and staff from three universities and two research programs. At the University of California at Santa Barbara, where I started my academic career as an assistant professor (1982–1989), my most earnest supporter and mentor was Dr. Juan-Vicente Palerm, then serving as director of the Center for Chicano Research. Funds from the Center, and from the UCSB Academic Senate, contributed to my being able to work on the initial parts of the research presented in these pages.

My affiliation with the University of Texas at Austin started in 1988–1989 when I was based there for my Ford Foundation postdoctoral research. During that year, I was mentored by Dr. Rudy de la Garza, who, in spite of his skepticism of the role of the mass media in Latino politics, was kind enough to connect me to his national network of colleagues and research on Latino scholarship. Then, as a faculty member (1989–2002), I enjoyed the blessing of the collegiality and friendship of Drs. John Downing, Emile McAnany, Charles Ramírez-Berg, and Dean Robert Jeffrey, who thoroughly validated my line of work, as did Drs. Mercedes de Uriarte, Neal Burns, Horace Newcomb, Tom Schatz, and many other faculty staff and friends from all across campus. Special funds from the University of Texas, the University of Texas Co-op, and especially the Teresa Long Institute of Latin American Studies, allowed me to enhance parts of the work related to this book and to venture into other creative research activities.

While at UT-Austin, I also received a Goldsmith Research Award from the Joan Shorenstein Barone Center for the Study of Press, Politics and Public Policy at Harvard University (1992), and was selected as Senior Fellow of the Smithsonian Institution's Senior-Junior Program of the National Museum of American History (1996). I appreciate each of those funding opportunities, which allowed me to delve deeper into my research about Latinos, media and politics.

Now, at Texas State University (since 2005), I currently owe a major debt of gratitude to Drs. Bruce Smith, Laurie Fluker, and Dean Richard Cheatham for welcoming me to join their outstanding team of colleagues, students, and staff, and whose support made it possible to conclude this volume and start new academic ventures about Latinos and media issues, while reaching out to more Latino students and others interested in this subject matter.

In addition to all the people recognized already, there are various others who deserve being acknowledged. My greatest appreciation related to my years as a professor goes to the dozens of students (many of whom already earned their doctorates) who enriched my teaching and research on Latino and other diversity issues. Among them are Laura Barbarena, Dr. Mary Caudle Beltrán, Loreto Caro, Dr. Susan Coulsant, Michael Coyle, Oscar de la Torres, Dr. María Denney, Dr. Vanessa Fonseca, Belinda García, Sara Harding, Dr. Raquel López-Godoy, Anthony Ozuna, Dr. Henry Puente, Susana Quintero, Dr. Diana Ríos, Dr. Viviana Rojas, Maryanne Schiffman, Luciana Tenaure, Dr. Raúl Tovares, Cristina Villareal, Dr. Joseph Villescas, Dr. Elizabeth Waiters; and contributors to this book, Marc Brindel, Dr. Stacey Connaughton, Dr. Patti Constantakis-Valdés, Renée Espinoza, María Flores, Amy Langenkamp, Dr. José Carlos Lozano, Dr. Victor Menayang, Dr. Juandalynn Taylor, and Dr. Kenton Wilkinson. I am truly proud of your own achievements, and certainly value immensely how all of you were so instrumental to helping me forge ahead with mine. To the co-authors in this book, and to all other authors in this volume, I sincerely appreciate your patience in waiting for your manuscripts to become published chapters.

Dr. Stacey Connaughton, moreover, deserves an additional paragraph of her own. As student she was stellar, especially when as research assistant she ventured into topics that enhanced this field exponentially. Most recently, during the last stretch of this project, she not only became a co-author, but also helped edit parts of the book. Your faith in and validation of this work mean so much more than what I can summarize in these few lines.

Closely tied to getting this book done, there are other very special people to whom I'm greatly indebted. Linda Bathgate (senior editor, Communications, Lawrence Erlbaum Associates, Inc.) believed in the potential value of this book and remained patiently supportive from the start until its conclusion. To you and the blind reviewers of the prospectus and chapters of this book, thank you for the validation and trust. I must also thank Susan McLelland and former students Kevin Hodges and Victor Jaramillo who, during the last few years, read and helped improve sections of the manuscripts and/or the bibliography.

On the periphery of my academic routines, but invaluable nonetheless, I extend my gratitude to Galia Sefchovich: your personal life coaching was a career saver and spiritual anchor during my transition years (2003–2005) between doing consulting work and returning to academia. Thanks also to the staff and friends at Texas Rowing Center: being able to practice this sport was more than just a physical exercise—it reconnected me to the spirit of nature so abundant in Austin.

Finally, as is usually the case in acknowledgments, there is a central and special place in the heart that is saved for family and friends who were always there to serve as cheerleaders and sounding-boards for the trials and tribulations related to academic and personal pursuits. Dear friends:

you are too many to list individually but I remember and thank all of you. A similar but infinitely more heartfelt appreciation goes to my extended family. But in this category of acknowledgments, the prizes go to my wife, Julia, and my daughter, Jalima (and since 2003 son-in-law, Mark Kassing), because *you've constantly provided your unconditional love and moral support*, even at times when I've been physically away from you because of my travels or to focus on the writing of this and other manuscripts. *¡Muchísimas gracias a todos!*

Federico A. Subervi-Vélez
Austin, Texas

# PREFACE

As this book reaches the hands of scholars, students, politicians and political communication strategists interested in learning something from the first book to bring together the study of Latinos, media, *and* politics, the 2008 presidential election campaign will be in full swing. Undoubtedly, as that campaign rumbles across the land, Latinos will be the center of attention during part or all of that process; perhaps more in some battlegrounds than in others. It will be interesting to observe if the patterns of media coverage, outreach strategies, and media influence discussed in this book remain the same or alter dramatically—for better or for worse—on the national scene.

The contributors to this book hope that whatever Latino-oriented political communication takes place in years to come will garner more attention and receive increased systematic analysis in both presidential campaigns and state and local elections, especially in regions where Latinos are a larger part of the population.

With that objective in mind, we are confident that the chapters that follow provide both a solid foundation for understanding the past and valuable guidance on a variety of topics, questions, and issues to be explored today and in the future. One of the strengths of what we offer in these pages is the interdisciplinary approach to this topic. Another is the variety of research methods and theoretical perspectives used to address the issues at hand. And while limitations or shortcomings in this text are certain to be noted by the more critical readers, the feedback that is generated should inspire improved studies about the mass media and Latino politics. We hope this book will be an important first step in ongoing and collaborative efforts to further develop scholarship and analysis in this important field.

We look forward to feedback so that we too can improve our research as we continue to forge ahead in the front lines of additional studies in this field. To this end, data are already being collected on the 2008 election period. The Resources and Research section of the Latinos and Media Project website (www.latinosandmedia.org) will have occasional updates listing those projects and data, and faculty and students involved in Latino communication research activities. Thus, the LaMP site is open to receive and share additional information and documents related to Latinos, media and politics received from various sources. And, for historical research, the site will also post documents we've gathered over the years but could not use for this book. This includes, for example, copies of Latino-oriented political TV, radio, and print advertisements, documents related to the Democratic and the Republican Parties' old internal Latino outreach strategies, and term papers and unpublished manuscripts from students' research projects.

In sum, the authors and the editor of this book welcome new opportunities to guide and/or collaborate in the research that contributes to enhance the knowledge about, and actual political participation of, Latinos in the United States. We trust that, in doing so, we will all be enhancing the democratic processes of this country to include a wider range of participants at all levels: politicians, voters and the media.

Federico A. Subervi-Vélez
Austin, Texas
January 23, 2007

# ABOUT THE CONTRIBUTORS

**Laurien Alexandre**, Ph.D., (lalexandre@antioch.edu) is vice chancellor of academic affairs for Antioch University. She also holds an appointment as director and professor of Antioch's Ph.D. in Leadership and Change program. Since the early 1980s, Laurien has been teaching and writing about mass media and foreign policy and, most recently, about media and Latinos. She has co-authored with her husband, Henrik Rehbinder, a number of articles about Latinos and the national media including a study of differences in local TV news in several major Latino markets in the United States, as well as an analysis of election news coverage.

**Marc Brindel**. Upon completing his M.A. degree at the University of Texas at Austin, he pursued various media and teaching jobs in Mexico and the United States, including a period of collaboration with Radio Bilingüe in California.

**Stacey L. Connaughton**, Ph.D., (sconnaug@purdue.edu) is an assistant professor in the Department of Communication at Purdue University. Her research interests include identification and leadership in geographically distributed contexts, particularly as these issues relate to virtual organizations and political parties. Her published work has appeared in the *Journal of Communication*, *Management Communication Quarterly*, *Communication Studies*, *Communication Yearbook*, and *The Howard Journal of Communications*. She is the author of *Inviting Latino Voters: Party Messages and Latino Party Identification* (2005, Routledge).

**Patricia Constantakis-Valdés**, Ph.D. After completing her doctoral studies at the University of Texas at Austin and spending a year as a University of California President's postdoctoral scholar at UC–Santa Cruz, she became a principal partner in Academic Systems, where she developed award-winning educational software programs for traditionally under-represented students in higher education. Continuing her endeavors in education/edutainment, she is currently executive producer at The b EQUAL Company, developing interactive titles for children and adults alike.

**Louis DeSipio**, Ph.D., (ldesipio@uci.edu) is an associate professor in the University of California, Irvine (UCI) Departments of Political Science and Chicano/Latino Studies. He is the author of *Counting on the Latino Vote: Latinos as a New Electorate* (1996, University Press of Virginia), the co-author with Rodolfo O. de la Garza of *Making Americans/Remaking America: Immigration and Immigrant Policy* (1998, Westview Press), and the author and editor of a seven-volume series on Latino political values, attitudes, and behaviors. The most recent volume in this series is *Muted Voices: Latinos and the 2000 Elections* (2005, Rowman and Littlefield). DeSipio serves as Chair of UCI's Department of Chicano/Latino Studies.

**Renée Espinoza** obtained her B.A. degree in Intercultural/Organizational Communication from Arizona State University, and went on to receive her M.A. from the University of Texas at Austin in Speech Communication/Rhetoric. While at UT–Austin, Ms. Espinoza focused her research on Latina representations in general market and Latino-oriented magazines. After working several years for various magazines, Ms. Espinoza now enjoys contributing as a freelance writer to local and national Latino-oriented magazines. Currently Ms. Espinoza is a real estate broker living in Phoenix, Arizona.

**María Flores-Gutiérrez** (mariaf@stedwards.edu) is an adjunct professor at St. Edward's University and a McNair faculty mentor/research director. Her areas of concentration are media content and audience research. Within those areas, Flores specializes in political communication and international/intercultural communication. Currently, she is team member of the "Mexico 2006 Panel Study," which is an extensive effort from distinguished Mexican and American professors. Flores and Dr. Maxwell McCombs are conducting research on the Mexican and Hispanic media by examining how they covered that country's most recent presidential election process. Her dissertation examined the agenda-setting process in the 2006 Mexican election.

**Erika Franklin Fowler**, Ph.D., (erikaff@umich.edu) is a fellow in the Robert Wood Johnson Scholars in Health Policy Research Program at the University of Michigan and an assistant professor of government at Wesleyan University. A recent graduate of the University of Wisconsin–Madison, Fowler served for five years as the research director of the University of Wisconsin NewsLab (www.polisci.wisc.edu/uwnewslab). Her dissertation examines the content and effectiveness of local television news coverage of elections and her work relating to communication and local television newscasts has appeared in law, policy, and medical journals. Fowler's primary research interests also include political behavior, public opinion, and research methodology.

**Matthew Hale**, Ph.D., (halematt@shu.edu) is an assistant professor in the Center for Public Service at Seton Hall University. In addition to his academic work on local television and elections, Hale has examined how the media cover nonprofits and philanthropies and has written extensively on the adoption and use of web pages by municipalities and neighborhood organizations. His work has appeared in *Nonprofit and Voluntary Sector Quarterly, Political Communication, Administration and Society,* as well as in several book chapters.

**James R. Henson**, Ph.D., (jhenson@mail.la.utexas.edu) is a lecturer in the Department of Government of the University of Texas at Austin. He coordinates the department's internship program and directs its Texas Politics Project. He is also assistant director of the University of Texas College of Liberal Arts Instructional Technology Services. Dr. Henson's interests include politics in Texas, the impact of the internet on politics, and the educational use of digital media.

**Amy G. Langenkamp** (amygill@prc.utexas.edu) is a postdoctoral fellow in the Department of Sociology and Population Research Center at the University of Texas at Austin. Her research interests are in the areas of education, race/ethnicity, and organizational stratification. Her current research uses school transitions as a way to understand paths of educational opportunity and examines the consequences of change on students' academic performance and integration into American high schools (www.prc.utexas.edu/ahaa/profiles/langenkamp.htm). She is also currently in the field with a project exploring the community role in access to post-secondary education for under-represented groups. Prior to graduate work, she was an elementary school bilingual educator.

**Katie Lever** (klever@rci.rutgers.edu) is a Ph.D. candidate at Rutgers University in the School of Communication, Information and Library Science, where she is also an instructor. She has taught classes on interpersonal communication, mediated communication theory and organizational communication theory. Her research interests include the social implications of new technologies, as well as the process of identification in mediated and organizational settings.

**José Carlos Lozano**, Ph.D., (jclozano@itesm.mx) is the director of the Center for Communication and Information Research at the Tecnológico de Monterrey, at Monterrey, Mexico. He is the author of books and journal articles in the areas of mass and international communication, including *Teoria e Investigacion de la Comunicación de*

*Masas* (2000, Addison Wesley Longman), a textbook widely used in Latin American communication schools. Currently, he holds the Audiovisual Media and Globalization in North America Chair at the Tecnológico de Monterrey.

**Maxwell McCombs**, Ph.D., holds the Jesse H. Jones Centennial Chair in Communication at the University of Texas at Austin. His most recent book, *Setting the Agenda: The Mass Media and Public Opinion* (2004, Polity Press), summarizes the five major aspects of Agenda-Setting Theory that have evolved since publication of the seminal Chapel Hill study by McCombs and Donald Shaw in 1972. His current research is focused on the consequences of agenda-setting effects for voters' attitudes and opinions in the 2006 Mexican presidential election and recent U.S. elections.

**Victor Menayang**, Ph.D. After completing his doctoral studies at the University of Texas at Austin, he returned to Indonesia, his home country, where he took on numerous teaching and administrative roles with the University of Indonesia, especially the Communications Department, at which he chaired the Graduate Studies Program. In 2004, his country's House of Representatives voted to include him as one of the members of the newly created Indonesian Broadcasting Commission.

**Dina Nekrassova** (dinanekr@eden.rutgers.edu) is a Ph.D. candidate in the School of Communication, Information and Library Studies at Rutgers University. Her research interests include emotion work and its implications for the processes of identification, control and decision-making in co-located and virtual organizations.

**Zachary W. Oberfield** (oberfield@polisci.wisc.edu) is a Ph.D. candidate in political science at the University of Wisconsin–Madison. His research interests include race, poverty, and public administration. He is currently completing his doctoral research on socialization into street-level bureaucracies with the support of the Institute for Research on Poverty. His project follows rookie welfare workers and police officers during their first two years of work to understand how they develop their beliefs about deservingness and workplace identities.

**Tricia Olsen** (tdolsen@wisc.edu) is a Ph.D. student of comparative politics and political science methodology at the University of Wisconsin–Madison. She has worked with the Wisconsin NewsLab since the fall of 2004, most recently serving as its project director where she is responsible for the implementation and data analysis of UW NewsLab's Spanish- and English-language content.

**Henrik Rehbinder** (henrik.rehbinder@laopinion.com) is the editor of the opinion section of *La Opinión*, the nation's largest Spanish-language daily newspaper. Born in Uruguay and raised in Argentina, Henrik has been a reporter and editor at *La Opinión* for more than 20 years. He has also co-authored with his wife, Laurien Alexandre, a number of articles about Latinos and the media, including a study of differences in local TV news in several Latino markets in the United States, as well as an analysis of election news coverage.

**Adam J. Segal** (adamjsegal@jhu.edu) is a faculty lecturer in the Master's in Communication Program, and director of the Hispanic Voter Project, at Johns Hopkins University in Washington, DC. He is the president of The 2050 Group (www.the2050group.com), a successful multicultural marketing and public relations agency in Washington, DC. Segal received his M.A. in government from Johns Hopkins University and his B.A. in political science and Judaic studies from the George Washington University.

**Federico A. Subervi-Vélez**, Ph.D., (subervi@latinosandmedia.org) is a professor at the School of Journalism and Mass Communication, Texas State University–San Marcos. Since the early 1980s, he has been conducting research, publishing and teaching on a broad range of issues related to the mass media and ethnic minorities, especially Latinos in the United States. In Brazil, he studied racial representations in that country's television commercials, and in Puerto Rico he analyzed the political economy of the media systems. Dr. Subervi also directs the Center for the Study of Latino Media and Markets, and the Latinos and Media Project (www.latinosandmedia.org), which includes a site dedicated to the dissemination of research and resources pertaining to Latinos and the media, and serves as chair of the Board of Directors of *Latinitas*, Inc., an organization and web-based magazine for Latina adolescents and teens (www.latinitasmagazine.org).

**Juandalynn Taylor**, Ph.D., J.D., writes on a broad range of subjects including the portrayal of race in media, political campaigns, and the law. Other research areas include organizational communication and jury persuasion. Dr. Taylor currently owns and operates a full service litigation consulting firm that specializes in capital defense cases. Dr. Taylor received her Ph.D. from the University of Texas at Austin in 2000 and her J.D. from the Thurgood Marshall School of Law at Texas Southern University in 2007.

**Kenton T. Wilkinson**, Ph.D., (kent.wilkinson@ttu.edu) is regents professor in Hispanic and International Communication in the College of Mass Communications at Texas Tech University. He is an international communication specialist who also studies U.S. Spanish-language media and Hispanic-oriented health communication. His recent publications explore media opening and democratization in Mexico, language and media policies in North America and Europe, and the efforts of Hispanic subgroups to influence U.S. Spanish-language television. Wilkinson collaborates with a multidisciplinary research team whose goal is to improve healthcare among West Texas Hispanics through improved communication. He directs Texas Tech University's Institute for Hispanic and International Communication.

# 1

# INTRODUCTION

*Federico A. Subervi-Vélez*

The subtitle of the book *The Latino Wave*, by Jorge Ramos (2004), states *How Hispanics will elect the next American president*. Published before that year's presidential election, Ramos—who during the last two decades has been the main anchor of *Noticiero Univisión*, the evening national news program of the leading Spanish-language television network in the United States—asserted that Latinos would be a deciding factor in the campaign that year. He also suggested that Latinos were a key to Bush's successful 2000 presidential campaign. Starting in chapter one, titled "Making history: How Latinos decided the 2000 election," and throughout his book, stemming primarily from interviews with Latino political leaders, scholars and field work, Ramos makes his case about the political impact of Latinos. He also points out, sometimes more implicitly than explicitly, that the media, particularly Spanish-language media, are an integral part of that process.

While the precise impact of the Latino vote in the presidential campaign may be argued, it certainly was a crucial factor in Los Angeles on May 24, 2005 when Antonio Villaraigosa became the first Latino mayor of that city since 1872. A few days later, the cover of the May 30, 2005 edition of *Newsweek* magazine proclaimed in bold letters "Latino Power: L.A.'s New Mayor—And How Hispanics Will Change American Politics." The inside pages of that edition featured not only the story behind Villaraigosa's electoral victory, but also an overview of some trends in the surge of Latino political power in the United States, as well as past and future strategies used by Republicans and Democrats to win Latino votes.

One of the main tenets of this book, *The Mass Media and Latino Politics*, is that it is more than long overdue time for political communication scholarship to assess how this ethnic group and the media directed to them have played distinct and niche roles in American electoral politics and, moreover, that political campaigns and research about those processes and events should pay more attention to the intersection between media and Latinos when assessing the political socialization and mobilization of Latinos. Building on historical assessments and on contemporary

1

social science-based research, the pages document how the language and rhythm of political communication in the United States are changing very rapidly, and that Latinos and the media and messages directed to them are at the core of that transformation. In ways and at rates not commonly observed in previous decades, the media and messages of electoral campaigns are being culturally diversified, but more specifically so, "Latinized."

Across the nation, from local elections to presidential campaigns, when there are potential Latino votes at stake, the strategies and operations, the news and propaganda, and the whole modus operandi of the image-makers and disseminators are being redesigned and directed with more precision. Thus, on the one hand, it can be observed that a goal of many candidates and their respective parties is to enhance the outreach—be it in Spanish, in English or in both languages—specifically targeted to win the favor and votes of Latinos. On the other hand, more frequently than in the past albeit still only occasionally, the general market (mainstream) media feature stories on Latinos, Latino issues, or on campaign efforts directed at them.[1]

As the writing for this book was coming to a close in fall 2006, the national focus on Latinos increased exponentially during the public discussions, Congressional deliberations, and the president's proposals to deal with immigration reform. The repercussions of the often heated debates were seen in the Congressional elections of November 2006 when Latinos voted heavily for Democratic Party candidates, a pattern that might well be repeated in the presidential campaign of 2008. Undoubtedly, more than in previous decades, Hispanic-related issues and themes will be part of the general political rhetoric and propaganda, and even more so in the efforts to attract or discourage Latino voters.

The changing demographics help explain part of these new trends in political communication. U.S. Census Bureau data suggest that Hispanics, after making the greatest proportional gains three decades in a row, are now the nation's largest "minority" group. With more than 43 million people nationwide (approximately 15% of the total), they now outnumber the African-American population of 38 million (13%).[2] The increase in economic power has also been evident, especially as the annual purchasing power surpassed $960 billion and advertising and marketing strategists sharpen their focus on the Latino niche or niches.[3]

Another explanation for the increased attention to Latinos is their large numbers in various states that have been major battlegrounds for deciding the outcome of presidential elections. New Mexico and Arizona, but even more so Florida, were pivotal states in the 1996 and 2000 elections. In 2004 the Latino voters were substantial and thus targets of focused attention in these three states plus four others also considered up for grabs or battlegrounds: Colorado, Illinois, Nevada, and New Jersey.

During the 2002 gubernatorial elections in Florida, Texas, New Mexico and New York, Latino voters were also heavily courted with Spanish-language and English-language campaign propaganda. Democrat and Republican candidates even tried to reach out by sprinkling Spanish-language phrases in selected stump speeches.

It should thus not be surprising that Latinos increasingly are an integral part of the emerging political dynamics at the start of the twenty-first century, and will continue to be so particularly in areas with large Latino concentrations (de la Garza and DeSipio, 1992, 2005; de la Garza, Menchaca and DeSipio, 1994; García-Bedolla, 2005; Geron, 2005; Estrada, 1997). The increased Latinized political communication trends are also certain to continue. As will be discussed further in this book, this is correlated with the growing—albeit still limited—media attention given to Latinos during political campaigns.

Even to the casual observer, it should be quite evident why it is important to study mass communication processes related to politics. In essence, the mass media are the main disseminators and transmitters of political information and, as a result, are central players in politics. Media contributions to U.S. politics have been debated and studied for many decades, including the political communication books by Bennett (1992, 2001, 2002), Bennett and Entman (2005), Graber (1994, 1997, 2000, 2005), Graber, McQuail, and Norris (1998), Hart (1999, 2000, 2005), Jamieson (1996, 2000), Jamieson and Campbell (2001), Jamieson and Waldman (2003), Kaid (2004), Patterson (1994), and Perlmutter (1999), among others.

Unfortunately, the academic evidence that highlights the relationships between media and politics stems almost entirely from studies of the U.S. Anglo European populations and general market English-language media. The field of political communication has for too long practically ignored Spanish-language newspapers and television, as well as other Latino-oriented media, which together comprise the largest and best established of all ethnic mass communication channels in the United States (Fishman, Gertner, Lowy and Milan, 1985; Subervi-Vélez et al., 1994; Subervi and Eusebio, 2005). With very few exceptions (primarily the previous works of this author and his associates), political communication research has even neglected assessing the coverage of "Latino candidates or issues" in general market media and of media effects on Latinos (or any other ethnic/racial minorities). Latino voters—actual or potential—and their uses of media in any language have also received minimal attention in academic circles.

This book begins to fill some of the void by focusing simultaneously on Latinos, the mass media, and politics. While numerous works have delved into Latino politics,[4] and a few into Latinos and the mass media,[5] studies that assess the intersection of these are scarce. In this book they are brought together in every chapter to show that studying the mass media can enhance the understanding of Latino politics in the U.S., including issues related to the political knowledge and participation of this population. It is also important to note that while parts of this book date back to the 1980s, they provide the historical foundations to explain why the language and rhythm of political communication in the United States are indeed being transformed.

Latinos are one of the foci of this book because, as alluded to above, they are an integral part of this country's political dynamics. The number of Latinos registering to vote has increased steadily since the 1980s as a result of strong voter registration drives around the country. Likewise, voter turnout also has increased steadily. In the 1988 presidential elections 3.7 million Latinos voted, representing 3.6 percent of the total votes cast (DeSipio and Rocha, 1992). Four years later, 4.2 million Latinos cast their votes, representing 3.9 percent of the total votes cast (The Tomás Rivera Center, 1996), and in 1996 it was 5 million, representing 5 percent of that year's votes.

In 2000—the closest and, at the time, most controversial national election—even more Latinos cast votes, anywhere from 5.9 million (5.6 percent) (de la Garza and DeSipio, 2005) up to 7.4 million (7 percent).[6] According to various analyses of the outcome of that year's presidential election, including the opinions of Ramos (2004) and a number of the people he interviewed for his book, Latinos' votes were instrumental in Bush's victory. The same is being stated about the outcome of the 2004 campaign, in which close to anywhere between seven and eight million Latinos voted, albeit the percentage of the share of the total number of voters did not increase notably.

One of the more telling factors related to the constant growth in the number of Latino voters is the impact they are having in countless state and local elections. Not surprisingly, the number of Latino elected officials has risen steadily since the 1980s (Hero and Tolbert, 1997; Moore and Pachon, 1985; NALEO, 2006; Vigil, 1988, 1997; Welch and Hibbing, 1988). According to figures compiled by the National Association of Latino Elected and Appointed Officials (NALEO),[7] in 1984 a total of 3,128 Latinos had obtained such distinction; as of June 2002, the figure then was 4,464, including one governor (Bill Richardson, Democrat, New Mexico), and 22 Congressmen. And greatly thanks to Latino votes in the 2004 and, subsequently, the 2006 elections, there are more than 5,129 Latinos in elected and appointed offices, including the three Latinos elected to the U.S. Senate, 23 to the House of Representatives, plus two Cabinet level appointees—Attorney General, Alberto Gonzales, and Secretary of Commerce, Carlos Gutiérrez. Clearly, Latinos embody a significant force in U.S. politics. As the population ages and obtains higher education and income levels, and as more of its members become U.S. citizens, its political clout should also increase.

4

De la Garza (1992), de la Garza and DeSipio (2005), and other researchers have pointed out, however, that Latinos have yet to realize their potential fully. For example, statistics indicate that Latino political participation is still lower than non-Latino participation, and that the number of Latino elected officials still lags in proportion to their concentration in most communities (Calvo and Rosenstone, 1989; DeSipio and Rocha, 1992; Leal, Barreto, Lee, and de la Garza, 2005; NALEO, 2006). This holds true even after the mid-term elections of 2002 and the presidential elections of 2004. As Lopes (1995) has asserted, political potential alone will not elect more Latino mayors, city council members or legislators. For Latinos to enhance their political power, be it in local, state or national elections, they need, among other things, information about how and why to become politically involved. When they speak, their views have to be covered and widely reported. In essence, to enhance political socialization and mobilization, ample mass communication efforts are vital and can be decisive. In other words, the media are indispensable and crucial in those processes.

This fundamental connection between information and community interests was observed decades ago by Tichenor, Donohue and Olien (1980: 11) who, in their well-documented study of community conflict and the press, affirmed:

> [I]t is quite clear that possession of information, or access to it, is a potentially crucial resource for the power position of groups that are seeking to realize or protect their collective interests.

Graber also has stated that the mass media serve as "powerful guardians of political norms" and that media "images are especially pervasive when they involve aspects of life that people experience only through the media" (1997: 3). And, she adds, "[a]ttention to the mass media is all-pervasive among twentieth-century Americans" (1997: 3).

The mass media are therefore the second foci of this book, because at all levels of society they are the most *pervasive* sources of news and information, particularly regarding issues and events with which the audience has no direct access or experience. For millions of Hispanics,[8] the media may be a very important source of current news and information about American political life and about Latinos' political life in America. For the U.S. population as a whole, general market media also provide information and representations—albeit limited and sometimes even distorted—about Latinos and their political representatives, interests, goals, etc. (Subervi, Torres and Montalvo, 2004, 2005).

Building on the above, an underlying axiom of this book is that analyzing the mass media is imperative for a better understanding of the politics related to this country's Latino communities. A corollary axiom is that political information about and for Latinos transmitted by way of the mass media is crucial for the mobilization and citizenship development of Hispanics and their interests in the United States. It is assumed that studies seeking to understand the dynamics of Latino politics in this country can benefit from analyses of the political content of the media. That understanding can also be enhanced with assessments of the mass communication strategies of this nation's major political organizations, i.e., the Democratic Party and the Republican Party. Knowing something about Latinos' use of the media and whether that is related to their political knowledge and participation can be quite revealing, too.

These axioms and assumptions are built on previous research in political communication and thus underlie the various chapters of the book, which correspondingly answer three fundamental questions: What are the political messages for or about Latinos disseminated by the mass media? How have the major political parties used the media to gain Latino votes? And, what evidence exists that exposure to the media influences Latino political participation?

The chapters that follow provide some answers to these and other related queries. Before turning to these, however, it is important to consider the reasons for studying ethnicity, particularly those pertaining to Latinos, in the context of political communication.

## ETHNICITY: A CORE AND PERENNIAL FACTOR IN U.S. SOCIETY

During the last part of the twentieth century and continuing on in the new one, the ongoing debates concerning ethnicity, ethnic identity and pluralism, and diversity in American society have been a distinguishing social concern (Ferrante, 2000; Fischer, Gerber, Guitart and Seller, 1997; Schaefer, 2006; Takaki, 1994). Not that ethnicity ever ceased to be important for many individuals and segments of the population—it always has been and continues to be (Parrillo, 1996). But a whole paradigm of social science theory and research was built on the tenets and ideology of a unidirectional assimilation process—one in which the ethnic heritage and identity of recent immigrants or minorities constantly decreased until they became "assimilated" into the great American "melting pot" (e.g., Gordon, 1964; Park, 1950). Similar theoretical foundations have been evident in writings about mass communication research on or about ethnic minority groups, e.g., the works by Kim (1988, 2001) and others summarized in Subervi-Vélez (1986).

More recently, it has been argued that "multiculturalism has always been part of the American scene and is no more a threat to the cohesiveness of society today than at any time in the past," (Parrillo, 1996: 3).

Parrillo even acknowledges that assimilation "remains a powerful force affecting most ethnic groups" but one that "has been relatively ineffective with racial minorities" (1996: 3). He thus postulates: "assimilation and pluralism are not mutually exclusive entities, nor are they necessarily enemies of one another" (1996: 3). In his view, "both assimilation and pluralism have always been dual realities within American society" (1996: 4).

What he and other scholars are pointing out is that the adaptation by ethnic minorities to the dominant society is more complex than the assimilationist model, and not necessarily linear. Ethnic identification continues to serve as a core and perennial value for many segments of the population. For example, instead of transforming their ethnicity from the original or minority group society to a full immersion into the identity of the dominant society, Royce (1982) and Padilla (1985) observe a phenomenon they refer to as *situational ethnicity*. In such cases, particular aspects and dimensions of the ethnic minority heritage are retained and/or expressed depending on a number of factors and contexts, such as the perception of in-group and out-group acceptance or rejection of the particular ethnic attribute(s). In chapter 3 of this book, the implications and applications of the concept of situational ethnicity become central to the formulation of a theory on political communication pertaining to Latinos.

Ethnic group classifications, ethnicity and ethnic identity also remain important in U.S. society because stereotyping and discrimination based on national origin, race, and/or culture persist in spite of the progress made in education, employment, housing, and media representations. Thus, there continue to be notable multidimensional differences between groups, including socio-economic status (Goldberg, 1997), media exposure and use patterns (Ríos, 1993), portrayals in the media (Gandy, 1998; Gandy and Matabane, 1989; Greenberg and Brand, 1994), intra- and interpersonal communication, and intra- and intergroup relations (Berger, 1986; Gudykunst, 1994; Gudykunst, Ting-Toomey and Chua, 1988; Kim, 1986, 1988, 2001). Numerous perceptions of group distinctiveness remain strong, even when some of the differences are not statistically significant, are not consistent for or representative of all members of an ethnic group, or do not hold true when class, age or gender factors are taken into consideration. The mass media may be contributing to such perceptions of distinctiveness or differences; if so, they merit scrutiny.

Furthermore, ethnic groups and ethnicity also are core factors in advertising and marketing. Until a few short years ago, ethnic group designations underlined discriminatory exclusionary practices; in more recent times ethnic groups are integral components in strategic targeting and inclusionary practices. Civil Rights struggles of the 1960s and 1970s, and the industries' recognition of the growth of ethnic minority populations and the steady increase of their expendable income have produced positive changes. For example, the U.S. Hispanic purchasing power was estimated at $279 billion in 1998, and was projected to reach $520.4 billion by 2020 (Vitucci, 1999). But, as mentioned above, that purchasing power has surpassed the $768 billion mark (Williams, 2005), and is projected to reach $trillion by 2008.

Thus, the persistence of ethnicity as a dynamic form of personal identity was elevated to help in the expansion, modification or creation of advertising and marketing strategies. The interaction of these factors concomitantly contributed to the expansion, modification and creation of ethnic-oriented, niche, or specialty messages and mass media, including a variety of print, broadcast and cable outlets (Wilson and Gutiérrez, 1995; Wilson, Gutiérrez, and Chao, 2003). Such messages and media, in turn, stimulate and validate ethnicity, ethnic identity, and/or group consciousness. In other words, they contribute to the re-emergence and maintenance of ethnic pluralism.

## LATINO ETHNICITY: ALSO CORE AND PERENNIAL

Latinos in the U.S. have been integral parts of the ethnic group dynamics mentioned above. To properly discuss these issues as pertinent to the theoretical and methodological foundations of this research, some demographic factors must be examined. First, the 1980s were heralded as "the decade of the Hispanic." Such designation resulted from the recognition of the rapid growth of this population, its economic attainments, and its political advances at the local and state levels. The particular statistics and implications of the progress and difficulties of Latinos in the U.S. have been widely discussed in other writings from political perspectives (as in the literature alluded to above and elsewhere in this text) and from communication perspectives (see the partial list in the Latinos and Media Project bibliographic database).[9] Many of the rationales for those studies still hold true today; a few relevant for this book are discussed further below.

Second, the next generation of research in this arena will have more reason to focus on Latinos even if only demographic figures are taken into account. As mentioned earlier, the number of Latinos in the U.S. has been growing steadily, making this population the largest ethnic minority group. The U.S. Census Bureau predicts that, by the year 2040, Latinos will greatly outnumber any other ethnic minority group with a population surpassing 80 million; more than one out of five U.S. residents (22 percent) will be of Hispanic heritage.[10] In many southwestern states, and in major metropolitan cities all across the country, the concentrations and growth of Latino populations are much more dramatic—a dynamic particularly noticed and being taken advantage of by marketing and advertising companies and professionals (see del Valle, 2005; Korzenny and Korzenny, 2005; Nevaer, 2004; Valdés, 2000; Valdés and Seoane, 1996). The implications of Latinos' increasing numbers in the U.S. electoral politics thus merits close attention. Even if Latinos do not determine the outcome of a presidential race, they certainly may influence the process of selecting the nominee for president, and the winners of numerous state and local elections.

Revealing as they are, the aforementioned statistics alone are not sufficient grounds for a special focus on Latinos. However, the impact of Latino identity, especially cultural connections to the country of origin or ancestors' heritage, does merit major consideration. That identity remains very strong even among those who have adopted economic, cultural, or social traits of the dominant Anglo-European society. As mentioned above, marketing and advertising companies and professionals, recognizing the power of the persistence of Latino identity and culture, have seized the opportunity to solidify and expand niches directed toward these populations. The music, media, literature and entertainment businesses generated with this population in mind certainly do not lose sight of its growing purchasing potential (see Dávila, 2001; del Valle, 2005).

Moreover, the impact of Latino culture is not just contributing to the maintenance of some traits among the members of this group, but also permeating into the mainstream society. A feature article claimed "Americans becoming Latin lovers" (Barrientos, 1997). The author mentioned how Latino-themed movies and Hispanic-based cuisine, literature, music and dance were making major inroads in dominant society. Commenting on how Latinos will become more significant players in political, social and economic arenas, García (1997: xi) suggests that "to the extent that there is an American core culture, it will continue to become more Latinized at the same time as Latinos become more Anglicized." Recent developments in the music and entertainment industries certainly attest to these cultural dynamics.

One other factor to keep in mind is that although some similarities exist, there also are significant differences between Latinos and non-Latinos in terms of media exposure and use patterns, portrayals in the media, intra- and interpersonal communication and intra- and intergroup relations (Ríos and Mohamed, 2003; Ríos, 1993; Quiroga, 1995; Subervi-Vélez, 1986; Subervi-Vélez et al., 1994; Torres, 1997). In the realm of politics, some similarities with non-Latinos have been noted, but so have persistent differences (de la Garza, DeSipio, García, García and Falcón, 1992; García, F., 1997). Researchers who assess housing, occupation, education, and income attainments have also noted numerous disparities between Latinos and other groups (Bean and Tienda, 1987; Goldberg, 1997; Hellerstein, 2005).

Therefore, two trends seem to be evident. On the one hand, acculturation is taking place in several dimensions of Latinos' life in the U.S.—including media use and exposure patterns and politics (Ríos, 1993; Subervi-Vélez, 1986; Suro, 2004; Zmud, 1992). On the other hand, there is ample evidence supporting the persistence of continued Latino pluralism (Padilla, 1994; Shoemaker, Reese and Danielson, 1985; Subervi-Vélez, 1984; Suro, 2004). Latino-oriented media in Spanish and/or English, which are growing in conjunction with the increase in Latino-oriented advertising and marketing, are major factors in sustaining national or pan-Hispanic Latino identities (Dávila, 2001). In effect, Latinos reflect a propensity toward selective distinctiveness, i.e., situational ethnicity (Subervi and Ríos, 2005). They are not abandoning all their Latino roots and ties, nor proceeding into a unidirectional assimilation of all of the dominant society's norms, values, or behaviors, etc., as have many immigrants in the past. Therefore, a question that merits attention is: What are some of the similar issues, as well as some of the distinct issues, for studying political communication among Latinos?

## COMMON GROUNDS IN POLITICAL COMMUNICATION

To begin this topic, we again turn to the aforementioned reasons for studying media in the context of politics. One is that possession of information and access to it is a crucial resource in the process of realizing collective interests (Tichenor, Donohue and Olien, 1980). Media are known to be conveyers of information valuable for the realization of collective political interests. Thus, they become important objects of analysis for understanding the processes of realizing such interests. Another reason is that media are pervasive, as are their images, especially pertaining to those aspects of life that are not experienced directly (Graber, 1997). To the extent that few political events can be experienced directly, the media become the most pervasive window through which nearly everybody who cares about such matters gets to "see" what is happening in politics. Studying the media can therefore reveal what the public is seeing and learning about the world of politics. It may even help us to understand variations in people's political knowledge and participation.

These and other arguments have long been made for studying the political contexts of the general market media. Such rationalizations undoubtedly hold true for the study of ethnic-minority populations, politics and media. But, as shown in chapter 2, few academic writings have applied these tenets to the study of Latino populations or Latino-oriented media. Hence, the focus of attention here turns specifically to explaining the value of studying media in political contexts for this population.

Building on the views presented above, we assume that there are sufficient grounds to contend that Latinos' relationships to mass media in political matters may be, at a minimum, similar to those of the general American public. The media are certainly crucial resources in the process of their realizing collective interests. For Latinos, too, the mass media are important objects of analysis when seeking to understand the processes of realizing such interests. Moreover, media also are relied upon as major sources for news and information regarding politics, given that for most people, few political events can be experienced directly.

## DISTINCTIVE LATINO FACTORS IN POLITICAL COMMUNICATION

On the other hand, factors related to Latinos' ethnic heritage, ethnic group membership, and/or ethnicity are potentially important in their search for and interpretation of political matters. While Latinos seek and consume news, commentary, opinions, partisan promotions and other political information that addresses needs and interests related to their social class, age group and political ideology, they also may search for "Latino angles" to such materials. What is proposed here, and discussed throughout the book, is that Latinos may seek information potentially relevant to some aspect of their Latino identity, however that is defined (Subervi and Ríos, 2005). They could seek information concerning campaign issues, or they could seek information regarding the difference (i.e., the potential power) their vote could make in the outcome of a campaign.

If such relevancy is found in media (and other sources of information), the implications for mobilization can be more significant than if Latinos do not perceive relevancy in a campaign. If nothing else, Latinos should find it interesting to listen to, watch, and/or read about Latinos like themselves, members of their family and/or about "Latino issues." If Latino-themed and oriented advertising and marketing strategies can enhance Latinos' purchasing of "mainstream" consumer products, Latino-themed and oriented political news, information and partisan promotions certainly enhance at least the attention offered to such matters. In either case, attention to media content, communication strategies and audience behaviors are invaluable for improving the understanding of Latino politics in the U.S.

## ORGANIZATION OF THE BOOK

The goal of this book is to explore the relationships between media and Latino politics. Part I, *Foundations*, starts by answering two questions:

"What is known?" (chapter 2) and "Why study the media for understanding Latino politics?" (chapter 3). Chapter 2 is an extensive review of articles, book chapters and other writings that have shed light on the connections between the media and Latino political life in the United States. The first segment of the chapter presents writings that illuminate the politics and the political functions of Latino-oriented newspapers both past and present. The second segment of the chapter points to research and documents that reveal strategic uses of the media by political parties seeking Latinos' allegiance and votes. The third section provides a detailed and critical analysis of survey research into the relationships between Latinos' exposure to, or use of, mass media and their political orientations, knowledge, attitudes and behaviors.

Chapter 3 answers its main question by building on political communication literature and logical deductive reasoning that justify the subsequent research-based studies presented in the book. Thus, theoretical foundations, contexts, and methodological considerations are presented for the data analyses of the print and broadcast news media, for studying the communication strategies of the main political parties, and for assessing the potential impact of media on Latinos' political orientations.

Part II of the book, *Studies of media coverage of elections*, has four chapters dedicated to assessing how Spanish-language media have covered elections, and four chapters on how English-language media have covered Latino-related issues and candidates during elections. For both types of media, historical and contemporary (up to the year 2004 election) data are analyzed. Altogether, the findings from chapters 4 through 11 provide a unique perspective on the similarities and differences in political news coverage for Spanish-language versus English-language media.

The Spanish-language press is the subject of chapter 4. Spanish-language television is analyzed in chapters 5 through 7. English-language newspapers are the subject of chapters 8 and 9, and national network news programs are the focus of chapters 10 and 11. The research question that each of these chapters provides answers for is "What are the political messages about or for Latinos disseminated by way of the mass media?" Across all media, patterns of limited coverage are evident, especially with respect to key electoral campaign issues—including education.

The historical data on the Spanish-language media are chapters 4 and 5. The first of these presents studies from four different presidential elections. It begins with a condensed version of Subervi-Vélez's (1988) previously published analysis of the political news in six Spanish-language daily newspapers during the 1984 presidential election. It then discusses his analysis of how five Spanish-language dailies covered the 1988 presidential campaign. Two other sections offer insights into how one Spanish-language daily covered the last months of the 1992 presidential campaign and how two others covered the final stretch of the 1996 elections. These sections relied on research respectively conducted by Marc Brindel and by Juandalynn Taylor and Renée Espinoza.

Chapter 5 offers the first in-depth look at the election campaign coverage provided by Spanish-language television. It presents the findings of the analysis that Patricia Constantakis Valdés conducted for her dissertation on how Univisión's and Telemundo's national evening newscasts covered the 1988 elections. The chapter also presents Constantakis' 1992–1993 analysis of how the newsroom operations of those television organizations are structured and how the news routines influence political news coverage and production. The chapter shows the ways in which the coverage is tailored to the ethnic audience—providing needed information for a growing political power—and the ways in which the coverage is similar to that provided by mainstream television. Findings indicate that the coverage is, in fact, quite similar to mainstream English-language election campaign coverage, but also has specific Latino-oriented characteristics and themes.

This is followed by a contemporary analysis of Spanish-language television. Shifting from the formal content analyses tradition, Laurien Alexandre and Henrik Rehbinder share in chapter 6 their "impressionistic assessment" of the year 2000 coverage of a convenience sample of Univisión's and Telemundo's national evening newscasts. Even without the methodological rigor of the typical political content analysis, this chapter reveals important patterns about the type of election-related information available to Latinos who watch these news programs.

Using the most advanced content analysis methods, in chapter 7 Matthew Hale, Tricia Olsen and Erika Franklin Fowler take a step away from the theoretical towards the practical by providing a descriptive analysis of the 2004 election coverage aired by Spanish-language television stations at both the network and local levels. Using a unique new method of capturing and analyzing television news content developed by researchers at the University of Wisconsin–Madison's Newslab and the University of Southern California's Norman Lear Center, this chapter provides the most comprehensive analysis of Spanish-language television coverage of elections ever conducted. The results highlight the complexity of the subject as they show that local election coverage varies significantly by media market and by station ownership, and remind us that the diversity of the Latino culture is reflected in the media that serve it.

The focus then turns to English-language media. Chapter 8 presents how Latino candidates and issues in the general market newspapers have been covered in presidential elections from 1988 through 2004. The first part of that chapter is an historical analysis that highlights how, during the 1988 presidential election period, five prestige daily newspapers in five major metropolitan areas with large Latino populations covered the "Latino angle" of that election, i.e., Hispanic candidates and that which could be identified as "Latino issues." These are explained in that chapter and the following ones, which also focus on this angle of the campaign coverage. The second section of this chapter builds on José Carlos Lozano's unpublished analysis of two of those papers in San Antonio also in 1988. The third section of the chapter focuses exclusively on the headlines that identified Latinos and Latino issues in 1992, 1996, 2000, and 2004. The findings of this section suggest that there are few explicit cues in the headlines of the political campaign stories that will signal an ethnic content.

The analysis by Louis DeSipio and James Henson in chapter 9 concerns how 40 newspapers covered Latino issues in their respective cities in 1989. The newspapers and methodology used by the authors are distinct from those used in the previous chapter. However, the general findings of the two chapters on the English-language newspapers are remarkably similar: they document the dearth of Latino-themed political news.

The last two chapters in Part II offer assessments of how English-language television news has covered Latino-themed political stories. Chapter 10 analyzes the 1988, 1992, and 1996 presidential election periods. Here, Kent Wilkinson focuses on coverage of the most notable Latino issues to assess how the network TV news represented the Latinos who were gaining political power. He also compares English-language and Spanish-language networks' treatment of "the little brown ones," the term that then President George H.W. Bush used to refer to his half-Mexican grandchildren in 1988. As was the case with the English-language newspapers, the television network news also offered little substance to understand politically relevant issues of concern to or about Latinos.

Chapter 11, by Amy Langenkamp and Federico Subervi-Vélez, explores one key issue for Latinos and politicians in the 2000 election: education. Through a content analysis of English-language television news stories on education, this study summarizes the candidates' education platforms and network news media coverage of that topic. While the platforms dealt directly with education issues important to Latinos, news coverage of this issue offered little depth. Furthermore, as Election Day approached and no clear front-runner emerged, the news stories on education neglected mentions of Latinos, other racial/ethnic minorities, and the poor.

Part III of the book, *Campaign strategies, political advertisements, surveys*, encompasses five chapters. The first three respond to the second general research question: "How have the main political parties used the media to gain Latino votes?"

Chapter 12 offers an historical overview of this rubric of Latino political communication by summarizing four previously published analyses of the Democratic and Republican Parties' mass communication strategies from the 1950s up to the 1996 presidential campaign.

In chapter 13, Zachary Oberfield and Adam J. Segal draw from a comprehensive database of national political campaign television advertisements, network and affiliate political files, as well as interviews with elite members of each political party and campaign in order to take a detailed look at the Democratic and Republican Parties' respective advertising expenditures and strategies behind these during the 2000 campaign. They also situate that year's elections historically to better understand the appeals made to Latinos in presidential elections and to suggest a strategy for Latinos to attract party attention.

In chapter 14, Stacey Connaughton, Dina Nekrassova, and Katie Lever offer a different look at the Democrats' and the Republicans' 2004 advertisements by investigating *which* issues each party constructed as salient to Latino voters and *how* they have done so in campaign discourse. Specifically, the authors examine 2004 Spanish-language presidential campaign ads and ask: What issues do the Democratic and Republican parties construct as Latino-oriented issues in Campaign 2004? In a departure from previous Latino-oriented campaign findings, results of this study suggest that the GOP presented more issues as salient to Latinos and utilized a denser structure in their ads than their Democratic counterparts. Democrats, on the other hand, did not mention issues in the vast majority of their message units and, when they did, couched the issues they discussed within values such as family and faith. The authors offer various interpretations of this data and directions for future research.

The last two chapters of Part III provide answers to the third general research question: "What evidence is there that exposure to the media influences Latino politics?" With the collaboration of Victor Menayang, Subervi-Vélez presents in chapter 15 the results of a distinct secondary analysis of the 1990 Latino National Political Survey, which was based on a nationwide sample of Mexican Americans, Puerto Ricans and Cubans. The findings of that study show limited but undeniable influences of the mass media in selected aspects of Latinos' political orientations.

In chapter 16, María Flores and Max McCombs bring together both content analysis and survey research that confirm the influence of the mass media on Latinos' political orientations. Their study examined the 2004 U.S. presidential election dynamic, analyzing the Latino voter's agenda and the Spanish television networks' media agenda. The results indicated that the first level of the agenda-setting effect was not significant but that the intermedia agenda-setting effect was evident.

The final chapter offers some conclusions and then answers the last major question of the book: "What steps should be taken and directions followed in the next generation of political communication research related to Latinos?" With the experience of the preceding chapters, it proposes an agenda with theoretical and methodological guidelines pertaining to content analyses, studies of campaign strategies and advertisements, and survey research.

Altogether, the book offers a diverse collection of studies that shed light on a growing body of research on the convergence of media, U.S. Latinos, and politics. It also shows that while such research is still in a genesis stage, it already contributes to the understanding of many aspects of Latino political life in the U.S. It is thus expected that future inquiries about the connections between communication and Latino politics can benefit from and build upon the foundations presented here. In sum, the book contributes to academic analyses of American politics by illuminating the implications of increased ethnic and cultural heterogeneity and the role the media—including Latino-oriented media—play in such dynamics.

## NOTES

1 See the National Association of Hispanic Journalists' Network Brownout Reports, which since 1996 have documented how news about Latinos and Latino issues have constituted less than one percent of the national television network news, and that a miniscule fraction of those stories have been Latino and politics. The 2005 report (Subervi, Torres and Montalvo, 2005) offers an analysis of the network news in 2004, plus a 10-year retrospect of the evening television news coverage of Latinos and Latino issues.

2 For the most recent population updates, see http://www.census.gov. For other information about Latino populations and trends, see also the demographics section of the Pew Hispanic Center's web site, http://pewhispanic.org.

3 See the December issues of *Hispanic Business* for information about the estimates of the Latino purchasing power.

4 See García, García, de la Garza, Falcón, and Abeyta (1991) annotated bibliography book on this subject. More recent works of notice are, for example: Bedolla, 2005; Cámara-Fuertes, 2004; de la Garza and DeSipio, 1999, 2005; de la Garza, DeSipio, García F., Garcia J. and Falcón, 1992; de la Garza, Menchaca, and DeSipio, 1994; de la Isla, 2003; García F., 1997; García-Bedolla, 2005; García, Falcón and de la Garza, 1996; Geron, 2005; Leal, Barreto, Lee and de la Garza, 2005; Montejano, 1999; and Navarro and Mejía, 2004.

5 The chapter by Subervi-Vélez, et al. (1994) contains an extensive bibliography on Latinos and the mass media. See also the database of the Latinos and Media Project (www.latinosandmedia.org). Notable books on Latinos and the media are Barrera, 2001; Berg, 2002; Dávila, 2001; Fregoso, 1993; García Berumen, 2003; Greenberg, Burgoon, Burgoon, and Korzenny, 1983; Keller, 1985, 1997; Mayer, 2003; Noriega, 1992, 2000a, 2000b; Noriega and Lopez, 1996; Rodríguez, A., 1999; Rodríguez, C., 1997; Soruco, 1996; Veciana-Suarez, 1987, 1990; Wilson, Gutiérrez, and Chao, 2003. See also, Cortés, 2000, who discusses how media teach children, including Latino children, about diversity.

6 The higher figure was suggested by Andy Hernández (but was based on initial estimates immediately following that year's election). Upon further analysis, the figure was lowered to conform to the data compiled and more accurately assessed by the United States Bureau of the Census. Hernández served as

Director of the Latino Outreach Office of the Democratic National Committee during the 1996 campaign. For Census estimates on voter turnout by Latinos and others, see www.census.gov/population/www/socdemo/voting.html.

7 See www.naleo.org/ataglance.html.
8 The terms Latino and Hispanic are used interchangeably.
9 See, in the Latinos and Media Project web site (www.latinosandmedia.org), the annotated bibliography in the Resources and Research section.
10 The African American population estimates for the year 2040 are 55 million, 15 percent of the nation's total. Data reported in this paragraph are from the Census Bureau's web site on population projects.

# Part I

# FOUNDATIONS

# 2

# WHAT IS KNOWN?

## Writings on contributions of newspapers and other mass media to Latino political life

*Federico A. Subervi-Vélez*

This chapter reviews writings related to the connections between newspapers—and a few selected other mass media—and Latino political life in the United States. Many of the works provide invaluable insights that support our basic proposition on the importance of studying media for better understanding Latino politics in this country. The first part of the chapter presents writings that illuminate the politics and the political functions of Latino-oriented newspapers both past and present. The second part points to discussions on the strategic use of media by political parties seeking Latino votes. The third part of the chapter provides a detailed and critical analysis of survey research that has studied relationships between Latinos' exposure to, or use of, mass media and their political orientations, behaviors, attitudes, etc. In some of the literature reviewed, the respective authors have clearly and directly established the political contributions of the mass media. In other works, the media-politics connections are stated only implicitly. Altogether, this chapter provides a panoramic view of the literature on the subject of political communication with respect to Latinos in the United States.

## POLITICS OF LATINO-ORIENTED NEWSPAPERS AND OTHER MEDIA[1]

The fact that newspapers have had political roles and functions since their beginnings, and have been important players in U.S. political affairs, has been recognized and documented quite extensively (see, e.g., Altschull, 1984, and citations he offers on pp. 310–311). Through the works cited in this chapter it is shown that Latino-oriented newspapers have likewise been politically oriented and have played significant roles in the political affairs of Latinos in the United States. The first references date back to the beginnings of the establishment of Hispanic settlements in what were then territories of northern Mexico. Political leanings and roles of the press also have been discussed with respect to the newspapers published for and/or by the immigrant Puerto Rican and the Cuban communities of past and present. This section begins with a discussion of the historical experiences of press and politics of each of these three ethnic groups, and ends with a review of a study of gatekeepers and the perceived political functions of media oriented to various Latino groups in Chicago.

## The Mexican American experience

In his essay on the history of the Mexican American press, Carlos Cortés indicates that the Spanish-language newspapers published during the early to mid-nineteenth century in the areas of New Mexico, Texas and Arizona—which were then part of northern Mexico—"established a tradition for what would become the Mexican-American press after 1848" (1987: 248). Although there is limited analysis of such newspapers, these undoubtedly had similar functions as the general market press of the time, i.e., to provide information to their communities, advertise goods and services, and emphasize or promote the political and economic interests of their owners or publishers. With names such as *El Crepúsculo de la Libertad* and *La Verdad*, one can confidently assume that these and other publications were involved in some form or another in political struggles of the times: first, to gain independence from Spain and subsequently in the battles for territorial control of Texas and the neighboring states where Mexicans became "foreigners in their native land" (Weber, 1973). Given the strong family, social, cultural and economic ties between people of Mexican heritage on both sides of the borders, active stances for or against the various political forces within Mexico also were integral to those early papers.

The first Spanish-language periodical within the United States was *El Misisipí*, published in New Orleans in 1808 by the Anglo William H. Johnson and Company. Wilson and Gutiérrez (1985: 179) write that this four-page publication "exhibited many of the characteristics that were to be found in the other Latino publications that were to follow it": it was directed toward the immigrant Spanish-speakers who came to the United States because of turmoil in their homeland; it was bilingual, its news content was heavily influenced by events elsewhere, and it was operated as a business venture.

While information for and about Mexican American concerns in the United States was not at the core of *El Misisipí*, politics apparently was an important component of many other Hispanic publications during the early part of the nineteenth century. Cortés, citing various sources

22

(e.g., Ríos and Castillo, 1970; Ríos, 1972; Oczon, 1979; Taylor, 1928–1934; Chacón, 1977; Pitt, 1966; and Stratton, 1969), indicates that Mexican Americans were very active in publishing weeklies and some dailies in the Southwest, California and even Chicago. He adds that many of these publications, as instruments of social activism, "protested against discrimination, pointed out the lack of public services for Mexican Americans, raised Chicano consciousness, and exhorted Mexican Americans to take action" (1987: 254). Cortés implies that politics of another nature (of social control and "Americanization") also have been evident in some of the Latino-oriented press. An example of this is found in David Weber's (1973) introductory paragraph about a newspaper published in 1904:

> *El Labrador*, published in Las Cruces, New Mexico, demonstrates the desire of the editor to have Mexican Americans work within the American system, yet preserve a sense of ethnic pride . . . to join organizations such as *La Alianza Hispano-Americana*; to become citizens and vote; to have pride in their own language, as well as to learn English.
>
> (Weber, 1973: 251–252)

Francisco Lewels' (1974) brief account of the first Mexican American press supports the notion of political activism, some of it much more radical, of many of the first publications of this type. The prime example he cites is *La Regeneración*, published by Ricardo Flores Magón, a Mexican national who fled from the revolution at that time to San Antonio, Texas. Lewels narrates that Flores Magón's crusade against the tyranny of Mexican dictator Porfirio Díaz and his articles about Mexican-Americans led to assassination threats against this journalist who was forced to flee to St Louis, to Canada, and eventually to Los Angeles where he again published his newspaper. However, in Los Angeles Flores Magón "was tried and convicted of sedition for an article he wrote calling for a labor movement of worldwide proportions. He was sent to the federal penitentiary at Leavenworth, where he died in 1922" (1976: 37).

From the early 1920s to the 1960s Mexican American newspapers were very volatile. Latino population shifts—which varied depending on labor opportunities offered by agriculture, industry, and government programs —resulted in the creation or folding of ethnic media. The existence of these media also was affected directly by the availability of capital, which was restricted owing to economic depressions and the World Wars (see Lewels, 1974; Cortés, 1987). Probably because of the few papers that were published for extended periods of time, and the scant number of these that have been archived and studied, little is known about the general characteristics—much less about the political roles or stances—of this press during those years.

Nevertheless, Robert Brand (1949) provides some insights on the politics of the Spanish-language press of the beginning up to the middle years of the twentieth century. As part of his "general view" of these publications from different parts of the country, he points out that a portion of the Mexican press in the Southwest was "under the influence either of certain elements in the Roman Catholic Church, the Sinarquista movement in Mexico or ultraconservative interests" and was thus most "vehement in its support of Franco" (1949: 369).

Juan Gómez-Quiñones (1990), referring to the period from 1941 to the 1960s, states that "compared to the past, publications declined in number and quality" (1990: 32). Politics were not absent in the Mexican American press, but a conservative trend in those media also was emerging. On the ideologically progressive side, Cortés (1987: 252) mentions in passing the "growing importance and social activism of . . . Ignacio López's outspoken *El Espactador* in Pomona, California." Gómez-Quiñonez (1990) also mentions that newspaper which served as the pro-active voice of that Mexican American community. He alludes to *El Progreso*, founded in 1933, as the newspaper of the progressive Asociación Nacional México Americana. On the other hand, this author also points to the moderate views of the two major Spanish-language dailies at that time—*La Opinión* (Los Angeles, 1926–present; see below) and *La Prensa* (San Antonio, 1913–1963),[2]—and adds that "except for their greater sympathy [towards Latinos], the smaller local papers, such as *El Sol* (Phoenix) and *El Universal* (Corpus Christi), were not markedly different in their views than other local English newspapers" (1990: 32).

The Civil Rights movements and struggles of the 1960s were the catalysts that brought about a new and dramatic explosion of politically oriented Chicano newspapers all across the country. Thus, a few writings from or about that time period mention the titles of those Chicano papers (e.g., *El Grito del Norte, La Raza, El Gallo, El Papel, El Chicano, El Popo, Con Safos, El Deguelle, El Malcriado*) and of their roles as activists, mobilizers, protesters of discrimination and oppression, and fighters for civil, farm and other labor rights (see Lewels, 1974; Cortés, 1987; Castro, 1974; del Olmo, 1971).

Unfortunately, little has been published about this highly political press. *El Malcriado* (1969–1976), the irreverent grassroots paper published by César Chávez' United Farm Workers' Union, is mentioned in barely three pages of Lewels' book (1974: 21–23). Gómez-Quiñonez (1990) only provides passing mentions of four publications: *Agenda* (1971–76), the magazine of the National Council of La Raza; *El Gallo* (1968–1980), the newspaper of the Crusade for Justice, a very progressive, confrontational political organization founded by Rodolfo "Corky" González in 1966; *La Causa* (1969–1972), the newspaper of the Movimiento Estudiantil Chicano de Aztlán (MEChA); and *Sin Fronteras*

(1974–1978), the newspaper of the Centro de Acción Social, the "most salient progressive organization functioning in the Mexican community" in the 1970s. Other accounts of these media also are very limited (del Olmo, 1971; Ríos, 1972; Ríos and Castillo, 1970).

After the 1970s, practically all of the most activist press declined owing to the divisions and transformations of the political movements, the increased costs of production and distribution, and most certainly as a consequence of the repressive efforts of state and/or federal government agencies. Although there has never been a national Chicano or Mexican American *daily* newspaper, much less a politically oriented one, there are still numerous regular publications directed primarily at the Mexican American populations.

Given the societal controls over these media, Lewels contends that "the Spanish language press has, for the most part, been exemplified by an orientation toward events in Mexico and Latin America rather than toward the problems of Mexican Americans" (1976: 37). Cortés summarizes it this way: "In general, conservatism has proved more palatable for advertisers and government and, as a result, most of the 'successful' Mexican-American newspapers in terms of longevity and financial stability have been of the more conservative variety" (1987: 255). Lewels, Cortés and others agree that San Antonio's *La Prensa* and Los Angeles' *La Opinión* are examples of this type of journalism: relatively conservative with respect to politics in Mexico yet at the same time active in promoting the Mexican and Hispanic culture and the social, economic and political rights [but not necessarily *activism*] of Mexican and other Latino immigrants in the United States.

Currently, there are no national *daily* publications—much less any primarily *political* daily newspapers—providing either voices for the heterogeneous Mexican American population or serving as coalescing channels for the multiple ideological views of that diverse community. Nevertheless, more than 500 local newspapers oriented towards Mexican Americans and other Latino populations are published on some regular basis across the United States.[3] While we have not located any writing that discusses the political or even social or cultural content and/or goals of those papers, an examination of the collections of these at the Benson Latin American Library at the University of Texas suggests that there are a few publications that carry the political torch as a primary mission. A few of the local papers are primarily profit-seeking businesses with heavy emphasis on advertising and little or no focus on the political mobilization of the Latino communities they serve. The few national magazines serving Mexican Americans and Latinos in general, e.g., the English-language *Hispanic* and *Vista*, are commercial ventures of this type (see Subervi-Vélez et al., 1994; Subervi and Eusebio, 2005).

The oldest daily Spanish-language newspaper serving Latinos in

Southern California is *La Opinión*. While the general political orientation of *La Opinión* has been discussed (see also Medeiros, 1980), the specific political content of this paper during a presidential election had not been studied until our first analysis of its coverage of the 1984 campaign (Subervi-Vélez, 1988). The findings of that study are presented in chapter 4 along with findings from the content analysis of *La Opinión*'s coverage of other presidential campaigns.

One additional media outlet that deserves attention in this section is Spanish-language radio. Even in its early days, this medium, in addition to broadcasting music and entertainment, offered political information and contributed to political mobilization of Mexican Americans. The documentaries *Ballad of the Unsung Hero* (1984) and *Break of Dawn* (1988) clearly illustrate the role that, during the late 1920s and early 1930s, Mexican radio show host, Pedro González, played in bringing to his audience's attention the discrimination and other social and economic problems faced by Mexican immigrants to the U.S.[4] Although historical records about the content and consequences of activist radio programs directed at Latinos are scarce, it is undeniable that select radio programs and voices were a major source for political information and mobilization of Latinos.[5]

## The Puerto Rican experience

The first political print media of the Puerto Rican community outside of the island were the periodicals that flourished in the United States during the latter part of the eighteenth and the early part of the nineteenth century. Joseph Fitzpatrick's (1987) historical review of the Puerto Rican press in this country indicates that, during that time period, New York was both a center of the revolutionary movements of the Caribbean colonies and the place where the "gospel of independence" was spread through a variety of small—but significant—newspapers. Thus, the Puerto Rican papers in this country emerged from the pens of prominent Puerto Ricans fighting to free their island from Spain and later the United States.

One of these distinguished patriots was Luis Muñoz Rivera, father of Luis Muñoz Marín, who was governor of Puerto Rico between 1952 and 1964. The senior Muñoz was founder of pro-independence newspapers on the island (*La Democracia*, 1890–1948) and later in New York (*The Puerto Rico Herald*, 1901–end date unknown). As Fitzpatrick explains, this latter weekly newspaper "was an important voice of Puerto Rican protest during the early years of discussion and controversy in the U.S. Congress about the status of Puerto Rico" (1987: 304). Fitzpatrick adds that in that paper "Muñoz Rivera published a blistering criticism of the Foraker Act, which marked the imposition of a governing system by the United States on Puerto Rico in 1898" and "publicized his views and those of his colleagues in their efforts to achieve autonomy for Puerto Rico" (1987: 304–305).

26

*The Puerto Rico Herald* and other similar publications during that period constituted a very powerful political press that brought together patriots exiled from the island and many of the revolutionaries back home. That press also served many other important functions in the lives of the early Puerto Rican communities in New York (Acosta-Belén, 1988; Sánchez Korrol, 1994). As Fitzpatrick notes, this press "had a brief but influential history in the struggle for a political status acceptable to the Puerto Ricans" (1987: 305). But, he adds, the 1917 Jones Act, which imposed United States citizenship on Puerto Ricans, terminated a great period for the Puerto Rican press in this country.

In the years that followed, politics were still part of the U.S.-based Puerto Rican publications, but these took a different turn as nationalistic activities were subjected to overt or covert repression on the island and in the United States.[6] From 1913 to 1948, the only significant daily newspaper serving the Puerto Rican community in New York was *La Prensa*, founded and edited by José Campurí, a Spaniard. While this paper was sympathetic to liberation and anti-colonialism causes in Puerto Rico and other parts of Latin America, its target audience was primarily the immigrant community from Spain. Thus, *La Prensa* was political from its start and even more so during Spain's civil war as it supported the Loyalist cause. However, as Fitzpatrick suggests, when the Puerto Rican community "needed a strong advocate in the press, the only general interest newspaper available in Spanish was directing its attention to Spain" (1987: 306).

In 1948 another Spanish-language newspaper, *El Diario de Nueva York*, was launched by Porfirio Domenicci, a prominent immigrant from the Dominican Republic. This newspaper was also a political force for Puerto Ricans in that city, starting with the appointment of the first editor— Vicente Geigel Polanco, a distinguished pro-independence lawyer from the island who had moved to New York. He was followed in 1952 by the experienced Puerto Rican journalist José Dávila Ricci, a close associate of Luis Muñoz Marín, who was then governor of the island. Even after Dávila Ricci had to leave that post in 1954 as a result of "questionable legal activities" (Fitzpatrick, 1987: 307), *El Diario*, under the editorship of Stanley Ross, continued its strong leadership and presence regarding Puerto Rican causes in New York and the United States (see Fitzpatrick, 1987: 307–309).

In 1963 *El Diario de Nueva York* and *La Prensa* were merged into *El Diario-La Prensa* by O. Roy Chalk, who had bought the former paper in 1961. This merger, coming at a time when Puerto Ricans were beginning to lose their status as the dominant immigrant population in that city, reduced their political clout. Although local Latino issues were and still are at the forefront of the mission of this newspaper (now with new owners[7]), the Puerto Rican political causes, especially those related to pro-independence ideals, took a back seat to issues pertaining many of the newer immigrant populations—such as Cubans, Dominicans and other Central and South American political and economic refugees (see McCardell, 1976).

In 1980, another daily newspaper oriented toward Latinos was launched in New York—*Noticias del Mundo*[8] (see Subervi-Vélez et al., 1994; Vidal, 1980). From its inception, this paper also was political; its founder is the anti-Communist crusader Reverend Sun Myong Moon and his Unification Church International. This and other publications in the United States and Latin America were organized under their New World Communications, Inc. Ana Veciana-Suarez cites then editor-in-chief, José Cardinali, as stating: "We are against dictatorships . . . We cannot abide Marxism" (1987: 21). Although she adds that the editorial stands were "decidedly conservative in international affairs and pro-Hispanic on domestic issues" (1987: 21), the perspectives on those domestic issues were predominantly conservative as well.

In addition to these two dailies, there is currently *Hoy* (launched in that city in 1998 by the Tribune Company), plus numerous local papers with commercial or political orientations serving the New York Puerto Rican and other Latino communities. These papers have generated little academic interest, including regarding their political orientations, roles or functions. Nevertheless, it seems quite evident that there has not been significant political press by or for Puerto Ricans in the United States for many years. Also, other than our own work on the political content of the two daily papers during the 1984 elections (Subervi-Vélez, 1988), and the analysis of their coverage of the 1988 elections (see chapter 4), very little is known about the politics of these dailies or other Puerto Rican oriented newspapers.

## The Cuban experience

Publications by and/or for the Cuban community in New York at the turn of the century were similar to the Puerto Rican press at that time: militantly pro-liberation from Spain and focal points for the expatriates residing in that city. Edna Acosta-Belén (1988: 95) states that "Cultural and political activity in the early Cuban community manifested itself through the proliferation of newspapers" which, as she cites from Poyo (1984: 53), "developed and defined separatist thinking and circulated in all centers of Cuban population in the country giving a sense of unity and commonality of purpose." After Cuba gained its independence from Spain, and subsequently from U.S. forces which occupied that island at different times between 1898 and 1917, the exile political press published by Cubans in this country apparently declined in number. However, significant Cuban publications continued in different locations including

Tampa, Florida. Brand, referring to the Cuban and Puerto Rican news-papers in this city and New York, labeled these as being "about half left wing, a somewhat vague term which in this case is meant to include liberal Democrats, Socialists, anarchists, Communists and pro-labor groupings of all types" (1949: 369).

The Cuban press flourished again in the 1960s when thousands of islanders fled the Castro-led revolution and began establishing their mili-tant political as well as commercial media in southern Florida and other cities where they became exiles. But this time the politics were quite different. While it is commonly known that the more recent Cuban communities in Miami and elsewhere in the U.S. have had numerous political newspapers and broadcast media, and that Cubans have made ample political use of whatever media they can influence, very little has been written about the subject.

One of the few authors to provide some insights into the political side of the Cuban media in the U.S. is Ana Veciana Suárez (1987, 1990). Among her analyses of the U.S. Hispanic media she states, for example, that "[b]y and large, the radio stations, particularly those with news/talk shows, are fervent advocates of Hispanic political issues, mainly anti-Communism. This is particularly true of *Diario Las Américas*" (1990: 48), and adds

> Because Miami is predominantly a community of political exiles—both Cubans and Nicaraguans have fled Marxist regimes —the media that serve them have strong political undertones. About half of Miami's radio stations, for example, have news/ talk show formats that carry plenty of political news. In other markets, no station does.
>
> (Veciana Suárez, 1990: 48–49)

For her previous work, Veciana Suárez interviewed Horacio Aguirre, edi-tor of *Diario Las Américas*, whose views (see 1987: 34–35) confirm the political activism and conservatism of that paper.

An earlier insight into the political orientation of *Diario Las Américas* was provided by Benigno Aguirre, who performed a content analysis of the coverage of the Watergate affair by this paper and *The Miami Herald*. Aguirre found that "In contrast to *The Herald*, *Diario* showed a less crit-ical view of Nixon" (1979: 161). He concluded that *Diario* offered the Cuban exiles an interpretation of the Watergate affair events as "an insidious communist attack on the political stability of this country. Nixon was perceived as the victim of a well orchestrated liberal and communist fabrication" (1979: 162).

The only other academic account we could find that provides some insights into the politics of the Cuban-oriented media in the U.S. is Gonzalo Soruco's (1996) book. In his chapter 3 on the media in Miami, he first describes the development of radio on the island and then points to the influence of that form of radio in Florida. Under a section titled "The Radio Wars," Soruco states

> That Spanish-language radio would become political in Miami under the direction of the exiles was not surprising, given its history in Cuba. The political conflict gripping the island and the conditions under which they had to leave their land only has-tened the process . . . To those left behind, they urged resistance, rebellion, and even sabotage. As relations between Cuba and the U.S. deteriorated, the broadcasts assumed an ominous tone. The exiles' militancy was assisted further by the U.S. government.
>
> (Soruco, 1996: 38)

In his work, Soruco describes the characteristics of the political radio wars that Cubans (with the support of the CIA) carried out both towards their compatriots on the island and in South Florida. In the U.S. part of these radio wars during the 1970s, various groups emerged with different perspectives on how to deal with Castro and how to present their views via the mass media. Soruco indicates that the "[f]anatical right-wing factions used a variety of methods to intimidate or silence radio personalities who advocated a more moderate line" (1996: 38), including picketing in front of Spanish-language stations, insulting political opponents on talk shows, temporarily taking over by force their radio stations, and even bombing their cars.

From Soruco's perspective, this type of radio changed in the 1980s when Miami's population had significant influxes of Nicaraguans, Dominicans, Colombians, Peruvians, Argentineans and other South Americans. Today, he states, there is "greater tolerance for dissent among the exiles" (1996: 39).

With respect to politics in the print media, Soruco's work focuses pri-marily on the battles between the Cuban exiles and *The Miami Herald*. He points out that this paper was accused of being insensitive to Cubans not only as an immigrant, ethnic minority population, but also to their polit-ical interests and perspectives. Numerous protests and other challenges by the Cuban community, including a critical advertisement in *The Herald*, pressured this paper to make a series of changes during the mid 1980s. As a result, Cubans were hired at *The Herald*, news about their community became more diverse, reflecting a wider spectrum of their activities, and the paper's editorial policy became more conservative.

As these battles were taking place, a parallel development was the estab-lishment of the daily *El Herald*, which subsequently was named *El Nuevo Herald*. It was established in 1976 as a Spanish-language insert of *The Miami Herald*; in 1987 it was published independently although it was still owned and operated as part of the Knight-Ridder Corporation

(Subervi-Vélez et al., 1994; Subervi and Eusebio, 2005; Veciana Suárez, 1987, 1990). The ideology of this newspaper is decidedly conservative, especially in its opinion pages where a number of Cubans, other Latinos and Latin Americans publish their columns about politics and a variety of other topics.

Chapter 4 presents the findings of the content analysis of these two Cuban papers and of the other three major Spanish-language dailies in order to assess their political content during presidential election periods. The findings of that analysis help explain part of the political functions these papers still may have in their respective communities. That data will also contribute to the theoretical discussion of the functions of the ethnic media, including the often-concomitant dual roles of pluralism (e.g., maintaining ethnic identity), and assimilation (e.g., helping in the process of adopting some of the characteristics of the dominant group).

## A gatekeeping study

The first study to directly test part of the assimilation-pluralism theory as it applies to the politics of Latino media was carried out in 1986–1987 by Ilya Adler in Chicago. Building on the literature about ethnic assimilation and pluralism, and the few writings about the functions of the press in general and ethnic media in particular, Adler sought to answer the question: "Do Latino media preserve a Latino presence *and* a Latino agenda in politics, or do they simply facilitate Latinos' incorporation into mainstream political life?" (1987: 3, emphasis in original). Adler then states: "Of interest to this study is the degree to which Latino gatekeepers perceive their role in regard to all three outcomes." To answer these queries, he surveyed 250 Latino media reporters, publishers, editors, managers, producers and broadcasters. He also conducted in-depth interviews with 12 of these journalists.

After explaining the Latino media environment in Chicago at the time of his study (which coincided with a mayoral election in that city), Adler describes demographic and other characteristics of his sample. He then discusses his data analysis in which he tested seven hypotheses proposing relationships between the respondents' background characteristics and the political roles they perceived that their publications played.

Among the findings, Adler indicates that "the higher the proportion of years spent in the United States, the greater importance gatekeepers are likely to assign to an assimilationist function (but not either a pluralistic or retentive function)" of their media. He also found a strong relationship between the degree of importance assigned to the pluralistic function and the importance assigned to encouraging Latinos to vote in large numbers; such correlation was not found with the assimilationist function. Thus, Adler states that this "supports the contention that a pluralistic vision [of the role of Latino media] is much more politically motivated than an assimilationist vision" (1987: 19). Ironically, Adler did not find any relationship between the pluralistic function and the importance assigned to political unity among Latinos, nor with that function and the perception of discrimination in the United States.

These and other findings led Adler to conclude that Latino gatekeepers' pluralism is "perhaps more conservative, in tune with the general political trends of the 1980s in the United States" (1987: 20). To this he adds that these journalists "appear to believe that simply voting in large numbers will bring about positive political responses toward Latino causes" (1987: 20) and that they "see the role of the Latino media as highly political and highly local, and see themselves as important channels for creating political consciousness and encouraging the development of a dynamic Latino presence in local politics" (1987: 21).

One final important point made by Adler is his observation that the Latino journalists he studied, in spite of their support for higher voter turnout, avoid any sense of political advocacy. This, he states, "might reflect traditional journalistic norms (i.e., inform, not advocate), but whether or not this more 'objective' posture aids social and political causes for Latinos remains to be seen" (1987: 22–23).

Other than Constantakis-Valdés' (1993) dissertation analyzing Spanish-language television network news (see summary and revised version in chapter 5 of this book), no other social science study has addressed the issue of the political functions of Latino media and how such functions reflect or conform to either assimilation or pluralism. Or as Adler (1987) found, how they play such dual roles.

To summarize this section, it can be stated that the historical reviews of the Mexican American press and the Puerto Rican press, as well as the passing references to those publications and the essays in the special edition of *The Americas Review* (1989), all attest to the fact that these media were instrumental in cementing Hispanic political organizations, identities and cultures, and in mobilizing Latinos living in this country. However, while progressive politics were at the core of numerous such newspapers that denounced discrimination, racism and other forms of injustice against Latinos, there were also other papers more moderate and even conservative in their views. Furthermore, as discussed by the authors cited and by others (e.g., Gutiérrez, 1977; Gutiérrez and Ballesteros 1979; Wilson and Gutiérrez, 1995), those publications served multiple social, cultural, and economic functions as well. Few of the newspapers discussed in these studies have had significant national circulation; most appear to be the product of very local or regional groups, organizations, or businesses.

The Cuban experience with politics and media has been somewhat different from that of the Puerto Ricans and Mexicans and Mexican Americans in the United States. While politics played a part in the early stages of the press for each of these groups, it is still central and most decidedly present in the contemporary daily press oriented toward Cubans. Another distinction is the political power of radio for this group. The same cannot be said—or at least has not been documented —with respect to Puerto Ricans and Mexicans. The political role of television has also not been documented for either group.

Altogether, what the literature from the first section of this chapter makes quite evident is that politics—be they of the homeland and/or of the local Hispanic communities—have been at the core of many of the local Latino-oriented publications.[9] More than 20 years ago Lewels (1974) found that, at least in some locations, the Chicano movement's activities were integrally connected with grassroots media channels. One of the major conclusions of his work is that, to make significant gains in political power, Chicanos (and other Latinos) need to improve their access and exposure to Anglo as well as Latino media channels dramatically. Adler's (1987) findings, if they were to hold true today and in other cities, lend support to Lewels' view. One final undeniable fact that emerges from this section is that the past and present politics of Latino-oriented media need more research.

## CAMPAIGN STRATEGIES
## AND ADVERTISEMENTS

Although very little has been written on this subject with respect to Latinos, it is evident in the works reviewed here that there is an assumption that the media do contribute to the goals of the political entities.[10] In other words, candidates for political office and party organizations (such as the Democratic National Committee and the Republican National Committee) make ample use of the media because these are considered crucial means to reach their audiences and to influence the outcome of an election (Bennett, 1992; Graber, 1993; Kern, 1989; Payne, 1989). As Latinos and other ethnic minority groups have become increasingly important electorates (see DeSipio, 1993; de la Garza and DeSipio, 1992, 2005; de la Garza, Menchaca and DeSipio, 1994; Jackson and Preston, 1991), they too have been targeted by the major political parties for communication outreach efforts that seek their ideological allegiances and votes.

One of the few academic works to discuss the communication strategy of a major political organization is Tony Castro's historical account of the emergence of Mexican American political power in the United States. In chapter 12 of his book, he analyzes the strategy developed by the GOP regarding Mexican Americans—a strategy that included "negative tactics in either attracting or neutralizing the Mexican American vote"

(1974: 202). Among the many efforts developed by Nixon's administration Castro mentions that the "Committee to Re-Elect the President, with all its complexities and political labyrinths, included a division assigned to woo the Spanish-speaking voter" (1974: 202). At the head of that effort was Alex Armendáriz, who wrote a memorandum from whom Castro quotes extensively that mentions, among other things, that the Republicans wished to "influence some middle class [Hispanic] people by careful use of presidential surrogates" (1974: 203), i.e., Latinos who could represent the views of the GOP and the President. That memo by Armendáriz quoted by Castro goes on to say that their program had not been completely successful as those surrogates were "speaking to the wrong audiences and press coverage is sparse . . . Someone must come up with a slick advertising package showing the President doing, or having done, something about jobs and housing" (1974: 203–204).

Castro does not elaborate on the specific use of the media by the GOP, but details of these efforts at the time can be found throughout Books 10, 13 and 19 of Presidential Campaign Activities of 1972. These books are part of the multivolume series stemming from the U.S. Senate's hearings and investigations related to the Watergate scandal and other activities associated with Nixon's re-election campaign. Book 13, for example, contains copies of numerous memoranda of the weekly activity reports of the "Spanish Speaking Task Force," one of the many committees that worked for the re-election of President Nixon. Practically each of those memos lists Latino-oriented media activities. This quote from the correspondence of April 28, 1972, from Mill Marumoto, chair of the Spanish Speaking Task Force, to Chuck Colson and Fred Malek (sic) offers one example:[11]

> A number of us, Henry Ramírez, Alex Armendáriz, Carlos Conde, etc., and myself [Marumoto], have each spent some time with the publishers and editors of La Luz, a Mexican American version of Life Magazine that is just getting off the ground. They need assistance in obtaining national advertisers, which we've given them leads. Of equally (sic) importance, we've got them committed to writing at least one feature per month on the Nixon Administration.
>
> (Book 13, Presidential Campaign Activities, 1972: 5566)

Another part of the same memo reads:

> Conde has completed an updated Spanish speaking media list. It has been made available to the Committee for the Re-Election of the President. . . . Conde met with PIO representative from OMBE to plan a Spanish speaking brochure. This is part of the

34

Spanish Speaking media plan and it will be done in Spanish and English.

(Book 13, Presidential Campaign Activities, 1972: 5574)

Some of the specifics of that media plan can be observed in a memo from Carlos Conde to Marumoto and others dated May 31, 1972, on the subject of "Spanish Speaking Task Force on Media Team." This document in Book 13 (1972: 5595– 5598) states that "The Spanish speaking media plan developed by this office is now underway."[12] This plan, a full copy of which is found in Book 19 (1972: 8617–8640), discusses in detail topics such as "background on the Spanish Speaking Community," "Campaign Strategy," "Campaign Organization" and the "specific action steps necessary to activate" that campaign strategy.

Evidently, at the highest circles of the Republican Party, the mass media—including Spanish-language media—were considered crucial tools in the efforts to mobilize the Latino population for the GOP's political purposes. While these were not the only tools used for that effort, they were a significant part of Nixon's and the Republican Party's master plan with respect to Latinos.

Another in-depth and historical look at the GOP's outreach to Latinos is offered by Santillán and Subervi-Vélez (1991). Also under the rubric of campaign strategies are the works by Subervi-Vélez (1992) and by Subervi-Vélez and Connaughton (1999), which offer assessment of the Democratic and Republican Latino-oriented communication efforts in 1992 and 1996, respectively. Because key findings by those authors are part of the historical overview presented in chapter 12 of this book, they are not repeated here.

The Republican's Latino outreach strategy in 2000 was the subject of Marbut's study in 2005. What he observed was very much in line with what has been noted by Subervi-Vélez and collaborators (alluded to above). As in previous presidential elections, the GOP strategists "developed well-funded, highly integrated Latino advertising campaign" (2005: 68) that included a mix of Spanish-language and English-language print and broadcast media advertisements in targeted states. The main characteristics of those spots, created by Sosa, Terrance, and other known architects of that party's Latino-oriented messages, were the emotional appeals, and the absence of specifics regarding critical social, economic, health or education issues of concern to Hispanics. One other common denominator of that year's Latino outreach efforts and those of previous years was the unity of the general market messages with those directed to Latinos: family values and the GOP as a conduit to help achieve the American Dream.

Additional documentation and discussions on the Republican and Democratic parties' Latino-oriented strategies are offered in chapters 12 to 14 of this book.

As revealing as these reviews of the literature on the politics of Latino-oriented newspapers and the strategies by the Republicans has been, it must also be recognized that, to date, no publicly disseminated opinion polls or systematic studies have empirically tested the effects of these tactics. With one exception,[13] no one has assessed whether any of the Mexican American, Puerto Rican or Cuban newspapers have specifically had any direct or indirect influence on the political behaviors or attitudes of Latinos in the United States either at the turn of the last century or in more recent times. Knowledge about, or potential influence of, specific campaign strategies also have not been studied in any survey research.[14] Nevertheless, there appear to be significant relationships between media exposure and political orientations among Latinos. What limited academically based research has been done on this line of inquiry is the subject of the third section of this chapter.

## CONNECTING MEDIA EXPOSURE TO LATINO POLITICS

While Latino political life has been the subject of various studies, especially since the decade of the 1980s (Cámara-Fuertes, 2004; de la Garza and DeSipio, 1999, 2005; de la Garza, DeSipio, García, and Falcón, 1992; de la Garza, Menchaca, and DeSipio, 1994; García F., 1997; García J., 2005; García-Bedolla, 2005; García, Falcón, and de la Garza, 1996; García, García, de la Garza, Falcón and Abeyta, 1991; Geron, 2005; Leal, Barreto, Lee, and de la Garza, 2005), there is still a scarcity of literature analyzing the role of mass communication variables in the context of this group's politics. No significant discussions about media are found in the most extensive compilations of research on Latino politics (García, de la Garza and Torres, 1985; Nelson, 1984). This subject also was left untouched in the seminal works on Chicano/Latino/Hispanic politics by (García, 1974, 1988, 1997; Gómez-Quiñonez, 1990; Guzmán, 1976; Hero, 1992; Vigil, 1978, 1987; Villareal, Hernández and Neighbor, 1988[15]) or about Puerto Rican politics in the U.S. (Cámara Fuertes, 2004; Jennings and Rivera, 1984).

Most recently, such as in John García's 2005 book, Latinos' use of the media is mentioned, but again only in passing. For example, García points out (2005: 138) how much money the political candidates and parties spent on placing advertising spots on Spanish-language television in the 2000 elections ($12 million) and in the 2002 elections ($16 million); no source is provided for these figures. Later, García states:

> The mass media, especially the Spanish-language media, as well as other high-tech forms of communication serve as vehicles

for maintaining, redefining and bridging communities among Latinos. The mass media and [their] influence on Latinos' attitudes, cultural practices and awareness, and political communication represent a vital area for more in-depth analysis.

(García J., 2005: 228)

This statement is not followed by any additional references to the media, other than to state that market media symbolically tend to characterize Latinos as a homogeneous group (2005: 251). Thus, no empirical tests are offered as to if, how and why the media—in Spanish and/or in English—affect Latino political socialization and mobilization.

A similar brief mention of the political role of the media is made by García Bedolla when she refers to author Griswold del Castillo, who points out that during the 1940s, a time during which Mexicans were experiencing hostility and discrimination, a broad multiclass Mexican identity was facilitated, in part, owing to the development of a Spanish-language press (2003: 46). García Bedolla's only other mention of the media is when she states that for a group of Latinas in Los Angeles (circa early 1990s), Spanish-language television contributed to activate their identities as Latinas and as women (2003: 124). Details of how that activation was produced are not discussed by that author.

Three major examinations of literature focusing specifically on Latinos and mass communication (Greenberg, Burgoon, Burgoon and Korzenny, 1983; Subervi-Vélez, 1986; Subervi-Vélez et al., 1994) also suggest that scholars have neglected the topic of media and politics. Nevertheless, the role of mass communication for some aspects of Latino political life has been recognized and studied in at least a few works.

The earliest empirical study we have found which assesses the relationship between exposure to the mass media and politics among Latinos was carried out in 1963 by Daniel Valdes y Tapia. As part of his dissertation at the University of Colorado, he conducted a panel survey "to determine if ethnicity alone or in combination with exposure to selected mass media communication had any significant relation to the amount of interest, intention to vote, and choice of candidates in a municipal election" (Valdes y Tapia, 1976). The panel of 208 subjects was derived from a probability sample of registered voters, a large number of them with Spanish surnames in the heavily Hispanic precincts in Denver.

Of particular interest to Valdes y Tapia was the surveyed subjects' exposure to:

(1) a television speech calling attention to the present mayor's (and one of the candidates) failure to eliminate discrimination against Hispanos and his failure to stop police brutality aimed primarily at persons from minority groups; (2) two issues of

> *El Tiempo* appealing to the Hispanos' pride and the need to "throw out of office" those responsible for their plight.
>
> (Valdes y Tapia, 1976: 114)

Valdes y Tapia—who, in addition to being a doctoral student, was, not coincidentally, the editor of Denver's English-language Latino-oriented newspaper, *El Tiempo*—also surveyed the subjects for other aspects of their media exposure, plus their demographic background and ethnicity as these related to their politics. The results, for which chi-square statistical analysis was used, showed that choice of candidates to vote for, amount of interest in voting, and intention to vote were different primarily among Hispanos and Anglos who had high exposure to the particular media items studied.[16] For example, he found that among Hispanos[17] who had been exposed to the critical messages on television and *El Tiempo*, there was a change in favor of the candidate who was supported by those messages, but that the same was not true among Anglos.[18] It should be pointed out that this analysis constitutes, to date, the only assessment of the influence of Latinos' exposure to a particular Latino-oriented newspaper. The other studies, as reviewed below, do not identify the particular print media to which the subjects of the surveys were exposed.

Another finding by Valdes y Tapia was that, across time, interest in the election increased when subjects were more highly exposed to the mass media. However, he noted that "when Spanish- and Anglo-oriented respondents (both equally highly exposed to mass media communication) are compared, the number of Hispano oriented respondents whose intention to vote increased is significantly greater than the number of Anglo-oriented respondents" (1976: 148). He goes on to say that for the purpose of his study "the important finding is the positive relationship between ethnicity and voting behavior" (1976: 148). It also seems evident that exposure to the selected media was more related to Latinos' than to Anglos' political orientations.

More than a decade later, Marilyn Buehler also found a positive relationship between media and Latino politics in her study of 465 Mexican American males living outside the Detroit metropolitan area. Her random sample of heads of households was chosen from a combination of sources such as "city directories, Catholic church parish listings, diocesan census, lists of Mexican-American organizations, agency lists and field interviews" (1975: 43–44). Migrant farm laborers and other foreigners, however, were excluded in this study. Using gamma for the statistical measures of associations between variables, Buehler found that voting turnout was related to, among other things, age, social status, length of residence in the area, and exposure to the mass media. Specifically, she observed that in high education groups (8 years or more of school), there was greater voter participation when the respondent was exposed to radio, newspapers and magazines.[19] In low education groups (0–7 years of school), exposure to magazines also was related to higher voting rates. Greater exposure to television, however, was not related to higher voting rates for either high or low education groups. Buehler concludes:

> In general the results support the hypothesis that exposure to mass media is directly associated with voter turnout. The relationship between media exposure and voting is only weakly supported using television as an indicator. This is probably because television may be used primarily as a source of entertainment rather than information. In the higher educational group, voting increases with exposure to radio, magazines or the newspaper. In the lower educational group, exposure to radio does not have a statistically significant effect, but exposure to magazines and newspapers does. In summary, exposure to mass media is generally positively associated with voter turnout regardless of education.
>
> (Buehler, 1975: 75)

Fortunately, the subsequent works on communication and Latino politics did not take another decade to emerge. In the 1980s, studies by Tan (1981, 1983), de la Garza, Brischetto and Vaughan (1983), de la Garza, Brischetto and Weaver (1984), Subervi-Vélez (1984), and Shoemaker, Reese and Danielson (1985a, 1985b) shed additional light on this subject.

In what appears to be the first multicultural research of this kind, Alexis Tan (1981 and 1983) tested a number of hypotheses on the relationships between exposure to the mass media and the political knowledge and behaviors of Latinos, Blacks and Anglos in Lubbock, Texas. The first of those studies was based on a March 1976 interpersonal interview survey of a random block sample of 139 Blacks, 137 Mexican Americans, and telephone interviews of 219 Anglos sampled from a telephone directory. Using regression and path analysis, he tested the proposition that the respondents' political attitudes (e.g., "sense of efficacy" and "diffuse support for the government") and behaviors (e.g., "active campaign participation") determine the respondents' use of the mass media.

The results showed some similarities as well as some differences among the three groups. For all three it was found that "political participation significantly predicts mass media use for public affairs information . . . Respondents who were politically active were more likely to use newspapers and TV for public affairs information than those who were not" (Tan, 1981: 144). However, the measures of political efficacy did not lead to greater public affairs use of the media among Latinos or Blacks.

Possibly because of these unexpected results, in his next study in 1983, apparently using the same data set, Tan hypothesized that "the mass media can socialize the majority (white) and ethnic minority members of the community to accept common values, norms and behavioral patters which are supportive of the system" (1983: 126). In other words, in this study, Tan proposed that the media acted more as independent variables on the subjects' political orientations and behaviors. Indeed, Tan found that exposure to the mass media[20] contributed to some aspects of the political knowledge and the participation of all three groups. Utilizing standard regression analysis to test the relationships between the studied variables, Tan states that

> [G]eneral public affairs knowledge is significantly predicted by newspaper and public affairs reading within the high education group of all three racial samples. In the low education group, newspaper public affairs reading predicts general public affairs knowledge only in the white sample.
>
> (Tan, 1983: 128)

In this study the low education group were the respondents who did not finish high school; the high education group were respondents who finished high school, attended some college or finished college. This variable was a strong differentiator as Tan also found that

> *Ethnic* political knowledge in the black and Mexican-American samples is significantly predicted by newspaper public affairs reading in the high education sample. . . . In the low education sample, TV public affairs viewing predicts ethnic political knowledge in the Mexican-American sample.
>
> (Tan, 1983: 128, italics added)

It is interesting and quite valuable that Tan inquired about the minority respondents' *ethnic* political knowledge. For Blacks and Hispanics, this was measured by asking subjects to identify some ethnic leaders and organizations; Mexican Americans, for example, were asked to identify César Chávez and La Raza Unida.

While no ethnic-relevant questions were asked about political participation, the media were again an important influence on it, although the relationship varied by ethnic group membership and education. For Mexican Americans and Blacks, political participation was not predicted by any of the media variables. However, with respect to Anglos, Tan states that "newspaper and public affairs reading predicts political participation in both the low and high education groups"; also, for the White high education group, he adds that "TV entertainment viewing is negatively related to political participation" (1983: 128). Interpersonal communication was the common predictor of participation among all three groups regardless of educational attainment.

The final intergroup difference observed by Tan was related to political efficacy—which was measured by the presence of the belief that political and social change is possible and that individual citizens make a difference in this process. In this case Tan found that exposure to newspaper public affairs reading made a positive impact for White respondents with higher education and for Black respondents of both education groups. Such media exposure, however, did not significantly affect Mexican Americans' political efficacy, which in turn was negatively affected by this sample's exposure to entertainment television.

Tan concludes his work by arguing that, upon taking into consideration the role of education, there is general support for the media's positive effects on politics. Among the caveats he posits with respect to ethnic minority groups, he states that "[p]olitical apathy, cynicism and feelings of alienation from the system may be more prevalent among less-educated ethnic minorities than among less-educated whites, thus neutralizing any reinforcing effects of the mass media" (1983: 131).

One of the key questions that Tan did not address was that of the language preference or ability of the Latino subjects and their exposure to or use of Spanish-language media. These issues were studied in the next two works of the 1980s that contributed to the emerging knowledge about the relationship between media and politics among Latinos.

Rodolfo de la Garza, Robert Brischetto, David Vaughan and Janet Weaver used data from a survey conducted in 1981–1982 by the Southwest Voter Registration Education Project (SVREP) in San Antonio and East Los Angeles to assess, among other things, the information sources, policy orientations, and political opinions and behaviors of Mexican Americans in those cities. In San Antonio, the 558-person sample was derived from a systematic random sampling of Hispanic households selected from that city's criss-cross Polk Directory. In Los Angeles, the 448 subjects for the study were selected based on a multistage cluster sampling strategy. While political communication was not at the core of that study, the survey did have some media questions, which produced findings of significance on this subject. For example, de la Garza, Brischetto and Vaughan found that

> [r]egardless of the language ability of the respondents, television is the most important source of information about what is happening in the local community. However, the second choice for Spanish monolinguals is radio, whereas for bilingual and English monolinguals, it is newspapers. As a source of news on the Mexican American community, television and radio are more important to Spanish monolinguals than to bilinguals, who rely most often on television and newspapers.
>
> (de la Garza, Brischetto and Vaughan, 1983: 18)

The impact of language ability on Latinos' media use is further evident in other findings, two of which are important for understanding aspects of the political socialization of this group. First, in that study it was observed that for Hispanics who speak only Spanish, the most trusted sources of political or community news were Spanish TV followed by Spanish radio (1983: 18, 20). On this question of most trusted media, de la Garza et al. also found that very few respondents selected Spanish-language newspapers. They attribute this to the "paucity of Spanish-language printed media in San Antonio and to possible low literacy rates among this group of respondents" (1983: 20). While the second reason may apply to Latino residents of both the cities studied, the first reason should not be true for Los Angeles, where *La Opinión*—one of the best and most pro-Latino Spanish-language dailies in the country—is published. The second finding on the impact of language on Latinos' political socialization was the fact that "English speakers, whether monolingual or bilingual, consider English news sources most trustworthy" (1983: 20). Among this group of respondents, television was the most trusted source followed by English-language newspapers.

Unfortunately, de la Garza et al. do not provide further elements for understanding the apparent lack of trust of the Spanish-language press among Spanish speakers, nor do they adequately expound upon the contextual or situational factors that could help explain the other political communication patterns. Nevertheless, the potential role of media for some aspects of Latino political life is clearly acknowledged in the conclusion of their work. Of particular note is their view that

> efforts to reach key sectors of the electorate should be tailored to the media use patterns of each community. Spanish-language radio may be very effective in reaching that sector of the electorate that is least likely to become electorally active. That electorate, though small, could play a major role in close elections. Moreover, because the great majority of Mexican Americans also listens to Spanish radio, efforts to mobilize the monolingual segment of the electorate should also contribute to mobilizing the electorate in general. . . . Overall, then, Mexican American voters make extensive use of the media to inform themselves about local, national and international issues.
>
> (de la Garza, Brischetto and Vaughan, 1983: 25–26)

In their following publication in 1984, de la Garza, Brischetto and Weaver analyzed other variables from the same data set and found further evidence on the relationships between media use and Mexican American political behaviors. In that part of their research, they used multiple regression analysis to assess the influence of various demographic, language, media and other variables on whether or not the respondents were registered to vote, had voted in the 1980 presidential election, chose particular candidates in that election, and otherwise participated in the electoral process. Media use[21] was positively related to some of the political behaviors. For example, for the combined sample (but not for the separate San Antonio and East Los Angeles samples) watching local news on television was positively related to voter turnout. In a curious way, the newspaper reading variable also contributed to the preference on who to vote for president. The authors state:

> The results of the analysis indicate that those who voted for Reagan tended to have higher incomes, included disproportionately large number of Protestants and were slightly less likely to read newspapers. Conversely, those who voted for Carter tended to be Catholics, have lower incomes, and were more likely to read newspapers.
>
> (de la Garza, Brischetto and Weaver, 1984: 8)

As a footnote to the first sentence of this citation de la Garza et al. state: "It is unclear why those who voted for Reagan read newspapers less than those who voted for Carter. Future studies will attempt to determine if this is a consistent pattern" (1984: 8). To the best of our knowledge, these authors have not provided any further explanations of this in their subsequent works. In fact, discussions of the potential role of the media in Latino politics was negligible in subsequent publications by these authors, except in the conclusion to Brischetto and de la Garza's 1985 work in which they summarize:

> Messages imported from outside the Chicano community either from establishment media or political institutions do not penetrate the electorate as deeply as messages transmitted from within the community. The survey also shows that while television is the main source of information for both ethnic groups, Mexican Americans rely more on radio than on newspapers than Anglos. The success of a media campaign strategy would be enhanced by including endorsements from Mexican-American officeholders and community leaders.
>
> (Brischetto and de la Garza, 1985: 26)

Altogether, it seems evident that for the Mexican American electorate studied by de la Garza et al., mass media—including Latino-oriented media—do contribute in important ways to political knowledge and mobilization. What those authors did not address is the relationship of media use and political behaviors among other major Latino groups.

Almost a decade after these studies de la Garza, DeSipio, García, García and Falcón (1992) did compare the politics of different groups of Latinos but then gave even less attention to media variables.

To date, the only study to assess simultaneously the interplay of media and politics among different groups of Latinos was conducted by Federico Subervi-Vélez for his doctoral dissertation. Utilizing data that Daniel Durán and Marcelino Miyares[22] gathered in 1977 from a stratified cluster probability sample of 400 Latinos in Chicago, Subervi-Vélez (1984) tested associations between the media use and political knowledge and participation among the respondents. Specifically, he investigated whether exposure to Hispanic and Anglo mass media was reflective of an assimilationist or a pluralist process, and whether exposure to such mass media influenced political knowledge of, and participation in, American society.

To assess this, the author used hierarchical regression path analysis controlling for and testing the influence of the usual demographic and socio-economic variables as well as the *proportion* of years in the United States,[23] English-language reading ability and Spanish-language reading ability. The dependent media variables were four measures of exposure to Anglo mass media, eight measures of exposure to Hispanic mass media, and two measures of dependency on Hispanic radio and television for information about the Latino community.[24] These variables were then analyzed as direct influences and as mediating variables on an index of political knowledge (knowing who was the mayor of Chicago, the recently elected Governor, and the two state senators), and an index of political participation (registering to vote and actual voting).

The findings indicated that exposure to the media was a function of a combination of different variables for each Latino group, but that there was a general assimilationist process in Latinos' increased exposure to the Anglo media and diminished exposure to the Latino-oriented media. The findings regarding political processes suggested there was an interplay of significant factors for each of the Latino groups.

Political knowledge, as operationalized in that study, was more a function of Latinos' demographic, U.S. residency and educational characteristics than it was a function of exposure to the mass media. However, various media measures had small, yet significant influences that merit notice. For example, controlling for the independent variables, political knowledge of Puerto Ricans was positively influenced by exposure to Hispanic and Anglo print media.[25] For Mexican Americans, especially those who were United States citizens, exposure to Anglo print media also had some positive influence on their political knowledge. Among Cubans in the sample who were United States citizens, political knowledge was positively influenced by exposure to Anglo print media as well as exposure to Spanish-language radio.[26]

Political participation, as measured in that study, was not as significantly related to the tested variables. Only for Puerto Ricans was Hispanic print media found to have some small, but statistically significant, association with the participation index; not so for Mexican American and Cuban American United States citizens. As Subervi-Vélez (1984) noted, of the possible reasons for the lack of significant relationships between many of the studied variables is the simplicity of both the media and political measurements themselves. For example, the question about the number of newspapers read (see endnote 25) was at best a gross approximation of exposure to this medium; no inquiry was made about exposure to Latino-oriented or general market media specifically for public or political affairs. The original data also lacked questions on ethnic political knowledge and participation that would be potentially more relevant to Latinos themselves. Furthermore, small sample sizes, especially in the Mexican and Cuban groups reduced the reliability of the regression analysis, which had to account for 11 control variables.

While the question remains as to whether a study with a larger sample of Latinos, including Puerto Ricans and Cubans, would lead to different results, this study, even with its shortcomings, supports our underlying proposition of the importance of studying media for understanding Latino politics. Such proposition was further supported in the final major research of the 1980s that analyzed some variables related to this subject.

In spring of 1984, Pamela Shoemaker, Stephen Reese and Wayne Danielson (1985a) directed a study that included half-hour interviews with a total of 1,218 Texas residents of which 308 were at least partially of Hispanic origin. The sample of subjects, drawn by using a two-stage, random-digit dialing process, were studied for assessing similarities and differences among Hispanics and Anglos regarding, among other things, "mass media usage and attitudes toward the media and journalists, including use of and attitudes toward Spanish-language media specifically," and "political behaviors and attitudes, including voting patterns and attitudes toward political parties and action groups" (Shoemaker, Reese and Danielson, 1985a: 5).

With respect to media use in general, Shoemaker et al. found patterns similar to those reported above, particularly regarding the high use of Spanish-language radio, and a declining use of print media in that language. In terms of the relationship between media and politics, the authors found that some media do make a difference in political behaviors but that there were significant differences between Hispanics and Anglos. For example, exposure to each of three media—TV news, radio news, and newspapers—were all significantly correlated with both political interest and political discussion. However, some of these associations proved spurious after the data were submitted to regression analysis with more rigorous controls. Then it was observed that Hispanics were less likely to vote than were Anglos of similar social, demographic, and media use patterns. This fact notwithstanding, it was also noted that some media still contributed to the mobilization of Latinos. Shoemaker et al. state:

> This study provides some evidence that media use and political behaviors like voting are related differently for Hispanics than for Anglos. Even after simultaneous controls for other political and media variables, as well as for demographic variables, there remained a small but statistically significant relationship between voting and newspaper reading for Hispanics, but not for Anglos. This supports our hypothesis that Hispanics may be more affected by media use than Anglos, perhaps because they exhibit low involvement with politics and may have fewer sources for political information. . . . When Hispanics read the newspaper, they may be more likely than Anglos to be activated to vote.
> (Shoemaker, Reese and Danielson, 1985a: 53–54)

It is interesting to observe that the significant media variable in this particular analysis was "days per week that the respondent reads a daily newspaper" with no distinction being made of the language of that publication. Possibly because the Latino subjects of this study indicated limited use of the Spanish-language media, Shoemaker et al. did not discuss any relationships between exposure to those media and the various measures of political attitudes and behaviors. However, even if such analysis would have been conducted, this type of report based on statewide phone survey data provides no relevant information on the community contexts that would explain the relationships.

More than a decade after the comparative study by Shoemaker et al. in 1985, no other research has systematically delved into the intersection of Latinos, mass communication, and politics.[27] Admittedly, the Latino national political survey by de la Garza et al. (1992) of 1,546 Mexicans, 589 Puerto Ricans, and 682 Cubans did include numerous questions on these subjects' political values (see their chapter 6), political attitudes and behaviors (see their chapters 8 to 10), and media use and exposure (see their chapters 5 and 10). Unfortunately, to date none of the principal researchers of that research team has published in depth analysis of the potential relationships between media and political variables. That data and analysis are the subject of chapter 15 of this book.

Evidently, there are major lacunas in the study of these matters during the last 10 years. Even the few works that have been published are limited in a number of ways. The absence of additional findings associating media and political variables may reflect more a problem of imprecise assessments of political variables that are functionally related to media messages, as has been discussed by McLeod and Reeves (1981). In the study by Subervi-Vélez (1984), for example, the measures of media exposure and of political knowledge and participation were crude indexes constructed from data originally gathered for other purposes. The fact that the associations between the media and political indexes showed statistical significance even after controlling for various other factors is very telling of the relationship between those variables. In other words, given what has been learned from the available limited data, the political effects of exposure to, and use of, the mass media could be even more properly assessed if adequate measures and procedures were followed.

Another shortcoming of the studies discussed in this third part of the chapter is that none offered any clues as to the quantity or quality of the respective communities' media coverage of political news and events that may have been relevant for the specific Latino communities in question. While researchers assume, and often verify, for example, that newspapers are related to Latinos' political behaviors, such as voting, no discussion is offered as to what was published in those papers that may have contributed to the mobilization. Discussions similar to those offered in the first section of this chapter on the political functions of the Latino-oriented press in the United States have not even been mentioned in most of the survey-based publications that queried Latinos' exposure to the Spanish-language press. That survey research also has left out assessments of Latinos' knowledge about and/or exposure to, or the potential effects of, specific campaign strategies, including political advertisements, directed at Latinos.

These limitations notwithstanding, each of the studies discussed in this section establish that there are a variety of often small but significant relationships between media variables and Latinos' political life. The challenge is to improve the methods and theories toward this end.

## CONCLUSION

It is evident that the writings reviewed above are very revealing about Latino political communication issues. However, they leave unanswered many questions about the role of the general market and Latino-oriented media in this group's political life. The remainder of this book presents the results of a series of studies related to Latino-oriented political content of media, and political strategies directed at Latinos. The data can provide some answers to the questions of what the media publish or broadcast that could lead to Latino mobilization, or lack thereof, and how the media have been used to reach Latino voters. Theoretical and methodological issues discussed here should contribute to the building blocks of future research on these matters.

## NOTES

1 In addition to the sources cited in this section, further information about the history of Latino-oriented press can be found in Fishman (1966), Fitzpatrick (1987), Gonzáles (1977), Griswold del Castillo (1977), Gutiérrez (1977, 1978), Gutiérrez and Ballesteros (1979), Hester (1979), Kanellos (1994), MacCurdy (1951), Medeiros (1980), Rendón (1974), Shearer (1954), and Wagner (1937).

2 See special edition of *The Americas Review*, Vol. 17, No. 3–4, 1989, dedicated to *La Prensa*.

3 The 2004 National Association of Hispanic Publications Media Kit & Resource Guide (2004) indicates, on page 11, that in the year 2003 there were 304 weekly papers and 322 less than weekly papers that could be considered Hispanic. Since then, these numbers have grown even more. However, a problem with the NAHP list is that it includes commercial non-news flyers and also Spanish-language publications that may partially circulate in the U.S. but are produced in Mexico and other countries. Another historical source is the *Library Microfilms, 40th anniversary issue: Materials on microfilm, historical collections* (p. 193), which indicates that, in the early 1990s, there were over 250 Chicano periodicals in its microfilm collection.

4 The power of González's rhetoric and its political mobilization led to his being falsely charged yet convicted and incarcerated for rape. Upon being released from a U.S. prison, he was deported to Mexico from where he continued to speak out via Mexican radio waves that crossed to the U.S. about the problems faced by Mexicans in this country.

5 The role of some Spanish-language radio stations in politically mobilizing Latinos was particularly noted during the pro-immigrant marches and rallies that took place across the country in spring 2006; see Navarro (2006).

6 For a discussion of the federal government's repressive activities against Puerto Rico's independence, including activities detrimental to the media favoring this status, see Bosque Pérez and Colón Morera (2006), Lewis (1974), and Varo (1973).

7 See chapter 4 for additional notes about *El Diario-La Prensa*, and Subervi and Eusebio (2005) for more details on the current status of the ownership changes.

8 *Noticias del Mundo* was launched on April 22, 1980 and closed on April 29, 2004.

9 Currently there are no U.S. Latino-oriented *daily* or weekly newspapers circulating widely or reaching the majority of Latinos at the national level. The largest circulating print media directed primarily to this group are *Hispanic*, an English-language monthly and *Vista*, another monthly English-language magazine with a brief Spanish-language section, whose format is similar to *Parade* magazine. Both are published out of Miami, Florida. Because *Vista* is distributed as an insert to local newspapers in selected cities with high concentrations of Latinos, its circulation is approximately one million. Neither of these can be considered regular and prompt providers of current events related to Latino political life in this country.

10 For this review we did not search for newspaper articles and columns that may have reported or commented on the media strategies of any party or specific candidate. In addition to the works cited here and our own research on this subject (see bibliography), the only other publication that mentions campaign strategies directed at Latinos is by John Knaggs (1986). His book discusses at length the Republican Party's 25-year effort to woo Mexican American voters

in Texas, but he does not shed details into the mass media activities, except to mention the participation of Lionel Sosa in the campaigns for electing Senator Jim Tower. Mr. Sosa's work on behalf of GOP presidential candidates is further discussed in chapters 12 to 14.

11 Charles Colson was Special Counsel to President Nixon; Frederic Malek was Deputy Director of Management and Budget as well as member of the Domestic Council.

12 That memo continues with discussions of the limitations of the "plan" such as the "lack of special expertise and experience of ethnic writers" (1972: 5595). Strategies for improving the overall plan are then reviewed and suggested (1972: 5595–5598).

13 The only test of the political effects of exposure to a particular newspaper, i.e., El Tiempo in Denver, was conducted by Valdes y Tapia (1976) whose work is discussed in this chapter.

14 We could assume that in their political interests, the Democrats and Republicans have conducted studies on these matters. But such information, which is most probably very confidential, has not come to our attention.

15 In Villareal et al.'s (1988) edited book, the chapters by Finke (1988: 69) and Regalado (1988: 97) allude to the media but do not elaborate on this subject. In the conclusion by Villareal and Neighbor (1988: 130–132) the media are mentioned in passing as important for the political education of Mexican Americans.

16 Frequency of exposure to "newspapers," "Spanish radio," "Spanish TV," "church or religious newspapers or magazine," "labor magazines or newspapers" was coded as "never," "sometimes," "quite often," and "daily" (1976: 215–216). Using similar ordinal level response options, Valdes y Tapia also inquired if the respondents read editorials, listened to political material on TV or radio, read editorials or articles on elections in El Tiempo.

17 Hispano is the term frequently used in Colorado and New Mexico to refer to people of Latino/Hispanic heritage, especially if the person is of Spanish origin.

18 Exposure to the critical messages in El Tiempo was coded as "did not read or see," "saw but did not read," "yes, read." Somewhat similar coding options were stated for the critical messages on TV and radio.

19 Media exposure was measured as "reported watching TV previous day" (yes or no), "reported listening to radio previous day" (yes or no), "last time respondent looked through or read a magazine" (today or yesterday, a few days ago, a week, longer than a week), "frequency of newspaper reading" (every day, 2–6 times a week, 1 or less times a week).

20 Tan's media exposure was operationalized as "multiplicative function of frequency of general use of the medium (e.g., hours TV is watched daily or days a newspaper is read) and frequency of attention to specific articles or programs in the content type" (1983: 127). Public affairs exposure was measured by asking respondents to indicate on a four-point scale their frequency of such exposure in newspapers and on TV.

21 This was operationalized with two dichotomous variables—"Do you ever watch local news on television?" and "Do you read a daily newspaper?"—for which the respondents could answer yes or no.

22 See the doctoral dissertations by Duran (1977) and Miyares (1978). Duran's work was published as a book in 1980 by Arno Press. Neither of these authors tested in any detail the relationship between the media and the politics variables.

23 In that study, the author found that *proportion* of years in the United States, measured by dividing the respondent's number of years in the U.S. into his/her age, was a stronger and more accurate variable for partially assessing the impact of immigration than the traditional variable that only assesses the number of years in the United States.

24 Given that this was primarily a mass communication based research, the operationalizations of all the media variables are quite extensive and cannot be easily summarized here (see Subervi-Vélez, 1984: 81–86). However, operationalizations of the key variables that were significantly related to politics are presented below.

25 Exposure to Hispanic and Anglo print media was measured by adding the number of newspapers and magazines in the respective language that the respondent "read regularly within the last year." This question was asked only to subjects who had answered yes to the question "Over the last year, have you read any newspapers regularly?" As discussed in the main text, this was certainly an inadequate measure for assessing potential influence on politics.

26 Exposure to Spanish-language radio was based on an index that brought together two measures: (a) "During the last seven days, how often did you listen to Spanish-language radio? Would you say you listened every day, a few days a week, about one day, or did not listen at all?," and (b) counting the actual number of programs that from a list of options from the interview schedule the respondents said they listened to on such radio.

27 A study by Austin and Nelson (1993) merits a brief mention here as it analyzed the influence of ethnic group membership (Hispanic, Native American, White) and indicators of family communication environment on socialization into U.S. politics among 10th to 12th graders from three rural Northwest towns. While the authors found some ethnic group differences, the specific influence of the media on the political socialization process of Hispanics youths was not dealt with in any detail or clarity. Discussions of the subjects' community contexts and environment, including the media in English or Spanish, were also absent from this work.

# 3

# THEORETICAL, CONTEXTUAL, AND METHODOLOGICAL CONSIDERATIONS

*Federico A. Subervi-Vélez*

Complementing the literature reviewed in chapter 2, this chapter discusses various theoretical, contextual, and methodological considerations that serve as foundations for political communication research centered on Latinos. The aim is to enhance the frameworks used to research and better understand (a) what influences people, in this case Latinos, to engage in the political dynamics of the United States (e.g., gain knowledge about issues and candidates, attend rallies, mobilize, vote, and other related political orientations and activities), and (b) the role of the media in such processes.

## THEORETICAL CONSIDERATIONS

As even a cursory literature review would show, there are numerous theories that help to explain a wide spectrum of dimensions of the political participation of the American public (Conway, 1991; Verba and Nie, 1972; Almond and Verba, 1963; Brady, Verba, and Schlozman; 1995; Jackman, 1987; Putnam, 2000; Rosenstone and Hansen, 1993). Some of those theories pertain to ethnic and/or immigrant populations (Danigelis, 1978; Leighley, 2001); others focus on Latinos (Chávez, 2004;[1] Connaughton, 2005). There are also theories that delve into the role of the media in politics (see especially Part 3 of Kaid, 2004). There is still a scarcity, however, of theories centered on *political communication* as related to ethnic minorities, in particular with respect to Latinos.

Nevertheless, there are frameworks that serve as building blocks for, or provide, valuable insights into theoretical constructions about Latino political communication. The concepts of assimilation and pluralism are one set; social comparison and relevancy are another.

Under the rubric of assimilation and pluralism, the focus turns to two interconnected yet distinct processes of adapting to the American way of life, both of which have implications for assessing Latino political communication. Assimilation implies, among other things, "the process by which a subordinate group or individual takes on characteristics of the dominant group and is eventually accepted as part of that group" (Schaefer, 1979: 37). Pluralism, by contrast, leads to sustained ethnic differentiation and continued heterogeneity. It implies conditions in which ethnic, national, or minority groups in general may practice their "own cultural traits and still participate in the dominant society" (Schaefer, 1979: 45).

However, instead of assimilation, the term acculturation will be preferred. It implies learning and adapting selected cultural traits and patterns of the dominant society and allows for discussing if and how an individual or group takes on characteristics of the dominant society, such as political socialization into the political party and voting system, without having to assess whether or not there is any particular acceptance by the dominant society (see Subervi and Ríos, 2005). Giving preference to the term acculturation also avoids having to assess whether the immigrant or non-dominant group member is casting aside and forgetting tenets related to his/her original nation or minority group. The focus is on what is being done congruent to involvement with and in dominant norms, in this case in the political arena.

Applying some of the tenets related to the process of acculturation, it can be proposed that Latinos adapt to the dominant ways of the U.S. society by enhancing their political knowledge, discussing politics, registering to vote, attending political rallies, and voting for the candidate or party that best represents their political ideology (somewhere along the liberal or conservative spectrum) or socio-economic interests as traditionally defined for the general American public. It is all part of achieving the "American dream," along with improving the education, occupation, income and other aspirations for self and family.

One extreme of the spectrum, a type of acculturation—the one that is best defined by the concept of assimilation—also entails leaving behind (neglecting, forgetting, ignoring, becoming indifferent to) the ethnic points of reference and values that are not congruent with the perceived American way of life.[2] For Hispanics pursuing this type of immersion, it can be proposed that they will have little, if any, exposure to or use of Spanish-language or other Latino-oriented media for learning about and immersing into American political, business, social or cultural affairs. Likewise, issues that may be of particular relevance to other Latinos (e.g., immigration, bilingual education) may be of limited concern to them, at least within the realm of politics.

Another consideration with respect to Latinos that are fully assimilated is that the path to obtain their votes is primarily via news stories and political commercials and ads in general market English-language media. This subset of potential voters may be interested in Spanish-speaking politicians or their representatives, but the fact that they speak Spanish would not necessarily be meaningful factors in their attention to, or preference for, a candidate or party.

It is probably rare, however, to find this type of assimilation that is oblivious to any connections to the Latino cultural inheritance.[3] In fact, for Latinos, the reality is probably more of acculturation (learning and adapting selected cultural traits and patterns of the dominant society) and pluralism (selectively keeping and expressing cultural and other traits of their Latino heritage) (see Subervi-Vélez, 1986; Subervi and Ríos, 2005).

Thus, even while pursuing the "American dream," most Latinos adapting to the dominant United States society are not totally disinterested in political, social, economic, or cultural issues that relate to their ethnic community, however that is defined.[4] This suggests that even highly acculturated Latinos would not be immune to the candidacy and messages of a Latino candidate, nor to the appeals that non-Latino candidates make to them as Latinos, or much less to messages from Latino operatives on behalf of their respective candidates, especially if the candidate is also Latino. If research had demonstrated that the majority of Latinos were acculturating in a way in which all elements of their national origin or at least pan-Hispanic identity was being irrecoverably lost, neither the Republican nor the Democratic Party and their candidates would spend the millions of dollars that they do in special—Latino-oriented—communication efforts (see chapters 12 to 14).

The proposition can thus be made that, with proper cues from the media and other campaign information, Latinos—including those who are acculturated or in the process of becoming fully immersed into the political norms of the United States—may be more prone to enhance their political knowledge, involvement, and/or activism when they perceive Latino connections to a candidate or a campaign. Most certainly, at least a minimal level of ethnic identity remains important and some political connection is plausible with that ethnic identity. In such a case, the acculturation theoretical framework needs to be broadened to consider the proposition that *the greater the perceived Latino relevancy of candidates or issues,[5] the greater the political involvement of Latinos—even among those who seek to fully acculturate in the dominant United States society.*

The previous proposition requires additional considerations, but from the framework of pluralism.[6] Applying some of the tenets more in line with the concept of pluralism, it can be argued that Latinos adapt to the dominant ways of the United States society but mostly in terms of selective acculturation, not full immersion into the United States and phasing out of the Latino culture. Thus, they maintain a sense of heterogeneity or distinctiveness even as they go about enhancing their political knowledge, discussing politics, registering to vote, attending political rallies, and voting for the candidate or party that best represents their political ideology or socio-economic interests. In this scenario, greater attention is potentially paid to the issues and candidates that are perceived as connecting to their ethnic identity or concerns as Latinos. Even in the process of achieving the "American dream," Latino identity is valued and serves more than just as an occasional nominal classification.

For Hispanics pursuing this type of adaptation,[7] issues such as immigration and education become more salient within the realm of politics. Thus, they pay special attention to the news that addresses such matters. During a political campaign, even more attention is directed to the news if the issues are explicitly framed with respect to Latinos, be it by the candidates or their representatives—especially if these are Hispanic. For the more pluralistic Latinos, exposure to or use of Latino-oriented media, including Spanish-language media, would be an avenue for learning more about American political, business, social or cultural affairs and the relevancy of these to Latinos' lives because Latino-oriented media provide more variety, depth and insights to the coverage of such matters from Latino perspectives.

Building on the above, a proposition that would follow from the pluralism framework is that a path to obtain the votes of these Latinos is via news stories and political commercials and ads in the media that they pay most attention to. For the bilingual pluralistic Latino, that could mean both general market English-language media *and* Spanish-language media. For the primarily Spanish-speaking Latino, the communication path to their vote would be more heavily paved in Spanish-language media and political commercials in that language. For either of these subsets of potential voters, politicians who can or try to speak Spanish, or their representatives who do the same, could attract significant attention and potentially be key factors in their preference for a candidate or party. Even if the candidates do not speak Spanish, the ability to use Spanish-language media to get their message and propaganda across via Spanish-language and other Latino-oriented media would be most effective (see Colín, 2004; Ramos, 2004).

Given these theoretical considerations, the questions that merit attention for assessing the potential impact of the news media on Latinos are: (1) In their coverage of political campaigns, do the news media provide information that could potentially help Latinos better understand from the framework of their own ethnic background the candidates and the issues and thus mobilize to vote? (2) More specifically, in the general market English-language media or in the Latino-oriented—especially the Spanish-language—media, are there headlines, lead paragraphs, pictures, opinion columns, or explicit audio and visual cues about the Latino candidates and/or issues? In essence, do the news media provide content that

54

can be considered relevant from a Latino perspective? The chapters in Part II of this book address these precise matters.

Discussion of that research data, however, first calls for some contextual considerations about the Spanish-language media as well as the general market media in relation to Latinos.

## THE AUDIENCES, COMMUNITIES, AND ROLES OF SPANISH-LANGUAGE NEWS MEDIA[8]

### The audiences

The primary audience that is regularly exposed to, and may be most influenced by, Spanish-language media is, obviously, the Latinos who can understand the language.[9] That audience includes established or temporary residents who have acquired the language either in their Spanish-speaking homeland (Mexico, Puerto Rico, Cuba, etc.), or in the United States by way of formal or informal instruction. Government and private industry sources vary in their assessments of how many Latinos in the United States are Spanish-speakers. Nevertheless, the fact remains that this language is prominent across the land and is now the most common foreign language taught in schools and colleges in almost every state of the union.

For example, one report of the U.S. Bureau of the Census (2003) indicates that in 2000, Spanish was spoken in the home by more than 28.1 million people of five years of age and older (approximately 12 percent of the total U.S. population). The report adds that 13.8 million of these did not speak English well or at all. Citing U.S. Bureau of the Census figures for 1990, Valdés and Seoane (1996) point to the distribution of the U.S. Spanish-speaking population as follows: California, 5.5 million; Texas, 3.4 million; New York, 1.8 million; and Florida, 1.4 million. The corresponding figures based on that 2000 Census were much larger: 8.1, 5.2, 2.4, and 2.5 million (U.S. Census Bureau, Census 2000 Special Tabulation 224), all of which imply potential interest and demand for Spanish-language media and other related consumer products.

Another perspective is offered by a private industry source, *El Nuevo Herald* (c. 1996). Citing figures from a Strategy Research Corporation study, this paper's marketing pamphlet lists the percentages of Latinos in Los Angeles, New York, Miami, San Francisco, and Chicago who "first learned to speak Spanish," were "most comfortable with Spanish," for whom "Spanish [was] most frequently spoken at home," and for whom "Spanish [was] most frequently used socially." The lowest percentage for any one these activities was 56 percent; it reflected San Francisco's Hispanics response to the last item. All other figures averaged more than 60 percent and were as high as 90 percent.

An overall approximation of the potential audience of Spanish language broadcast media in the cities from which some of the data of the studies presented in this book is illustrated in figure 3.1. The numbers in that figure illustrate the distribution of language dominance or preference of Latinos in Los Angeles, Miami, New York, Chicago, San Antonio, and Houston. What their data show is that at least 27 percent of the Latino residents of each of these cities are Spanish dominant, or prefer that language. In Los Angeles the number is significantly higher: 75 percent

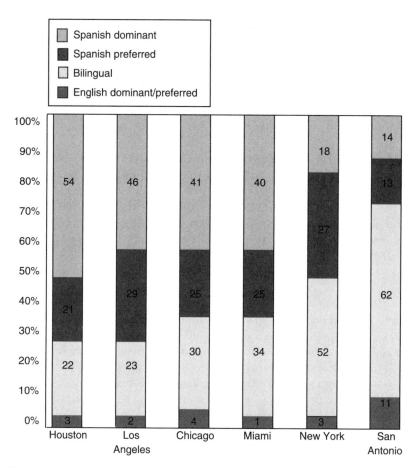

*Figure 3.1* Language segmentation by key Hispanic markets, male and female of household, ages 18–54

*Note:* At least six months in United States and five hours of Spanish media per week.

*Source:* Valdés and Seoane, (1996), Figure 5.5, p. 239; reprinted with copyright authorization

of the Latino population indicates such language characteristics. In San Antonio, the majority of Latinos are bilingual.[10]

The number of Latinos who can read Spanish is another important language factor that merits consideration. On this topic, Valdés and Seoane (1996) provide data for Southern California and Chicago where at least 80 percent of the Latinos they have interviewed claim the "ability to read Spanish either very well or well" (see their tables 5.3 and 5.4). Based on a survey of a national sample of Latinos, Strategy Research Corporation (1991) found a higher number, 88.9 percent, of Latinos claiming ability to read Spanish well or very well.[11] Evidently, what these numbers suggest is an ample potential audience for Spanish print media. However, as can be expected, there are regional and state variations in Latinos who can read Spanish, and in the level of that ability.

Variations will also stem from a person's place of birth and subsequent socialization. De la Garza, DeSipio, García, García and Falcón (1992) found notable differences in the "home language," "overall language ability," and English and Spanish literacy among foreign born versus native United States-born Mexicans, Puerto Ricans and Cubans. For example, among the foreign born, 79 percent of the Mexicans, 59 percent of the Puerto Ricans, and 81 percent of the Cubans speak only Spanish or more Spanish than English in the home. Among the United States-born, the respective numbers of members of these groups who speak only English or more English than Spanish are 63 percent, 50 percent and 31 percent. As can be expected, the figures for overall language ability and literacy in English and Spanish are similar to these.

In a subsequent section of their book (e.g., 1996: chapter 6), Valdés and Seoane provide numerous figures of media use among Latinos in various parts of the country. Figures of Spanish-language and general market media use and exposure also are found in the annual studies of the Strategy Research Corporation, as well as in the proprietary studies of numerous other marketing companies seeking to gauge the media in which to place advertisements and promotions directed at Latino populations. While variations can be found from one source to another, they coincide in pointing toward a large and significant audience for Spanish-language media.

In the cities about which we studied the political content of Spanish-language dailies, there was evidently a sufficient number of readers in that language to justify the daily production of those newspapers. Even with declining circulation among some of the older or more established papers, the five newspapers analyzed in this book are still commercially viable enterprises and potential sources for political news and information for some segments of the Latino communities they serve. Moreover, the exponential increase in the number of Spanish-language dailies in the last five years is even stronger testimony of a viable audience for these media (see Subervi and Eusebio, 2005).

A similar assertion can be made about the audience for the Spanish-language television networks and stations, which continue to flourish in spite of fluctuations in advertising revenues. In fact, Spanish-language radio is one medium that has been enjoying a constant increase in number of stations, audience and advertising revenues. When Clear Channel announced in September 2004 that it was changing the format of 20 to 25 of its stations from English to Spanish, it was a definitive recognition of the existence of a growing and commercially viable Spanish-speaking audience (Leeds, 2004).[12]

Spanish-monolinguals are not the only audience that could use and be affected by Spanish-language media. When the figures for bilingual (Spanish and English) speakers are added, the potential circle of influence of those media is expanded. Except for Latinos who are highly acculturated in the sense of being English monolinguals and very isolated from their family roots and country of origin, numerous Latinos are bound to be in regular contact and interaction with Spanish speakers—be they Spanish monolinguals or bilinguals. This is most likely for Latinos who live in large cities that historically have also been primary immigration points (such as is the case for Miami, Los Angeles, Houston and New York).[13] This suggests that through interpersonal communication processes, the circle of potential influence of the Spanish-language media extends beyond the monolingual Spanish-language speakers.

Access to Spanish-language media, however, can limit its audience and thus impact. For instance, because of the restricted circulation areas of most of the Spanish-language press—including the daily newspapers studied in subsequent chapters of this book—many Spanish-speaking Latinos not reached by this medium live beyond the limits where the papers circulate via home delivery or on newsstands.[14] For these Latinos and for others who live in cities where there are no regularly published Spanish-language newspapers, little is known about if and how that press has much influence in the community's politics or any other matters. At the time of the 1984 and 1988 studies (see chapter 4), only New York, Los Angeles and Miami had locally produced Spanish-language dailies.[15] And while there are now some 20 Spanish-language dailies being published in this country, these remain easily available in only about a dozen metropolitan cities plus a handful of border communities.[16]

Spanish-language television also has some boundaries in many Hispanic markets. While Univisión and Telemundo claim to reach more than 90 percent of the Hispanic households in the United States, there are variations in the availability of that access. Major metropolitan areas have Univisión and Telemundo owned-and-operated local stations or affiliates broadcasting over the air via UHF channels. In metropolitan areas and elsewhere, some cable carriers not only offer the main programming of these two networks, but also of their respective cable operations Telefutura and Mun-Dos, and of other companies such as Galavisión, Gems, and HNTV. In various communities, however, the VHF signals are low powered. This requires the viewer interested in Spanish-language TV to have to subscribe to cable—*if* he or she can afford it and *if* the cable company carries that programming. In smaller markets, especially with few Latinos, the cable operators may offer one but not the other networks.

In sum, aside from the few Latinos who may be geographically or linguistically isolated, there are sufficient potential audiences for Spanish-language media and thus sufficient grounds on which to justify studying the political content of Spanish-language media. Whether or not the Latino residents pay attention to and are affected by the political news and information of their Spanish-language media is the subject of other discussions further on in this book.

## The communities

Latinos living in the communities where Spanish-language newspapers do not circulate are not totally immune from the political news and information of that press. The same can be said about the Latinos living outside the reach of Spanish-language broadcast media. The potential impact of Spanish-language print and broadcast media includes their influence on community leaders and their function as outlets for those leaders and other members of the community. It can be further argued that in serving the traditional surveillance, correlation and transmission roles, the Spanish-language and other Latino-oriented media may concurrently serve the dual roles of acculturation *and* pluralism.

First, Latino community leaders and activists are *unlikely* to be among those removed or detached from the media that cater primarily to their communities. Regardless of their language orientations or abilities, these leaders monitor Spanish-language newspapers, television and other Latino-oriented media to keep abreast of what is happening in their environment (see Lewels, 1974; Nicolini, 1986). Furthermore, Latino leaders are not the only ones who monitor the Spanish-language media, especially the newscasts. It is common practice for elected officials, prominent business leaders and others aspiring to such distinction to keep tabs on their community news sources regardless of the language in which they are printed or broadcast. In other words, both Latino and non-Latino leaders and activists often use the Spanish-language media to, at a minimum, survey the Hispanic issues of their environment. It can thus be proposed that, to the extent that the Spanish-language media help, inform and/or persuade Latino leaders or others regarding some public policy, it can be said that such media have some potential influence on the Hispanic community and, in fact, on the community at large.

A second way in which the Spanish-language media affect Latinos is by providing outlets for the expression of community concerns. Again, community leaders and activists are among the first to make use of the Spanish-language print and broadcast media to "get their message out" (see Lewels, 1974). Likewise, the Latino leaders are often sought as spokespersons and sources for stories published or broadcast by the Latino-oriented media—be they produced in Spanish or in English. Furthermore, Latino leaders are also sought (although usually not as often) for stories produced by the general market media. It can thus be proposed that, to the extent that the Spanish-language (and other Latino-oriented) media provide opportunities for the expression of community concerns, be it via the general public or by way of the Latino leadership, they have the potential to affect that community. In the first instance, those media can be said to be providing a "surveillance" function; in the second case, they are serving "correlation" and "transmission" functions (see Wilson and Gutiérrez, 1995).

## Dual roles: acculturation and pluralism

Two other roles played by the Spanish-language newspapers, television, and other Latino-oriented media are political acculturation *and* political pluralism[17] (see Subervi-Vélez, 1986; Riggins, 1992). Spanish-language and other Latino-oriented media promote political acculturation in various ways. They report about the national, state and local governments, about leaders, events and issues. This includes news on legislation, rules and regulations that affect the American polity and population at large, as well as Latinos. They also report on the mainstream political parties (including their leadership) and their activities, events and issues that take place at the national and local levels. During campaigns for elected office or related to a proposition or a referendum, Latino-oriented media of all types may feature information about where and how to register and vote. Spanish-language media, especially the major daily newspapers, may feature translations of the candidates' qualifications and platforms, as well as translations of the propositions or referendum items.

Reading or watching news about any of such political matters can be one of the factors—possibly an important one—in Latinos' learning about American political life. If that happens, it can be said that those media had a political acculturation role at the cognitive level. If learning about dominant society politics via Spanish-language and/or other Latino-oriented media also helps Latinos become more actively involved in U.S. politics, e.g., registering to vote and voting, it can be said that such media also played a political acculturation role at the behavioral level.

The Spanish-language and other Latino-oriented media may also contribute to political pluralism.[18] Spanish-language and other Latino-oriented media promote political pluralism in various ways. For example, they report about the elections and appointments of Latinos to leadership positions in government and political parties. While general market English-language media also do this, Spanish-language and other Latino-oriented media usually provide a Latino perspective to the news of such elections and appointments. This means additional information about the national heritage and other ethnic factors related to the candidates' and appointees' life and community, including their stands on issues that may be of special concern to Latinos.

Another political pluralism activity, this one specifically carried out by the Spanish-language press, is the publication of news, opinion columns and editorials that highlight uniquely Latino perspectives to political events, including propositions and referenda. This takes place on a regular basis regarding the political workings of government and parties, and possibly more so during elections. Latino perspectives are particularly discussed with respect to laws, legislation and regulations that are proposed (or should be proposed) which affect Latinos in a unique way. When the editors of a newspaper and/or community leaders consider that an act of discrimination—political or otherwise—has taken place or is threatening to take place, Latino perspectives are usually published very prominently in this press. Community-wide mobilization campaigns may even follow. Occasionally, when Spanish-language television stations offer special newscasts or programs on Latino-oriented political or social concerns, they too play a pluralistic role.

Reading or hearing through Spanish-language or other Latino-oriented media about Latino elected and appointed leaders, or about issues that are deemed important to or affecting Latinos in a particular way, can be one of the factors—possibly a very important one—in the learning by readers of *Latino* perspectives to political life, albeit as part of the dominant U.S. political life. This would imply that those media foster political pluralism at the cognitive level. If learning about dominant society politics also helps a print media reader or broadcast media listener to become more actively involved in Latino politics, such as promoting and voting for a Latino candidate, or voting in favor of or against a proposition or referendum that affects Latinos in a particular way (e.g., California's propositions 187 and 209), it can be said that those media also encouraged political pluralism at the behavioral level.

A pluralist role of such media can be inferred if they contribute to readers or listeners supporting Latino-oriented community activities or events. This includes the enhancement of the status or candidacy of non-Hispanic leaders or candidates who distinctively promote the well-being and interests of Latinos and their communities. An even more pluralistic political role is played when Latino-oriented media, upon reporting on alternative Latino political groups such as La Raza Unida Party in South Texas in the 1970s (see Santillán, 1973), contribute to the learning about and involvement with such group. Evidently, it is assumed that Latino news, information and perspectives in the Spanish-language media can be valuable for and contribute to the political mobilization of the Hispanic electorate.

The content analyses in chapter 4 of Spanish-language newspapers and in chapters 5 to 7 of Spanish-language television network news provide partial evidence as to if and how these media carry out any of these political roles and functions within the Latino communities they serve, especially the dual roles of acculturation and pluralism. Given what is known of the political history of some of the Latino print media, as alluded to in chapter 2, it is proposed that the newspapers studied herein do play such dual roles. For broadcast media, there is less data on which to make a similar proposition at this time. However, the chapters in this book that offer empirical data about the national network newscasts suggest those news programs play similar roles. Based primarily on personal observations, it can be affirmed that some radio stations, especially the Cuban American ones in the Miami area, have also played both roles quite prominently.

Another important political function of the media, in this case Latino-oriented media as well, is agenda-setting (McCombs, 2004; Protess and McCombs, 1991; Weaver, 1981; Winter and Eyal, 1981). Building on analysis of media content and public opinion, the agenda-setting function implies that the media influence what people are thinking about (e.g., what is important, salient, worthy of attention) in terms of the elections and electoral processes. As shown in chapters 15 and 16, Spanish-language newspapers and television news are indeed playing this function in Latino communities. Interpreting whether that function and its corollary effects correspond more to an acculturation or a pluralism perspective is debatable. What the chapters do show is that Latino-oriented news media are important and integral factors related to the political socialization of Latinos.

An alternative dual role perspective about ethnic minority media has been offered by Riggins (1992), who proposes that these media have two ideologies. One is a dominant ideology (defined as information consistent with the interests of the elite). The other contains traces of counter ideology (defined as information opposing elite interests). He suggests that ethnic minority media have elements and characteristics of mainstream media, as well as elements and characteristics unique to ethnic media. The merits of Riggins' dual role perspective will be discussed in light of the findings of the content analysis of the Spanish-language media and their acculturation/pluralism roles.

Summarizing this segment, we can affirm that the analyses of the political content of the Spanish-language media allow for two outcomes. First, the study of these media will reveal the characteristics of the political messages disseminated to a particular and distinct segment of the population. In other words, the analyses provide a window on how the dominant United States polity was presented to the audiences of the newspapers and TV newscasts. Second, the study provides elements for comparison with numerous writings about the English-language news-papers and networks coverage of politics (e.g., Stempel and Windhauser, 1991). The most direct comparison is that which will come in chapters 8 and 9 of this book, which look at how selected general market English-language newspapers covered "Latino" candidates and issues. In conclu-sion, studying the political content of the Spanish-language media will contribute to a better understanding of part of the political life and dynamics of Latinos in the United States.

## ASSESSING LATINO PERSPECTIVES IN GENERAL MARKET PRINT AND BROADCAST NEWS MEDIA

The previous section began with the question "Which media should be studied for better understanding Latino politics and why?," to which we responded "all, each for different reasons." This section delves into the rationale for studying English-language print media (analyzed in chapters 8 and 9) and English-language broadcast media (analyzed in chapters 10 and 11).[19] For studying these media, there are also some distinct Latino perspectives in terms of audiences and the communities at large.

Before expanding on those points, it is important to reiterate that the foundations for the study of these media are built on the same justifica-tions and assumptions given by the numerous authors who have studied the politics of the general market United States news media. That ration-ale was summarized by stating that mass media may have some influence on the public. Concomitantly, by studying their content, something can be learned also about the world of politics they cover.

### The audiences

First, general market mass media are pervasive among Hispanics, too. Time and again, studies of media use and exposure show that Latinos do read English-language newspapers and watch English-language television news (de la Garza, et al., 1992; DeSipio, 2003; Suro, 2004). While differences abound in the number and demographic characteristics of the Latinos who engage in these media activities, and in the time spent with various media, no study has found Latinos to be isolated from society's dominant channels of mass communication. Moreover, the literature reviewed in the third section of chapter 2 offered considerable evidence of Latinos' use of, and exposure to, general market media, and of the relationship this had to the political orientations of some members of this group. Thus, when we propose that English-language media are important vehicles for transmitting news and information about politics, it follows that assessing the political content of these media also is indispensable for better understanding the dynamics of Latino politics in this country.

The second point about Latinos as audiences comes from the realization, as described in the previous section, that in some locations Latino-oriented media are not easily available. For example, in cities such as Albuquerque, Boston, Philadelphia, San Francisco, and Tampa, where thousands of Latinos reside, no *daily* newspapers are published primarily oriented to members of this group. Until recently, the same was true in Chicago, Dallas, Orlando, and San Antonio. Thus, for many Latinos the main source of printed news relevant to Latino politics would be the general market English-language dailies. That is the reality faced by Latinos regardless of their Spanish or English language abilities.

The issue of language brings us to the third point about the audience considerations. For Latinos who are monolingual English speakers, English-language media are unequivocally a more accessible source of political information than are Spanish-language media. This would hold true even in cities where Spanish-language media abound. Therefore, understanding this population's media experiences with Latino perspectives in political news requires assessments of the English-language sources.

Fourth, most Latinos who have become United States citizens have learned some amount of English. That language should not be unfamiliar even for Puerto Ricans who were born and educated on the island because that language is taught and required there from grade school through the second year in college. Thus, for Latinos who are United States citizens residing in this country, English-language media may be among the outlets used on a regular basis for various types of news and information, including that relating to politics.

The question remains—What are the messages of English-language media that may be of distinct Latino appeal to members of this population?

## The community

Whatever the media say or don't say about Latino politics can significantly affect not only Latinos, but also the community at large. The media's responsibility to present properly diverse populations and issues of particular importance to those populations, and the consequences of inadequate representations of these, has been made in reports and studies ranging from the 1960s to date (e.g., U.S. Kerner Commission, 1968; Keever, Martindale, and Weston, 1997; Martindale, 1986; Murphy and Murphy, 1981; de Uriarte, 2003). In essence, the lack of portrayals of minorities, as well as a preponderance of negative portrayals of minorities, definitively affect minorities' self-esteem and their relations to other members of society; they also affect how *non*-minorities relate to minorities (see Berry and Mitchell-Kernan, 1982).

Without a doubt, similar concerns apply to the realm of political communication. Graber asserts that mass media "images are especially pervasive when they involve aspects of life that people experience only through the media" (1997: 3). Since most non-Latinos have very limited opportunities to directly experience "Latino politics," it will be the English-language news media (and other general market media) that will provide the mediated experience, if any at all. The exception is the non-Latinos, such as many government officials and community leaders, who deliberately tune in to the Latino-oriented media.

Nonetheless, studying English-language media to assess if and how they cover Latino-related political news, information, and perspectives is invaluable for various reasons. First, because those media may contribute to Latinos' knowledge and actions about politics in general and about Latino politics in particular. Second, because those media contribute to non-Latinos' knowledge about and behavior towards Latino politics. In essence, understanding Latino-related political content of general market media can help us better understand some of the dynamics of Latino political life.

## FOUNDATIONS FOR STUDYING COMMUNICATION STRATEGIES OF POLITICAL PARTIES AND CANDIDATES

Under this heading, two issues require attention for building the case to study communication strategies in the context of Latinos politics. One pertains to the functions of Latino-oriented strategies for political parties and their candidates. The second pertains to the functions of those strategies for Latinos and Latino communities. They are related and interdependent, yet also distinct.

In the first case, the marketing of a political party and its candidates for elected office is akin to the marketing of almost any other consumer product. The potential consumers are identified, the specific messages are designed and developed for them, and appropriate channels are selected and used for the dissemination of those messages. If properly created and delivered, the messages will be consumed as will the "product" being promoted. Ultimately, the main function of the targeted campaign will have been served if the party and/or its candidate have won.[20]

A critical element in this whole process is connecting the product to the consumer in a way that offers a very special relevancy, at least in appearance. Generic messages may *reach* the potential consumer, but, lacking a unique or special connection, the value of the product could be diminished or disregarded altogether. In the field of marketing, segmented targeting and niche strategies have been replacing the mass approaches (Kotler, 1986), especially with respect to the growing Latino markets (del Valle, 2005; Korzenny and Korzenny, 2005; Valdés, 2000). The outcome of such focused efforts has not always been successful, but neither has it been predominantly negative. If that were the case, by now we would have seen the return of generic, across-the-board strategies in which ethnic groups and other distinct populations are practically ignored. The opposite has been true, thus the increase in the focused media campaign strategies for consumer products as well as political campaigns (see Newman and Perloff, 2004).

In the Latino political communication arena, the situation is quite similar. The "potential consumers" are the Latino constituencies; the "specific messages" are the ethnic-sensitive and ethnic-oriented political promotions and other propaganda; the "appropriate channels" are Spanish-language and English-language media known to reach these consumers. The evidence that establishes the "consumption" of the promoted product is the number of Latinos who turned out to vote for the party or candidate in question. Here, too, the formulation and execution of images heralding special connections between product and consumer are indispensable. Generic or general market messages may work in reaching the Latino constituencies, but marketers assume that distinct messages directed specifically to the targeted Latino populations or subgroups are much more effective (del Valle, 2005; Korzenny and Korzenny, 2005; Valdés, 2000).

This means that campaigns that specifically target Latinos for selling a product—be it a consumable good or a political candidate—must take the above factors into consideration if they are to win the Latino market/vote in a particular locality, state, region or the nation. Thus, national campaigns require, for example, themes, sounds and/or images that serve as common denominators among various Latino groups. In statewide or other more focused campaigns, efforts should be made to strike a chord of relevance with the predominant Latino national group(s) in the locality.

Still lacking, however, are the theories and the systematic gathering of long-range empirical data to best assess the full spectrum of issues related to Latino-oriented political communication strategies. As was observed in chapter 2, there is a dearth of academic literature delving into the development and implementation of such strategies during campaigns and non-campaign periods.

Nevertheless, there have been numerous campaigns that have successfully focused on obtaining the winning margin of the Latino vote. Even if causal relationships between a particular Latino-oriented strategy and the outcome of the election in question are speculative, some of the attributed results are very telling.[21] Examples of elections which, according to some analysts, would have had different outcomes if not for the auspicious mobilization of the Latino vote are the triumphs of Chicago Democratic Mayor Washington (1983 and 1987), and two Texas Republicans— Senator Tower (1966, 1972 and 1978), Governor Clements (1978 and 1984), and George W. Bush (1998), to name a few. In 1996, President Clinton won New Mexico, the state with the largest percentage of Latinos, and Florida a key electoral state for his win, thanks to the Latino votes. George W. Bush's presidential wins in 2000 and 2004 were also the outcome of concerted efforts via the media (Colín, 2004; Ramos, 2004). Each of these campaigns exhibited some form of successful Latino-oriented tactics, including communication strategies. Chapters 12 to 14 in this book discuss examples of the processes and outcomes of Latino-oriented efforts during the last three presidential campaigns.

Most importantly, however, are the victories of Latinos and Latinas themselves to prominent offices. A few recent examples are Democrat Ken Salazar (Colorado) and Republican Mel Martínez (Florida) to the United States Senate in 2004, Democrat Bill Richardson as Governor of New Mexico (2004), Democrat Antonio Villaraigosa as Mayor of Los Angeles (2005), Democrat Henry Cisneros as Mayor of San Antonio (1981 and 1985), and Democratic Peña as Mayor of Denver (1983 and 1987). Thanks to the mobilization of Latino voters, various Hispanics have also been elected to Congress, state senates, city councils and school boards across the country. One of the most surprising and heralded victory in the Congressional arena has been Loretta Sánchez' 1996 win over Bob Dornan in Orange County, California. Colorado also elected a Democratic Congressman, John Salazar, in 2004.

In the scenarios described above, the primary function of Latino-oriented strategies is the victory of the candidate and party that uses them. Even when there is no electoral success, a Latino-oriented strategy may enhance a candidate's and a party's recognition, e.g., name identification, among this segment of the population. Such recognition could be utilized in future political campaigns or mobilization efforts. Under this rubric, whether or not the campaign in general or its specific messages served any other functions for the Latino voter is another matter. The functions or even worthiness of the product purchased (i.e., the party/candidate who won) also is extraneous. That is, until the next election campaign when the selling process begins anew.

What about the functions of the communication strategies *for* Latinos themselves (i.e., the Latino community at large)? In this case, the applicable analogy is that which brings together the tenets of community service and public relations campaigns. Two issues are of central importance: (a) infusing resources that contribute to help members of the community, while (b) building the good will that enhances the probabilities of the consumption of the product at a future date. The former implies acknowledgment and validation of a community's population, values, needs and institutions, and investing time and financial resources to help the community. The latter implies assuring that those efforts bring about positive name recognition and good will that can contribute to subsequent support and purchase of products or services.

In the Latino political communication arena this overall sketch is valid, but a few additional caveats are called for. The resources to be infused are the campaign or party operational funds, including those for political advertising. The members of the community that can be helped are the individuals and companies contracted for the technical support and other infrastructure needs of the party or a campaign. For example, consider the numerous food service, transportation, construction, audiovisual, office supply and other services contracted for establishing party/candidate offices, or for running special events such as meetings, assemblies or rallies.

When a Latino communication strategy is launched, the Latino community that can benefit is even larger. For example, under the rubric of communication, there are many companies hired to create, produce, and distribute special political propaganda such as political spots for print or broadcast media, campaign buttons, brochures and other literature. Other members of the community that can benefit are survey or polling companies. Also benefiting are Latino-oriented radio and television stations, and community newspapers that cater to Latinos. Space or time for political advertisements are often purchased in these media.

The diverse entities contracted for many of these jobs or for dissemination of propaganda—be it paid or free media—are often (although not necessarily always) selected because they are owned or operated by Latinos. It is thus not coincidental to find that many of the owners of the companies and Latino-oriented media hold strong friendships or loyalties to the political party, the candidate or their surrogates that contract them. Thus, the products and services purchased are also of mutual benefit. On the one hand, the contracted entities receive some income, which is augmented significantly during campaign periods. On the other hand, political parties and their candidates earn the good will, loyalty, and even votes and campaign donations from the contracted entities, their relatives, friends and other members of the community who directly or indirectly benefited from the contracts.

The final aspect to consider regarding the functions of the communication strategies for Latinos themselves is the benefits they can receive when Latino-oriented political advertisements and media messages are generated and disseminated. When those messages are assertive and positive and also refer to relevant issues, needs and values of the Latino constituencies, members of this community, especially potential voters, can build a sense of empowerment and mobilize into voting or other types of political action. If nothing else, assertive and positive messages can enhance Latinos' perception that they and/or issues of importance to them are part of the mainstream political agenda. This occurs especially if some positive aspects of a Latino-oriented communication strategy reach non-Latinos and such messages, in turn, lead to some understanding or valuing of Latino contributions to the shared polity. This may be especially true if the communication strategy is not merely general messages that happen to be channeled to that group, but instead includes verbal and visual messages of either prominent Latinos or of Latinos with whom other Latinos and non-Latinos can positively identify.

These scenarios provide plausible foundations upon which to base the studies of the communication strategies and advertisements discussed in chapters 12 to 14. For now, it seems evident that the study of the communication strategies of political parties and their candidates also can be very revealing and insightful for better understanding Latino politics in the United States.

## FOUNDATIONS FOR POLITICAL COMMUNICATION SURVEY RESEARCH WITH LATINOS

After affirming how the study of media content and partisan communication strategies can help us better understand Latino politics in the United States, what remains for elaboration are the arguments for including mass media variables in survey research that aims to expand the knowledge about Latinos' political affairs. To such end, this section begins by reiterating some key considerations from mainstream political communication writings that merit attention for the works in this book. It then turns to a few relevant studies that have focused on ethnic minorities (other than Latinos). Finally, it builds on the previous findings in order to discuss distinct caveats that require attention when Latino populations are surveyed to assess the relationships between their media use and/or exposure and their political orientations.

The notion that the political dynamics of the United States have been affected, often unduly, by the press is something that emerged alongside the birth of the American republic (Stempel and Windhauser, 1991). Two hundred years later, the U.S. public continues to believe that the press and more modern media "have an important impact on the conduct of politics and on public thinking" (Graber, 1997: 13). The social science-based studies about media effects have yet to render conclusive and consistent evidence about how media do or do not work in these matters. Nevertheless, there are sufficient grounds upon which to assert the importance of studying the role of the media in political processes—including those pertaining to Latinos.

Graber (1997) offers three major reasons for the disjunction between public beliefs and the outcome of research: (1) the narrow approach to the study of media effects in early studies; (2) minimalist interpretations of media use theories; and (3) the difficulty of synthesizing the complexity of factors that, along with media, influence public opinion and behaviors in the realm of politics.

Over 20 years ago, when McLeod and Reeves (1981) discussed the complexities of assessing media effects, they pointed to the improper methodological and procedural assumptions, inferences and generalizations that often are made in studies that seek to establish direct relationships between media and human opinions or behaviors. According to these authors, it is possible that the limited findings associating media and politics may reflect more a problem of imprecise assessments of the political variables that are functionally related to media messages than a lack of correlation between media and behaviors.

A similar opinion is stated by Wagner (1983: 411) who, upon reviewing a wide range of studies assessing media influence on politics, summarizes that "One reason why scholars have had difficulty discovering media effects arises from the problem of obtaining a good methodological fit with the sort of data available on media audiences." After discussing some examples of methodological limitations, he adds: "a second reason for difficulty in identifying media effects involves selecting a measure of media use" (1983: 412). He argues that imprecise indexes that confound the amount and diversity of media exposure must be rejected in favor of measures that discriminate among the kind, quality and quantity of media use. In other words, it is not just exposure to the media that may have some effects on political cognitions, attitudes, or behaviors. Instead, it is exposure to specific media and specific content of the particular media.

In his own study of media effects, Wagner made some assumptions about media content and statistically controlled exposure by creating a media variable out of concrete questions concerning actual media use. He then was able to assess more effectively the effect of media exposure on respondents' perceptions of issue differences between two presidential candidates (Carter and Ford). Even after taking into account factors such as education, class and interest in public affairs, Wagner found that exposure to different media led to systematic variations in the perceptions of the candidates and even the level of voting turnout.

What these and other works attest to is that, in spite of some limitations of past works, media effects can be found when research is conducted with measures and procedures that account for media specificity and relevance. The certainty that media can and do affect politics is most evident at the conclusion of Graber's summary of past and more recent studies on this subject. After pointing to the contributions of such works, as well as to their continued limitations, she nonetheless asserts:

In light of what we have discussed so far, it seems totally unrealistic to deny that the media are important in setting the stage for ongoing political developments, in shaping the views and behaviors of political elites and other selected groups, and in influencing the general public's perception of political life. . . . Even if one argues that the media are nothing but conduits of information over which they have no control, one cannot deny that people throughout the world of politics consider the media to be powerful and behave accordingly.

(Graber, 1997: 18)

In the scant political communication research on ethnic minority populations, support for the "media effects perspective" also is observed when improved measures of media and politics are utilized. Since the pertinent literature on Latinos was reviewed in chapter 2, and will be assessed again below, this discussion turns to works on African Americans and other ethnic groups.

The seminal work in this category, and unparalleled more than 25 years hence, is the survey by Allen and Chaffee (1979) of a sample of 268 Black adults in San Francisco. A key finding of their work was that measures of media use *doubled* the amount of variance explained on a number of political participation indicators. Using hierarchical regression analysis, these authors first assessed the influence of various demographic/ background variables (e.g., age, education and socio-economic status) and a set of subjective orientation measures (e.g., anomie, black identity). Allen and Chaffee observed that, even with statistical controls for these factors, media exposure, including black news magazines, predicted campaign participation and other forms of political involvement. Thus, they conclude that

[i]n general, media use can be seen as an important stage in the process by which education is consummated in political activity. . . . If the news media containing specialized content designed specifically for the black community were not available to blacks—which was the case historically, and continues to be in some places—we can imagine that black political participation would be significantly retarded.

(Allan and Chaffee, 1979: 520)

Another of their conclusions, which is central to the theoretical and methodological foundation for the studies presented later in this book, states that

[t]he most reasonable interpretation of media exposure, then, is not as an independent variable isolated from other social

processes but as a facilitating factor that helps to explain the translation of background and psychological variables into political participation.

(Allan and Chaffee, 1979: 521)

Kennamer (1987) also observed relationships between discrete political variables and specific media measures in a study for which 80 percent of the sample were Whites and 20 percent were Blacks. For both groups, "intent to vote" was directly influenced by exposure to television and indirectly, via cognitions, by attention to newspapers. The media influence was significant even with statistical controls for sex, age, race, education, interest in the election, strength of party identification, and discussion of politics. With adequate measures and procedures, the political effects of exposure to, and use of, the mass media were properly assessed and found to be statistically significant. Missing in Kennamer's study, however, were assessments of potential effects of ethnically relevant media.

Two other studies of Blacks have also found significant associations between the media exposure and political information (McCombs, 1968) and voting (Latimer, 1983). Apparently, basic measures of media use and exposure have been valuable in studies of the political dynamics of ethnic groups other than Latinos.

But more consistent measures of media exposure, such as those used by Jeffres (1999, 2000) in his panel studies of primarily European ethnic heritage populations, have made stronger cases for the influence of media, including ethnic media, in political socialization and participation.

Applying the lessons from the literature cited above, two conclusions could be drawn. First, survey research about politics should incorporate appropriate inquiries about media use and exposure. Then, to the extent that Latinos are similar to non-Latino populations in terms of their general market media practices, the justifications for studying media variables in survey research should be sufficiently stated and need not be further elaborated here. In other words, propositions similar to the findings of Allen and Chaffee, Kennamer, and others about the influence of the media on political knowledge, attitudes and/or behaviors should apply to some members of this group. In the survey research chapters of this book, the applicability of common foundations, as well as the limitations of mainstream theories and methodologies, will be made evident.

Second, ethnic minority populations may also have distinct relationships with media, especially if ethnic-oriented media are available. The differential use and potential impact may be more pronounced if the ethnic media provide political content of particular interest to the group in question. Thus, given the Latino-oriented media in this country, inquiries about Latinos' media practices in general, and relations with Latino-oriented media in particular must be undertaken. The value of this proposition also will be tested in the survey research chapters.

Before turning to the caveats in survey research about Latinos, it should be recalled that chapter 2 of this book reviewed in detail the available literature that shows the contributions of media variables in politically related survey research studies with this population. Therefore, that literature needs no further presentation. What is pending is the discussion of issues that merit careful attention for the case studies, as well as for future survey research with Latino populations. The first concerns Latino-oriented media. The second concerns characteristics of general market media.

## Caveats regarding Latino-oriented media

The first precaution that should be kept in mind is that any survey of Latinos' media use and/or exposure requires attention as to whether or not Spanish-language and other Latino-oriented media are readily *available* (in terms of whether or not they are published) and *accessible* (in terms of easily obtainable via subscriptions or on newsstands) in the community being studied. Second, if Latino-oriented media are available and accessible in the community, it is important to have at least some basic understanding of their political coverage practices and orientations. Such understanding is indispensable when examining whether or how those media are used specifically for political knowledge, mobilization, etc.

As explained in an earlier section of this chapter, Spanish-language and other Latino-oriented media are not published regularly in all communities with Latino populations. Even in cities that publish Spanish-language dailies, those papers may be hard to find beyond the core Latino enclaves. Nevertheless, the history of social and political advocacy of the Spanish-language daily press in at least three metropolitan cities (New York, Miami, Los Angeles—see chapter 4 and sources cited therein) plus in the other cities with recent daily publications (Brownsville, Dallas, Houston, Laredo, McAllen, San Antonio, Chicago, Orlando, and Lawrenceville) allows us to say that Latino-oriented political news, as well as political news in general, are at least available to the Latino Spanish-language readers *in those particular locations*. Because of this reality, it is in those locations, and those locations only, that it would be appropriate to inquire in a survey questionnaire about exposure to or use of Spanish-language newspapers for political information in general and/or for Latino political news and issues in particular. Yet even in those locations, the first matter that should be assessed is whether the respondent has easy *access—and whether the respondent can afford*—the Spanish-language papers. While the publication of Spanish-language daily newspapers may have some political repercussions or serve some political functions for the Latino community at large, it would be inappropriate to ask about exposure to or use of a medium that is not regularly and easily accessible.

In other locations where Spanish-language newspapers are not published on a daily basis, survey questions about Latinos' exposure to or use of the Latino press for political reasons would require contextual explanations about the availability of that print media. The research, and subsequently the reader of the outcome of the research, should explain whether or not there are Latino-oriented weekly or monthly newspapers, and how easily accessible these may be. Studies about such media also would have to offer background information about the frequency, orientation, and prominence of the political content of those periodicals. If the weeklies or monthlies are nothing more than entertainment and/or advertising giveaways or supplements, it would be wrong to expect that exposure to these media should be related to much of anything in the political arena.

The caveats with respect to Spanish-language broadcast media are some-what different from that of the press. Both types of broadcast media— radio and television—are widely available in most major cities with large Latino populations. For example, there are at a minimum four full-time Spanish-language radio stations catering to Latinos in each of the large metropolitan areas of greater New York/New Jersey/Connecticut, Miami/ Fort Lauderdale, Los Angeles and its vicinities, the San Francisco Bay area, the Washington, DC, area, and in cities such as San Antonio, El Paso, Houston, Dallas, Chicago, Albuquerque, and San Diego. Also, in each of those metropolitan areas, Univisión and Telemundo, the two major national Spanish-language networks, have either owned-and-operated or affiliated television stations with local news productions. In places such as these, survey research that inquires about Latinos' exposure to, or use of, Spanish-language broadcast media for political news, information or issues would seem quite appropriate and may be very revealing.

Researchers must also keep in mind other particular caveats for each medium. With respect to television it should be recalled that, even in those communities served by Spanish-language television, not all Latinos have equal *access* to the Spanish-language TV signals. In some locations, the signals of one or both networks' stations are available only in the proximity of the stations' antennas. Outside those areas, the signals are available exclusively via cable subscription. For Latinos who live in the outer limits of the over-the-air signals, or for those who do not or cannot subscribe to cable, the news and other programs from this medium are out of their direct reach. Therefore, for Latinos in such situations, a sur-vey item inquiring about the political use of Spanish-language television is of limited value and potentially unreliable.

When studying radio, the problem is not of the accessibility of the signal or the availability of channels. With this medium the biggest issue is the lack of *political* content—be it in news, information or public affairs programming. If our findings of the political content of more than 30 of these stations across the country continue to be the norm (see Santillán and Subervi-Vélez, 1991), there is little base on which to expect major relationships between Latinos' exposure to, or use of, this medium and their political orientations.

The exception, and possibly the only metropolitan area where political content is a standard and common offering via radio, is in Miami. Because of the decades-long anti-Castro activism and conservative mobilization of Cuban exiles, radio stations in that area offer not only news, but also mostly very political commentary practically 24 hours a day (Soruco, 1996).

Otherwise, in most radio stations the norm is an only occasional two- to five-minute newscast at the top of the hour. Some AM stations also broadcast extended (half hour or one hour) morning or late afternoon news programs. However, many news providers originate in or are linked to U.S. mainstream news agencies such as United Press International, ABC, CBS and the Associated Press, which primarily offer translations of their regular wire news. The other major source of Spanish-language radio news are Latin American news agencies such as Notimex or Cadena Latina, which emphasize little, if any, information about U.S. Latino political life. To date, there is no equivalent to National Public Radio's *Morning Edition*, or *All Things Considered*.

Among the few Latino-oriented radio news providers (see Subervi-Vélez, Báez and Saenz, 2005), we can point to CNN en Español Radio, which offers top-of-the-hour news programs from 6 a.m. to 1 a.m. (Eastern). Approximately 50 Spanish-language stations in the United States subscribe to this service, produced exclusively for the U.S. Latino audiences. Another commercial radio broadcast news network directed mostly to U.S. Latinos is Univisión Radio. Via Radio Cadena, it provides talk and news programming at different schedules for 15 AM stations in the United States. From 1998 to 2003, the major commercial radio network at the national level was Radio Única, which at the time offered to over 40 markets round-the-clock news and commentary, including interviews with Latino and non-Latino political figures. Since its closure in fall 2003, there has not been another national network offering similar news content and format.

In the realm of public radio, Radio Bilingüe, a non-commercial radio network, offers Latino-oriented news to its affiliated stations. Its *Noticiero Latino*, a weekday series of news and news bulletins that lasts for 8–10 minutes, is broadcast across the network's 40 stations in the United States, two in Puerto Rico, and five in Mexico. The network also airs *Línea Abierta*, a two-hour weekday program of news, news-related interviews, debates, and other information on current events.

For Latinos who can understand English, another radio source for news

75

is *Latino USA*, a weekly half-hour program that airs over 200 stations, most of them publicly owned but some community and commercial stations as well. This "radio journal of news and culture" offers Latino perspectives to many of the most important news events of the week, as well as interviews, commentaries, and feature stories on a diversity of topics related to Latinos—including politics. However, listening to *Latino USA* is possible only for people who live in areas covered by one of the stations that carry this program. Many public radio stations do not, and even among those that do, the schedule for this once-a-week program can be quite challenging—such as very early in the morning or late at night and only on weekends.

As can be discerned, other than the Miami area and in communities that can tune into Radio Bilingüe's news and interview programs, there may be few places where Latino radio audiences may have regular political news and information over the radio. Of course, there may be some other communities that also have access to political voices over the local radio stations. But that programming is not available at the national level. Moreover, the characteristics of the political news offered by commercial and non-commercial networks and programs have not been studied. The last systematic approximation to the study of the political role of community-based Latino-oriented radio was Lewels' (1974) research in the early 1970s.

Given these contexts, it would be theoretically unsound to expect that there would be significant positive relationships between Latinos' exposure to, or use of, most entertainment-focused Spanish-language radio and Latinos' political knowledge, attitudes, or behaviors. The exception, again, would be among Latinos living in an area served by radio stations that regularly offer politically-orientated news and commentary. As will be observed in chapter 15, the survey data we have analyzed does show a significant influence of exposure to that medium among Latinos from that area. In sum, positive political effects from exposure to Spanish-language radio should not be expected; that is, unless the respondents live in cities in which the fieldwork shows that the radio stations do provide relevant political news and information on a regular basis.

Turning to magazines oriented to U.S. Latinos, some additional caveats merit attention. As of this writing there was no United States produced and nationally disseminated *Latino-oriented* Spanish-language or English-language equivalent to *Newsweek, Time,* or *US News & World Report.* Typically, the major national and general content publications (e.g., *Hispanic* and *Vista*) or business publications (e.g., *Hispanic Business*[22]) provided only occasional stories directly related to political content, even during elections.

The only magazine with frequent political content related to Latinos is *Hispanic Link*. This publication, however, is a weekly 8–12 page news-letter with a limited circulation of approximately 5,000 copies that pri-marily reaches politically minded readers in Washington, DC, and other centers where Latino political matters are regularly debated.

Thus, as pointed out with respect to Spanish-language radio, it would be of limited value to develop survey queries expecting to find that among Latinos there are significant political effects stemming from exposure to, or use of, Latino-oriented magazines—except if that exposure was to *Hispanic Link*.

## Caveats regarding general market media

Attention turns next to characteristics of general market media that can influence the outcome of survey research about the potential effects of the media on Latinos. The justifications for discussing those character-istics were discussed earlier in this chapter, but merit reviewing. First, ethnicity, including Latino identity, is part of a core and perennial value in American society. Second, general market media are conduits through which many Latinos (and, of course, non-Latinos as well) learn about other people like themselves. If we assume that both of these are true, then it can be proposed that many Latinos (especially those interested in political affairs) will look for, or pay attention to, Latino-themed or oriented political news.

This leads to the first general market media characteristic that merits attention for subsequent queries about the potential political effects of such media on Latinos: the frequency and orientation of the news cover-age about Latinos in those media. As past research about overall coverage of Latinos has shown, Latinos have more often than not been ignored or covered in predominantly negative ways in general market media (see summary overview in Subervi-Vélez et al., 1994; and the studies by Kraeplin and Subervi-Vélez, 2003; Pease, Smith, and Subervi-Vélez, 2001; Salwen and Soruco, 1997; Subervi, Torres and Montalvo, 2004; 2005).

If issues about Latino politics, including the candidacies of Latinos run-ning for office, receive similar or worse treatment, especially during cam-paigns, there is little that can be proposed about distinctive Latino-related positive influence coming from exposure to such media. If exposure to, or use of, such media contributes to political knowledge, attitudes or behaviors, it would be indispensable to discern in survey research ques-tions whether or not such effects are with respect to politics in general, or about political issues that can be associated with Latinos per se.

The second general market media characteristic that merits attention for queries about the potential political effects of these media on Latinos relates to material other than news. In print media this refers to editorials, opinion columns, editorial cartoons, and advertisements. With broadcast media this refers to public affairs programs, public affairs announcements, and political commercials. In each case for both types of media, the caveat is whether Latino materials appeared under any of these categories, and whether they were conducive to Latinos' increased knowledge and/or mobilization.

In this context, the term "conducive" can imply two different and opposite reactions. When the materials presented value and promote Latino candidates, issues or concerns, the results have the potential to enhance Latinos' political development. When the materials are presented in ways construed as negative or detrimental to Latino candidates, issues or concerns, the results may be the opposite. If such is the case, survey research and any discussions about the potential role of general market media on Latinos should also reflect these potential distinctions.

In essence, survey research that seeks to link Latinos' exposure to or use of the mass media to some political outcome must aim to establish *a priori* two things: knowledge about the various media accessible and available to the Latino population being served, and a basic understanding of the quantity and quality of the Spanish-language and English-language media content in terms of if and how such content may relate to Latinos at the local and/or national level. With this in mind, questions about media use and exposure can and should be tailored to the particular contexts of the community being studied. Under such conditions, inquiries about the effects of media on Latino politics are certainly bound to be much more fruitful.

## CONCLUSION

The literature and propositions of this chapter affirm the value of studying the mass media for better understanding politics relating to the complex and heterogeneous dynamics of Latino communities across the United States. The chapter also makes clear that there are many factors about the Latino communities and the media oriented to them that must be taken into consideration in political communication research. Evidently, the potential political effects of exposure to and use of the mass media could be properly assessed if measures and procedures that are more adequate are followed.

The remaining chapters of this book offer studies that, in their research methodologies and findings, provide important lessons about past relationships between Latinos, media, and politics. They should also serve as foundations for future studies in this arena.

# NOTES

1 Chávez summarizes the numerous models that have been proposed to explain Latino political participation. The list is too long to present here. However, she categorizes the analytical frameworks used to study Latino politics into "three main models or core analytical frameworks: the historical/identity politics model, the mainstream political science framework, and the nationality and gendered framework" (2004: 36). None of the models discussed by Chávez makes direct reference to the mass media or acknowledge the mass media as playing a major role in the political participation/mobilization of Latinos.

2 From this immersed acculturation, often labeled as assimilation perspective, ethnic identity may be just a "nominal" classification (see Subervi-Vélez, 1986; Subervi and Ríos, 2005). It would reflect a point in time that established a distinct ethnic heritage owing to parental place of origin or that of the person's birth or early years of life. Yet that connection offers little or no relevance for the daily routines of the individual who seeks total assimilation. At most, it may emerge only sporadically when, for example, that person responds by checking the box designated for Hispanic or Latino for the Census survey or on a form for a job or school application. This type of full ethnic assimilation would be in line with Gordon's (1964) perspective a few decades ago.

3 Full assimilation is indeed rare and sociologists and anthropologists disputed Gordon's (1964) proposals of full assimilation. For reviews of a broad range of literature on this subject of adaptation from a communication perspective, see also Kim (1988; 2000).

4 See, for example, the findings by de la Garza, DeSipio, García, García, and Falcón (1992).

5 For the purposes of this discussion "Latino relevancy of candidates or issues" refers to candidates who have Latino heritage and make that known, non-Latino candidates who make explicit appeals to Latinos, and issues that are identified by public figures and/or the mass media as especially important for Latinos as a whole or for some component of the Latino population such as Puerto Ricans, Mexican Americans, Cubans.

6 Of course, a connection could be made from a variety of identities, interests, or points of reference, which may or not have to be related to ethnicity. The theoretical framework shifts to pluralism because it is assumed that a person who pays attention to issues and campaign cues that seem relevant from an ethnic (i.e., Latino) perspective is prone to hold a sense of identity that is more than just nominal. It is distinctive and as such open to consideration from a vantage point in which the value of being Latino (be it in pan-Hispanic mold or from a particular national origin) remains active in the person's mind and/or social milieu, and thus relevant.

7 The term "adaptation" is used here to encompass assimilation and pluralism—as well as acculturation or retro-acculturation—because all are processes that require some type of adjustment in the individual's life when dealing with a dominant society different from the one in a previous setting (see Subervi-Vélez 1986; Subervi and Ríos, 2005).

8 The discussion of these factors focuses primarily on newspapers and television, but many of the tenets are certainly applicable to radio and magazines. Less emphasis is given to justifying the analysis of these latter two media because of the limited data available for this book on the political content of these outlets.

9 Anglos and other people of any ethnic background who can understand this language and follow some of the news reports in these media are secondary audiences for Spanish-language media. Nowadays, this includes some government officials or politicians—and/or their assistants—who seek to connect to their respective Latino constituents.

10 See also the 2003 Census report cited above for the most recent figures on the top ten cities, in terms of percentage of the population that speaks Spanish. These are: Hialeah, FL (91.9), Laredo, TX (91.3), Brownsville, TX (86.6), East Los Angeles, CA (86.4), McAllen, TX (74), Santa Ana (69.7), El Paso, TX (68.9), Miami, FL (66.6), El Monte, CA (61.8), and Pomona, CA (55).

11 According to a Strategy Research Corporation researcher interviewed by telephone (April 25, 1997), that figure has not changed significantly since then.

12 Data about the market trends of Spanish-language and other Latino-oriented media are published in the December issues of *Hispanic Business* magazine and are also regularly available at the magazine's web site www.hispanicbusiness.com.

13 Since September 11, 2001, immigration routes from Mexico may have shifted to other areas—for example, to smaller communities where the demand for agricultural, poultry and construction work is highly needed. Even there, Spanish-language media may be in greater demand as the main source for socializing into the new environment.

14 Mail subscriptions are still an option for people interested in knowing what is happening in their communities, even if the news is two or three days late. But only a very small fraction of the subscribers to the Spanish-language dailies subscribe by mail.

15 Those newspapers were *La Opinión* (Los Angeles), *El Nuevo Herald* and *Diario Las Américas* (Miami) and *El Diario-La Prensa* and *Noticias del Mundo* (New York). In 1984, there was also the now defunct daily *El Mañana* in Chicago. New York's *Noticias* was also defunct as of 2004.

16 As the following list shows, Spanish-language daily newspapers are now much more numerous. *El Día*, owned by the Budini family enterprises, was launched in Houston, Texas, in 1995. The Tribune Company started its own chain of Spanish language dailies, *Hoy*, which circulate in New York (since 1998), Chicago (2003), and in Los Angeles (2004). *La Visión*, owned by CHL Communications Inc., began operations in Lawrenceville, Georgia in 2000. In 2003, two Spanish-language dailies were launched in Dallas. The first was *La Estrella*, formerly a weekly, owned by the Knight Ridder Company, the second largest newspaper publisher in the United States and also engaged in Internet publishing. The second was *Al Día*, published by the Bello Corporation, owners of various media companies, including *The Dallas Morning News*. In 2003, *El Nuevo Día—Orlando* was launched, owned by the Ferré Family Enterprises of Puerto Rico, which also own the island's largest daily, *El Nuevo Día*. And in 2004, AztecaAmerica, with capital investors from Spain, started their own chain of dailies in San Antonio, Houston, the Valley (South Texas), and Austin (although the edition for this latter city was closed in 2006). The Texas–Mexico border region also has daily newspapers: *El Tiempo*, which since 1926 has been an insert to the *The Laredo Morning Times*; *El Nuevo Herald*, a daily since 1934 out of Brownsville; and McAllen's *La Frontera*, launched in 2004 by Freedom Communications, Inc., which also owns that city's English-language daily *The Monitor*.

17 This discussion focuses on the political acculturation and political pluralism roles of the press. However, similar arguments can be made about the cultural,

social, and economic acculturation and pluralism roles of minority media. See Subervi-Vélez (1986) and Riggins (1992).

18 Again, for the sake of brevity, the focus is on *political* pluralism. However, it should be acknowledged (at least in this note) that for obvious reasons one of the most distinctive cultural pluralism roles of the Spanish-language media, including the Spanish-language press, is that of language maintenance. For more information on this type of function of ethnic mother-tongue media, see Fishman (1966).

19 The discussion of these considerations focuses primarily on newspapers and television because none of the chapters provides data on general market radio and magazines. However, many of the tenets may apply to these media, too.

20 Whether or not the overall campaign or its specific messages served any concurrent or ulterior function for the consumer is of less importance, as are the functions or worthiness of the product purchased. Of course, this applies to the first time a product is purchased. The second time a similar product is needed personal experience will certainly influence the purchasing decision more than will almost any propaganda, except maybe that which claims to be "new and improved."

21 Each of the political campaigns alluded to in this section may have had some unique strategies pertinent to the mass media, community organizations, and/ or grass-root committees to reach out to the variety of Latino voters. Yet, beyond brief accounts in newspaper or news magazine articles, or the opinions recollected and relayed to us during our research, it is evident that most of these milestone cases went unnoticed in empirical political communication research and literature.

22 *Hispanic Business* provides additional political news and information via its web site, and through weekly e-mailed news bulletins to subscribers of this electronic service.

# Part II

# STUDIES OF MEDIA
# COVERAGE OF ELECTIONS

# Section A

## The Spanish-language media

# 4

# SPANISH-LANGUAGE DAILY NEWSPAPERS AND PRESIDENTIAL ELECTIONS

*Federico A. Subervi-Vélez*

in collaboration with
*Marc Brindel* (1992 campaign)

and
*Juandalynn Taylor and Renée Espinosa* (1996 campaign)

Newspapers, including the Spanish-language press, contain and convey more political news and information than any other mass medium. This assertion holds true regardless of the actual or potential size of the audience of this medium, and whether or not the press contributes to any particular effects that could be assessed in conventional public opinion surveys. Word for word, on a regular basis and even more so during election periods, no other medium provides more coverage of politics than do newspapers. Assessing the campaign-oriented political content of the Spanish-language dailies reveals, if nothing else, the characteristics of the political materials upon which some members of the Latino community can build part of their knowledge and form their opinions about the political parties, their candidates, and issues.

The search for answers to one of the main queries of the book— "What are the political messages for or about Latinos disseminated by way of the mass media?"—begins by assessing the press precisely because of the potential role of this medium. Thus, the specific question addressed by this chapter is: "How have the *Spanish-language daily newspapers* covered presidential elections?" The answers are derived from the findings from four separate studies of the 1984, 1988, 1992, and 1996 election periods. The historical data presented here offer a cornerstone for this media-centered look into Latino politics.

For the reader unfamiliar with the Spanish-language press, the next few pages offer a capsule history of the daily newspapers analyzed herein. It is an important foundation for understanding these papers and the characteristics of their political coverage. The rest of the chapter presents the analyses of the data divided into four sections. The first integrates and summarizes the findings of how six dailies covered the 1984 elections. It is followed by the analyses of how five of those dailies covered the 1988 elections. The final two sections are summary versions of the findings from the study of one of the dailies in 1992, and of a study of two of the dailies in 1996.

Altogether, the chapter confirms that political (i.e., campaign) news and information are an integral part of the material that Spanish-language dailies offer their readers in their respective local communities. At the same time, the partisanship of these papers is more evident than that which has been observed in studies of the elite English-language press in the U.S. The data also show that, while the partisanship of some of the dailies reflects the dominant political orientations of the Latino communities they serve, such is not the case for all newspapers or in all of the types of material (i.e., news vis-à-vis editorials and op-ed pieces) they publish.

## HISTORICAL SYNOPSIS OF SELECTED SPANISH-LANGUAGE DAILIES

Spanish-language newspapers within the national boundaries of the United States have been published since the beginning of the nineteenth century (Cortés, 1987; Fitzpatrick 1987; Gutiérrez, 1977). The Vargas and de Pyssler (1999) study of many other Latino-oriented papers speaks of the continuity and penetration of that media all across the country. As summarized in chapter 2, those papers in Spanish, as well as a few English-language and bilingual publications aimed at Latinos, have had political roles and functions since their beginnings.

However, during the latter part of the last century, at the time of the studies presented in this chapter, only five daily newspapers had a continuous and strong presence in three major metropolitan areas with large concentrations of Latinos.[1] The names of these are La Opinión (Los Angeles), El Diario-La Prensa and Noticias del Mundo (New York), El Nuevo Herald and Diario Las Américas (Miami). Except for Noticias del Mundo, which ceased operations in 2004, these daily papers have survived numerous transformations and persevered in serving their communities in many ways, including providing political news and commentary, especially during elections. These five are the ones that were analyzed for their coverage of presidential elections and are thus the subjects of this chapter. Other papers, including the dailies of more recent arrival, have yet to be studied for political content. Before delving into what the research has shown about the patterns of coverage during presidential elections, a few background notes on each are indispensable.

La Opinión began publishing in Los Angeles on September 16, 1926. It was founded by Ignacio E. Lozano, Sr., a Mexican national who "wanted to provide news of the native homeland as well as of the new country for the growing Mexican population in Southern California" (Subervi-Vélez, et al., 1994: 318). The Lozano family still runs the newspaper's editorial policies and operation, but the corporate ownership has gone through changes since the 1980s.[2] Overall, La Opinión editorial orientation has historically been more liberal than conservative, especially in its stands regarding the status and problems faced by the Mexican and other Latino communities in the Southern California region. La Opinión is a broadsheet paper, of approximately 60 pages and with a circulation of about 128,000.[3] Today, as has been the case since its foundation, the vast majority of the papers are sold from street stands and in neighborhood stores; home delivery in person or by mail has continued to grow but remains more limited than is the case for general market English-language dailies.[4]

El Diario-La Prensa is a New York City tabloid-size daily with front pages characterized by large, bold, graphic-less headlines that dramatize one major event. It averages 56 pages and has a circulation of approximately 50,000 daily.[5] The difficulty of home delivery also forces this paper to depend almost entirely on street sales. The corporate ownership of this newspaper has undergone many changes, the most recent of which was in 2003.[6] Although oriented to the Spanish-speaking population of which Puerto Ricans have historically constituted the vast majority, practically no members of this group have had *ownership* interests in this daily, the oldest of its type. However, Puerto Ricans have had, and continue to hold, important management positions. In spite of these ownership characteristics, Puerto Rican and other Latino concerns are at the heart of this newspaper. But the changing demographics in New York have led El Diario-La Prensa to cater to a more diverse Hispanic population which, although still principally Puerto Rican, is increasingly Dominican and Central and South American. In her summary of the editorial policy of El Diario-La Prensa, Veciana-Suárez stated over a decade ago that "the primary focus of the editorial, without a doubt, is on Hispanic issues, whether local, national, or international" (1987: 28). Policies generally associated with the poor and the Democratic Party have historically been supported by El Diario-La Prensa (see Fitzpatrick, 1987: 310). These observations held true at least until prior to the recent change of owners; time will indicate if that editorial policy changes.

From April 22, 1980 through April 29, 2004, Noticias del Mundo was the other New York City Spanish-language daily newspaper. It circulated Monday through Friday as a 20-page broadsheet.[7] It was operated by the

CIUDAD — O.J. Simpson llega caso de acoso sexual — 1B

DEPORTES — Hoy el choque México vs. Honduras — 1C

ESPECTACULOS — Alejandra Ávalos cánta ahora rancheras — 1D

MIERCOLES 6 de NOVIEMBRE de 1996

# La Opinión

Los Angeles, California

35¢

1926 1996

# Bill Clinton arrasa

■ Republicanos retienen el control del Congreso; se aprueba la Proposición 209

El presidente Bill Clinton, su hija, su esposa y el vicepresidente Al Gore saludan a sus partidarios en una celebración de victoria en Little Rock, Arkansas. FOTO AP

**■ Los votantes autorizan la Proposición 215 y derrotan las medidas relacionadas con los HMO**

María del Pilar Marrero
Reportera de La Opinión

El presidente Bill Clinton hizo historia ayer al obtener fácilmente su reelección con el primer mandatario de los Estados Unidos, la primera vez que lo logra un demócrata desde Franklin D. Roosevelt en 1936.

El de Clinton será además el séptimo nombre en la corta lista de presidentes elegidos para dos períodos consecutivos desde el nacimiento de la república estadounidense y también el último presidente del siglo XX.

El mandatario fue declarado ganador por los medios de comunicación a las 6:00 de la tarde, hora del Pacífico, mucho antes del cierre de las votaciones en California, cuando ya había anticipado los votos del colegio electoral necesarios para el triunfo.

Al cierre de esta edición, sin embargo, ya era claro que los republicanos mantendrían el control de ambas cámaras del Congreso que recuperaron en 1994, tras muchos años de control demócrata.

En California, los votantes favorecieron a Clinton, pero apoyaron mayoritariamente la medida a la que el Presidente se opone. La Proposición 209, diseñada para desmantelar los programas de Acción Afirmativa que facilitan el acceso.
LEA CLINTON, pág. 16A

**▼ ADENTRO**

■ Congreso Republicanos retienen control del Congreso. Pág. 6A
■ Legislatura Continúa indeciso el control en la Legislatura. Pág. 6A
■ Las elecciones Las elecciones en nuestro estado. Pág. 7A
■ Los Cerros Ligera desventaja de Correa en contienda inicial. Pág. 8A

---

## Latinos votan en números récord

■ Según las encuestas, volcaron masivo apoyo a Clinton, incluso en Florida

María del Pilar Marrero
Reportera de La Opinión

Un número sin precedentes de electores latinos, entre ellos muchos nuevos ciudadanos acudió ayer a las urnas, volcando su creciente poder electoral contra los republicanos, principalmente en respuesta a las medidas y la retórica antiinmigrante.

De acuerdo con la encuesta realizada a la salida de las urnas por la cadena CBS-Telenoticias y los analistas se volcaron en un masivo apoyo al presidente Bill Clinton a nivel nacional y en estados clave como California, Florida y Texas.

Al menos un 70% de los votantes latinos apoyaron al presidente Bill Clinton, que logró fácilmente la reelección para un segundo gobierno, impulsándose incluso en estados como Florida, que tradicionalmente vota por los republicanos.

De acuerdo con la encuesta de CBS-Telenoticias, entre los votantes que salían de ejercer su derecho al sufragio, un 71% de los latinos a nivel nacional votó por Clinton, mientras que tan sólo 20% favoreció al candidato republicano Bob Dole y un 8%, a Ross Perot. En 1992 Clinton recibió un 62% del voto latino.

De igual manera, los latinos favorecieron a Clinton en California y
LEA RECORD, pág. 7A

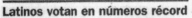

**VOTANTES NACIONALES**
Dole 13%
Perot 8%
Clinton 20%
75%

**PROPOSICION 209**
SI 34%
NO 66%

FUENTE: CBS-Telenoticias
Estudio muestra cómo votaron los latinos.

---

## Lynch aventaja a Garcetti

Leticia García-Irigoyen
Reportera de La Opinión

Al cierre de esta edición, el subprocurador del distrito de Los Ángeles John Lynch aventajaba por un margen de siete puntos porcentuales al Gil Garcetti, quien podría perder su reelección para un segundo término.

Los resultados del conteo de la votación por correo mostraban a Lynch a la cabeza con un 53% del voto -EEUU-T sufragio- contra un 46% -107,833 obtenidos por Garcetti.

Por otra parte, en la contienda por el Distrito 4 de la Junta de Supervisores del condado.
LEA GARCETTI, pág. 16A

---

**PROPOSICION 209**

## Los votantes dan el sí a la Prop. 209

Mary Ballesteros-Coronel
Reportera de La Opinión

Los resultados preliminares de las elecciones indicaban ayer que los votantes de California se inclinaron a favor de la Proposición 209, el cual eliminaría los programas de Acción Afirmativa que facilitan el acceso a minorías y mujeres a la educación, empleos y contratos del sector público.

Los grupos opuestos a la iniciativa declararon que estan listos pa-
LEA 209, pág. 16A

**Proposición 209**
Sí 59%
No 41%

**Proposición 210**
Sí 61%
No 39%

---

## Buenas y malas noticias para el presidente Clinton

■ El mandatario entra en la historia por su reelección, pero enfrenta un Congreso republicano poco amistoso

Maribel Hastings
Corresponsal de La Opinión

WASHINGTON — El presidente Bill Clinton ya pasó a la historia como el primer demócrata en obtener la reelección en 60 años. Ahora, en su segundo período, tiene la oportunidad de dejar su marca en esta historia.

El legado dependerá en gran medida de las fuerzas políticas que controlan el Congreso, en este caso los republicanos, y de cómo interactúen con el mandatario.

Lo primero es analizar el porcentaje del voto popular alcanzado por el Presidente. Al cierre de esta edición Clinton obtenía cerca de 47%, lo que aún se habría requerido para sostener su agenda política.

Lo segundo es ver quién controló el Congreso, que se mantuvo en manos de los republicanos tras las recientes elecciones, dato que tiene buenas y malas noticias para Clinton.

Buenas noticias, porque al mandatario se ha colocado al centro del espectro político como un demócrata de tendencia moderada que ya ha demostrado su capacidad de negociar y trabajar con un Congreso republicano.

Al mismo tiempo, las cerradas contiendas en que se vieron enfrascados los republicanos durante las elecciones.
LEA PRESIDENTE, pág. 16A

**▼ ANALISIS**

---

## Nueva generación de electores llega a las urnas

■ Muchos esperaron durante varios años el momento de poder expresarse políticamente en este país

Jenny Llanos y Roberto Hipp
Especial para La Opinión

Virginia Mújica voto por primera vez en una elección del Este de Los Ángeles.
LEA JOVENES, pág. 16A

---

Figure 4.1 Courtesy of La Opinión

*Figure 4.2* Courtesy of *El Diario-La Prensa*

News World Communications, Inc.—an organization founded in 1976 by the anti-communist crusader Reverend Sun Myung Moon and his Unification Church International.[8] Although *Noticias del Mundo* claimed to function more independently from its staunch conservative founder, it is known for representing politically conservative positions as observed by author Veciana-Suárez, who noted that the editorial stands were "decidedly conservative in international affairs and pro-Hispanic on domestic issues" (1987: 21). Fitzpatrick also alluded to this ideological bend when he observed that the paper's orientation was "more conservative and reflects the attitudes of the Reagan administration" (1987: 310). We could add that, until the paper's demise, it also reflected the opinions of the subsequent Republican administrations.

*El Nuevo Herald* is one of two Spanish-language dailies published in Miami. This broadsheet paper was started in November 21, 1987, as an improved version of *El Miami Herald*. This predecessor had been regularly published since March 29, 1976, as an insert to the English-language daily *The Miami Herald*. In 2004 *El Nuevo Herald* averaged 48 pages with circulation of over 88,000.[9] Both *Herald* newspapers are owned by The Miami Herald Publishing Company, a subsidiary of the Knight-Ridder newspaper chain. Since its beginnings, the principal readers of *El Nuevo Herald* have been immigrant Cubans and Latin Americans residing in Miami and its surrounding communities. Prominent Cuban and Latin American columnists regularly publish their views about politics and other issues relevant to the life and concerns of these communities whether they reside in the U.S. or in their home countries. Veciana-Suárez, writing about the *Herald's* op-ed policy prior to the change in 1987, stated "When dealing with politics, [the columns] tend to be anti-communist and conservative, a reflection of the overwhelming feeling of Miami's Cuban community" (1987: 41). This general policy seems to still hold true today.

*Diario Las Américas* is the other Spanish-language daily published in Miami and the oldest of its type in the city. It was launched on July 4, 1953, by Horacio Aguirre, a Nicaraguan lawyer, and is published by The Americas Publishing Company owned by the Aguirre family. In spring 2004, this broadsheet paper published 24 pages Tuesday through Friday (it is not published Mondays), with a circulation of 61,000. Its distribution is based primarily on home delivery and by mail subscriptions.[10] The principal readership of this paper is the Cuban and other Latin American residents of the Miami and southern Florida area. As with most Cuban-oriented media in that region, the newspaper is explicitly politically conservative and makes this known in its large and lengthy front-page headlines, which often present more than just a caption of the news; they also contain opinion statements of the event being reported. The conservative leanings are also evident in the editorials and opinion columns.

With this context in mind, just what are the characteristics of the political messages that these daily papers have disseminated during presidential elections? Fractional as it is, the evidence summarized below is very revealing.

*Figure 4.3* Courtesy of *El Nuevo Herald*

## COVERAGE OF THE 1984 PRESIDENTIAL ELECTIONS[11]

In the first systematic analysis of how Spanish-language daily newspapers in the United States covered a presidential election, Subervi-Vélez (1988) concluded that this ethnic press appeared to be more imbalanced and partisan than what has usually been found to be the case among the general market press. In four newspapers, *Noticias del Mundo, Diario Las Américas, El Mañana*,[12] and *El Miami Herald*, the Republican campaign was by far better covered than the Democratic campaign, which, in turn, was better covered in *La Opinión* and *El Diario-La Prensa*. This was observed in terms of the number of articles, space, placement, and characters in photos. *La Opinión* was also found to be editorially favorable to the Democrats but its opinion columns were more balanced than those of the other papers. *Noticias del Mundo* and *Diario Las Américas*, on the other hand, were the most partisan, clearly favoring the Republicans in their editorials and opinion columns as well.

93

# DIARIO LAS AMÉRICAS

Por la Libertad, la Cultura y la Solidaridad Hemisférica.

Miembro de la Soci...
Interamericana de Pre...

AÑO XLVIII     NUMERO 306     Miami, Florida Jueves 9 de Noviembre de 2000   EDICION DE 28 PAGINAS - 2 SECCIONES   35 CENTAVOS EN MIA...

| Hillary Clinton da las gracias a los neoyorquinos por abrir corazón y mente | Sila María Calderón: primera mujer Gobernadora de Puerto Rico | Empate 50-50 en el Senado con el triunfo Debbie Stabenow |
|---|---|---|
| Página 8-A | Página 10-A | Página 11-... |

# Ojos del mundo fijos en la Florida

## Comenzó el recuento oficial de los votos

### Boletas ausentes son clave

Por HELEN AGUIRRE FERRE

Clay Roberts, de la División de Elecciones del Departamento de Estado de la Florida dijo a DIARIO LAS AMERICAS que ya ha comenzado, este miércoles, el recuento de los votos. La oficina de Katherine Harris, Secretaria de Estado de la Florida, emitió un informe a las seis de la mañana del miércoles 8 de noviembre confirmando que el candidato republicano para la presidencia, el Gobernador de Texas, George W. Bush, estaba por encima del Vicepresidente demócrata Al Gore, con 1,784 votos, faltando sólo por contar las boletas ausentes del extranjero. La diferencia en votos es menos de un medio por ciento, por lo cual, de acuerdo con la Constitución de la Florida habrá un recuento de votos para verificar los resultados. La oficina de la Secretaria Harris informó que se hará todo lo posible porque los resultados del recuento se separ... al final del día laboral del jueves, 9 de noviembre.

Esta información viene después de una larga y dramática noche llena de suspenso y tensión —la del martes 7 de noviembre— en la que los medios de información a nivel nacional dieron por sentado a las diez de la noche que Al Gore había ganado la Florida, hasta que el Gobernado... de dicho estado y hermano del Gobernador de Texas, Jeb Bush, alert... a su hermano de que las encuestas estaban erradas y que la Florid... efectivamente votó por George W. Bush.

Como si esta historia fuese sacada de una novela, a las dos de la... mañana de este jueves 8, las cadenas de televisión y periódicos anunciaron a Bush como el vencedor, para luego desestimar es... predicción a las cuatro de la madrugada con la noticia de que n... se sabía quién había ganado la Florida. Tanta fue la confusión... que el Vicepresidente Gore había llamado a George W. Bush par... felicitarlo por su victoria y a la hora y media llamó de nuevo par... retirar su concesión de derrota hasta que no se hubiese un recuent...

(Pasa a la Pág. 12-A Col. 2)

Los candidatos a la presidencia por el Partido Demócrata, Al Gore, y por el Partido Republicano George W. Bush están a la espera de un nuevo conteo de votos en el reñido estado de Florida. Si se confirma la victoria de Bush, además de conquistar la presidencia, los republicanos conservan además el control que tienen desde 1994 en la Cámara de Representantes -cuyos 435 escaños estaban en juego- y en el Senado, que renovaba un tercio de sus 100 curules. La democracia de Estados Unidos vivió esta madrugada las horas más alocadas e increíbles de su historia con la sucesión de acontecimientos que han obligado a retrasar el anuncio del resultado final de las elecciones presidenciales. (Telefoto AFP)

Figure 4.4  Courtesy of *Diario Las Amèricas*

That study was based on quantitative analysis of the September 1 through November 6, 1984, issues of those six dailies.[13] Altogether, they published 713 articles, accompanied by 260 photos, related to that year's presidential elections.[14] The analysis summarized here was based on the 653 articles that were directly related to the *campaigns* of the Democratic and Republican presidential candidates.[15]

It is important to point out that because the study was conducted almost two years after the 1984 elections, old copies of four papers and microfilms of the other two were used for the analysis. Obtaining these was often extremely difficult[16] and resulted in incomplete samples for two of the papers.[17]

The coding instrument allowed for notations of, among other things: (a) the type of article; (b) source; (c) page number and zone location; (d) square centimeters[18] of headlines, text, photos and other graphics; and (e) party affiliation of the subjects in graphics (up to four photos, cartoons, and/or drawings were coded for each article).[19]

Findings, discussed in terms of the coverage by party and orientation, are divided into three general topics: (1) number and types of article; (2) amount of space (in square inches) dedicated to the electoral coverage; and (3) zone location of page one news articles. Findings about the photographs are also discussed, but only in terms of their distribution by party. A final section summarizes some general findings about the article sources, letters to the editor, and advertisements.

## Number and types of article

The distribution of types of article published by each Spanish-language daily, table 4.1, illustrates the imbalance and partisan campaign coverage by these papers. It shows, for example, that in *La Opinión*, although many of the news articles were neutral for both the Democratic and Republican Parties, there was a larger number of news classified as unfavorable toward the Republicans (25.1 percent) as compared to the unfavorable news about the Democrats (5.8 percent). This difference in the distribution of the news and editorials by party and orientation was statistically significant. The imbalance is also evident in the editorials: 27.8 percent were favorable, none unfavorable, toward the Democratic Party. In contrast, 22.2 percent were unfavorable, none favorable, toward the Republican Party. No significant differences were found in the distribution of the other types of article. At odds with the previous pattern, however, is that in this otherwise seemingly pro-Democratic newspaper, there were no favorable opinion columns for the Democrats, yet 20 percent of the columns were coded as unfavorable.

The other pro-Democratic Party paper was *El Diario-La Prensa*, where the difference in the distribution of the news articles was also statistically

Table 4.1 Percentage of articles dedicated to the coverage of the presidential campaign from September 1–November 6, 1984, by newspaper, type of article, party, and orientation towards party

| Newspapers / type of article | Democratic | | | Republican | | | Both | | | Total no. of stories |
|---|---|---|---|---|---|---|---|---|---|---|
| | 0 | + | – | 0 | + | – | 0 | + | – | |
| *La Opinión* | | | | | | | | | | |
| News | 19.3 | 5.8 | 5.8 | 14.0 | 7.0 | 25.1 | 22.2 | – | 0.6 | 171 |
| Editorials | 22.2 | 27.8 | – | 11.1 | – | 22.2 | 11.1 | – | 5.6 | 18 |
| Opinion columns | 6.7 | – | 20.0 | 16.7 | 10.0 | 23.3 | 16.7 | – | 6.7 | 30 |
| Editorial cartoons | – | – | 33.3 | – | – | 52.4 | – | – | 14.3 | 21 |
| *El Diario-La Prensa* | | | | | | | | | | |
| News | 23.9 | 9.0 | 9.0 | 14.9 | 11.9 | 9.0 | 22.4 | – | – | 67 |
| Editorials | – | – | 33.3 | – | – | – | 66.7 | – | – | 3 |
| Opinion columns | – | 11.1 | 55.6 | – | 22.2 | 11.1 | – | – | – | 9 |
| *Noticias del Mundo* | | | | | | | | | | |
| News | 18.3 | 6.7 | 4.8 | 25.0 | 22.1 | 1.9 | 18.3 | – | 2.9 | 104 |
| Editorials | – | – | 42.9 | – | 42.9 | 14.3 | – | – | – | 7 |
| Opinion columns | 5.9 | – | 11.8 | 11.8 | 52.9 | – | 17.6 | – | – | 17 |
| *El Miami Herald* | | | | | | | | | | |
| News | 19.1 | 2.1 | 2.1 | 25.5 | 10.6 | 2.1 | 38.3 | – | – | 47 |
| Editorials | 10.0 | 10.0 | – | 20.0 | 30.0 | – | 30.0 | – | – | 30 |
| Opinion columns | 33.3 | – | 16.7 | – | 16.7 | 16.7 | 18.2 | – | 16.7 | 6 |
| Editorial cartoons | – | – | 36.4 | – | 18.2 | 18.2 | 18.2 | – | 9.1 | 22 |
| *Diario Las Américas* | | | | | | | | | | |
| News | 3.3 | – | 16.7 | 21.7 | 33.3 | 5.0 | 18.3 | 1.7 | – | 60 |
| Editorials | – | – | – | – | 100.0 | – | – | – | – | 2 |
| Opinion columns | – | 2.5 | 30.0 | 2.5 | 57.5 | – | 5.0 | – | 2.5 | 40 |
| Editorial cartoons | – | – | 33.3 | – | – | – | – | – | 66.7 | 3 |
| *El Mañana* | | | | | | | | | | |
| News | 18.8 | 6.3 | 18.8 | 31.3 | 6.3 | – | 12.5 | – | 6.3 | 16 |

significant suggesting more favorable *news* coverage of that party and its candidates. On the other hand, the imbalance is not evident in the opinion pages, where over half of the op-ed columns were unfavorable toward the Democrats, as was the case with one of the three campaign related editorials; the other two were coded as "neutral" toward both parties.

The imbalance changes party lines with the other newspapers. Thus, Republicans were significantly better off in all aspects of coverage by *Noticias del Mundo* and *Diario Las Américas*. Combining the neutral and favorable categories, 47.1 percent of the news, and 64.7 percent of the opinion columns were about the GOP in the first paper, while in the latter the distribution was 55 and 60 percent respectively. Not even one opinion column favorable toward the Democratic ticket was published in these papers, which were conservative-oriented in their editorial support as well. *Diario Las Américas* published only two editorials about the campaign and both were favorable toward Reagan-Bush. Of the seven campaign-related editorials in *Noticias*, three were favorable, and only one unfavorable, about them; the remaining three were all unfavorable about the Democrats.

In *El Miami Herald* and *El Mañana*, neutral or favorable news items about the Republicans were also found in greater proportions.[20] Likewise, favorable or even neutral opinion columns about the Democrats were absent in this paper, which published three favorable editorials about the Republicans, but additionally at least one favorable editorial about the Democrats.

## Space dedicated to the election coverage

Table 4.2 shows each newspaper's total space distribution by party and orientation. The pattern found here corresponds to the distribution of the number of articles and it holds mostly unchanged even when the text and headline spaces are analyzed separately. In another analysis it was also noted that the percentage distribution of total space is generally within five points of the percentage of number of articles; a few exceptions merit review. Although *El Diario-La Prensa* published six favorable and six unfavorable news articles about the Democrats, the former received three times as much space. In *Noticias del Mundo*, favorable news about the Republicans received more space than would be suggested by the percentage of number of articles, while the opposite was true for neutral Republican news. In *El Miami Herald*, the proportion of space for neutral articles about both parties was also larger, while it was smaller for the neutral stories of either the Democratic Party or Republican Party individually. This suggests that neutral stories about both required more space for presenting the various perspectives. *Diario Las Américas* and *El Mañana*, however, used more space to present the unfavorable Democratic news.

Table 4.2 Total square inches of news articles devoted to the coverage of the presidential campaign from September 1–November 6, 1984, by newspaper, party, and orientation towards party

| Newspapers | Democratic | | | Republican | | | Both | | | Total sq. inches |
|---|---|---|---|---|---|---|---|---|---|---|
| | 0 | + | – | 0 | + | – | 0 | + | – | |
| La Opinión | 2,582 | 706 | 736 | 1,639 | 758 | 3,097 | 3,361 | – | 62 | 12,941 |
| El Diario-La Prensa | 1,056 | 806 | 252 | 516 | 588 | 419 | 1,489 | – | – | 5,126 |
| Noticias del Mundo | 1,509 | 585 | 248 | 1,809 | 2,789 | 252 | 2,060 | – | 308 | 9,560 |
| El Miami Herald | 669 | 203 | 92 | 856 | 535 | 29 | 2,781 | – | – | 5,165 |
| Diario Las Américas | 79 | – | 1,338 | 979 | 2,157 | 220 | 936 | 91 | – | 5,800 |
| El Mañana | 125 | 71 | 322 | 524 | 32 | – | 95 | – | 106 | 1,275 |
| Totals | 6,020 | 2,371 | 2,988 | 6,323 | 6,859 | 4,017 | 10,722 | 91 | 476 | 39,867 |

To consider variation in coverage over time, the campaign was divided into four periods of 14 days (starting with September 1) and one, the last, of 11 days. For each period, the percentage of neutral, favorable, and unfavorable news article space each paper published about the Democratic and Republican parties and "both" was calculated from that paper's total news space. The distributions of space over the time periods (table 4.3) show that each paper had a unique pattern with hardly any linear trends. Coverage during the September campaign kick-off period was followed by a variety of erratic ups and downs for the various parties and orientations until the end of the campaign. Nevertheless, the pattern of better coverage of the Democratic campaign by *La Opinión* and *El Diario-La Prensa* is evident as is the better coverage of the Republican campaign by the other four papers.

## Zone location of page one news articles

In this dimension too, the Democrats fared generally better in *La Opinión* and *El Diario-La Prensa*. For example, in the first paper 11 of the 15 neutral or favorable front-page news items about the Democrats were above the fold. The two favorable and four of the 10 neutral news items about the Republicans were below the fold but most of the unfavorable GOP news items were placed above. In *El Diario-La Prensa*, there were four neutral/favorable page one news items for the Democrats but only one for the Republicans.

*Diario Las Américas* published on page one 88 percent of its 33 neutral and positively oriented news about the Republicans; 36 percent of these were above the fold. Only one of the three unfavorable news stories about the GOP was also above the fold. In contrast, 80 percent of its 10 unfavorable news about the Democrats were on page one; 62 percent of these were above the fold. Of the two neutral news stories about the Democrats in this paper, one was printed on the front page below the fold.

A major characteristic of *El Miami Herald*'s front page placement of political news is that only one neutral article about the Democrats and nine of the 12 neutral stories about both parties were above the fold. All other page one stories, regardless of orientation, were below the fold. However, the GOP candidates may have been treated better because a greater proportion of neutral and favorable stories about the Republicans (47 percent) than of the Democrats (18 percent) were printed on the first page. Unfavorable stories were balanced with one for each Party.

*Noticias del Mundo* did not print on page one either of the two unfavorable stories about the GOP; yet it did print there, below the fold, three of the five unfavorable news articles about the Democrats. Also, 49 percent of the neutral and favorable news items about the Republicans

Table 4.3 Percentage of space for Democratic (D), Republican (R), and "Both"(B) in each of five time periods, 1984 campaign (neutral and favorable space combined)

| | Time periods | | | | | | | | | | | | | | | | | |
| | 9/9 to 9/14 | | | 9/15 to 9/28 | | | 9/29 to 10/12 | | | 10/13 to 10/26 | | | 10/27 to 11/6 | | | Total | | |
| Newspapers | D | R | B | D | R | B | D | R | B | D | R | B | D | R | B | D | R | B |
|---|---|---|---|---|---|---|---|---|---|---|---|---|---|---|---|---|---|---|
| La Opinión | 7.2 | 2.4 | 3.8 | 2.4 | 3.7 | 2.0 | 2.6 | 3.3 | 7.0 | 1.3 | 3.1 | 5.9 | 11.5 | 6.0 | 7.2 | 25.0 | 18.5 | 25.9 |
| El Diario-La Prensa | 6.0 | 3.1 | – | 2.9 | 2.4 | 2.4 | 4.9 | 0.4 | 3.1 | 7.3 | 1.6 | 8.2 | 14.8 | 14.1 | 14.8 | 35.9 | 21.6 | 28.5 |
| Noticias del Mundo | 4.6 | 5.6 | 2.9 | 3.2 | 9.5 | 0.7 | 3.9 | 5.5 | 5.3 | 3.8 | 8.1 | 6.6 | 6.3 | 20.3 | 5.2 | 21.8 | 49.0 | 20.7 |
| El Miami Herald* | 3.3 | 3.0 | 5.5 | 5.3 | – | 3.0 | 5.8 | 12.8 | 16.3 | – | 4.3 | 21.2 | 2.4 | 6.8 | 7.3 | 16.8 | 26.9 | 53.3 |
| Diario Las Américas | 1.4 | 5.6 | 2.8 | – | 5.1 | – | – | 5.0 | 5.2 | – | 17.2 | 7.7 | – | 20.9 | 2.1 | 1.4 | 53.8 | 17.8 |
| El Mañana | 11.8 | 26.7 | 5.0 | 3.6 | 0.8 | – | – | 16.1 | 2.3 | ** | ** | ** | ** | ** | ** | 15.4 | 43.6 | 7.3 |
| All newspapers | 5.3 | 4.3 | 3.2 | 2.7 | 4.6 | 1.7 | 3.2 | 5.4 | 7.0 | 2.3 | 6.2 | 8.4 | 7.6 | 12.6 | 6.7 | 21.1 | 33.1 | 27.0 |

* Original name at the time
** Data missing owing to incomplete samples

were on page one, although for the most part below the fold. Only 23 percent of the neutral news and one of the favorable news of the Democrats were page one items; two thirds of these were below the fold. In *El Mañana*, two of the four front page stories were unfavorable about the Democratic Party (one was above the fold) but no Republican story was printed on that page.

## Photographs

*La Opinión* and *El Diario-La Prensa* published significantly more pictures of Democratic candidates than of Republican candidates (63% to 35%, n=65; and 52% to 27%, n=33 respectively[21]). The opposite was true for *Diario Las Américas* and *Noticias del Mundo* where the distribution, also statistically significant, was favorable to the Republican candidates (68 to 16 percent, n=19; and 52 to 34 percent, n=79). In *El Miami Herald* each received 43 percent (n=44); *El Mañana* had 4 percent Democrats and 3 percent GOP (n=10). No particular pattern was found in the use of photos in neutral, favorable or unfavorable articles.

## Summary of other findings of the 1984 elections

Only *El Miami Herald* had more than half of the news articles filed by the paper's staff. At least 25 percent of such news was staff-produced in *El Diario-La Prensa*, *La Opinión*, and *Noticias del Mundo*. *Diario Las Américas*, on the other hand, relied on wire services for almost 90 percent of its campaign news articles. United Press International is the wire service most used by four of the five large papers. *El Miami Herald* relies mostly on Associated Press copy while *Diario Las Américas* also uses copy provided by Spain's major news agency (EFE) and the French agency (AFP). The source of *El Mañana*'s articles was mostly coded as "other," with Germany's Deutsche Presse-Agenteur (DPA) providing the plurality of these. For photographs, UPI services were the most used, with AP second. No other agency was found to have provided photos about the presidential campaign.

Except for 12 letters to the editor published in *El Miami Herald* and four in *La Opinión*, Latino readers either refrained from writing about the campaign to their papers, or the editors did not publish letters on the subject. Political ads for the presidential candidates[22] were also scarce in the Spanish-language newspapers. Only three were found in *La Opinión* and another three in *Diario Las Américas*; all were for Reagan. The Mondale camp had two full-page advertisements: one in *El Diario-La Prensa*, the other in *Noticias del Mundo*. However, pro-vote promotions (nonpartisan announcements, ranging in size from 1 square inch to about 4 square inches, telling readers to register and vote) were published in large numbers in *Noticias del Mundo* (at least 88 were coded); a few were coded in three other papers.

## Discussion of the 1984 findings

Limited as it was, this first systematic analysis of political campaign coverage offered by the United States' Spanish-language dailies shows that in 1984 the press was indeed more partisan than has typically been the case with major general-market English-language dailies. The two Miami papers, *Diario Las Américas* and *El Miami Herald* leaned toward the Republican side in news and editorial content, thus matching the political orientations of that city's primarily conservative Cuban population. Reflecting its very conservative ownership, the same is true of New York's *Noticias del Mundo*, although the majority of Latinos in that city, especially Puerto Ricans, are traditionally more liberal in their voting patterns.

The pro-Democratic leanings of the news and editorials of *La Opinión* in Los Angeles and of the news in *El Diario-La Prensa* in New York match the voting patterns of the majority of Latinos in those two cities. Interestingly, the opinion pages of the former, and the editorial pages in general of the latter, did not reflect the same liberal tendencies. Why the editorial content of these two dailies offered few pro-Democratic viewpoints is subject for future research.

Aside from the partisan leanings discussed above, the data also show that of the six dailies studied, *La Opinión* stands out in the coverage given to the 1984 campaign. By far, it printed more news (see table 4.1), dedicated a larger amount of space (see table 4.2), and published more pictures about the campaign than did any of the other papers. The second place, in terms of news coverage, corresponds to New York's *Noticias del Mundo*. However, as was evident in the preceding pages, the partisan orientation of these two newspapers was diametrically opposite. The top spot for the number of opinion columns on that year's campaign goes to *Diario Las Américas*; and the paper with the most editorials was *El Miami Herald*. The least amount of coverage was offered by Chicago daily *El Mañana*, which published only 16 news stories with no editorials, opinion columns, or editorial cartoons. Thus, during the 1984 electoral period, Latinos seeking *news* about the presidential contention would be better off by reading this Los Angeles daily, albeit that coverage would be more about Democrats than about Republicans. For editorials and opinion columns, Latino readers would best turn to the Miami papers where they would find that pro-Republican viewpoints were the norm.

## COVERAGE OF THE 1988 ELECTIONS

The second systematic political communication study of the Latino-oriented press focused on the 1988 elections.[23] Five Spanish-language dailies—*La Opinión, El Diario-La Prensa, Noticias del Mundo, El Nuevo Herald,* (formerly *El Miami Herald*) and *Diario Las Américas*—were coded and content analyzed following procedures similar to those used for the 1984 elections.[24] For this study, however, all the published editions from January 1, 1988 to November 14, 1988 were coded.[25]

The units of observation were all news stories, news-briefs, opinion columns, editorials, and cartoons about or related to the 1988 campaign published during that time period.[26] The coding instrument allowed for notations of, among other things: (a) newspaper, (b) date, (c) section, (d) page, (e) location on page, (f) headline size and rank, (g) text size and rank, (h) number of photos, (i) article type, (j) news source of article, (k) geographic location of news, (l) type of political race, (m) candidate or party, (n) candidate's ethnicity, (o) topic of the political message, and (p) specific ethnic (e.g., Latino) topic of the story and the proportionate amount of space (relative to the rest of the story) dedicated to the Latino angle.[27] In addition, the headlines were copied and entered into computer data files for subsequent analysis.[28]

As can be discerned from items (n) and (p) above, special attention was paid to the articles that had ethnic content, particularly if it was Latino. Thus, a code was set to distinguish Latino candidates; these were identified by their surnames and/or ethnic references in the political messages of the story. With respect to Latino topics, these were defined as explicit statements in the article that indicated that any particular issue was related or of interest to Latinos, affected by or could be affecting Latinos. This included, but was not restricted to, education, housing, employment, health, abortion, and human rights.[29] No attempt was made to define *a priori* which would be the Latino issues.

### Overview

Altogether, between January 1 and November 14, 1988, the nation's leading Spanish-language daily newspapers published approximately 5,180 items relating to that year's electoral processes, including three types of news article, four types of editorial and opinion content, letters to the editor, and political advertisements (see table 4.4).[30]

The data analysis that follows, however, focuses on selected findings from five distinctive time periods that were considered to be the most important for the campaign: the weeks around three major primaries, the weeks of the Democratic and Republican Party conventions, and the final stretch comprising September through Election Day. While it is

Table 4.4 Total coverage of the 1988 campaign: January through mid-November: number of stories in each paper by category

| Newspapers | News n (%) | News-briefs n (%) | Graphics/photo stories n (%) | Editorials n (%) | Opinion columns n (%) | Editorial cartoons n (%) | Letters to the editor n (%) | Political ads n (%) | Totals n (% for col) |
|---|---|---|---|---|---|---|---|---|---|
| La Opinión | 968 (67) | 43 (3) | 96 (7) | 43 (3) | 98 (7) | 155 (11) | 14 (1) | 25 (2) | 1,442 (29) |
| El Nuevo Herald | 538 (68) | 33 (4) | 28 (4) | 29 (4) | 16 (2) | 109 (14) | – | 37 (5) | 790 (15) |
| Diario Las Américas | 709 (57) | 14 (1) | 38 (3) | 29 (2) | 19 (2) | 296 (24) | – | 138 (11) | 1,243 (24) |
| El Diario-La Prensa | 395 (67) | 17 (3) | 20 (3) | 36 (6) | – | 65 (11) | 8 (1) | 45 (8) | 586 (11) |
| Noticias del Mundo | 728 (65) | 33 (3) | 33 (3) | 108 (10) | 9 (1) | 97 (9) | 2 (<1) | 109 (10) | 1,119 (22) |
| All newspapers | 3,338 (64) | 140 (3) | 215 (4) | 245 (5) | 142 (3) | 722 (14) | 24 (1) | 354 (7) | 5,180 (100) |

important and valuable to observe the whole campaign process, the chosen time periods adequately represent the dynamics of the 1988 elections.[31] The discussion of the findings turns to the number and types of news, editorials, and opinion articles, the topics of these articles, and whether or not these had Latino content.

## Patterns of the 1988 coverage

Table 4.5 presents a summary of the data collected about the *news* and *editorial* content published by the five newspapers during the selected campaign periods. As was the case in 1984, once again *La Opinión* stands out for providing its readers the largest number of campaign news, newsbriefs, photos, and editorial cartoons. *Diario Las Américas* repeats its distinction of publishing the largest number of opinion columns. It also printed more political advertisements than any of the other dailies (see table 4.4.) For *Noticias del Mundo*, the distinctive figure is the number of editorials. Of the five dailies assessed in 1988, the least coverage was offered by *El Diario-La Prensa*, which, the reader should recall, is a tabloid-size paper; the other four are printed in broadsheet format.

More revealing is the data summarized in table 4.6. Under the five respective time periods, the first row for each newspaper shows the number of stories published about all types of electoral campaigns. The second row indicates the number of those stories that were about the *presidential* campaign only. The third row specifies which of those presidential campaign stories had some *ethnic* content.

To explain the table with an example, observe first the data about *La Opinión*. The last column on the right (which totals the three categories of news), shows that this newspaper published 648 news items (news, news-briefs, and photo stories) about political campaigns and elections during the selected time periods. The vast majority of these news items, 500 (77 percent) were about the presidential campaign; the remaining 23 percent were about other federal, state, or local elections. Of the 500 presidential campaign stories, 145 (29 percent) had some identifiable ethnic reference.

With this explanation in mind, various patterns and characteristics of each newspaper become evident. First, across the various time periods studied, the presidential campaign was the dominant political story for most of the papers. This is particularly the case for *La Opinión*. On the other hand, *Noticias del Mundo* and *Diario Las Américas* offered the lowest percentage of political stories about the presidential campaign.

Second, while the percentage of presidential stories was higher for *La Opinión*, the proportion of those with ethnic content was under 30 percent, as was the pattern with *El Diario-La Prensa*. Thus, even though it printed more stories about elections and about the presidential campaign,

Table 4.5 Coverage of the 1988 campaign during the major selected time periods of Feb 24–Mar 15, May 31–June 14, July 4–25, Aug 1–22, and Sept 1–Nov 3: number of stories in each paper by category

| Newspapers | News n (%) | News-briefs n (%) | Graphic/photo stories n (%) | Editorials n (%) | Opinion columns n (%) | Editorial cartoons n (%) | Totals n (% for col) |
|---|---|---|---|---|---|---|---|
| La Opinión | 551 (67.0) | 42 (5.1) | 55 (6.7) | 28 (3.4) | 95 (11.5) | 52 (6.3) | 823 (31.8) |
| El Nuevo Herald | 317 (72.7) | 16 (3.7) | 18 (4.1) | 15 (3.4) | 59 (13.5) | 11 (2.5) | 436 (16.8) |
| Diario Las Américas | 355 (60.9) | 3 (0.5) | 21 (3.6) | 15 (2.6) | 178 (30.5) | 11 (1.9) | 583 (22.5) |
| El Diario-La Prensa | 163 (72.8) | 6 (2.7) | 5 (2.2) | 18 (8.0) | 32 (14.3) | – | 224 (8.6) |
| Noticias del Mundo | 383 (73.0) | 20 (3.8) | 13 (2.5) | 61 (11.6) | 42 (8.0) | 6 (1.1) | 525 (20.3) |
| All newspapers | 1,769 (68.3) | 87 (3.4) | 112 (4.3) | 137 (5.3) | 406 (15.7) | 80 (3.0) | 2,591 (100.0) |

Table 4.6 News articles by time period, political race, and ethnic reference in each paper

| | | Time periods | | | | | |
| | | 2/24 to 3/15 | 5/31 to 6/14 | 7/4 to 7/25 | 8/1 to 8/22 | 9/1 to 11/3 | Total |
| Newspapers | Political race/ Ethnic reference | n (%) | n (%) | n (%) | n (%) | n (%) | n (%) |
|---|---|---|---|---|---|---|---|
| *La Opinión* | All races | 52 | 67 | 117 | 98 | 314 | 648 |
| | Presidential | 42 (81) | 45 (67) | 108 (92) | 85 (87) | 220 (70) | 500 (77) |
| | Ethnic | 12 (29) | 19 (42) | 49 (45) | 17 (20) | 48 (22) | 145 (29) |
| *El Nuevo Herald* | All races | 41 | 11 | 57 | 52 | 190 | 351 |
| | Presidential | 33 (80) | 10 (91) | 47 (82) | 41 (79) | 99 (52) | 230 (66) |
| | Ethnic | 11 (33) | 6 (60) | 30 (64) | 16 (39) | 17 (17) | 80 (35) |
| *Diario Las Américas* | All races | 18 | 20 | 56 | 67 | 218 | 379 |
| | Presidential | 10 (56) | 11 (55) | 33 (59) | 48 (72) | 111 (51) | 213 (56) |
| | Ethnic | 5 (50) | 5 (45) | 13 (39) | 14 (27) | 40 (36) | 77 (36) |
| *El Diario-La Prensa* | All races | 19 | 18 | 28 | 17 | 92 | 174 |
| | Presidential | 12 (63) | 7 (39) | 22 (79) | 12 (71) | 73 (79) | 126 (72) |
| | Ethnic | 7 (58) | 5 (71) | 8 (36) | 1 (.08) | 13 (18) | 34 (27) |
| *Noticias del Mundo* | All races | 56 | 49 | 56 | 56 | 199 | 416 |
| | Presidential | 30 (54) | 24 (49) | 35 (63) | 33 (59) | 104 (52) | 226 (54) |
| | Ethnic | 13 (43) | 12 (50) | 16 (46) | 8 (24) | 23 (22) | 72 (32) |
| *All newspapers* | All races | 186 | 165 | 314 | 290 | 1,013 | 1,968 |
| | Presidential | 127 (68) | 97 (62) | 245 (78) | 219 (76) | 607 (60) | 1,295 (66) |
| | Ethnic | 48 (38) | 47 (48) | 116 (47) | 56 (26) | 141 (23) | 408 (31) |

The percentages to the right of the second rows of numbers for each newspaper represent the proportion of news articles that were about the presidential campaign. The percentages in the third row are the proportion of the presidential stories that have an ethnic content (see text for full explanation).

*La Opinión* limited the identifiable ethnic references in those stories; so did *El Diario-La Prensa*. This means that readers of the two liberal Spanish-language dailies would find the news about the presidential campaign less explicitly connected to the Latino community. The pattern with the three traditionally more conservative newspapers—*Diario Las Américas, El Nuevo Herald,* and *Noticias del Mundo*—was different. The political news covered by these papers was proportionally less dedicated to the presidential campaign, but the percentage of these items that had ethnic references was slightly higher.

A third pattern discerned from this table is that, almost across the board, the emphasis on ethnic references in the presidential election stories was typically higher during the primary campaign period than was the case from September through Election Day. Because political news principally reflect the activities of the political parties and candidates, this pattern may be very revealing about the importance given to Latinos at different phases of a campaign (at least in 1988).

As pointed out by DeSipio, de la Garza, and Setzler (1999), Latinos have been more heavily courted during the primaries, when every candidate for his respective party's nomination needs every vote possible to gain that thin margin that may define victory or defeat, than during the final stretch. During this latter time period, votes from Latinos and other minorities may be perceived as less crucial (especially if the polls suggest an easy victory for one of the contenders).[32]

. A different set of patterns emerges from the analysis of the data in table 4.7, which shows the placement of the *presidential* campaign news stories about the Democrats and the Republicans during the final phase of the campaign: September 1 through November 3, 1988.[33] For this table, the figures on the first row show the number of stories related to each party published in the corresponding page sections. The numbers in parenthesis right next to these indicate the percentage distribution of the stories throughout the paper. The last numbers to the right under each party are for the total of stories about that party, while the numbers in the brackets represent percentages across the two parties. As was the case in the previous table, the *second row* for each paper indicates the number and percentage of presidential stories that had *ethnic references*. The figures in parentheses and brackets to the right of these follow the same pattern as those in the row above them.[34]

The example to better explain the table again refers to *La Opinión*. The first row shows that 36 (41 percent) of its 87 news stories about the Democratic Party or its nominees to the presidency or vice presidency were published on page 1. 21 (24 percent) were printed on page 2 or 3, and the remaining 30 (35 percent) on the other inside pages. In contrast, 16 (29 percent) of *La Opinión*'s 54 news stories about the Republican Party and its top candidates were printed on page 1, another

Table 4.7 Location of news about the presidential campaign related to each party and news about this campaign with ethnic references related to each party published by each paper from Sept 1–Nov 3, 1988

| Newspapers | Political race/ Ethnic reference | Democratic Party related news | | | | Republican Party related news | | | |
|---|---|---|---|---|---|---|---|---|---|
| | | page 1 n (%) | pp 2–3 n (%) | inside n (%) | total n [%] | page 1 n (%) | pp 2–3 n (%) | inside n (%) | total n [%] |
| La Opinión | Presidential | 36 (41) | 21 (24) | 30 (35) | 87 [61] | 16 (29) | 23 (42) | 15 (28) | 54 [38] |
| | Ethnic | 10 (48) | 6 (29) | 5 (24) | 21 [70] | 5 (56) | 3 (33) | 1 (11) | 9 [30] |
| El Nuevo Herald | Presidential | 5 (26) | 6 (32) | 8 (42) | 19 [35] | 17 (49) | 10 (29) | 8 (23) | 35 [65] |
| | Ethnic | 1 (50) | 1 (50) | – | 2 [22] | 5 (56) | 3 (33) | 1 (11) | 9 [78] |
| Diario Las Américas | Presidential | 5 (36) | 2 (14) | 7 (50) | 14 [30] | 27 (57) | 8 (17) | 12 (26) | 47 [70] |
| | Ethnic | 3 (38) | 2 (25) | 3 (38) | 8 [27] | 14 (64) | 3 (14) | 5 (23) | 22 [63] |
| El Diario-La Prensa | Presidential | – | 6 (21) | 23 (79) | 29 [58] | – | 1 (5) | 20 (95) | 21 [42] |
| | Ethnic | – | 5 (56) | 4 (44) | 9 [75] | – | – | 3 (100) | 3 [25] |
| Noticias del Mundo | Presidential | 5 (14) | 15 (42) | 16 (44) | 36 [51] | 10 (29) | 17 (50) | 7 (21) | 34 [49] |
| | Ethnic | 5 (42) | 4 (33) | 3 (25) | 12 [50] | 5 (42) | 6 (50) | 1 (8) | 12 [50] |
| All newspapers | Presidential | 51 (28) | 50 (27) | 84 (45) | 185 [49] | 70 (37) | 59 (31) | 62 (32) | 191 [51] |
| | Ethnic | 19 (37) | 18 (35) | 15 (29) | 52 [49] | 29 (53) | 15 (27) | 11 (20) | 55 [51] |

23 (42 percent) on page 2 or 3, and the remaining 15 stories (28 percent) on the other inside pages. As could be expected, given the coverage patterns observed about the 1984 campaign, *La Opinión* had almost twice as many Democratic Party related stories (61 percent) than Republican Party related stories (38 percent). Of the front page stories published by this paper, a greater number (n=36) and proportion (41 percent), were about Democrats and published on the first page. *La Opinión's* emphases were even more notable with presidential campaign stories that had ethnic (typically Latino) content. Seventy percent of those were about the Democrats, and almost half were on the first page.

The emphasis in the coverage of the Democrats is also evident in *El Diario-La Prensa*. Fifty-eight percent of its 50 news stories about the presidential campaign focused on the Democrats. And of the 12 stories with ethnic content, nine (75 percent) were about this party. In this tabloid newspaper, none of the stories about either party was featured on page 1. In the inside pages, stories about the Democrats were proportionally more evident on page 2 and 3 than was the case for stories about the GOP.

A different and more marked emphasis on the Republicans is evident in the data from *Diario Las Américas*, which published 47 news stories about the GOP, almost three times more than the 14 about the Democrats. Most of *Diario Las Américas'* stories about the Republicans (57 percent) were printed on page 1; whereas only five of the stories about the Democrats (36 percent) received the prime space. This newspaper's political leaning was even more notable in the 30 stories with ethnic content: 22 (63 percent) were about the GOP and 14 (64 percent) of these were on page 1.

Similar patterns emphasizing the Republicans can be observed in *El Nuevo Herald*. Thirty-five (65 percent) of its 54 presidential campaign news items were about Republicans. And of the 11 stories with ethnic content, nine (78 percent) were also about the GOP. Only two stories related to the Democrats that also had some ethnic content were printed during the last three months of the campaign.

Contrary to its partisanship in 1984, *Noticias del Mundo* shows a more balanced approach, at least in terms of the percentage of stories published about the two main parties, and also in terms of the placement of these. The number of presidential campaign news items was almost equally divided between Democrats and Republicans, with a slight edge of two extra stories for the former. Where the Republicans gained advantage was in the placement: twice as many of the items about them were printed on page 1.

## Topics

Another set of data from the coverage of the 1988 elections focuses on the topics of the stories about the Democrats and the Republicans, also during the September to November period. Table 4.8 summarizes the findings showing that, almost invariably, the newspapers focused on general campaign activities. Stories emphasizing issues were not frequent in the coverage of the presidential campaign, not even for the news that had ethnic references. For example, in *La Opinión*, not even one of its 21 presidential campaign stories with ethnic reference pertaining to the Democrats was coded as focusing on "issues"; 19 were about general campaign activities. However, two of its ethnic-related stories about the Republicans did focus on issues. Across most newspapers, thus, the norm was less than three stories about "issues."

A notable variation to this pattern is observed in *Diario Las Américas*, which, under the rubric of ethnic-related presidential campaign news, offered its readers seven "issue" stories about Republicans and four about Democrats.

Yet another lacuna in the way the Spanish-language dailies covered the last months of the campaign pertains to news about the "horse race" (i.e., who is ahead in the preference polls), and in stories that primarily featured profiles of the candidates. While fewer news items in both these categories can be expected, the table shows that in some newspapers there was not even one item on either of these subjects, not even in the stories with ethnic angles.

## Editorials and op-eds

The final section of the data analysis of the 1988 campaign turns to the editorial and opinion voices across the selected time periods. Table 4.9 shows the number of editorials, opinion columns and editorial cartoons about all races, the presidential campaign only, and those with ethnic references. The most evident overall finding here is that, while these Latino-oriented newspapers do express opinions about politics, they do not do so consistently and the explicit ethnic content of these is quite limited.

Only *La Opinión* offered its readers editorials, opinion columns and editorial cartoons with electoral content throughout all five of the time periods. During the first four time periods, practically all of the perspectives were about the presidential campaign but, toward the latter part of the campaign, a few were about other races. Yet even in this paper, editorials and editorial cartoons with ethnic references were very scarce. What is consistent and incremental as the presidential campaign progressed was the publication of opinion columns. As can be seen in table 4.9, during the final stretch of the campaign, *La Opinión* published at least a dozen op-ed pieces with ethnic content.

*Diario Las Américas* published more than twice the number of opinion columns than did *La Opinión* for all races and also twice as many about

Table 4.8 Frequency distribution of topics, controlling for political party, of news about the presidential campaign and news about this campaign with ethnic references published from Sept 1–Nov 3, 1988

| Newspapers | Political race/ Ethnic reference | Democratic Party related news | | | | | | Republican Party related news | | | | | |
|---|---|---|---|---|---|---|---|---|---|---|---|---|---|
| | | Number of stories by topics | | | | | | Number of stories by topics | | | | | |
| | | Horserace | Issues | General campaign activity | Candidate profiles | Other* | n | Horserace | Issues | General campaign activity | Candidate profiles | Other* | n |
| La Opinión | Presidential | 7 | 12 | 59 | 7 | 2 | 87 | 4 | 12 | 20 | 14 | 4 | 54 |
| | Ethnic | – | – | 19 | 1 | 1 | 21 | 1 | 2 | 6 | – | – | 9 |
| El Nuevo Herald | Presidential | 6 | 3 | 10 | – | – | 19 | 2 | 4 | 24 | 5 | – | 35 |
| | Ethnic | – | 1 | 1 | – | – | 2 | – | 2 | 7 | – | – | 9 |
| Diario Las Américas | Presidential | – | 4 | 5 | 5 | – | 14 | – | 13 | 28 | 4 | 2 | 47 |
| | Ethnic | – | 4 | 3 | 1 | – | 8 | – | 7 | 14 | – | 1 | 22 |
| El Diario-La Prensa | Presidential | 1 | 10 | 11 | 6 | 1 | 29 | 2 | 4 | 6 | 8 | 1 | 21 |
| | Ethnic | – | 2 | 5 | 1 | 1 | 9 | – | 2 | 1 | – | – | 3 |
| Noticias del Mundo | Presidential | 6 | 3 | 23 | – | 4 | 36 | 6 | 2 | 23 | – | 3 | 34 |
| | Ethnic | 2 | 2 | 6 | – | 2 | 12 | 2 | 1 | 7 | – | 2 | 12 |
| All newspapers | Presidential | 20 | 32 | 108 | 18 | 7 | 185 | 14 | 35 | 101 | 31 | 10 | 191 |
| | Ethnic | 2 | 9 | 34 | 3 | 4 | 52 | 3 | 14 | 35 | – | 3 | 55 |

* Other political news not related to specific candidate or combination of other topics

Table 4.9 Number of editorials (Ed), opinion columns (OC), and editorial cartoons (C) by time period, political race, and ethnic topic in each paper

| Newspapers | Pol-Political race/Ethnic reference | Time periods | | | | | | | | | | | | | | | | | Total | | |
|---|---|---|---|---|---|---|---|---|---|---|---|---|---|---|---|---|---|---|---|---|---|
| | | 2/24 to 3/15 | | | 5/31 to 6/14 | | | 7/4 to 7/25 | | | 8/1 to 8/22 | | | 9/1 to 11/3 | | | | | | | | |
| | | Ed | OC | C | Ed | OC | C | Ed | OC | C | Ed | OC | C | Ed | OC | C | | | | Ed | OC | C |
| La Opinión | All races | 2 | 7 | 8 | 4 | 10 | 4 | 2 | 12 | 2 | 3 | 20 | 8 | 17 | 46 | 30 | | | | 28 | 95 | 52 |
| | Presidential | 2 | 6 | 8 | 1 | 10 | 4 | 2 | 12 | 2 | 3 | 18 | 8 | 6 | 38 | 27 | | | | 14 | 84 | 49 |
| | Ethnic | 1 | – | – | – | 5 | – | 1 | 5 | 1 | 1 | 4 | 1 | 1 | 12 | 1 | | | | 4 | 26 | 3 |
| El Nuevo Herald | All races | 3 | 7 | 2 | – | – | – | 4 | 4 | – | 8 | 10 | 3 | – | 38 | 6 | | | | 15 | 59 | 11 |
| | Presidential | 3 | 4 | 1 | – | – | – | 4 | 4 | – | 7 | 8 | 3 | – | 21 | 6 | | | | 14 | 37 | 10 |
| | Ethnic | 1 | 4 | 1 | – | – | – | 3 | 4 | – | 2 | 5 | – | – | 7 | 1 | | | | 6 | 20 | 2 |
| Diario Las Américas | All races | – | 6 | – | – | 12 | – | 2 | 26 | 3 | 3 | 30 | 2 | 10 | 104 | 6 | | | | 15 | 178 | 11 |
| | Presidential | – | 5 | – | – | 12 | – | 2 | 22 | 3 | 2 | 24 | 2 | 3 | 81 | 6 | | | | 7 | 144 | 11 |
| | Ethnic | – | 1 | – | – | 4 | – | – | 10 | 1 | – | 6 | 2 | 1 | 14 | 1 | | | | 1 | 35 | 4 |
| El Diario-La Prensa | All races | – | 1 | – | – | – | – | 1 | 2 | – | 1 | 4 | – | 16 | 25 | – | | | | 18 | 32 | – |
| | Presidential | – | 1 | – | – | – | – | 1 | 1 | – | 1 | 4 | – | 11 | 19 | – | | | | 13 | 25 | – |
| | Ethnic | – | – | – | – | – | – | 1 | 1 | – | 1 | 2 | – | 6 | 6 | – | | | | 8 | 9 | – |
| Noticias del Mundo | All races | 5 | 5 | – | 4 | 4 | – | 8 | 4 | 1 | 13 | 1 | – | 31 | 28 | 5 | | | | 61 | 42 | 6 |
| | Presidential | 2 | 5 | – | 3 | 3 | – | 6 | 4 | 1 | 10 | 1 | – | 17 | 20 | 4 | | | | 38 | 33 | 5 |
| | Ethnic | 1 | 3 | – | 2 | – | – | 2 | – | 1 | 2 | – | – | 4 | 8 | – | | | | 11 | 11 | 1 |
| All newspapers | All races | 10 | 26 | 10 | 8 | 26 | 4 | 17 | 48 | 6 | 28 | 65 | 13 | 74 | 241 | 47 | | | | 137 | 406 | 80 |
| | Presidential | 7 | 21 | 9 | 4 | 25 | 4 | 15 | 43 | 6 | 23 | 55 | 13 | 37 | 179 | 43 | | | | 86 | 323 | 75 |
| | Ethnic | 3 | 8 | 1 | 2 | 9 | – | 7 | 20 | 3 | 6 | 17 | 3 | 12 | 47 | 3 | | | | 30 | 101 | 10 |

Table 4.10 Number of Democratic and Republican related editorials, opinion columns, and editorial cartoons about the presidential campaign in general and about that campaign but with ethnic references published from Sept 1–Nov 3, 1988

| Newspapers | Political race/ Ethnic reference | Democratic Party related items | | | | Republican Party related items | | | |
|---|---|---|---|---|---|---|---|---|---|
| | | Editorials | Opinion columns | Editorial cartoons | Total | Editorials | Opinion columns | Editorial cartoons | Total |
| La Opinión | Presidential | 1 | 4 | 1 | 6 | — | 19 | 11 | 30 |
| | Ethnic | — | 3 | — | 3 | — | 6 | 1 | 7 |
| El Nuevo Herald | Presidential | — | 3 | — | 3 | — | 3 | — | 3 |
| | Ethnic | — | 2 | — | 2 | — | 2 | — | 2 |
| Diario Las Américas | Presidential | 2 | 24 | 4 | 30 | 1 | 21 | — | 22 |
| | Ethnic | 1 | 4 | 1 | 6 | — | 5 | — | 5 |
| El Diario-La Prensa | Presidential | 1 | 5 | — | 6 | 1 | 5 | — | 6 |
| | Ethnic | — | 1 | — | 1 | — | 1 | — | 1 |
| Noticias del Mundo | Presidential | 11 | 3 | — | 14 | 2 | 6 | 1 | 9 |
| | Ethnic | 1 | 1 | — | 2 | 1 | 2 | — | 3 |
| All newspapers | Presidential | 15 | 39 | 5 | 59 | 4 | 54 | 12 | 70 |
| | Ethnic | 2 | 11 | 1 | 14 | 1 | 16 | 1 | 18 |

the presidential race. However, it was during the last three months of the campaign that these newspapers published opinion columns about all types of race—especially regarding the presidential campaign.

Finally, table 4.10 shows the number of editorials, opinion columns, and editorial cartoons about the presidential race that referred primarily to either the Democrats or to the Republicans during the last three months of the campaign. In the absence of any assessments as to whether any of these published items were favorable or unfavorable to the main party referred to, it is difficult to affirm whether the newspapers expressed any partisanship in the editorial/opinion pages. Nonetheless, it would be plausible to consider that, for example, the majority of the 21 opinion columns that *Diario Las Américas* published about the Republicans were probably favorable to the presidential candidate and/or his party, while most of the 24 columns about Democrats were probably unfavorable to its candidate and party. Meanwhile, in the pages of *La Opinión*, it is plausible that there would be more favorable opinions about Democrats than about Republicans. This pattern, however, may not hold true if the sources of the columns were conservative voices or operatives of the GOP (see Santillán and Subervi-Vélez, 1991; Subervi-Vélez, 1992). Future studies should certainly assess the partisan leanings or preferences expressed in the editorial pages of the Spanish-language newspapers and the Latino-oriented press in general.

## COVERAGE OF THE 1992 ELECTIONS[35]

In this section, the focus turns to how *La Opinión* covered the 1992 campaign. Following the same methods used in the previous two studies, this study also coded for political candidates, article types, subject matters, whether there was Latino mention in the articles, sources of these, the length of the articles, and their location in the paper. The sample for this study was from September 1 through November 3 (Election Day) that year. Altogether, 362 articles were coded during this time period (almost 50 more than was the case for the same period during the previous presidential campaign).

### Summary of findings

Overall, *La Opinión* presented a generally balanced coverage of the two main presidential candidates, Bill Clinton and George Bush. As table 4.11 illustrates, an almost equal number of news, features, and graphics were printed about the two main candidates—a pattern notably different from the 1988 coverage. Ross Perot and other independent candidates received less attention in terms of allocation of articles and print space.

Table 4.11 Summary of La Opinión's coverage of the 1992 campaign from Sept 1–Nov 3, 1988

|  | Clinton | Bush | Perot | Clinton and Bush | All | None |
|---|---|---|---|---|---|---|
| Headline inches | 124 | 139 | 54.8 | 203.5 | 80.38 | 58.25 |
| Text inches | 776.88 | 1,020.7 | 498 | 1,682.5 | 823.25 | 488 |
| Graphic inches | 373.5 | 560.88 | 190.75 | 465.5 | 278 | 91.88 |
| Total inches | 1,274.38 | 1,720.98 | 743.55 | 2,351.5 | 1,181.63 | 638.13 |
| Number of photos | 26 | 20 | 9 | 20 | 7 | 3 |
| Number of stories | 62 | 96 | 35 | 91 | 44 | 34 |
| Above/below the fold | 45/16 | 57/39 | 22/13 | 53/18 | 29/15 | 19/15 |

In terms of the space and location treatment of articles, Bush received approximately one-third more text and graphic space coverage—an imbalance that stems from the extra number of editorial material that focused on him and his campaign. However, Clinton was presented in 25 percent more photos than was Bush, and was also favored in terms of placement of headlines above the fold with 75 percent on the preferable location. Only 59 percent of Bush's headlines were placed as prominently.

Perot appeared in only half as many stories as Clinton and a third as many as Bush. That discrepancy between the candidates of the two main parties and the independent becomes even more pronounced when stories involving both Clinton and Bush are considered. One of the factors that certainly contributed to this pattern is that Perot had backed out of the race prior to the Democratic Party's convention and did not re-declare his candidacy until late September, halfway into the period studied, after which he never approached the poll standings of his two principal competitors.

What was dissimilar to the 1988 coverage was the greater number of opinion columns and editorial cartoons about the Democrat. Clinton was clearly favored in both of these op-ed items. The opinion columns were authored primarily by independent journalists who, as such, may have enjoyed an aura of authority derived from the columnist's own individual stature. This is of particular significance in a newspaper such as La Opinión, which relied largely on wire reports without bylines, thus making each bylined story stand out as though it were written especially for its pages.

In the editorial cartoons, much criticism of Bush and Perot was evident. In fact, Bush was most prominent in this section of the paper, but most often serving as the object of mordant satire. When Clinton was included in this type of item, he was usually portrayed in a neutral or positive light as the attractive candidate next to the foils of Bush or Perot. For example, in one editorial cartoon, Clinton is shown waiting patiently for Bush at a debate podium as the "chicken" President Bush cowers in the wings, and a "Dumbo-eared" Perot astonishes his counterparts by appearing behind a very short debate lectern, which is actually an oversized money bag overflowing with bills.

Summarizing additional analysis of this newspaper, it was evident that La Opinión's choice of subject matter favored Clinton. The issue this candidate had chosen as the central theme of his campaign—Bush's alleged failure to improve the economy—received constant mention, especially in articles focusing on Bush himself.[36] Foreign policy issues also occupied a large share of La Opinión's news sections, focusing attention on Bush's controversial involvement in Iraqi affairs and his polemical approval of arms sales to Taiwan and Saudi Arabia. Few stories shed light on Clinton's experience or prospective performance in the international arena, an issue the Republican sought unsuccessfully to raise throughout the campaign—often in the form of attacks against Clinton for his alleged evasion of military service.

Feature articles, often subtitled "analysis," tended not to editorialize. Nevertheless, some bias was evident, especially in ignoring Perot, who received little coverage even after his declaration of candidacy. The analyses most commonly compared only the positions of Clinton and Bush on the main campaign issues such as the economy and domestic policy. Debates did receive some attention in the form of analysis of the horse race, other polling results, and conventional wisdom regarding the effects of the debates on the race. Some features also instructed readers about the election process itself, such as registration dates, polling places, and the dynamics of the Electoral College and party patronage.

Turning to the analysis of ethnic (i.e., Latino) references, it was observed that about one out of every four items coded from La Opinión's coverage of the 1992 campaign explicitly allude to Latinos. Table 4.12 shows the distribution of the Latino angle by type of story. The highest percentage under this rubric was the opinion columns (30 percent). However, no graphics (such as could have been printed to show the results of surveys) or editorial cartoons were found to refer explicitly to Latinos or Latino issues.

A more detailed analysis of the content showed that of the few articles that did have Latino themes, most focused on the North American Free Trade agreement but addressed U.S. Latinos only peripherally. As such, they might have well been coded as international or economic issues. Most of such articles were either editorials or opinion columns written by the editors of La Opinión or by Latino leaders who did not necessarily mention the Latino community per se.

In La Opinión's opinion pages, Latino leaders lent their support exclusively to Clinton. For example, Henry Cisneros (former Mayor of San Antonio), Gloria Molina (member of the Los Angeles County Board of Supervisors), and various Latino pundits all supported the Democrat. So did La Opinión's governing board, which in its editorials explicitly endorsed the Democrat. Bush was, for the most part, criticized or ignored in these pages.

## Discussion of the 1992 findings

During the last three months of the 1992 campaign, La Opinión offered its readers an ample number of news and opinion pieces about the political candidates and even published some features on the election process. The pattern is similar to its coverage of previous campaigns. Overall, in terms of news articles, this Spanish-language daily offered its readers a balanced coverage of the two main presidential candidates that year.

Table 4.12 Latino references in *La Opinión*'s coverage of the 1992 campaign from Sept 1–Nov 3, by article type

| Type of reference | New n (%) | Graphics n (%) | Opinion columns n (%) | Editorials n (%) | Editorial cartoons n (%) | Feature articles n (%) | Total n (%) |
|---|---|---|---|---|---|---|---|
| Latino | 40 (25) | – | 13 (30) | 3 (23) | – | 4 (24) | 60 (17) |
| Non-Latino | 120 (75) | 18 (100) | 30 (70) | 10 (77) | 65 (100) | 13 (76) | 256 (83) |
| Totals | 160 | 18 | 43 | 13 | 65 | 17 | 316 |

However, it covered the Democratic Party candidate more favorably than was the case for either of his opponents in terms of placement, number of photos, and the actual content of the editorials and opinion page pieces. As in previous campaigns, what remains limited is an explicit connection of Latinos and the Hispanic communities to the campaign, the candidates, and/or issues.

## COVERAGE OF THE 1996 ELECTIONS[37]

The final section turns to the 1996 campaign and presents, as was the case for the previous study, primarily a narrative on the findings on the coverage during the last three months of that year's election period: September 1 through November 5. The study, however, encompasses two dailies—La Opinión and El Nuevo Herald—for which articles pertaining to the *presidential campaign* as published in each paper's A and B sections were selected and coded applying some of the protocols followed in the other studies discussed above. Altogether, the analysis of La Opinión yielded 82 news articles, plus 19 editorial page items; the numbers from El Nuevo Herald were 72 news articles, plus 15 from its editorial section.[38]

For the presidential campaign stories selected for this study, the headlines and first few paragraphs of the articles were examined together and treated as one specific unit of analysis.[39] Four coders independently assigned articles to five mutually exclusive categories pertaining to topic of story.[40]

Each unit of analysis was classified as being favorable, unfavorable, or neutral in content. Favorable coverage was considered to specify a positive reference to the candidate, including polls reporting a lead or recognition of an activity as being positive. Unfavorable coverage was seen as a negative reference to the candidate, including attacks on character or forms of criticism. Neutral coverage included articles that documented general campaign activity.[41]

### Summary of findings

The wire services were relied upon heavily as sources of the published articles (including those in the editorial pages) for both newspapers: 49.5 percent for La Opinión and 52.9 percent for El Nuevo Herald. Also, in both newspapers the majority of the coverage was centered on President Clinton, who was portrayed primarily in a positive way. Such coverage is consistent given the findings from the previous studies, and also in light of La Opinión's endorsement of President Clinton in 1996. However, the results were different from what was observed about El Nuevo Herald's more pro-Republican coverage in 1984 and 1988, and somewhat at odds given the endorsement of Bob Dole by the parent newspaper—*The Miami Herald*.

The theme "strength of character" dominated the coverage in both papers. This was marked by references to candidates' qualifications, virtues, abilities, and experience, predictions about chances of winning, and endorsements received by each. A common feature found in articles under this rubric was the subject of Dole's attacks on Clinton's virtues, and Clinton's reactions to such attacks. The analysis did not reveal any articles showing Clinton making direct attacks on Dole's character.

*La Opinión* covered the candidates' positions on immigration policy and social services issues more than did *El Nuevo Herald*. In those articles, the emphasis was on the interests of Mexican Americans—a large percentage of *La Opinión*'s audience. This observation also stems from articles that made reference to other political initiatives that appeared directly to affect Mexican Americans in the Los Angeles area. *El Nuevo Herald*, on the other hand, reported more on issues of foreign policy, especially U.S. relations with Cuba. This finding is congruent with other research that alludes to the divergent range of political concerns among Latinos (Garcia, Falcón and de la Garza, 1996).

The "horse race" stories were also common in both newspapers. These were marked by references to who is leading, especially in polls, debates, general campaigning activities and fundraisers. A salient number of articles were dedicated to talk about the debates followed by discussion of standing in the opinion polls.

Finally, consistent with the news coverage (and findings from previous studies) *La Opinión*'s editorials and columns generally featured Clinton more favorably than not. This paper's op-ed articles also dealt more with immigration and welfare issues, and with Mexican and Latin American politics. *El Nuevo Herald*'s editorials and columns were more evenly distributed between the two candidates, and discussed Latin American themes and politics, particularly issues concerning Cuba.

## Discussion of the 1996 findings

With the exception of *El Nuevo Herald*'s relatively favorable coverage of Clinton, the findings are consistent with previous assessments of the partisanship of how these Spanish-language dailies cover presidential campaigns. It was also interesting to observe that the issues emphasized by *La Opinión* pertained primarily to immigration and welfare, while at *El Nuevo Herald* the focus was on international matters with an emphasis on Cuba. These differences again affirm the importance of not treating the Latino community as monolithic, particularly in political matters.

The findings are comparable to other assessments of general market print media coverage of elections. For example, comparable to the analyses by

Jamieson and Waldman (2003) of the coverage by select general market newspapers of political campaigns, it can be suggested that the emphasis on the attributes of the candidates over issues seems to be a consistent pattern between Spanish-language and English-language newspapers.

## CHAPTER SUMMARY AND CONCLUSIONS

The main question of this chapter was "How have the Spanish-language daily newspapers covered presidential elections?" The data allow for a few answers and thus at least a partial understanding of how some of these media outlets convey American politics to Latinos.

For *La Opinión*, the largest Spanish-language daily serving Los Angeles and Southern California, the coverage across election periods is generally pro-Democratic—and thus congruent with the political orientations of the Latino readership in that region. But the favorable orientation toward Democratic candidates is not always as evident in the op-ed pages, not so much because of negative items, but instead for the few editorials and opinion pieces supportive of the Democratic Party and its candidates. Likewise lacking across various campaigns was the explicit connections in headlines and stories between a particular party or candidate and Latinos and/or Latino issues. The Southern California region Latinos reading this paper for political content would have to seek other sources to learn more directly or explicitly the relevance of the presidential campaign to the Hispanic community in general or the local community in particular.

Similar patterns were observed with New York's *El Diario-La Prensa*, at least during the two election periods for which it was analyzed. In EDLP there was, on the one hand, a more pro-Democratic coverage in a number of stories, while, on the other hand, even less attention to either party in terms of editorials, op-ed pieces, and explicit connections between presidential candidates and Latinos and/or Latino issues. Latinos reading this paper for political content would also have to search for alternative sources to find explicit connections between the presidential campaign and the Hispanic community.

At *El Nuevo Herald*, the only other newspaper that was also studied in two or more campaign periods, a transition was observed from the Republican partisanship in 1984 and 1988 to a more balanced coverage—at least in news space and op-ed focus—given to both major presidential candidates. What distinguishes this paper from the other two is the greater proportion of stories and op-ed pieces that explicitly connect the political parties and candidates to Latinos and Latino issues, however these are defined. The campaign coverage is not just about American politics detached from the local community. What is at stake for Latinos, at least from the local/regional base, is alluded to on a more regular basis.

Interestingly, the ethnic (i.e., most certainly Latino) "relevance" factor was also observed in the other papers whose content was also more pro-Republican—*Noticias del Mundo* (no longer in circulation) and *Diario Las Américas*. And as was noted in previous pages, the latter of these two also offered its readers a regular diet of editorials and opinion columns about the presidential campaigns. Latino readers of these Spanish-language daily newspapers would probably have a larger repertoire of political information that would also make references to the national and/or local Latino communities.

In essence, during election periods, Latinos who wish to follow in Spanish-language newspapers the developments of the campaign can count on finding ample coverage if they gain access to *La Opinión* and *El Nuevo Herald*. Latinos can also easily find campaign coverage, although not as extensively, in *El Diario-La Prensa* and *Diario Las Américas*. Yet even when reading these papers, explicit connections between the campaign and ethnic (Latino) issues may be scarce or diffused.

We could expect that the newest Spanish-language dailies in the country, *El Día* in Houston, and *Hoy* in New York City, Chicago and Los Angeles, will also offer on a regular basis ample coverage of electoral campaigns. How explicitly relevant or connected to Latinos and Latino issues is unknown at this time.

Also unknown is the actual or potential influence that directly or indirectly these newspapers have on the political knowledge, orientations, and actual behaviors of Latinos, be they U.S. citizens, resident aliens or just recent immigrants. That will have to be the subject of subsequent research that properly assesses the relationships between reading the political content of these newspapers and Latinos' political cognitions, attitudes, etc.

That type of research will have to keep in mind the fact that the daily Spanish-language newspapers—be they the older ones or the newest arrivals—albeit being the most extensive sources of campaign news and information, are still available in print format in only a few cities. This means that survey research that assesses the potential political effects of Spanish-language newspapers on Latinos must recognize that little or no effects—direct or indirect—are realistically possible in cities where those newspapers do not circulate.

Yet it should also be pointed out that, given the recent availability of most of these papers via the Internet, it will be most valuable and interesting to delve extensively into the political socialization effects these sources may have. Assessing the influence of other Internet sources in Spanish and/or English should also be on future research agendas. Of course, this line of research will have to take into serious consideration, and statistically control for, the concomitant effects of income and education on both access to computers and the Internet and how these would affect political socialization.

What is missing? Too much. Certainly, more quantitative and qualitative analysis of the political news printed by the respective papers. Although we may know in a general way the political leanings of some of the papers, we do not know if that is the case for the newer publications, nor the specific language used in that preference. The number of stories about one party (the 1988 study) and the assessments of the orientation (positive, negative, neutral) of the stories about the parties (1984, 1996 study) offer the only evidence, yet still limited, of the partisanship.

Another important question that merits attention—even if just in the study of the content of the dailies, albeit even more so in the weeklies—is how much of the content is generated by the newspaper's staff and how much is generated by the political communication operatives of the respective parties? Different outcomes could certainly be expected when the Latino electorates who rely on Spanish-language newspapers build their orientations based on "objective" news offered by professional staff of the newspapers against that based on "planted" stories that stem from the parties or their propaganda offices.

But, again, what effect does exposure to this coverage have? Most importantly, how mobilizing is that content? In other words, how much does it not only inform the reader with the news information, but also call to action and get people active, not just for the sake of being part of the U.S. political system, but also because there is something at stake for the Latino community at large or the regional or local Hispanic group? Moreover, if mobilization is a key factor for Latino political participation and empowerment, in what form or fashion does that mobilization news and information take place in the headlines and/or text of the news and opinion content of the Spanish-language dailies?

These and many other questions wait for the next generation of research in this arena.

## NOTES

1 The five newspapers focused on in this chapter had been, until the 1990s, the *major* Spanish-language daily publications circulating in the *metropolitan* centers with the largest numbers of Latino populations. As the following list shows, the current Spanish-language daily newspapers are much more numerous. *El Día*, owned by the Budini family enterprises, was launched in Houston, Texas, in 1995. The Tribune Company started its own chain of Spanish-language dailies, *Hoy*, which circulate in New York (since 1998), Chicago (2003), and in Los Angeles (2004). *La Visión*, owned by CHL Communications Inc., began operations in Lawrenceville, Georgia in 2000. In the year 2003, two Spanish-language dailies were launched in Dallas. The first was *La Estrella*, formerly a weekly, owned by the Knight Ridder Company, the second largest newspaper publisher in the United States, and also engaged in Internet publishing. The second was *Al Día*, published by the Bello Corporation,

owners of various media companies, including *The Dallas Morning News*. In 2003, *El Nuevo Día-Orlando* was launched, owned by the Ferré Family Enterprises of Puerto Rico, which also own the island's largest daily, *El Nuevo Día*. And in the year 2004, AztecaAmerica, with capital investors from Spain, started their own chain of dailies in San Antonio, Houston, the Valley (South Texas), and Austin. The Texas–Mexico border region also has daily newspapers: *El Tiempo*, which, since 1926, has been an insert to the *The Laredo Morning Times*; *El Nuevo Herald*, a daily since 1934 out of Brownsville; and McAllen's *La Frontera*, launched in 2004 by Freedom Communications, Inc., which also owns that city's English-language daily, *The Monitor*. For additional information about these dailies and other Latino-oriented media, see Suberri and Eusebio (2005). The political news coverage of these has not been subject to any systematic or scholarly content analysis.

2 Subervi-Vélez et al., (1994: 318) observe from a 1990 profile of the newspaper's readers that the majority were Mexican and Mexican American (66 percent), with the rest comprising Central American (15 percent) and South American (5 percent). Between 1990 and 2003, *La Opinión* was part of the Times Mirror Company, although the Lozano family always maintained a majority on the Board of Directors and its full editorial policy and operational control. After the Times Mirror became part of the Tribune Corporation, this latter company proceeded with its plans to launch in Los Angeles in March 2004 a local edition of *Hoy*, a Spanish-language daily similar to the Tribune's other Spanish-language dailies in New York and Chicago. This led *La Opinión* to cease its partnership with the Tribune Company and the *Los Angeles Times* and subsequently to establish in January 2004 a joint corporate venture with *El Diario-La Prensa* and that company's new owners. The venture capital group, CPK Media Holdings, owns ImpreMedia LLC, the new corporation that combines both dailies. Fitzgerald (2004), writing for *Hispanic Business*, quotes José Ignacio Lozano, Chairman of the new company, ImpreMedia, as stating that the goal of the new partnership "is to create a national group of Latino newspapers that covers issues impacting our community nationally, regionally and locally on a hard hitting and timely basis." As a continuation of that plan, in 2004, ImpreMedia purchased Chicago's weekly, *La Raza*.

3 The number of pages and the circulation figures listed for this newspaper and the others studied here are averages and approximations. As with all newspapers, the page numbers vary by edition, and the circulation figures tend to be higher for Wednesdays and weekend editions.

4 *La Opinión's* circulation in the specific years of the studies presented in this chapter were as follows: in 1984, 54,567, in 1988, 68,415, and in 1992, 109,558. For the circulation figures of this and other major newspapers, see *Burrelle's Hispanic Media Directory* (1984) and later editions for the corresponding years.

5 *El Diario-La Prensa's* circulation in 1984 was 65,000, in 1988, 70,000, and in 1991 it was 54,481.

6 In their summary history, Subervi-Vélez et al. (1994) indicate that *El Diario-La Prensa* (*ED-LP*) was launched in the summer of 1963 from the merger of *La Prensa* and *El Diario de Nueva York*. They add that the first of these was founded in 1913 and was operated by José Campubrí, "a Spaniard who kept the paper until 1957 when it was purchased by Fortune Pope . . . In 1963 Pope sold *La Prensa* to O. Roy Chalk who had been owner of *El Diario de Nueva York* since he purchased it in 1961 from Porfirio Domenicci, a Dominican who had started in 1948" (1994: 319). Chalk, an American Jewish businessman,

merged these papers in 1963 and then directed the operation until 1981 when he sold it to the Gannett Company, which is a major media conglomerate. Gannet held this paper for eight years, after which it has changed owners four additional times. In 1989 ED-LP was sold to a group of investors headed by Peter Davidson. In early 1995, ED-LP was purchased by another group of investors, which included Time Warner, Inc., the Massachusetts Mutual Life Insurance Company, Malayan United Industries,·and Wertheim Schroder & Company (Glaberson, 1995). That same year, this group of investors had formed "Latin Communications Group," and Peter Davidson and Carlos Ramírez, whose company "El Diario Associates," had owned ED-LP, became part of that group. Entravisión, a California-based media company affiliated with Univisión and Mexico's Televisa, owned the paper from April 2000 until July 2003. At that point, another group, led by Clarity Partners, a Los Angeles-based private equity firm focusing on media and communications, obtained this newspaper. A New York Times story of the latest sale of ED-LP indicates that the other purchasing partners included BMO Halyard Partners, a New York-based private equity investment arm of BMO Financial Group; ACON Investments, a private equity firm in Washington, with investments in Latin America and Europe; and Knight Paton Media Corporation, a newspaper investment consulting practice based in Toronto (Kelly, 2003). The most recent development at the corporate is the partnership, as of January 2004, under ImpreMedia LLC, and thus with La Opinión, as alluded to above (see Fitzgerald, 2004). Impre-Media currently owns not only the dailies ED-LP in New York, and La Opinión in Los Angeles, but also the weeklies La Raza in Chicago, La Prensa in Orlando and El Mensajero in San Francisco.

7 Noticias del Mundo's circulation hovered at maximum at about 30,000.

8 In the late 1980s and early 1990s, News World Communications also published, among other titles, the politically conservative Washington Times, the New York City Tribune, and Ultimas Noticias, a daily newspaper in Uruguay.

9 El Miami Herald's circulation in 1984 was approximately 63,000, in 1988 it was approximately 96,4000, and in 1992 approximately 102,289.

10 Diario Las Américas' circulation in 1984 was 62,520, in 1988, 64,093, and in 1992 it was 66,021.

11 The complete version of this study can be found in Journalism Quarterly, 65 (3), 1988, pp. 678–685.

12 In 1984, El Mañana of Chicago was published on a daily basis, although not regularly. This paper was established in May 1971 by Gorki Tellez, who at the time was a community activist and owner of a small truck catering business (Subervi-Vélez et al., 1994). It was a 16-page tabloid published Monday through Friday; it was very graphic, moderately sensational, usually void of editorials, letters to the editor, and opinion columns.

13 All editions of the six dailies from July 1 through August 30, 1984, were also coded but analysis of that data has never been conducted. Anyone interested in analyzing that data should contact the principal author, Federico Subervi-Vélez.

14 For the coding of all this material, I wish to express my special thanks to Susana Quintero, Margarita Rodríguez del Valle, Piedad Palacios, and María Denney, who at the time were students at the University of California at Santa Barbara.

15 Articles dealing primarily with the candidates' functions as public officials were excluded. And because the focus of the analysis was on the presidential

campaigns, articles of state or local candidates and issues were also excluded unless directly related to that campaign.

16  *La Opinión* and *El Miami Herald* were the only Spanish-language daily newspapers for which microfilms were produced and easily available shortly after the publication of the papers. *El Mañana* and *Noticias del Mundo* were not archived on microfilm, nor available via any library. Old copies were purchased, with difficulty, from the newspapers' main offices where for some of the dates no extra copies could be found even in the corporations' archives. *El Diario-La Prensa* and *Diario Las Américas* were supposed to be reproduced on microfilm but the dates needed for this case study had not been prepared even two years after the papers' publication. When copied, the Library of Congress can make them available through interlibrary loans. But no library in New York City or State, or anywhere in the U.S., archived *El Diario-La Prensa* on a regular or consistent basis. The only place where there were old copies of this publication was in the paper's central offices in New York City. *Diario Las Américas* did not even have old copies of its own product. Libraries of some major universities (e.g., Miami, California–Berkeley, and Texas–Austin) did have back copies of this and other Spanish-language papers, but they are not lent outside the holder's premises. Analysis of both these papers was possible because, during the summer of 1986, two of the research assistants (Margarita Rodríguez del Valle, and Piedad Palacios) traveled to New York and Miami respectively and, during their vacation time, continued to work on the project to complete the coding of these newspapers.

17  The missing editions were the following: *El Mañana*: September 3, 27, October 3, 11 to 31, and November 1 to 6; *Noticias del Mundo*: October 1, 18, 31 and November 3.

18  To increase accuracy at the time of coding, measurements were in centimeters but later converted to inches to present the findings.

19  In addition, the headlines were copied along with summary notations of the major events and political issues of the story. The headlines and notations were then read by at least three of the four coders who independently assigned each article three topic codes for classifying the main character(s) (e.g., candidates), what he/she was doing (e.g., campaigning, being praised or endorsed, criticized or not supported); and, if endorsed or criticized, by whom (e.g., another candidate, politician, a community or labor leader). Of the 2,139 codes assigned to all the articles (713 x 3) by each coder, there was agreement in approximately 95 percent of the cases. Finally, the codes were classified as favorable, unfavorable, or neutral. Favorable classifications were for the codes denoting, for example, that the candidate was ahead in the polls, had "won" a debate, had been supported or endorsed by another politician or community leader. Unfavorable classifications were given to codes indicating that the candidate was behind in the polls, had "lost" a debate, had been criticized or not endorsed. Codes indicating general campaign activities (e.g., candidate "X" gives speech in New York, campaigns in Chicago, favors a particular policy) were classified neutral. Since the whole article was not subjected to statement analysis for an in-depth determination of the story's leaning or bias, these classifications are conservative estimates of what might be perceived from reading the headline and first few paragraphs of an article. Chi-square tests were run to determine if the proportion of different types of article (favorable, unfavorable, or neutral) published by each paper for each party were significantly different.

20  The chi-square tests of those distributions were not significant because of the small numbers or lack of cases in some cells.

21 In all the figures about photos, the 100 percent total is made up by pictures of "both" or "other" (e.g., non-partisan people). Also, the percentage of news articles which had at least one photo was as follows: *El Miami Herald* and *El Mañana*, 65; *Noticias del Mundo*, 53; *El Diario-La Prensa*, 42; *La Opinión*, 29; and *Diario Las Américas*, 28.

22 In contrast to the scarcity of advertisements from the presidential candidates, it was observed that state and local candidates did advertise extensively in Miami's two Spanish-language dailies.

23 Special thanks to Rosa Acero, Lisa Acosta, Suzanne Avellano, Lorena Castellanos, María Denney, Daniel Escalzo, Karen Gavin, Tony Ozuna, Prisi Quijada, and Susana Quintero, who at the time were students at the University of California at Santa Barbara. A special note of appreciation to Ms. Quintero, who took on supervisory responsibilities, especially during the time I was in Brazil on a Fulbright Research grant.

24 That year, the newspapers were obtained via subscriptions; they were delivered via mail to the research office, which at the time was at the University of California at Santa Barbara. *El Mañana* was excluded because it was not being published on a regular basis. It was also difficult to obtain on a reliable basis for the research.

25 Data were coded up to a week after the campaign was over. Most of the findings presented in this chapter, however, focus on particular time periods. Anyone interested in conducting secondary analysis of the full data set should contact the principal author, Federico Subervi-Vélez.

26 Articles dealing primarily with the candidates' functions as public officials and not as candidates, even if these individuals were Latinos, were also excluded from that year's study. Thus, for example, news about Henry Cisneros' performance as Mayor of San Antonio with no references to electoral issues or activities were not coded. Neither were news about Latino Congressmen's activities that were void of references to their political campaigns for re-election or to other electoral issues such as endorsing other candidates, criticizing opponents, and so on.

27 Special thanks to Dr. Klaus Schöenback, University of Amsterdam, who provided numerous suggestions for developing the coding instrument.

28 The national project included other variables for the content analysis of both English and Spanish-language newspapers. However, they were not relevant to the research questions posed above. Anyone interested in analyzing that data should contact the first author, from whom further information about the coding can also be obtained.

29 In cases where the political message was not devoted completely to Latino topics or candidates (i.e., if approximately 80 percent of it was devoted to Anglo candidates and/or issues, and only 20 percent referred to Latino candidate or topic), the news story as a whole continued to be the unit of analysis for all variables, with the exception of the Latino candidate, topic and the proportionate amount of space dedicated to the Latino mention. In that case, the unit of analysis was the specific sentence or sentences referring to Latino candidate or topic.

30 This table 4.4, with the descriptive statistics for all the coded stories during the whole time period from January 1 through November 14, is presented in order to offer the reader a benchmark for future studies about these newspapers. However, as is evident in the main text, the analyses focus on a narrower range of the data.

31 A review of the headlines of the dates that were excluded from the more

detailed analysis confirmed that no major issues, especially related to Latinos, were omitted in the process.

32 This pattern was evidently altered during the year 2000 presidential campaign, when candidate Bush and the GOP pursued the Latino vote from the pre-primaries up to Election Day. See Villescas (2002).

33 Excluded from this table and analysis are the stories about the federal, state, and local elections.

34 Before discussing the actual data, it should be noted that the coding of these news did not include assessments of whether the particular items were favorable or unfavorable towards one party/candidate or the other. What was observed was that the preponderance of the stories about the elections were about the general campaign activities of one candidate or the other. Thus, when a story was coded as (for example) Democrat, this means it was about what the Democratic Party or its candidates were doing in their efforts to win the elections. Likewise regarding stories coded as Republican.

35 This section and the data presented herein stem from a class term paper project developed during fall 1992 by Marc Brindel, who wrote this while pursuing his masters studies at the University of Texas at Austin.

36 Even more news of the declining U.S. economy appeared during this period than is presented in this study. But those articles did not address the presidential election and therefore were excluded from the analysis. Prominent mention of high unemployment and slow economic growth, for example, clearly bolstered Clinton's appeal to voters stressing a need for a change of administration.

37 This section and the data presented herein stem from the term paper research developed in fall 1996 by Juandalynn Taylor and Renée Espinosa, who wrote this while pursuing their doctoral and masters studies, respectively, at the University of Texas at Austin.

38 For the limited time period of September 1 through Election Day, the number of articles identified in this study is much lower than those found in the other three discussed in this chapter. This reflects the narrower selection parameters for coding: only sections A and B of the newspapers, the focus on the presidential campaign stories, and among those only stories about the Clinton and Dole campaigns. Stories about other candidates and campaign issues were excluded.

39 The coding instrument was developed following Stempel & Windhauser (1991), King (1990), and other guidelines alluded to in the previous studies of this chapter.

40 The category definitions include: **War and diplomacy**: references to war, diplomacy and foreign relations, defense activities, and military use of space. **Economic activity**: stories dealing with prices, money, inflation, transportation, travel, agribusiness, labor and wages, and natural resources. **Public and moral problems**: references to human relations problems such as alcohol, divorce, sex, drugs, race relations and personal or ethical standards. **Public health and welfare**: references to public health, public welfare, safety, pollution, child welfare, and social problems. Social problems were inclusive of immigration issues. **Strength of candidate**: reference to candidates' qualifications, virtues, abilities, and experience, predictions about chances of winning, and endorsements. This category included some articles, which referred to polls to make predictions, but did not focus on polls as a central part of the story. **Horse race**: references to who is leading, especially in polls, debates, general campaigning activities and fundraisers. These categories were applied

to all sections; however, separate observations are made for editorial sections to account for differences in the stated purposes of the newspaper sections. Inter-coder reliability was approximately 92 percent for the assigning of articles by these topics.

41 Inter-coder reliability was approximately 86 percent for designating the articles into the favorable, unfavorable and neutral rubrics.

# 5

# UNIVISIÓN AND TELEMUNDO ON THE CAMPAIGN TRAIL: 1988

*Patricia Constantakis-Valdés*[1]

Television is by far the most pervasive of the modern mass media. Whatever political news and information it airs reaches more people than any other media combined. This is certainly true also for Spanish-language television in the United States, which is potentially available to more than 80 percent of Hispanic households across the country. Hence, what are the political messages for or about Latinos disseminated by this form and language of mass media? The first answers to this question are provided in this chapter analyzing how the nation's two largest Spanish-language TV networks, Univisión and Telemundo, covered the 1988 presidential campaign.

As a context for better understanding the political role of these networks, the first section offers a capsule history of Spanish-language television in the United States. It is followed by the methodology and specific research questions guiding the content analysis. The findings are then presented in various subsections addressing general market and minority media characteristics of the political news during the 1988 campaign. The final section ponders on the implications of the findings, some of which are discussed in the light of theoretical foundations offered in the previous chapters.

## SPANISH-LANGUAGE TELEVISION IN THE UNITED STATES: BACKGROUND OVERVIEW[2]

During the last decades of the twentieth century, Spanish-language broadcast media in the United States experienced tremendous growth.[3] At the beginning of the 1980s, there was only one national television network that offered primarily foreign programming. But today Spanish-language television consists of two major national broadcast networks—Univisión and Telemundo—plus a few cable operations. Potentially, these media now reach over 90 percent of the Latino audiences from north to south and from coast to coast. No other non-English language medium could claim such growth, including increased advertising sales and revenues.[4]

The first Spanish-language television programs in the United States were aired shortly after the dawn of general market English-language TV—in 1951 in San Antonio and a year later in New York City. The initial programs in those two cities were part-time music variety shows broadcast from the studios of English-language stations.

In 1961, Emilio Azcárraga, a Mexican media businessman who was seeking an export market for the movies and television programs he was developing in Mexico (see Paxman and Fernández, 2000), gained significant control of, and thus helped solidify, the first full-time Spanish-language TV station in the United States. Within three years, that station, KWEX in San Antonio, Texas, and another SLTV station, KMEX in Los Angeles, California, were part of an emerging national network linked to Televisa, Mexico's own looming television oligopoly. First under the name of Spanish International Network, and in 1982 renamed as Univisión, this media enterprise consisted of several network-owned stations across the United States, many affiliated stations, and programming carried on more than 250 cable systems.

During the time of the 1988 study, a Univisión media kit promotional brochure claimed it could potentially reach over 80 percent of the Hispanic households across the United States. Also during the end of the 1980s, this network underwent transitions when it was sold to Hallmark Industries, Inc., as the result of a lawsuit alleging foreign ownership of Univisión and the misdirection of profits to Mexico. Under Hallmark's ownership, the production headquarters were moved from Laguna Niguel, in Southern California, to Miami, Florida, and the percentage of programming actually produced by Univisión increased from 6 percent to 30 percent.

In 1993, Univisión was sold once again, this time to a group of investors headed by U.S. media entrepreneur, A. Jerrold Perenchio,[5] as well as Mexico's Televisa and Venezuela's Venevisión. As of fall 2006, during which Univisión was going through another ownership transition (Sorkin and Edmonston, 2006), the network consisted of 18 full-power and eight low-power owned-and-operated stations, and distributed via 66 broadcast television affiliate stations, and 1,834 cable carriers; it also owned one full-power station in Puerto Rico (see corporate information section of Univisión's web site http://www.univision.net/corp/en/utg.jsp).

Telemundo is the other major national Spanish-language television network in the United States. It was established in 1986 by a group of investors, Reliance Group Inc., who were interested in breaking into the Latino-oriented television market to compete with Univisión. Reliance purchased several stations across the country and set up headquarters and facilities to produce programs. From the outset, executives sought to include more U.S.-produced programming that reflected the U.S. Latino experience (Subervi-Vélez, et al., 1994). At the time of the 1988 study, Telemundo's promotional information claimed the network could reach approximately 80 percent of the Latino households in the United States.

In fall 1997, this network was purchased by Sony, Inc., bringing a new and major general market entertainment corporation into the world of Spanish-language television. In spring 2000, Telemundo's programming underwent significant changes as the strategies developed to attract the United States Hispanic were not as successful as expected. In the midst of this situation, the network was sold to NBC, which acquired it for $1.98 billion in October 2001 (Sorkin, 2001). At the time of this writing in fall 2006, the Telemundo Group Inc. consisted of 15 full-power and nine low-power owned-and-operated stations, and distributed via 36 broadcast affiliates and 684 cable and wireless systems across the U.S.; it also owned one full-power station in Puerto Rico (see corporate information section of Telemundo's web site—http://tv.telemundo.yahoo.com/corporativo, click on either "Corporación" or "Corporation" in the box headed "Información Corporativa").

All told, Spanish-language television in the United States is the largest ethnic minority broadcast medium in the country. Given the theoretical arguments presented in chapter 3, the political potential of the medium is certainly worthy of notice.

The question remains: When it comes to politics, what have these networks offered their Latino audiences, particularly during a presidential election period such as the 1988 campaign? Is it something similar to or different from that which was broadcast by the general market English-language networks? Was all or part of that political fare Latino-oriented, potentially contributing to the political socialization of the Latino communities? If so, could this content be characterized as assimilationist, pluralist, or both? These were the general questions posited for the analysis of these media outlets. The following findings from the analysis of that campaign provide some answers to these questions and reveal what aspects of this particular coverage contribute to testing the dual-role theory of ethnic minority media.

## METHODOLOGY AND SPECIFIC RESEARCH QUESTIONS

The primary method used for this study was the content analysis of Univisión's and Telemundo's national evening newscasts, which were videotaped from January 1 through November 3 (Election Day) in 1988.[6] Because, at the time, Univisión broadcast its national newscasts seven days a week and Telemundo five days a week, the total number of newscasts recorded from each network was not equal: 307 from the former and 219 from the latter. The newscasts selected for analysis[7] centered around five time periods that were considered most newsworthy:[8] the major primaries (divided into early and later periods), the two party conventions, and the general campaign season of September 1 through Election Day. Specific dates were:

- February 24 through Super Tuesday to March 15.
- May 31 through the California primary to June 14.
- July 4 through the Democratic convention to July 25.
- August 1 through the Republican convention to August 22.
- September 1 through Election Day, November 3.

A detailed coding sheet, patterned after those used in traditional studies of English-language election coverage (see, for example, Graber, 1989; Patterson, 1980) was developed for the analysis of the selected individual stories.[9] It provided a means of cataloguing information about the following elements (described in further detail below): length of story (measured in minutes and seconds); the display of graphic/key box over anchor's shoulder, if any; the inclusion of any video; story topics; ethnic subtopics; identification and classification of on-screen information sources (subjects used for newscast sound-bites); length of sound-bites; and references to other media sources.

Additionally, each coding sheet included a section in which a very brief summary of the story was entered.

Analytical categories focused on four general areas: substance of coverage, bias or objectivity, prominence of coverage, and uniformity of coverage.[10] These categories closely paralleled those used in studies of English-language television election coverage. Specific variables were identified for each general area.

Because the primary goal of this segment of the study was to provide a description of the election coverage on Spanish-language television, the bulk of the analysis consisted of simple univariate and bivariate analyses. Frequency distributions of these variables were conducted, and several pairs of variables (for example, length of story and party of story) were cross-tabulated. Data were also cross-tabulated between networks to assess the differences, if any, between the frequency distributions of the variables between one network and the other.

## FINDINGS

The major findings of the content analysis segment of this study support the hypothesis that Spanish-language media in the United States manifest a dual orientation. Coverage of the 1988 presidential election included both content that was similar to that produced by English-language networks and content that was noticeably dissimilar to the general market. These two types of content structure the following section of this chapter, which will first explore those patterns within Univisión and Telemundo that resemble traditional English-language television network campaign coverage. This section is divided into four subtopics: (1) similarity of coverage, (2) substance of coverage, (3) bias/balance in coverage, and (4) prominence of election coverage.

The second part of this section describes the patterns of the Univisión and Telemundo coverage that seem supportive of the ethnic minority identity of these networks. It outlines those elements in the presidential campaign coverage that diverge from general market coverage and are specifically ethnic or Latino in nature. The major subtopics in this section are: (1) similarity of coverage, (2) substance of coverage, and (3) bias/balance in coverage.

For assessing the *similarity of coverage*, the following variables were compared across the two networks: substance of coverage (story topic and ethnic subtopic), bias/balance for party favoritism (the party the story is about, the candidate the story is about, length of story by party, number of sound-bites by party, length of sound-bites by party), and for ethnic group favoritism (number of Latino stories, mentions, sound-bites, and length of the Latino sound-bites), and prominence of coverage (newscast date and segment of the newscast).

For assessing the *substance of coverage*—which was defined as the extent to which election news focused on substantive issues of the campaign or on superficial aspects of the "horse race,"—the variables included were "Story topic" and "Ethnic subtopic." Under the heading *bias or balance*— which is defined in terms of the amount of news space given to either or both sides of an argument, to both political parties or candidates, or to representative interests of particular issues—the two broad categories of variables are "party favoritism" and "ethnic group favoritism." A final area of *prominence of coverage* was addressed by two variables: "newscast date" and "segment of newscast."

## General market characteristics

### *Similarity of coverage*

One of the major findings common in studies of both print and broadcast news is the similarity in product between outlets. This is particularly true in election coverage (Graber, 1989). Usually all newscasts report the same stories in just about the same way. Findings in this study indicate that the same phenomenon is true for Spanish-language television news programs. When the Univisión and Telemundo coverage is compared across all variables, there are very few significant differences. In order to illustrate these strong similarities, in each of the following sections, each network's coverage is described separately and the two networks' stories are then compared.

### Substance of coverage: story topic

One of the major findings of the research about English language United States presidential coverage by the media, in both television and print, is the heavy emphasis on the "game" of the campaign. According to a number of scholars (e.g., Graber, 1989; Patterson, 1980), the coverage provided by U.S. media concentrates on the campaign itself, strategies involved in winning the contest, activities involved in pulling ahead in the race, and identification of the current front runner.

Spanish-language election television coverage follows similar patterns. More than 65 percent of the 711 stories on both *Noticiero Univisión* and *Noticiero Telemundo/CNN* focus on the "horse race" between candidates or about "campaign activities." As table 5.1 indicates,[11] a crucial concentration of stories focused on the campaign or "game" itself. Moreover, no other topic category (other than the Principally Latino Category that will be discussed later) approached this level of frequency. As table 5.1 also indicates, only a small percentage of the election coverage focused on the issues of the campaign.

### Horse race

As is typical for these types of news article, the stories coded here as "horse race" focused on the identification of the candidate leading at particular

*Table 5.1* Number of stories by topic

| | Univisión | | Telemundo | |
|---|---|---|---|---|
| | Number | (%) | Number | (%) |
| Horse race | 114 | (22) | 36 | (14) |
| Issues | 27 | (5) | 12 | (5) |
| Campaign activities | 237 | (46) | 136 | (53) |
| Personality profile | 16 | (4) | 5 | (2) |
| Primary results | 9 | (2) | 4 | (1) |
| Other | 10 | (2) | 5 | (2) |
| Combination | 18 | (4) | 7 | (3) |
| Scandals | 12 | (2) | 12 | (5) |
| Principally Latino | 68 | (13) | 39 | (15) |
| Total | 511 | (100) | 256 | (100) |

$X^2 = 12.31$ n.s.

moments in the race. On Telemundo/CNN most of these stories were limited to the reported results of polls released by various polling organizations or by other news media. They tended to present the results of CNN and its affiliated polls (for example, CNN with *USA Today*). *Noticiero Univisión* dedicated significantly more coverage to the "horse race" than did Telemundo. When the categories used in table 5.1 were collapsed into four categories (horse race, campaign activities, principally Latinos and all others), statistically significant differences ($X^2 = 7.998$, $p<.05$) were found. Univisión was found to have more stories about the "horse race" than Telemundo. Univisión network also tended to report poll results in its own "horse race" stories. Since this network was affiliated with Bendixen and Associates, a Los Angeles-based Hispanic polling company, campaign coverage included exclusive polls of the Latino community around the nation. Several reports on which candidate was favored among Latinos in various states were broadcast throughout the entire campaign. For example, one report discussed whether Dukakis or Bush was ahead in California, and another focused on Florida.

### Campaign activities

In addition to the direct coverage of the "horse race" itself, coverage of the other elements that make up the "game" of presidential campaigning also was high. As table 5.1 shows, a total of 237 stories on Univisión and 136 stories on Telemundo focused on campaign activities. Both networks had more stories about the campaign activities of the two candidates than they did about any other topic. The stories varied from accounts about the activities of the candidates to summaries of the debates. On Telemundo/CNN, in particular, coverage concentrated on summaries of both candidates' daily activities. The typical story began with a look at one candidate and his campaign stop for that day. It then focused on the other candidate and his day's activities. This type of coverage results from Telemundo/CNN's news gathering practices, which will be discussed in segment 3 of this chapter.

According to researchers who have examined general market presidential coverage (e.g., Sigelman, 1991; Graber, 1989; Brady and Johnson, 1987; Joslyn, 1984), television election news has not emphasized policy issues of importance to the nation because it concentrates on the "game" and the drama of the contest. Graber (1989) points out that rarely do the media include stories that explore a candidate's position on a specific issue or examine how that position will affect voters. Telemundo's coverage fits this model. Only 12 of its 256 stories focused on "issues" of the campaign (table 5.1). Occasionally, the candidate's position on a specific issue was mentioned within the context of his daily campaign stop. However, the candidate's position was rarely detailed, and issues received little emphasis.

## Substance of coverage: story subtopic

Even those stories that were focused on Latinos or that merely mentioned Latinos (coded as having an "ethnic subtopic") emphasized the activities of the candidates within that community. Table 5.2 indicates the general distribution of the stories coded as having an ethnic subtopic.

Overall, Univisión had a total of 45 stories (27 "horse race" and 18 "campaign activities") that concentrated on the "game" of the campaign and at least mentioned Latinos. A chi-square test comparing the frequency breakdown for "ethnic subtopic" across the two networks yielded a statistically significant distribution of "ethnic subtopic" stories on the two networks. Instead of focusing on which candidate was ahead in the race among Latinos ("horse race"), the ethnic coverage on Telemundo tended to summarize the activities of the candidates in Latino communities, and thus could be coded as "campaign activities." Only two of the 67 stories with an "ethnic subtopic" on Telemundo focused on the "horse race." However, the majority of coverage mentioning Latinos still did not focus on "issues." Only 16 of the 112 stories on Univisión and nine of the 67 stories on Telemundo concentrated on "issues."

Overall, the presidential election coverage found on both *Noticiero Univisión* and *Noticiero Telemundo/CNN* primarily concentrated on the "game" of the campaign rather than on issues of substance, not only in general stories, but also in those stories with a direct Latino focus and those that mentioned Latinos in passing. Issues of importance to the Latino community were virtually ignored in reports about the two candidates. What has been found to be the case for mainstream television election coverage is also true of Spanish-language election news coverage.

*Table 5.2* Number of stories by ethnic subtopic

| | Univisión | | Telemundo | |
| --- | --- | --- | --- | --- |
| | *Number* | *(%)* | *Number* | *(%)* |
| Horse race | 27 | (24) | 2 | (3) |
| Issues | 16 | (14) | 9 | (13) |
| Activities | 18 | (16) | 20 | (30) |
| Personality profile | 0 | (0) | 1 | (2) |
| Other | 41 | (37) | 31 | (46) |
| Combination | 10 | (9) | 4 | (6) |
| Total | 112 | (100) | 67 | (100) |

$X^2 = 21.14$ p<.005

## Bias/balance: party orientation

Spanish-language television election coverage was similar to English-language television coverage in its effort to produce objective journalism. Journalists clearly worked to present the facts, stories or narratives of events, without favoring either candidate or party. This balance is reflected in table 5.3, which describes the number of stories about each party.

### Number of stories about each party

Neither network had a significantly greater number of stories about one of the two parties. *Noticiero Univisión* did air slightly more stories about the Democrats, but the difference between the number of stories about each party was not statistically significant. On *Noticiero Telemundo/CNN* the difference also was not significant. Instead, Telemundo had more stories about both of the candidates rather than about each one individually. Overall, neither party received significantly more news stories than the other. This trend is consistent with the literature on mainstream election coverage (Graber, 1989; Patterson, 1980; Joslyn, 1984).

### Number of stories about each candidate

The amount of news space given to each candidate is also an important measure of balance. Political leaders and interest groups continually criticize the press for showing favoritism to one candidate over the other. In this case, when examining only the number of stories about each candidate rather than about the party as a whole, the pattern of balance holds true for the Spanish-language television newscasts. Neither network presented significantly more stories about either Bush or Dukakis.

As table 5.4 demonstrates, of the 511 stories on Univisión, 18 percent were about Bush and 16 percent about Dukakis. Telemundo presented 15 percent about Bush and 12 percent about Dukakis. Overall, there were slightly more stories on both networks about George Bush. Part of this

*Table 5.3* Number of stories by party orientation*

|  | Univisión | | Telemundo | |
| --- | --- | --- | --- | --- |
|  | Number | (%) | Number | (%) |
| Democratic Party | 174 | (35) | 76 | (31) |
| Republican Party | 147 | (30) | 71 | (29) |
| Both parties | 171 | (35) | 96 | (40) |
| Total | 492 | (100) | 243 | (100) |

$X^2 = 2.614$ n.s.
* Excludes stories not about either party

*Table 5.4* Number of stories by candidates

|  | Univisión | | Telemundo | |
| --- | --- | --- | --- | --- |
|  | Number | (%) | Number | (%) |
| Dukakis | 82 | (16) | 31 | (12) |
| Bush | 93 | (18) | 38 | (15) |
| Others | 336 | (66) | 187 | (73) |
| Total | 511 | (100) | 256 | (100) |

$X^2 = 4.250$ n.s.

may be accounted for because of the higher national profile he had as Vice President.

Although no specific code was developed to ascertain a positive, negative or neutral evaluation of the candidates in each story, detailed reviews of these stories allow for a few observations. Early on in the primaries when no particular candidate had taken the lead in the polls, the coverage of Bush and Dukakis was essentially neutral, mostly including their activities in daily summaries. By early May, both networks were projecting Bush as the nominee for the Republican Party using terms such as "el eventual candidato" (the likely candidate). Such terms were not used to describe Dukakis until the Democratic convention because of the close race between Dukakis and Jesse Jackson. During the general campaign season, Dukakis' image slowly declined. By two weeks before the election the words being used to describe Dukakis were "desperate," "last chance," and "glimmer of hope," giving the impression that Dukakis was a long shot to win the election. Bush, on the other hand, seemed to get stronger and closer to a sure victory every day. From my observations of the mainstream media during the same period of time, these trends seemed to be consistent with how the English-language media presented the two candidates.

*Number of sources from each party*

In terms of the number of sources or sound-bites used from both parties, the pattern of balance does not hold true (table 5.5). Chi-squared tests conducted within each network indicate that Univisión had a significantly greater number of Democratic sources/sound-bites who appeared on the air ($X^2 = 21.74$, p<.001) than Republicans or others who had no party identification. Univisión aired 181 Democratic sound-bites versus 140 aired with Republicans. Those same tests also indicated that Telemundo had a significantly greater number of Democratic sources ($X^2 = 21.21$, p<.001) than Republicans or others with no party identification. Telemundo had

Table 5.5 Party orientation of sources by network

| | Univisión | | Telemundo | |
|---|---|---|---|---|
| | Number | (%) | Number | (%) |
| Democrats | 181 | (43) | 115 | (45) |
| Republicans | 140 | (33) | 86 | (34) |
| Others | 103 | (24) | 55 | (21) |
| Total | 424 | (100) | 256 | (100) |

$X^2 = 0.745$ n.s.

115 Democratic sources and only 86 Republicans. A cross-tabulation across the two networks reveals that there are no differences in the way Univisión and Telemundo used Democratic and Republican sources. Thus, they are once again similar in this characteristic.

However, neither Bush nor Dukakis appeared on the air as sources or sound-bites significantly more often than the other on either network. Bush appeared 62 times on Univisión to the 52 times Dukakis appeared. Telemundo aired 29 appearances by Bush to 49 by Dukakis. Overall, evidence did not indicate imbalance toward the sound-bites of one candidate over the other.

Another measure of objectivity is the amount of time allocated to each party and each candidate. One way to determine the presence or absence of such objectivity is to examine the *length of stories* and the *length of the sound-bites* themselves. The analysis of this dimension found that the majority of stories about the presidential election were less than one minute. Of the 511 total stories on Univisión, 281 were less than one minute long. On Telemundo, 144 out of the 256 total stories were this short. This finding is consistent with others that have found that news stories are generally short (Hallin, 1992).

### Length of stories about each party

Table 5.6 summarizes findings analyzing the length of stories about each party. There were no statistically significant differences in the lengths of the stories about the Democrats and Republicans or about both parties together.

As table 5.6 illustrates, most of the stories were under two minutes in length. On Telemundo, the stories about Democrats were slightly longer: 32 of the stories were longer than two minutes whereas 25 of the Republican stories were longer than two minutes. However, the stories about both parties together on this network that were over two minutes long outnumbered the stories about Democrats or Republicans. On Univisión, the Democratic stories were slightly longer than were those about

Table 5.6 Length of story by party by network*

| | Univisión | | | | | | Telemundo | | | | | |
|---|---|---|---|---|---|---|---|---|---|---|---|---|
| | D | (%) | R | (%) | B | (%) | D | (%) | R | (%) | B | (%) |
| 1 min. or less | 89 | (51) | 82 | (56) | 97 | (57) | 33 | (43) | 38 | (53) | 43 | (45) |
| 1 min. 30 secs | 10 | (6) | 6 | (4) | 16 | (9) | 11 | (14) | 8 | (11) | 14 | (15) |
| 2 to 3 min. | 45 | (26) | 36 | (24) | 29 | (17) | 17 | (22) | 20 | (28) | 26 | (26) |
| Over 3 min. | 30 | (17) | 23 | (15) | 29 | (17) | 15 | (20) | 5 | (7) | 13 | (14) |
| Total | 174 | (100) | 147 | (100) | 171 | (100) | 76 | (100) | 71 | (100) | 96 | (100) |

Univisión $X^2$ = 30.05 n.s. Telemundo $X^2$ = 23.21 n.s.

* Excludes stories about neither party

Note: Percentage figures in parentheses are expressed to the nearest whole figure.

Republicans and those about both parties together. Of the 174 stories about Democrats, 75 were longer than two minutes while 59 of the Republican stories and 58 of the stories about both parties were longer than two minutes. This indicates slight leaning towards the Democrats on this network in terms of the length of stories about each party. Overall, however, both Univisión and Telemundo were similar in that there was an overall balance in this area.

*Length of sound-bites from each party*

It is also important to examine the length of the sound-bites. To what extent did one party receive more sound-bite time than the other? Did Dukakis appear on the air overall for more time than Bush? Did Latinos receive more air time than non-Latinos?

We found no evidence of imbalance in the length of sound-bites by those identified as Democrat or Republican. As shown by table 5.7, neither network allocated significantly more time to sources from one party or the other. Cross-tabulations of "length of sound-bites" across the two networks yielded no statistically significant differences in the distributions of this variable. Thus, sound-bites by Republicans are no longer overall than those by Democrats on either network.

Overall, the majority of the sound-bites, regardless of party or network, are between 10 and 25 seconds long. In fact, the average sound-bite length for both Univisión and Telemundo is 21 seconds. This number is longer than the 8.5 seconds Hallin (1992) found in his study of the 1988 presidential campaign. This difference might be accounted for by the difference in what was included in the definition and coding of a sound-bite for this study: both the actual words said by the source *and* the translation. If one assumes that the translation is approximately the same length as the

*Table 5.7* Length of sound-bites by party by network

| | Univisión | | | | | | Telemundo | | | | | |
|---|---|---|---|---|---|---|---|---|---|---|---|---|
| | D | (%) | R | (%) | N | (%) | D | (%) | R | (%) | N | (%) |
| 5 seconds | 14 | (7) | 7 | (5) | 14 | (13) | 11 | (10) | 6 | (8) | 2 | (4) |
| 10 seconds | 28 | (15) | 20 | (14) | 27 | (25) | 16 | (15) | 13 | (16) | 7 | (14) |
| 15 seconds | 38 | (20) | 34 | (23) | 15 | (14) | 26 | (25) | 11 | (14) | 9 | (18) |
| 20 seconds | 35 | (19) | 29 | (20) | 18 | (17) | 19 | (18) | 20 | (25) | 6 | (12) |
| 25 seconds | 26 | (14) | 16 | (11) | 10 | (9) | 9 | (8) | 10 | (13) | 12 | (24) |
| 30 seconds | 14 | (7) | 12 | (8) | 7 | (6) | 10 | (9) | 8 | (10) | 4 | (8) |
| 45 seconds | 20 | (11) | 22 | (15) | 12 | (11) | 9 | (8) | 7 | (9) | 7 | (14) |
| 1 min. & over | 13 | (7) | 6 | (4) | 5 | (5) | 8 | (7) | 5 | (5) | 3 | (6) |
| Total | 188 | (100) | 146 | (100) | 108 | (100) | 108 | (100) | 80 | (100) | 50 | (100) |

Univisión $X^2$ = 22.69 n.s. Telemundo $X^2$ = 21.72 n.s.

English segment, then the average sound-bite length is actually 10.5 seconds which is closer to the figure of 8.5 seconds that Hallin found. Spanish-language network news, therefore, uses sound-bites in a way similar to English-language networks.

### Bias/balance: ethnic group favoritism

The amount of news space allocated to Latinos and issues explicitly referring to them is an important measure of bias/balance serving a predominantly Latino audience. One would expect that a Latino medium would provide a balance between Latino sources and non-Latino sources as well as a balance of stories focused on Latinos and non-Latinos. Overall evidence demonstrates an imbalance of a non-Latino perspective in the presidential election coverage on both *Noticiero Univisión* and *Noticiero Telemundo/CNN*.

As table 5.1 shows, the majority of stories on both news programs were not about Latinos. Eighty-seven percent of the election stories on *Noticiero Univisión* did not have a Latino focus; 85 percent of those on Telemundo did not. The majority of sources or sound-bites also were non-Latino (table 5.8). Of the 422 total sound-bites on Univisión, 263 were non-Latino; 167 of the 254 sound-bites on Telemundo were non-Latino. T-tests within each network indicate that these differences were indeed statistically significant.

There appear to be some differences in the length of non-Latino sound-bites and Latino sound-bites (table 5.9). On Univisión, the sound-bites of the non-Latinos were only slightly longer than those of the Latinos: 65 percent of the Latino sound-bites were less than 25 seconds long, while only 63 percent of the non-Latino sound-bites were less than 25 seconds long. Chi-squared tests within Univisión did not reveal any significant

*Table 5.8* Ethnicity of sound-bites by network

|  | Univisión | | Telemundo | |
|---|---|---|---|---|
|  | Number | (%) | Number | (%) |
| Latinos | 159 | (37) | 87 | (34) |
| Non-Latinos | 263 | (63) | 167 | (66) |
| Total | 422 | (100) | 254 | (100) |

Univisión t = 3.172, p<.005 Telemundo t = 3.316, p<.005
$X^2$ = 1.065 n.s.

*Table 5.9* Length of sound-bites by ethnicity by network

|  | Univisión | | | | Telemundo | | | |
|---|---|---|---|---|---|---|---|---|
|  | Lat. (%) | | N-Lat. (%) | | Lat. (%) | | N-Lat. (%) | |
| 5 seconds | 14 | (9) | 19 | (7) | 1 | (1) | 17 | (13) |
| 10 seconds | 38 | (24) | 37 | (13) | 10 | (11) | 26 | (19) |
| 15 seconds | 27 | (17) | 60 | (22) | 20 | (22) | 21 | (16) |
| 20 seconds | 23 | (15) | 59 | (21) | 19 | (21) | 24 | (19) |
| 25 seconds | 15 | (10) | 37 | (13) | 16 | (17) | 14 | (10) |
| 30 seconds | 10 | (6) | 23 | (8) | 8 | (9) | 12 | (9) |
| 45 seconds | 22 | (14) | 31 | (11) | 11 | (12) | 10 | (7) |
| 1 min. & over | 8 | (5) | 15 | (5) | 6 | (7) | 10 | (7) |
| Total | 157 | (100) | 281 | (100) | 91 | (100) | 134 | (100) |

Univisión $X^2$ = 13.13 n.s.; Telemundo $X^2$ = 12.74, p<.001

differences. On Telemundo, however, statistically significant differences were found showing that non-Latino sound-bite lengths were shorter than Latino sound-bites ($X^2$ = 12.74, p<.001). Only 56 percent of the Latino sound-bites on Telemundo were less than 25 seconds long, while 67 percent of the non-Latinos sound-bites were less than 25 seconds long.

By combining these results with the number of Latino sources shown in table 5.8 an interesting picture emerges. On Univisión, significantly more non-Latino sources appeared on the air *and* those sources got slightly more air time than Latinos. This demonstrates an imbalance, and potential bias, toward non-Latino sources. Telemundo also used significantly more non-Latino sources, but since the Latino sources had more air-time the network balanced the non-Latino perspective with a Latino one more successfully.

### Prominence of coverage

As Graber (1989) and others have demonstrated, election coverage is no more prominent than any other newsworthy event on mainstream television. What this means is that the number of stories about the elections is not significantly greater than those about other news events. This study of Spanish-language television could not make such claims because news unrelated to the 1988 presidential elections was not examined. Certain measures, however, suggest that many of the patterns in English-language television regarding the ratio between campaign-related and unrelated coverage recur in the 1988 Spanish-language election news.

One such measure is the average number of stories per day. In this case, for mainstream television, Graber (1989) found that, because of the nature of the contest, the networks provide more coverage the closer it is to Election Day and important campaign events such as conventions and debates. It would be expected, then, that the average number of stories would increase similarly if patterns of coverage were similar for Spanish-language television.

This was, in fact, the case. The number of stories increased overall as Election Day neared. Figure 5.1 depicts the average number of stories broadcast about the election per day on both networks during selected dates. In March, when the Super Tuesday primaries were held in 20 states, Univisión had an average of 3.8 stories per day as compared to Telemundo's 1.5 stories. Univisión provided much heavier coverage of the Super Tuesday contest with 12 stories broadcast on March 9, the day before the primary. By June, and after the California primary on June 7, the average number of stories per day on Univisión had dropped slightly to 3.2, while Telemundo's had increased to 2.5. During the period surrounding the Democratic National Convention in July, Univisión broadcast only four stories per day as compared to Telemundo's average of 5.3 stories. In fact, Telemundo provided as much coverage of the Democratic Convention as it did during the final four days of the general election. In August, the period surrounding the Republican National Convention, Univisión broadcast an average of 5.8 stories per day, while Telemundo's coverage fell to four stories. Many of the stories on Univisión following the Republican Convention focused on the controversy surrounding Dan Quayle and his service in the National Guard. While Telemundo covered the controversy, it merely mentioned it in other campaign news roundups rather than dedicating a full story to it.

In September, neither network provided an extraordinary amount of coverage, averaging three stories per day. During the final stretch of the campaign, both networks increased the number of stories aired about the election; however, Univisión did so more drastically than Telemundo. In October, Univisión averaged six stories per day to Telemundo's four. By the final four days of the campaign in November, Univisión was broadcasting nine stories per day, while Telemundo had only five. Overall, then, both networks seem to follow the pattern of English-language television election coverage that indicates that more stories are broadcast around important events, such as the conventions, and as Election Day draws closer.

The increase in the variety of types of story can be seen in the following example. On October 31, just one week before the election, Univisión aired seven stories. The first was a report on an ABC poll that showed Bush ahead of Dukakis 51 to 44 percent in California. Next, Univisión introduced two reports about the day's activities of each of the candidates. The first story examined Dukakis' place in California as he campaigned in that state, particularly among the Latino community. The second story reported on Bush's campaign activities in Missouri. This was followed by a segment from a series about key states that could make or break the election for the candidates. On this day, the focal state was Michigan. The last story on Univisión reported on Kitty Dukakis' hospitalization and her husband's subsequent cancellation of campaign appearances later that day.

On November 1, Telemundo aired six stories about the election. The first was an introduction to one story about both candidates' daily activities. The story reported that Dukakis was campaigning in Milwaukee and Ohio on his birthday. Bush was in Indiana. The third story was a report on Kitty Dukakis' hospitalization. Following that, Telemundo reported on Reagan ridiculing Dukakis for comparing himself to JFK and Truman. The last two stories focused on the Latino population, their growth and their increased voting power that could influence who would win in states like California and Florida.

Another important indicator of the prominence of election coverage is where the stories appear within the newscast. Are they considered important enough to appear at the beginning of the newscast, or does their placement vary? Generally, the findings indicate that both Spanish-language television networks ran election stories during the first 15 minutes of the

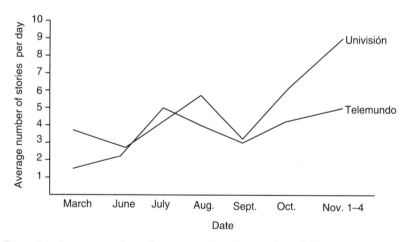

Figure 5.1 Average number of stories per day during selected date

newscast. More than half of the stories on both Univisión and Telemundo were in segment A or B (table 5.10). The segments indicated here are reflections of the divisions between commercial breaks the networks use for their newscasts. Segment A is usually the longest, running an average of six to eight minutes. Successive segments are shorter with the last one often including only one report. A chi-square test across the networks reveals that Univisión had significantly more stories in the first segment than did Telemundo.

In sum, several elements of the Spanish-language election coverage were found to be similar to mainstream English-language television election coverage. First, both Univisión and Telemundo concentrated on the "game" of the campaign rather than on the issues that are central to the campaign. This was the case in those stories that mentioned Latinos or focused on Latinos. Very little of the coverage focused on campaign issues of particular importance to the Latino audience. Instead it focused on the campaign events in the Latino community. This aspect of the coverage suggests that there are important similarities between Spanish-language and mainstream news.

Neither Univisión nor Telemundo appeared to favor either political party in the number of stories, length of stories, number of sound-bites/sources, and length of the sound-bites. However, the amount of news space given to Latinos was quite small. Like mainstream news outlets, presidential election coverage on Univisión and Telemundo is also built around non-Latinos.

As with mainstream coverage, the closer to Election Day, the more campaign stories were aired on both networks. Most election stories on both Univisión and Telemundo were aired during the first part of the newscast, usually during the first segment. Throughout the analysis, the coverage provided by Univisión was remarkably similar in all aspects to that found on Telemundo.

These findings are consistent with other studies about presidential

Table 5.10 Number of stories by segment by network

| | Univisión | | Telemundo | |
|---|---|---|---|---|
| | Number | (%) | Number | (%) |
| Segment A | 231 | (45) | 101 | (39) |
| Segment B | 115 | (23) | 63 | (25) |
| Segment C | 86 | (17) | 53 | (21) |
| Segment D | 33 | (6) | 29 | (11) |
| Segment E | 46 | (9) | 10 | (4) |
| Total | 511 | (100) | 256 | (100) |

$X^2 = 15.91$ p<.001

election coverage on mainstream English-language television news. These characteristics display—in the content and coverage—the mainstream view of the electoral process and provide support for the argument that Spanish-language media have largely mainstream-like content and thus a mainstream identity in terms of political news coverage.

## Minority media characteristics

The findings presented up to now have focused on the way that election coverage on *Noticiero Univisión* and *Noticiero Telemundo/CNN* and English-language television are alike. This section turns to the distinct minority component of the Spanish-language coverage that was found in this study. How is the election coverage provided by *Noticiero Univisión* and *Noticiero Telemundo/CNN* unique in comparison to the coverage of English-language networks? What are the elements that reflect a distinct minority perspective? The results of the content analysis reveal distinguishing characteristics in each of the main topics of the previous section.

### *Substance of coverage*

Although most campaign stories in this study were not about Latinos, more stories with an exclusive focus on Latinos appeared on both news programs than the number of stories on Latinos found on English-language news programs (see chapters 10 and 11). A full 13 percent of the stories on Univisión and 15 percent on Telemundo were about Latinos and the 1988 presidential election campaign (table 5.1). Furthermore, 112 stories of the 511 election stories on Univisión and 67 of the 256 on Telemundo had an ethnic subtopic; that is, they referred to Latinos at least once during the story. What these figures reflect is an effort to find what might be termed "the Latino angle" in many of the stories focusing on the 1988 presidential elections. This effort is not characteristic of mainstream television.

Another important indicator of the Spanish-language networks' "minority" focus is the type of story that focuses primarily on Latinos. Of the stories that were coded as "principally Latino" or as having an ethnic subtopic (making at least one reference to Latinos), the majority were not about the specific candidates themselves. Instead, they were on other news and issues that were related to the campaign in general (table 5.11). Forty-one of the 112 stories with an ethnic subtopic on Univisión and 31 of the 67 stories on Telemundo were about "Other news not related to the Specific Candidate."

On Univisión, the majority of the "other" stories focused on the importance of the Latino vote or on propositions as they related to Latinos, specifically propositions establishing English as the official language of several states. The same trend was present in Telemundo's coverage. Fifteen

148

*Table 5.11* Number of stories by ethnic subtopic

| Univisión | | Telemundo | |
|---|---|---|---|
| *Subtopic* | *Number* | *Subtopic* | *Number* |
| *Horse race* | **27** | *Horse race* | **2** |
| Non-Latino candidate's place vis-à-vis other non-Latino candidate in race | 6 | | |
| Results indicated by polling organizations | 3 | | |
| Opinions about who is ahead, who won or lost | 17 | Opinions about who is ahead, who won or lost | 1 |
| Other | 1 | Other | 1 |
| *Issues* | **16** | *Issues* | **9** |
| Relations with other countries | 7 | Relations with other countries | 3 |
| Education | 1 | Racial prejudice | 2 |
| Combination | 1 | Combination | 2 |
| Other/local issues | 7 | Other | 2 |
| *Campaign activities* | **18** | *Campaign activities* | **20** |
| Non-Latino speaking in favor of or endorsing a non-Latino candidate | 1 | Non-Latino speaking in favor of or endorsing a non-Latino candidate | 1 |
| Latino politician or leader speaking in favor of or endorsing a non-Latino candidate | 6 | | |
| Non-Latino candidate appealing to Latino voters | 5 | Non-Latino candidate appealing to Latino voters | 13 |
| Other general campaign activities | 6 | Other general campaign activities | 6 |
| *Personality profile* | **0** | *Personality profile* | **1** |
| | | Neutral information regarding candidate's beliefs, ability to lead, his physical or mental health, or his family | 1 |
| *Other news not related to a specific candidate* | **41** | *Other news not related to a specific candidate* | **31** |
| Importance of the Latino vote | 20 | Importance of the Latino vote | 15 |
| Need to mobilize Latino vote | 1 | Need to mobilize Latino vote | 2 |
| Political activity of Latino organizations | 3 | Political activity of Latino organizations | 2 |
| Propositions as they relate to Latinos | 11 | Propositions as they relate to Latinos | 8 |
| Intimidations/attempts to discourage Latino vote | 1 | Intimidations/attempts to discourage Latino vote | 1 |
| Other | 5 | Other | 3 |
| *Combination* | **10** | *Combination* | **4** |

of the stories with ethnic subtopics were about the importance of the Latino vote and six were about the English-only proposition. These stories comprised much of the ethnic component (i.e., Latino-oriented characteristics) in the 1988 election coverage.

### Bias/balance in coverage

The majority of the sources/sound-bites that appeared on the air on both networks were non-Latino. However, what the analysis also showed is that 37 percent of sources/sound-bites on Univisión and 34 percent of those on Telemundo were Latinos (table 5.8).

In addition, it is important to note that if Dukakis and Bush are excluded from the count of sound-bites, then 147 of the 424 (35 percent) sound-bites on Univisión were non-Latino as compared to the 159 (38 percent) Latino sources on the same network. Similarly, if one excludes the candidates from Telemundo's sound-bite count, the result is 94 (37 percent) non-Latinos versus 87 (34 percent) Latinos. The numbers are quite impressive. They point to the efforts of Spanish-language television reporters to actively seek out members of the Latino community to express opinions and give information about the candidates and campaigns. This is one important way that the networks make the stories they report more accessible and understandable to their Latino audience. Admittedly, this is often the only Latino "angle" present in the story, but it is present nevertheless.

Overall, findings from this segment of the analysis indicate that Spanish-language election coverage included several non-mainstream or minority-ethnic (as opposed to minority-immigrant) elements. First, stories that mentioned Latinos or focused exclusively on Latinos represented a sizable minority of both networks' coverage. Both networks also attempted to explain to the audience that the Latino vote was important, and to provide stories about propositions such as the English-only initiative that affected the Latino population in the United States. Second, Latinos also appeared frequently as sources or as sound-bites. These characteristics suggest that the coverage was not entirely mainstream in focus and orientation. The presence of these elements suggests that Spanish-language media have a minority-ethnic identity as well.

## CONCLUSIONS AND IMPLICATIONS

Overall, this study supports the proposition that Spanish-language television election coverage has a dual orientation. Still, mainstream characteristics are much more salient than Latino characteristics. Latino audiences receive political news information that is similar to that received by mainstream audiences from mainstream news outlets. These findings could be related to the type of methodology used in this study. Coders performed content analysis using a coding scheme developed with categories already found in mainstream election coverage, which may have influenced the ways in which the content was viewed. However, since the study was intended to parallel research that had been carried out on mainstream television, this kind of approach was essential. What is important to note, however, is that the results of this particular segment of research, which allowed for direct comparison with previous studies of mainstream election news, might also have been responsible for the fact that mainstream elements appeared to be salient.

Two other analyses performed concurrently for the dissertation from which this chapter is drawn provides a different view of these networks. Those examinations point to a different blend of mainstream and Latino elements. First, qualitative analysis of stories that were coded as principally Latino reveals more characteristics that are Latino than mainstream. The majority of the themes and frames identified revealed clear Latino foci and tones. Themes that stressed the growing number of Latinos, their growing political power, and their strong potential to affect the outcome of the election in key states revealed a strong minority presence in these stories. A few mainstream themes that reflected a concentration on the strategies and game of the campaign were also identified. While it could be argued that Latino themes were salient in this analysis because of the stories selected, it is doubtful that content analysis alone would capture the specifically Latino tone and texture of election news. Had the content analysis been conducted without this frame of reference, Latinos would appear to be of little importance in these networks' coverage of the presidential elections.

Second, the third segment of this study, the organizational analysis, also revealed that the two news organizations have a mainstream orientation with strong ethnic characteristics as well. The news-gathering and production routines, the sources of information, and the editorial hierarchy are characteristic of mainstream news organizations. The nearly all-Latino staff and the perception of the Latino audience as a unique one with different needs, problems and interests from the mainstream audience were characteristics identified as Latino. This third segment suggests that the structure of the news organization, which is itself dual in nature, affects the content, which has also been found to have dual orientation. In sum, while content analysis indicates that Latino interests and needs were largely ignored by Univisión and Telemundo, this impression may be caused by the lens with which we chose to view that coverage rather than the coverage itself.

Despite these reservations, the findings presented in this chapter (as well as those of the other two analyses of the dissertation) indicate that political news coverage of the 1988 presidential elections on Univisión and Telemundo exhibited a dual orientation. That is, content patterns reflected both a mainstream orientation *and* a minority orientation. Elements of the election coverage found with a mainstream orientation support the postulate that ethnic minority media (in this case Spanish-language television) provide information about mainstream society and play an acculturation role. At the same time, minority oriented elements support the postulate that ethnic minority media (i.e., Spanish-language television) help to maintain cultural ties and promote cultural pride.

In essence, both Univisión and Telemundo offer the Latino population in the United States the basic news and information-related presidential campaigns. And they do so with perspectives that can be interpreted as being particularly relevant for that audience. If and how that content influences Latinos at the cognitive, attitudinal, and/or behavioral level cannot be empirically assessed with these data. Nevertheless, this first political content analysis of these networks provides the foundation for future examinations in this arena.

## NOTES

1 The core of this chapter presents a condensed and modified version of the author's doctoral dissertation, which stemmed from a larger study of the 1988 campaign. The dissertation consisted of three main segments: (1) a content analysis of Univisión's and Telemundo's coverage of the 1988 presidential election; (2) an in-depth analysis of the "frames" used in the stories geared specifically to the Latino audience; and (3) a study of the news organizations of Univisión and Telemundo and how these actually produced election coverage (see Constantakis-Valdés, 1993).

2 See Subervi-Vélez, et al., (1994) for an encyclopedic history and extensive bibliography on the genesis, development, and tribulations of the United States' Spanish-language television, including Univisión and Telemundo.

3 Spanish-language radio in the United States also has grown exponentially during the last two decades. For example, between 1980 and 1992, the number of Spanish-language radio stations increased from 64 to 233 (Constantakis-Valdés, 1992). While, owing to different counting methods, the exact number of these stations is not known, some media directories offer good approximations. See Whisler and Nuiry (1999) and Orozco (2005).

4 For annual estimates of the advertising expenditures and profits stemming from Spanish-language television and radio, see the special reports on media markets in the December issues of *Hispanic Business* magazine.

5 Here it is important to point out that, over the years, Perenchio has contributed more than a million dollars to the Republican Party (Notingham, 2005). No research has been conducted to ascertain if and how Mr. Perenchio's contributions to the GOP may influence the news departments of the Univisión network and/or its stations. But his political preferences are a well-known fact inside the industry and, of course, in political circles.

6 The original 1988 elections study focused only on election coverage in the

newscasts. As a result, the team recorded and collected the corpus of tapes of videotaped newscasts but not the special programs that were aired about the elections in general (e.g., the presidential and vice presidential debates, extended special convention programs). These events were captured only as they were reported in the regular news programs. It is on this coverage that Constantakis-Valdés conducted the part of her dissertation analysis on which this chapter is written.

7  The review and selection of newscasts to be analyzed was initiated during the academic year 1990–1991. Coders reviewed all newscasts presented during the selected dates for stories that related (however slightly) to the November 1988 elections. All stories that were about the presidential campaign, other political candidates/races to be decided in the November 5 elections, or propositions or amendments in any state on that ballot were included in the analysis. It is important to note, however, that, because the national news focuses attention almost exclusively on national races, very few stories about state and local candidates for office could be expected, and indeed few were identified. Within the selected dates, coders analyzed a total of 511 stories for Univisión and 256 for Telemundo.

8  All the other newscasts were recorded and are available for additional analysis. For further information, contact the principal author, Federico Subervi-Vélez.

9  The full coding was completed by a total of five bilingual coders, all of whom underwent a significant period of training under the direction of the chapter's author. Each story was viewed by at least two coders who completed one coding sheet for each story viewed. For further reliability assessments, the author also independently coded each story. Inter-coder reliability between the principal researcher and other coders was 88 percent. The inter-coder reliability was determined by assessing the percentage of instances in which there was disagreement between coders and the author. Reliability improved as the analysis proceeded. When there were disagreements, stories were viewed again and attempts were made to reach a consensus. In those few instances when this was not possible, the principal researcher (Constantakis-Valdés) made the final decision. Once coding was completed, the data from each coding sheet were entered into a Macintosh computer using a specially designed Double Helix program for use with the Data Desk statistical package. Special thanks to Eliut Flores for his help with this study.

10  For a complete description of the categories, see chapter 3 in Constantakis-Valdés (1993).

11  These tables reflect the order in which the variables appeared on the coding sheet. Results are kept in this order so as to show the differences between Univisión and Telemundo in a consistent manner.

# 6

# WATCHING THE 2000 PRESIDENTIAL CAMPAIGN ON UNIVISIÓN AND TELEMUNDO

*Laurien Alexandre* and *Henrik Rehbinder*

*Figure 6.1* Pedro Sevcec, anchor of *Noticiero Telemundo*
*Source:* Telemundo Network Group LLC

Being mindful of media messages is an important and intentional act of awareness that can inform us about our culture, provide a window into the American polity, and enable us to reflect on our own perceptions and ourselves. Media scholar Todd Gitlin (1986: 4) states: "Television bears special watching. It needs criticism and understanding, which cut beneath annoyance or apologia. To be seen properly, it has to be seen as the place where force-fields intersect: economic imperatives, cultural traditions, political impositions." Yet, the act of "serious seeing," (Gitlin, 1986: 8) does not come naturally, it takes practice and study and dialogue with others.

Serious viewing can produce substantial contributions to our understanding of media coverage on significant issues and events, such as a presidential campaign. Informed watching must take into account such elements as routine media practices, production constraints, content biases, and the effects of organizational and stakeholder strategies, as many of the chapters in this book suggest.

When serious watching is brought to the task of understanding how and what Spanish-language television networks offered to Latino audiences during the presidential campaign of 2000, substantive insights can be gleaned about the successes and failures of the candidates to reach out to the Hispanic electorate, about the routine media practices that are shared by both Spanish-language and English-language news, and about the ways in which Univisión and Telemundo provided news with a Latino angle and emphasis.

In the case of the study at hand, the authors—one a journalist for the nation's largest Spanish-language daily, *La Opinión* in Los Angeles, and the other, a media scholar—watched nightly network news coverage during the final months of the 2000 presidential campaign on Telemundo and Univisión. Based on the viewing, the authors wrote a biweekly analysis of the news, discussing and interpreting the coverage's lenses and the lapses. These analyses were then submitted to Hispanic Trends, where they were edited and published as a web column, *MediaWatch*, mounted on the site of HispanicTrends.com.

Every Monday to Friday, 6:30–7:00 p.m., national newscasts of Univisión and Telemundo from July 24 through November 7, 2003, were videotaped. Each half-hour newscast was watched two times by each author, the first time to count relevant stories and the second to take detailed notes on sources, quotations, and content. The authors' notes were compared and, if discrepancies existed, the newscast was reviewed again. Finally, the authors discussed the coverage and prepared the biweekly analyses, which were then sent to Hispanic Trends for editing and online publication.

The number of stories devoted to national political news in general was counted, as were those that specifically focused on the presidential campaign. Special news show segments like Univisión's "Titulares" and "En Un Minuto" and Telemundo's "En Su Bosillo" and "En Escena" were each counted as one story when they appeared. *That said, counting stories was not the emphasis of this effort.* The process was more about an approach to watching than a method to quantifying, with the intention of establishing a grounded interpretation to the content. There was no notion of a fundamental coding "unit" and its frequency, and it is entirely possible that other investigators would draw different interpretations from watching the same news segments.

The *MediaWatch* analysis was neither strict content analysis nor, at the other extreme, entirely impressionistic. Rather, it took a hybrid approach, which strove to bridge interpretive real-time media criticism with a more rigorous media scholarship. In traditional social science research "the central requirement for content analysis is that there should be objective indicators which can be applied (also objectively) to determine the presence, absence or frequency of qualities of interest to an investigator" (McQuail, 1987: 181). Such research claims a measure of scientific reliability and replicability. In the case of *MediaWatch*, the authors made no such claims.

This chapter presents excerpts from the original analyses submitted for publication on Hispanic Trends' *MediaWatch*. The first reason for reprinting them here is because they are examples of critical and grounded media watching, a skill which is important to nurture in media consumers and students of media studies. As suggested above, these columns now provide a valuable record of Spanish-language television coverage of the 2000 presidential campaign and offer a unique approach to making meaning of that coverage. The very fact of their inclusion in a book on mass media and Latino politics affirms the merit of serious media watching as a valuable enterprise.

Second, as an actual record of media coverage, they provide evidence of force fields and strategies discussed in other chapters in this book. For example:

- Many of the excerpts reprinted below describe television news coverage that suggests the success of the GOP's strategy to promote itself as a party with a Latino future, as discussed in chapters 12–14 of this book.
- Many excerpts describe television news coverage that evidenced an invisibility of Democrats, suggesting a failure of the Democratic Party to connect with the Latino vote and to develop a coherent and consistent strategy early enough in the campaign, also discussed in chapters 12–14 of this book. Other researchers have also made note of the differences in GOP versus DNC outreach efforts to Hispanic voters. One recent report notes that the Democratic Party did not make outreach to Hispanics a top priority, as did the GOP, but rather included Latinos "on a list with other constituencies" (Segal, 2003: 16). The *MediaWatch* columns may well be a record of the failures of this strategy.
- Many excerpts affirm that there are media practices—such as framing presidential campaigns more as horse races than issue-oriented challenges for governance—which are similar in both in Spanish-language and English-language television, as suggested by Constantakis-Valdés in chapter 5. The excerpts that follow show a shared practice of overuse and imprecision with polls, for example, as well as with an

accessibility to candidates and campaign stops being a determinant of the extensiveness of coverage.

- At the same time, excerpts also demonstrate that the Spanish-language TV news presents Latino angles and issues and does cover national news with a lens that often differs from their English-language counterparts. This is consistent with the dual orientation hypothesis, also articulated by Constantakis-Valdés. Important issues for Latinos relate to barriers to their progress, such as education, health care, and immigration policies, all themes highlighted by the Spanish-language network newscasts in the 2000 campaign. Similarly, extensive use of Spanish-language spokespersons and Hispanic experts was evidenced on both networks.

Finally, these *MediaWatch* excerpts are "texts" themselves, demonstrating to students of journalism and to the more general audience of media consumers ways to critically watch the media. In fact, the chapter concludes with a set of guidelines for watching future campaign coverage.

## MEDIAWATCH ANALYSES OF THE 2000 CAMPAIGN

### July 24–August 4

The first *MediaWatch* covered the period from July 24 to August 4, 2000, during which time the Republican Convention and its lead-up events took place. This was a period when the Republicans dominated the national political news coverage. The Republican strategy to make itself over into the compassionate conservative party that now welcomes minorities worked extremely well on Spanish-language TV during this two-week period. Given the primacy of Convention-related events, the bias of sources between and imbalance of number of news stories about the two parties was not surprising.

#### *Excerpts*

The Republican Convention offered a celebration the likes of which Latinos had rarely, if ever, seen in a national campaign. As they covered the Convention, both networks offered the sounds and faces of "*sabor Latino.*" That Univisión's anchor broadcast live from the Convention floor and often chatted with his reporters over the sounds of mariachi music only added to the feeling of being inside the party, literally. Telemundo's anchors remained in Miami, but its reporters also broadcast direct from the Convention floor. Reporters from both networks interviewed

Spanish-speaking Republicans and Latino delegates. Both networks gave substantial time to Bush's Philadelphia arrival at a mostly Latino celebration where the candidate spoke Spanish to the musical presence of the likes of John Secada, Vicente Fernández, and Celia Cruz,[1] and to coverage of the Republican's "not-so-secret" weapon, nephew George Prescott Bush. It was, indeed, news to see the son of a governor and grandson of a former United States president speaking Spanish and representing the immigrant's American dream.

More time was devoted to coverage of issues that evidenced the party's transformation, particularly its new inclusiveness, than to issues that showed continuation with the party's past. Both networks ran pre-Convention platform stories noting the "drastic changes" (Univisión, 7/28) that showed that the "hard line of the past" was over (Telemundo, 7/28). Evidence of the turnaround was cited in the removal of the English-only clause, for example. Univisión led Convention-week coverage with the education issue, even visiting a local school in a Latino neighborhood of Philadelphia, consistent with the Convention's official first-day theme: "No Child Left Behind." Interestingly enough, Telemundo's first-day Convention coverage seemed to miss the education mark. However, neither station mentioned the day's other announced platform issue—health care—for which, it should be noted, there was also no prime-time podium speaker.

Platform planks that may have represented a continuation with the party's hard line past rather than a turnaround were barely presented on the broadcasts. Univisión noted that the Republicans wanted to strengthen defense and spoke briefly about this (8/1). One Telemundo piece mentioned Latin American issues with which the party will have to contend—relations with Mexico, Cuba and Colombia—but did not go into the party's platform positions on these foreign policy issues (8/1). Only one piece, a pre-Convention Telemundo story, included a few words about how the abortion issue may still divide the party (7/28). In conclusion, a citizen who watched only the Spanish-language nightly newscasts for these two weeks would have been woefully underinformed about the Republican Party's platform and positions.

In general, stories favored a roster of Spanish-speaking Republican strategists and representatives. With few exceptions, stories were not internally balanced with Republican and Democratic sources. Perhaps that is to be expected during the Republican Convention, but the imbalance was striking. During Convention week, not one Democratic "counter voice" on Univisión appeared until Thursday, when Congresswoman Loretta Sanchez (D-CA) attacked the reality behind the GOP image (8/3). The network followed with a Friday wrap-up piece with a number of Democratic reactions, including Speaker of the California Assembly, Antonio Villaraigosa (D-CA), among others (Univisión, 8/4). Telemundo had even fewer official Democratic sources during its Convention week period. However, Telemundo did bring in critical "unofficial" voices in its "man-on-the-street" story that included a number of Latinos questioning the sincerity of the Republicans' commitment to their community (8/2).

## August 7–18

This analysis covered a period of the Democratic Convention and its lead-up events. In striking ways, the Democratic Party did not enjoy the virtual monopoly of air-time that the Republican Party had experienced in the previous two weeks. Throughout this coverage period, there were GOP-related stories, such as McCain's cancer, as well as another Clinton-scandal grand jury activity. The Democratic Party also had to contend with a significant amount of news time devoted to the protests on the streets of Los Angeles outside the Convention center.

### Excerpts

Whereas the Democratic campaign was virtually invisible during the Republican Convention and lead-up period, Republican-related stories appeared during the Democratic pre-Convention week (8/7–8/11). Univisión aired a minute-long piece with excerpts of Bush speaking Spanish in Oxnard, CA (8/9) and an almost three-minute Jorge Ramos interview with Bush on the campaign train (8/10). In that interview, conducted in both Spanish and English, Univisión's Ramos sought the candidate's reactions upon learning that his nephew, George Prescott Bush, had encountered racism and anti-Latino slurs, to which Bush responded, "Que lástima!" (What a shame!).

The Democrats competed for airtime with coverage about the street protests in ways that the Republican Convention did not. For example, at least eight minutes of Univisión's Democratic Convention week coverage were devoted to the street protests; in fact, the demonstrations actually led the nightly newscast on two days (8/15, 8/16) of the four-day Convention.

The Democratic VP nominee, Joseph Lieberman, received more in-depth coverage than had his counterpart, Republican Dick Cheney, in the previous two-week period. On the one hand, there were positive pieces. In her first of two solid pre-Convention Lieberman pieces, Lori Montenegro noted that the nominee was often referred to as the "conscience of the Senate," and provided specifics on his actual voting record on the Persian Gulf and welfare (Telemundo, 8/7), a specificity lacking with regard to Cheney's voting record. In her second piece, Montenegro explored Latino angles of the selection, such as his family's immigrant roots and Lieberman's positive relations with his state's Puerto Rican community (8/8).

*Figure 6.2* Jorge Ramos, News anchor

However, during the Democratic Convention week, the Lieberman coverage was more mixed as Latino doubts about the nominee's approach to affirmative action and school vouchers, in particular, surfaced. Lieberman was seen meeting with Hispanic leaders and defending his civil rights commitment (8/16). Former Speaker of the Assembly, Antonio Villaraigosa (D-CA), noted his disagreement with the nominee over affirmative action (Univisión, 8/16). The complexities of the dilemma were exposed. Finally, there was the overall context of the Latino community's disappointment that Bill Richardson was not the vice presidential nominee. Richardson was quick to note his support of Lieberman and that "our turn will come in the future" (Telemundo, 8/8). However, when asked during an interview by Univisión's María Elena Salinas if he would have accepted the nomination, Richardson responded, "in a minute" (8/16).

Inclusion was more than window-dressing on the Democratic set. The presence of Latinos in the Democratic Convention (15 percent of the delegates) and the party's historic commitment to civil rights were given extensive and positive coverage. Both networks sought out Latino delegates and spokespersons, incorporated clips of the musical group Los Lobos and Spanish pop-star idol Enrique Iglesias,[2] and engaged the Spanish-speaking capabilities of Kareena Gore Schiff. Even more notably,

160

*Figure 6.3* María Elena Salinas, anchor for Univisión

Univisión ran a long interview with the young and articulate Lydia Camarillo, the first Latina to head a Convention Planning Committee (8/14). Both networks quoted her extensively throughout the week's stories. Telemundo's Monday Convention wrap-up piece had images and words from the many well known Hispanic leaders (8/14) and Univisión's main Convention piece on Tuesday (8/15) similarly focused primarily on the substantial presence of Hispanics on the Convention's second day, listing the names and clips of many Latino leaders.

Overall, the Democratic Party's message of solidarity with working peoples rooted in the spirit of John F. Kennedy and Cesar Chávez came across during this two-week period. Viewers witnessed the involvement of, and heard the comments from, many notable state and national Latino Democratic leaders throughout the week. The Party's position on immigration issues was prominently reported, as was Gore's long-standing record in support of health care, environmental issues, and public education. Lieberman's immigrant roots and historic nomination were recognized. But, to get its message across, the Democrats had to compete with other top political news stories such as Clinton scandals, George W.'s campaign train, and street protests.

The news wasn't all good for George W. Bush on Spanish-language television, however. The Texas governor's refusal to grant a stay of execution for Oliver Cruz, a debatably mentally retarded rapist and murderer, captured the news on both networks (Telemundo 8/7, 8/9; Univisión 8/9). On the day of the execution, Cruz's aunt cried out "He's [Bush] talking Spanish, he wants our votes, and all the while, he is executing Mexicans" (Univisión, 8/10). And Telemundo's piece noted that Bush opposed the law that would have made executing the mentally retarded illegal in his state (8/9).

## August 21–September 1

From mid-August through early September, the campaigns were well underway. While U.S. presidential campaigns were clearly taking the Hispanic voter seriously, there were questions about how seriously the Spanish-language media were taking the U.S. presidential campaign during this week. In an illustrative example of the challenges of Spanish-language news media's dual orientation, while there was a paucity of stories about the U.S. presidential campaign there was extensive coverage of the important visit of Mexico's president, Vicente Fox.

### Excerpts

The campaigns were not given high priority in the immediate post-Convention weeks, especially, it seemed, on Univisión. According to Univisión's second-week broadcasts (8/28–9/1), no presidential campaign was apparently underway. Except for a very brief (20-second) voice-over story closing the Friday broadcast about the candidates' position on the best barbecue, not one story on the campaign or campaign-related issues aired during the first week of this period—nothing about the candidates' positions on health care, education, defense, their campaign stops, the debate over the debates, not even a poll. In this specific case and for the period under review, Univisión shirked its responsibility to inform its viewers—the Latino electorate—of a presidential campaign in which their vote may well be the deciding one.

Telemundo broadcast three campaign stories during the same week: a brief poll story on Monday (8/28), a two-minute wrap-up piece in which reporter Montenegro talks about the campaign heating up over education and health care (8/29), and a three-minute interview with Dick Cheney (9/1). Since neither network had previously devoted much time to Cheney's positions, the interview was illuminating. Framed by reporter Guillermo Descalzi's context of "votes now in the balance," Cheney was asked about such issues as bilingual education ("I look to the results and favor English immersion"), about amnesty ("In the 80s, it might have been appropriate but I am not sure now"), about Cuba ("There will be no deals with Cuba until Castro is gone"), about Puerto Rican statehood

("If that is what the Puerto Ricans want, then it is OK with me"), and about Colombia ("Drugs are a serious national security issue"). To this last point, Descalzi noted that this opened the door to militarization.

Both networks aired revealing interviews with Al Gore (Univisión 8/24, 8/25; 7:30 minutes); Telemundo 8/25, 8/26; 5 minutes) during which the candidate was questioned rigorously about issues of high priority to Latinos. Some questions were the same on both networks' interviews—exploring Gore's position on amnesty, relations with the Hispanic community, the border, Colombia, Cuba, and the now famous nomination night "kiss" with Tipper. In the two-part Univisión interview, anchor María Elena Salinas in addition asked Gore about Richardson's presence on the VP list ("I have declined to name names but yes, there were Latinos on the list"), on the Drug Certification program ("To eliminate it will depend on what to replace it with"), on Peru ("I will continue to work with and encourage the democratic process"), on the Cuban child Elian González ("I would have handled it differently") and, on his relationship with Clinton ("I am running as my own man, but I am thankful for the opportunity to have worked with him for eight years"). In Telemundo's two-part interview, reporter Lori Montenegro in addition asked Gore about the U.S. military target-testing in Puerto Rico ("I think they should find another place to do it"). And, when asked why the Hispanic electorate should vote for him, Gore told Montenegro that "It's not palabras [words], it's my policies" (8/25). Telemundo's second-part broadcast of its important two-day Gore interview (8/25) was slightly over two minutes. But on that same day's broadcast, the newscast chose to devote two-and-a-half minutes to a "marriage rumor" involving pop singer Enrique Iglesias. It is questionable whether rumors of a star's marriage would ever warrant more time on a national newscast than a presidential candidate's one-on-one interview, but to make matters even worse, this Iglesias rumor was, itself, a media hoax, one in which the scripted wedding plan for Iglesias was to marry Telemundo's own reporter.

The border and its related issues, such as immigration and U.S.-Mexico relations, are of paramount concern to Hispanic voters. Thus, it is not surprising that the U.S. visit of Mexico's President-elect, Vicente Fox, was covered extensively on both networks' newscasts (Univisión 8/22, 8/23, 8/24; Telemundo 8/24, 8/25, 8/26). Since Fox met with both candidates, as well as with President Clinton, the visit clearly had campaign implications. As Univisión's Guzmán noted, Gore received Fox "more as a candidate than as the [standing] vice-president" (8/24). The presentation of the candidates' position toward Fox's oft-radical border proposals provided viewers with important information about the future president's position toward Mexico. While being interviewed by Univisión's anchor Salinas, Gore (speaking in Spanish) said he hoped to continue to work with Fox in the future and followed in English that "while the U.S.

doesn't favor unlimited immigration" he "wanted to hear what Fox had to say." He concluded that he found it "better to be confronted with ideas that are too big than those that are too small" (8/24). George W. Bush, speaking to a Miami-based group of Cuban Americans, was quoted as saying that "Mexico is number one on my Latin American agenda" (Univisión, 8/25) and, in juxtaposition to Gore's reaction to Fox's border proposals, Bush told the group he would hold the border. Said Bush, "I support the hold-the-line operation" (Telemundo 8/25).

## September 4–15

This Labor Day period saw the campaign heat up and the two Spanish-language networks captured the intensification. The number of campaign stories and the extent of the ongoing coverage increased from the previous two-week period, most significantly on Telemundo. Mixed in with stories of Bush's unscripted microphone chatter was the coverage of prescription drugs for seniors and immigration reform. The coverage of these and other related national issues demonstrated interesting differences in style between the two networks. Both networks had problems with the balancing of sources within some stories.

### Excerpts

Consistent with the tradition of Labor Day's intensification of the campaign, Telemundo started the two-week period very strong, with three separate campaign-related stories on Monday (9/4). Telemundo continued to run more campaign-related stories throughout this two-week period, a total of 14; Univisión ran a total of 10. A number of these stories covered issues such as health care and immigration reform, and differences between the two networks in the selection and treatment of the candidates' positions marked their coverage.

The main health care story of these two weeks was the candidates' prescription drug plan for seniors. In their drug plan stories, both networks used visual charts and compared the plans on basic points. In Univisión's informative piece (9/5), reporter Armando Guzmán presented both proposals, and brought in experts to comment. Telemundo went a different way: after presenting the plans and charts, Guillermo Descalzi, in his commentary-reporter-populist fashion, chose to then interview several "common folk" none of whom, unfortunately, could articulate much about the plans (9/5). Descalzi concluded that the campaigns were "talking above the level of the voter."

Coverage of the debate over the debates also demonstrated some differences in coverage between the two Spanish-language networks. Univisión referred to the debate about debates in five separate campaign stories during the two weeks under review (9/4, 9/5, 9/6, 9/14, 9/15). Following the story in this way provided viewers with continuity and an understanding of the story as it unfolded. In its final piece (9/15), Univisión's reporter Lourdes Meluza noted that Bush "tried in vain" to push his debate plan. Obviously, he lost. Telemundo made reference to the debate in just two stories, at the beginning and then its resolution (9/4, 9/15).

Coverage of the Bush campaign problems also differed. Telemundo ran a substantial piece on the problems (9/7), in which reporter Descalzi noted that "panic is spreading" in the Bush campaign. Telemundo did not, however, air a subsequent story noting the official change in strategy, which was announced the following day. Univisión registered the "change in strategy" within its longer campaign piece (9/8).

Finally, Univisión covered several other campaign-related stories that Telemundo ignored—in particular, the fundraising scandal against Gore (Univisión, 9/14) and Cheney's failure to vote in past national elections (Univisión, 9/8). And, if Gore's personality (or lack thereof) was a campaign concern for the Democrats, they could be happy with Univisión's footage of Lieberman singing on the O'Brien Show and Gore cracking jokes on the David Letterman Show (9/15). Clearly the two weeks were a lighter and happier period for the Democrats than for the Republicans.

## September 18–29

The campaign entered the final weeks, now in the "la recta final" (the home stretch) of the presidential horse race. The most striking aspect of these two weeks was that George W. Bush seemed everywhere on Spanish-language television with exclusive interviews, guest appearances, prominence in the campaign stories themselves, and his more favorable positioning in the polls. If Bush hadn't yet "conquered the West" (Univisión, 9/27), he was definitely conquering Spanish-language TV. This may well have been the outcome of the GOP's effective outreach to Hispanic voters in which the Bush campaign and the RNC, for example, outspent Gore and the DNC two-to-one in Spanish-language media advertising dollars as detailed in chapter 13 in this book. The continuing sloppiness in both networks' presentation of polls was also an issue for *MediaWatch* during this period.

### Excerpts

Bush seemed to be everywhere in and around the news. Teasers for the Republican candidate's guest appearances wrapped around the newscasts. Telemundo announced Bush's appearance on its brand new morning show, *Esta Mañana*, hosted by the brother of vocal Cuban-American Republican Congressman Lincoln Díaz-Balart (R-FL) (9/27). And on two different news nights, Univisión aired teasers announcing Bush's appearance on its late-night show, *Ultima Hora* (9/26, 9/27). It seemed like George W. Bush was appearing all over Spanish-language TV.

Within the newscasts themselves, Bush seemed well positioned. The exclusive Los Angeles Bush interview with Univisión's Jaime García (9/27) ran under the title "Conquistando el Oeste" (Conquering the West). During the two-and-a-half minute piece, the candidate made his pronouncement in Spanish, "Voy a ganar aquí" (I am going to win here in California). Included in this Bush campaign story was also a clip of wife, Laura, talking about how her husband really cares about women's welfare. Gore's brief appearance within the piece was far less than desirable. In contrast to the close-up shots and exclusive Bush footage, the Democratic candidate was seen only at a distance (which visually diminishes him and his stature) and, if that wasn't enough, the camera shot was shaky.

### Using polls without precision

With the presidential horse race down to the wire and the two candidates virtually neck-to-neck, polls were mentioned frequently on both networks' newscasts. After a Guillermo Descalzi story that used a Zogby poll showing Hispanics were 44 percent for Gore and 44 percent for Bush to illustrate the determining role of the Hispanic vote, anchor Pedro Sevcec commented with concern that "es un poco raro" (this is quite odd), since a previous week's poll had Hispanics at 57 percent for Gore, 28 percent for Bush. How could the numbers be so different in such a short amount of time? And how would viewers interpret these volatile figures? Sevcec's concern prompted *MediaWatch* to take a closer look at how the Spanish language media were using polls.

Clearly, employing polls and keeping tabs on "the presidential horse race" are an integral part of any campaign coverage. Twenty-eight separate stories broadcast since the beginning of *MediaWatch* (which began on July 24) highlighted polls, often citing two or more polls in a single piece. *MediaWatch* concluded that the Spanish-language broadcast media would do their viewers a better service by using polls with more discrimination and precision. Four different but common media decisions about the presentation of polls complicate the viewers' ability to understand the implications and limit the value of the poll as a snapshot of opinion in the moment.

### Confusion about the poll's origins and reach

At times, the sponsoring entity is identified but the poll's scope is not. For example, in one Univisión piece (8/24) both a Field and a University of Quinnipiac poll were presented, but it was not stated that they were only measuring California and New Jersey voters respectively. By not mentioning the limited scope of these two polls, Gore's *statewide* leads would be assumed to be national figures. In fact, the statewide leads were in excess of national polls released on the same day. In addition, examples were aired when reference was made to percentages in "other polls" but no identification was given of the poll or its sponsoring entity. Or the poll's originating entity was loosely referred to as "an Internet poll" (Univisión, (9/25).

### The non-existent margin of error

In all but three of the 28 instances of references to polls (Univisión, 8/16; Telemundo, 9/8, 9/20), the networks failed to mention the margin of error. While these margins are not exact, when poll figures are within the margin, providing viewers with the information may assist in their ability to understand the relative lead of one candidate over the other.

### Silence about the interviewed

Pollsters generally provide figures regarding registered voters and about likely voters. While the difference is technical, it may net different results. The networks, however, used one or the other indiscriminately, and in almost every case reviewed failed to inform which one was being used.

### Limiting the races to two

Some polls measured the expanse between Bush and Gore only; others included third party candidates Ralph Nader and/or Pat Buchanan. However, the newscasts used one or the other indiscriminately, and commonly failed to inform its viewers of which one was being used. In only three cases during these ten weeks (Univisión 7/28, 9/8, 9/25), were figures on, or mention of, third party candidates presented.

### A final point deserves comment

Only twice was a poll presented that referred to the extremely important electoral college votes (Telemundo, 9/11, 9/19). And, only twice during these ten weeks was a poll used that noted Hispanic voters specifically (Telemundo 9/13; 9/26).

## October 2–20

October was the month of the presidential debates, a time when—in the most ideal vision of American democracy—issues and views are robustly debated before the citizenry. Public debate should be at the core of an informed population. While the staged reality of presidential debates leaves much of the American electorate wanting, the Spanish-language media performed its dual orientation role well. Univisión devoted far more time and resources to the coverage. However, Telemundo struck some deep cords with several excellent pieces on campaign-related issues. The lack of presidential candidates' attention to issues of specific interest to Latino voters was a recurrent theme in the coverage by both networks.

## Excerpts

### October 2–6

Both networks carried virtually the same number of campaign-related stories during this first presidential debate week (Univisión's eight to Telemundo's seven), yet the differences in coverage were significant. Univisión's total time devoted to these stories was 21 minutes to Telemundo's 12 minutes. Univisión's correspondent, Armando Guzmán, broadcast direct and live on location from the Boston presidential debate site and then responded live to split-screen questions from anchor Jorge Ramos (10/3). Telemundo's correspondent Cristina Londoño broadcast live but not on location (10/3). The first presidential debate was the top story on both networks' broadcasts: Univisión devoted almost five minutes to Telemundo's approximately 3:45 minutes.

"Who won?" was the essence of both networks' post-debate Wednesday night stories. Univisión gathered 18 undecided Latino voters to watch the event (10/4) and only two of the 18 had made up their minds after the debate. One of the predominate themes running through the group's reactions was that neither candidate had touched upon many of the issues of great interest to Latino voters. This theme was to recur throughout the following weeks. In Telemundo's Wednesday night post-debate story, Cristina Londoño cited three polls, all showing that Gore was perceived to have won the debate (10/4). The piece also included voter reactions.

The Thursday vice-presidential debate was handled by both networks differently than the presidential debate and, once again, differently from each other. In this case, neither network had a reporter live from the site of the debate. Univisión ran the story on Thursday night, with footage from the debate (10/5). Meanwhile, Telemundo ran no Thursday night story about that debate.

On Friday, however, both networks carried post-debate stories. Univisión's Lourdes Meluza summarized the feeling that the vice-presidential candidates were more presidential than those running for the White House, listing characteristics demonstrated in the debate such as experience, intellect, oratory, and great style (10/6). The piece carried excerpts from the debate and reactions from Congresswomen Loretta Sanchez (D-CA) and Ileana Ross-Letheinen (R-FL). Telemundo's Friday wrap-up announced that the VP debate had occurred the previous night, noting the central themes (10/6).

*October 9–13*

With the period experiencing heightened conflict between Palestinians and Israelis in the ongoing Middle East crisis, the domestic political campaign was not the top story on either network on any night of this week. Both networks ran several pre-debate stories early in the week summarizing the candidates' campaign activities, citing recent polls, and analyzing the expectations for the upcoming second. In contrast to the first debate's coverage, Univisión did not place its correspondent live from the debate location and its report carried only the briefest clip of the actual debate, which was underway at the time of the broadcast. Telemundo pre-empted its West Coast Wednesday night newscast with a soccer game, thus, obviously, no live debate coverage was aired. Both networks aired post-debate stories, including polls and spins. Neither carried a Friday wrap-up report.

*October 16–20*

While the primary emphasis for both networks during this third and final debate week continued to be the crisis in the Middle East, Univisión aired more campaign-related stories of any week since the beginning of *MediaWatch*, with a total of nine stories and approximately 17 minutes compared to Telemundo's four stories and approximately eight minutes. Univisión once again placed its correspondent, this time Lourdes Meluza, live and direct from the debate's Missouri location. Meluza's approximately four-minute report summarized the debate's first questions, showed footage of the arrival of both candidates, and the correspondent responded live to questions from anchor Jorge Ramos. Telemundo did not broadcast live from the debate, and the night's three-minute report only devoted a brief initial part to the start of the debate underway and then went on to other campaign issues. Both networks ran post-debate stories later in the week.

As mentioned above, one of the recurrent themes covered throughout these three weeks on both network newscasts was the candidates' absence of attention to political issues of great import to Latino voters. One of Univisión's undecided voters said at the time, "Más de lo que se dijo, fué lo que no se dijo" (More important than what was said, was what they didn't talk about). Univisión returned to this theme in its report on the candidates' positions on foreign policy issues (10/16). Noting that Latin America was largely absent in the campaign, one analyst told correspondent Lourdes del Rio that the candidates shared similar positions regarding free trade, the Colombia Plan, pro-democracy efforts in the region, and concluded that while Bush was closer to Mexico it wasn't a priority for either.

Telemundo's Descalzi took this neglect and ran with it in two consecutive and powerful campaign-related stories. In the first of the two stories, aired on the night of the third and final presidential debate, Descalzi asked several undecided Latino men and women what questions they would like to ask the candidates. The street interviewees had no problem coming up with their list: What about immigration? What about amnesty? What would they do for us, the Latinos? (10/17). The following post-debate day, Descalzi screened the debate proceedings for these and other themes of interest of Latinos and concluded: "Immigration: zero; amnesty: zero; Cuba: zero; bilingual education: zero" (10/18). In a poignant observation, Descalzi scanned the faces of those in the third debate's town hall audience and commented "No había piel canela excepto la de George Prescott Bush" (There was no brown skin except that of George Prescott Bush, the candidate's handsome nephew). And, in remarkable similarity to Univisión's undecided voter three weeks earlier, Raul Yzaguire of the National Council of La Raza, was quoted stating that "More than surprising, it is ignorant that Latinos are not represented in this presidential event" (10/18).

Both networks also aired stories about voter apathy, an important issue during a campaign in which the Hispanic vote was so critical in key states. Univisión's Blanca Rosa-Vilchez focused her piece on Latino youth, citing figures of up to 50 percent of them not being registered to vote in New York (10/3). Telemundo's Carlos Botifoll included in his voter-apathy story a young Latino man saying "No tengo mucho interés" (I'm not very interested) (10/6). Noting that there was less than a week to do so, the Botifoll report provided viewers with practical information about how to register and showed efforts to combat the apathy, including an intense Spanish-language campaign to register voters. The theme was returned to in subsequent weeks, with Univisión running a third-week story on the lack of motivation to vote among Latino citizens (10/19). Perhaps the lack of candidates' attention to many issues considered extremely important to Latinos, and noted in the paragraph above, has contributed to this significant apathy.

Univisión began a major campaign-related series with a weekly in-depth piece examining the candidate's differences on major issues. The three themes addressed during these three weeks were immigration (10/2), education (10/9), and foreign policy (10/16). In the first of the series, correspondent Armando Guzmán began his immigration report by asserting that neither candidate has an overall plan on immigration and that they are mostly reacting to what is already out there (10/2). In a wonderfully clear presentation, Guzmán laid out major immigration legislation currently on the table, including amnesty, the new bracero program, dividing the INS into two services and other current proposals, and then lined up Bush and Gore either in favor or against these. The table clearly showed Gore as more positive on the issues listed, certainly a significant comment for Latino viewers.

The second of the series, the education report, concluded that in the campaign's home stretch "the conservatives have liberalized a bit, while the liberals have promoted ideas that are more traditional" (10/9). While a Bush spokesperson was used in the story, no Gore advisor was included—a significant oversight in a story specifically focusing on the candidates' positions regarding education. In Telemundo's education report (10/9) correspondent Lori Montenegro detailed the candidates' specific education proposals including, among other things, their positions on vouchers, a proposal which was not even mentioned in the Univisión piece. The third piece in the Univisión series was on foreign policy issues (10/16).

At this point, attention has to be drawn to a troubling sloppiness in the identification of spokespersons and sources used in the stories. This problem was noticed by *MediaWatch* on both networks on different occasions, but during these final three weeks, several examples stood out. In Univisión's Supreme Court report (10/2), neither the pro-choice spokeswoman, the anti-abortion spokeswoman, nor the quoted law professor were identified by name. In Univisión's immigration report (10/2), of the three sources used only the Bush supporter, Lincoln Díaz-Balart (R-FL), was identified as a Republican spokesperson and footage was shown of him in Congress. However, the Gore spokesperson in the story remained unidentified. Because he was neither named nor identified, the contrast with the high profile Congressman Díaz-Balart shown at the congressional podium could be construed as detrimental to the story's balance of sources. Finally, in another example, in a debate story, Univisión identified one on-camera source as a spokesperson for the Gore–Cheney campaign, which certainly would be an interesting but improbable ticket (10/11)!

## October 23–29

During the final weeks of the campaign, news coverage definitely increased and differences between the two networks in time and story placement were again notable. One of the most interesting features of this period's news coverage, especially given the determining role played by the Green Party in Florida's final vote (in hindsight), was that Spanish-language television news finally found the third party.

*Excerpts*

Campaign stories were always placed within the first five pieces in the Univisión newscast's line-up, whereas Telemundo's placement was within the *final* three pieces of the evening on three of the four nights that it ran campaign stories. The stark differences between the two networks was not only apparent in terms of placement and quantity, but the quality of the coverage was more substantive on Univisión, with an exclusive interview with vice-presidential candidate, Joe Lieberman, by anchor María Elena Salinas (10/25), and number of special in-depth reports.

The contrast in coverage demonstrates a break in patterns established in previous weeks. During the home stretch of the presidential campaign, it appears that one network took the lead. Univisión's Monday night newscast overflowed with campaign coverage. The fourth in its series on "Campaign Themes" focused on health (10/23). Correspondent Lourdes Meluza had a three-minute in-depth report on health insurance and Medicare. The use of a counterpoint technique between the two candidates' positions was highly effective. The evening's "Primer Plano" segment with correspondent Luis Megid focused on the theme of education and, in particular, the issue of vouchers in California (10/23). This was the second week in a row in which Univisión dedicated its "Primer Plano" segment to campaign issues. The newscast also included a campaign update, a daily feature throughout the week.

While third-party candidates had barely received notice in the Spanish-language networks, be it in stories or referenced in poll figures, this week was different, at least on Univisión. Reflecting the current circumstances of the tight race, a story on Ralph Nader was shown on Univisión (10/24). Correspondent Lourdes Meluza made note of the Green Party candidate's voter percentages as damaging to Gore's success. But it was in a report labeled "El Factor Nader" in which Meluza spent over two minutes exploring Nader's "spoiler" role (Univisión, 10/25). The theme was picked up again on Friday (10/26), when a Los Angeles-based analyst told correspondent Jaime García that the decrease in Gore's lead in California is "less about increasing support for Bush, and more about a decline in support for Gore and a rise for Nader." Telemundo, on the other hand, did to Nader what Gore would like to do to the Green Party candidate— they simply made him "disappear."

One of the week's best reports was Univisión's "Voto Hispano" (10/24), in which correspondent Lourdes del Río made note of a recurrent theme on the networks throughout the campaign, that "Despite a few words in Spanish, neither Bush or Gore have given Hispanics very much in terms of immigration." The report included immigration activist organizations calling upon the presidential candidates to intercede in the week's congressional battle over the Latino justice legislation. It should be mentioned

that both networks provided viewers with extensive and high quality coverage of the fight between Congress's Republicans and the White House
over passage of the immigration legislation and the president's impending
veto of the federal budget.

## October 30–November 5

It must have been that the Gore campaign finally got the message that the
Spanish-language media mattered because the Democratic candidate
finally came across as strong and accessible on both networks during this
week. As alluded to in chapter 13, the DNC allocated too little money
too late in the campaign, and this period of *MediaWatch* excerpts reflect
that turnaround in the Gore campaign.

### Excerpts

Gore finally made Spanish-language TV. The experience of Univisión's
senior correspondent Armando Guzmán was apparent in his reports
throughout the week and in his exclusive interview with Gore inside the
candidate's airplane. As he accompanied the vice president for 24 hours,
Guzmán explored questions about the campaign, the polls, and the Latino
vote (11/3). Telemundo also aired an interview with Gore, exploring a few
lighter topics in a much shorter report (11/3).

Added to the increased access to Gore, Univisión's anchor María Elena
Salinas aired an exclusive two-part interview with President Clinton,
which both dignified the standing president and gave emphasis to the
Democrats' positions on immigration legislation, a few foreign policy
issues of interest such as Mexico and Colombia and, as well, explored
Clinton's reflections on his personal mistakes (10/31, 11/1). Of particular
note during the eight-and-a-half minute interview is that Salinas made
note of the Republicans' success in reaching Latino voters and asked why
Latinos should vote for Gore. Clinton responded that: "Latinos should
look at the issues." In a year when the Spanish language itself has become
a political protagonist, the President further noted, "Both candidates
speak Spanish. I hope I will be the last President of the United States that
doesn't speak Spanish." To which Salinas inquisitively asked, "Nada?"
He replied, "A little."

### That handsome face

It is often said that television content just fills in the time between ads.
If that is the case, this week's news filled in space around the handsome
face of George Prescott Bush. In this week alone, three different Bush
ads appeared and all of them featured the handsome Spanish-speaking

nephew of the presidential candidate. On Univisión, even multiple versions appeared on a single evening newscast. The campaign ads appeared but much less frequently on the Telemundo broadcast. Not one Gore ad was spotted on either network during the week. It should be mentioned that *MediaWatch* is monitored from California and the appearance and frequency of the ads may be different on different newscasts.

## Election Night, November 7

### Excerpts

On this suspense-filled election night both Spanish-language networks covered the tightest presidential race in history in much the same way as the English-language counterparts—for good and bad, including the state-by-state count, the electoral college speculations, the magnificently premature declaration of George W. Bush as the winner, and the subsequent long hours of confusing impasse.

In a race which may well come down to the voting of the small Florida-based Cuban-American community, both networks used polls and analyst assessments to explore the multifaceted voting patterns within the Hispanic population. In particular, Univisión's Enrique Gratas provided insightful segments "Así Votamos" (How we voted). As the night wore on, and all eyes focused on the Florida numbers, Telemundo's Pedro Sevcec speculated about future frictions between the overwhelmingly Democratic Latino voters nationwide and the Republican Cuba-American community in Florida.

In the tightest presidential race in modern history, and one in which the Latino vote was so critical, Univisión's decision to air its regular *telenovelas* between 7:00 p.m. and 9:00 p.m. (Pacific Time), interspersed with occasional election briefs, was nothing short of shocking. Based on *MediaWatch*'s observation at the time, Univisión was the only major national network in the entire country—among Fox, CNN, CBS, ABC, NBC, PBS, Telemundo—that failed to pre-empt regular programming and replace it with continuous election coverage. While Univisión aired its *Locuras de Amor* and *Mujeres Engañadas*, Telemundo covered national Latino congressional races, the dramatic switches of Florida from the Gore to the undecided column, the live and fully translated acceptance speech of Senator-to-be Hillary Clinton, the Puerto Rican gubernatorial race, and reactions from Mexico. Not only was Univisión's coverage during these hours almost absent, but viewers learned of important election night occurrences in a delayed fashion, for example, the critical switch of Florida from the Gore to undecided was broadcast at 7:00 p.m. (PST) on Telemundo, but not until 7:25 p.m. on Univisión.

On the other hand, as the night progressed the two networks seemed to switch roles. Telemundo chose to move operations entirely from the network broadcast to its local Los Angeles affiliate (*MediaWatch* was monitored from the West Coast) at 10:00 p.m. and did not return to the network anchors until midnight. Telemundo went off the election coverage immediately after the campaign spokespersons told the assembled victory crowds that there was an electoral impasse and a recount was imminent. Telemundo then began airing its popular *telenovela*, *Betty La Fea* (*Ugly Betty*). Univisión, on the other hand, started its continuous national network coverage at 9:00 p.m. (PST) and stayed on the air with network anchors well past the spokespersons' statements.

## CONCLUSION

The intense "special watching" illuminates media practices, cultural traditions, and the effects of stakeholder strategies—to mention a few of the more salient aspects of this attention to Spanish-language television news coverage. One of the most significant observations that can be made is the degree to which Spanish-language television news is constructed and constrained by many of the same media routines and norms which frame English-language news coverage of political campaigns. The focus on the horse race aspect of the campaign, the imprecise and partial use of polls, and the lack of attention to third parties were all apparent aspects of the coverage that is commonplace in both Spanish-language and English-language coverage.

At the same time, Spanish-language media's dual orientation contributes an additional pressure on the medium's allocation of time and resources in that it is expected to cover both "mainstream" issues as well as the news most specifically of interest to its audience: the large and heterogeneous Spanish-speaking population in the United States. To a degree, Spanish-language television news must take into account the cultural and political traditions of its viewers while, at the same time, furthering those viewers' understanding of the political landscape in which they now find themselves. In addition, the degree to which reports try to draw out politicians' positions and parties' platforms on issues such as Latin America, immigration and education are noteworthy. The degree to which the candidates and their parties address these issues also provides viewers with an understanding of the perceived importance of the Latino voter in American politics.

Another observation related to the 2000 presidential campaign is the degree to which the Republican Party made its candidate and its spokespersons highly accessible to the Spanish-language media. It appeared that the Democratic Party came to that strategic decision much later in the race and, clearly in hindsight, to its detriment. For most of the campaign, it appeared that Bush and the Republican Party either made themselves more available to the Spanish-language TV news, or the networks themselves sought them out more often, or some other combination of decision making and stakeholder strategies. While viewers are unlikely to know the reasons behind the decision, the outcome was more GOP presence during many of the critical weeks of the campaign.

Finally, each Spanish-language network made decisions based on time, resources, and/or editorial determinations, which were hard to fathom. How or why, for example, did Univisión decide to air its regular *telenovelas* during pivotal hours of the election night debacle? Or why, later in the night, Telemundo ended its election night coverage once campaign spokespersons indicated there was an impasse? Clearly, and again in hindsight, the story was just beginning.

## RECOMMENDATIONS FOR SERIOUS WATCHING 2008

We can count on the political parties and presidential candidates to develop significant outreach strategies for the Hispanic voter in 2008. We can assume that millions of dollars will again be spent in advertising in Spanish-language media and hundreds of photo opportunities made available for television newscasts. As students of journalism and as media consumers, what can be learned from the *MediaWatch* initiative of the 2000 presidential campaign to help engage in serious watching of the presidential campaign for 2008?

- Be attentive to specific issues and ideas which have been regularly noted in the weeks of *MediaWatch* excerpts. For example: What issues are being covered? What issues are not? What issues are most relevant to Latino voters? Who are the sources? What expertise do they have? Do they represent multiple points of view? How much time is devoted to the presidential campaign?
- Always remember that news is produced; it is not reality but a particular construction of reality. Keep in mind that individual decisions have been made all along the way in order to compose the evening's newscast—decisions about what to cover and what not, what visuals to use and which ones to ignore, what sound-bites to include and from whom, and the like. Try to identify what decisions were made and understand that determinations based on resources, audiences, advertisers, media routines, and the political climate weigh heavily on the final product: the newscast you are watching. Imagine if different decisions had been made.
- Remember that every political story has more than two sides. In our

complex, multicultural and politically divided world, there are many positions and perspectives. As you watch the news, ask yourself whether or not a range of opinions are being presented within one story, across the newscast, and/or throughout the week. What opinions are dominating the story? What opinions are not being aired? Who is representing those diverse opinions? Remember, not all sources are equal. Some have more access to stakeholders or are more informed about issues. Some are Latino and some not. Do these positions make a difference in the news you are watching?

• Don't just absorb the newscast. Pause. Ask the sort of questions presented above. Discuss with others. In fact, watching TV communally is one of the best ways to develop your critical watching skills.

• Finally, seek out additional information about the candidates and issues beyond the nightly newscast. It will be difficult to know what is missing in the story. Read newspapers and, if possible, read from sources that seek opinions outside the mainstream. For example, look at third party bulletins, make use of Internet sites, advocacy groups and special interest resources, and seek out as much information as you can from those leads.

## NOTES

1 John Secada is a contemporary Cuban-American singer-songwriter; Vicente Fernandez is one of Mexico's most popular singers of traditional music, referred to as the King of Rancheros; and Celia Cruz was the influential and legendary Cuban-born Queen of Latin music, especially Salsa.

2 Los Lobos are the highly popular Los Angeles-based rock-folk-Tex-Mex band, and Spanish-born Enrique Iglesias is one of the best-selling Spanish-language artists in the world.

# 7

# HABLANDO POLÍTICA: HOW SPANISH-LANGUAGE TELEVISION NEWS COVERED THE 2004 ELECTIONS[1]

*Matthew Hale, Tricia Olsen* and *Erika Franklin Fowler*

As documented throughout this book, missing from the extensive literature on Latinos and politics, and largely missing from the less extensive literature on Latinos and mass communication, is systematic empirical work focusing on how Spanish-language media cover politics.

There are obviously several reasons for this gap, but three are particularly important. The first is that capturing and coding media content is extremely labor intensive and time consuming. This is especially true of television news content, which only exists in archival form if there is the capacity to capture it digitally. While most researchers can hook up a VCR and capture local news in their own city, very few have the time or money to capture news programming outside of their own media market. This leads many scholars to focus on single market studies (Entman, 1992; Stevens et al., 2006), on a few stations in a limited number of markets (Carter, Fico and McCabe, 2002; Just et al., 1996), or on national media or newspapers where data are more readily available (Kahn and Kenney, 1999; Beck et al., 2002; Farnsworth and Lichter, 2003).

Second, a central reason for studying the media is to determine under what circumstances messages matter and why. Political communication scholars are generally more interested in media if they can also show how it affects people in terms of voting behavior, civic participation, and political attitudes, or even how it might influence political/cultural assimilation or separatism. In an effort to demonstrate media effects, researchers are often content to rely on survey data and self-reported media use alone (Brians and Wattenberg, 1996; Krosnick and Brannon, 1993) or to design experiments that involve exposing individuals to small samples of media content (Gilliam and Iyengar, 2000; Iyengar and Kinder 1987; Valentino, 1999).

Finally, although the first two reasons can explain the gap in academic studies of local news generally (whether in English or Spanish), there may be an additional reason why *Spanish*-language news is often overlooked: the importance of English-language news to Latino voters may lead many researchers to focus solely on English media. A recent nationally representative survey of Latinos found that more than half (53 percent) of Latino voters get all of their news in English, four in ten (40 percent) get their news in both languages, but fewer than one in ten (6 percent) get all of their news in Spanish.[2] However, that same survey also reported that a growing number of Latinos switch between English and Spanish media for their information. It is our contention that, just as it is important to understand the content and influence of English-language media, it is equally important to understand the content and influence of Spanish-language media, especially if an increasing Latino population is tuning into news in both languages.

In this chapter, we argue that answering the question of effects about campaigns and elections without a solid understanding of what the public actually sees—in Spanish or English—is, at best, problematic. Although experiments are good at demonstrating effects minutes after exposure, they shed little light on how exposure amidst the chaos of everyday life translates into real world effects. Outside the laboratory, as several scholars have shown (Ansolabehere, Iyengar and Simon, 1999; Goldstein and Freedman, 2002), self-reported media use is notoriously inaccurate. Others have argued that education circumvents the problems of self-reports in providing a better proxy for reception (Price and Zaller, 1993); however, we contend that any studies of media effects must start with accurate measures of exposure that include the market-based variation in media content, and there is every reason to suspect that there are very real differences in how local television stations cover the news (Hale et al., 2007; Fowler et al., 2007). In a sense, then, we are taking a step back and making the case that a more detailed, systematic description of news content is needed to help future researchers more accurately gauge what news content means to the average citizen.

We begin this chapter by reporting on the quantity and quality of 2004 election coverage on both national network and local Spanish-language television stations in New York, Los Angeles and Miami. Overall, we examined a total of 205 stories airing on the two Spanish-language networks and 782 aired on the six local Spanish-language stations.[3] All of the stories were extracted from a universe of all prime-time programming (5:00 p.m.–11:30 p.m.) airing on the two major Spanish-language stations (Univisión and Telemundo) from October 4 through November 1, 2004.

The capture and analysis operations that made this study possible were based out at the University of Wisconsin NewsLab (www.polisci. wisc.edu/uwnewslab). Three important elements aided in creating significant advances in the capture, analysis and management of news content: (1) the methodology developed by UW NewsLab in conjunction with the Norman Lear Center at the University of Southern California, (2) the InfoSite media analysis system developed by CommIT Technology Solutions, Inc.,[4] and (3) technological advancements in digital media encoding. A full description of each of these elements, including the research methodology used for this study and an online searchable archive of election stories can be found at www.localnewsarchive.org. In a very real sense, the UW NewsLab solves the first problem described above by making the capture, analysis and management of large volumes of television news possible. By using this exciting new resource, we hope to provide researchers with, if nothing else, a more solid footing for future work.

## KEY RESEARCH QUESTIONS

Since our primary goal is to provide a basic understanding of what viewers of Spanish-language news actually see about campaigns and elections, the bulk of this chapter is descriptive. We focus on two fundamental dimensions: the quantity of election news and the "quality" of election news.

Measuring the quantity of election news is fairly straightforward. We first report the overall total of election coverage over the four-week period analyzed. Second, we report the amount of election news a viewer might see in a typical half-hour news broadcast. Third, we report the length of an average election story. We assume that, at least to some extent, more exposure to election news is normatively better for the viewer than less.

Measuring the quality of election news is somewhat more complicated, since "quality" is more subjective. Again, however, we focus on the viewers of Spanish-language television and frame our questions around what components of election coverage *might* lead them towards participating in the electoral process.

First, we examine which races received the most election coverage. We compare the percentage of election stories that focused on the 2004 presidential election with the percentage of stories that focus on "local" races (e.g., U.S. House, state legislature and other county and regional offices). The balance between presidential coverage and down-ballot races is especially important given how little most Americans (Latinos or otherwise) know about their legislative officials. The amount of coverage of "local" elections is also important given the recent policy debate over raising the number of media outlets that can be owned by a single entity in one media market. In response to an attempt by the FCC to raise these so called "ownership caps" (FCC Report and Order, 2003; FCC Review, 2003), a 3rd circuit court decision (*Prometheus Radio Project v. FCC*, 2004) harshly criticized the FCC for failing to address how media consolidation may affect the amount of localism in news content. A central criticism leveled by the court was that, because the FCC did not have a systematic way of collecting or analyzing local news programming, the methods the agency used to measure localism were woefully inadequate. While the court stopped short of mandating new FCC rulemaking on the issue, the agency has agreed to more review and study before implementing any policy changes. With this in mind, we also report the percentage of stories that focus on voting issues, which we define as stories about the mechanics of voting, and are generally locally focused. This is especially important given that many of the viewers of Spanish-language television are presumably less experienced in the voting and participation processes.

Next, we report how election stories are framed. The conventional wisdom in terms of English-language media is that election stories are focused on campaign strategy and the horse race as opposed to substantive political issues (Cappella and Jamieson, 1997; Graber, 2005; Bartels, 1988 and 1993; Bennett, 2002). Understanding how Spanish-language television frames its election coverage may be even more important owing to its audience. Since many viewers of Spanish-language news presumably have less experience of voting in the United States, they may know less about policy differences between candidates. To the extent that issue-based coverage helps viewers understand candidate differences, more substantive coverage may be better.[5]

As outlined elsewhere in this book, the extent to which Spanish-language media connects with its viewers is essential to understanding how it might influence them. One way of specifically connecting to Latino viewers in terms of elections is by including a "Latino" perspective in them. While we understand that broadly framing a singular "Latino" perspective misses a great deal of subtlety and subgroup differences, we will leave the question of "which" Latino perspective for future work. The broad measure, however, is still an important indication of how the television stations are attempting to reach their viewers. As such, we will report how often election stories include this perspective.[6]

Just as talking about a singular "Latino" perspective may ignore subgroup difference, it is also problematic to discuss "Latino" media in a monolithic way. We recognize this and will attempt to address it by examining our basic questions from two additional perspectives, which are described below.

## Local market variance

New York, Los Angeles and Miami are very different cities and the Latinos living in these cities are, of course, also quite different. For example, Miami and Los Angeles clearly have a dominant Latino subgroup (Cuban and

Mexican Americans, respectively), whereas New York is more diverse.[7] Market variance in the context of election coverage, however, is important because, regardless of the language they speak, journalists are more likely to cover competitive elections. Of the three local news markets, Miami was the only one considered to be competitive in the presidential race. Florida also had a highly competitive race for the United States Senate.[8] As a result, almost half (43 percent) of all local campaign stories aired in Miami. Yet the two New York stations provided substantially more election coverage than the stations in Los Angeles. This was despite the fact that, while most pundits agreed neither market was competitive at the presidential level, many rated the U.S. Senate race in California as being more competitive than that in New York.[9] So while election competitiveness is important, it seems clear that it is not the only explanation for market variance. By making market-to-market comparisons we hope to discover some additional factors in market variance.

## Station ownership

The second perspective is station ownership. As pointed out in earlier chapters, Univisión and Telemundo dominate Spanish-language television. By some accounts, the two companies control as much as 90 percent of the market. Yet, as distinct entities, they have fundamental differences. Dávila (2000) picks up this theme in her analysis of both networks programming and marketing strategies.

To begin, she describes Univisión, the older and by far the larger of the two networks as

> [a] self appointed keeper and broker of Latin American culture and primary conduit between U.S. Latinos and their culture. Univisión thus positions itself as the primary venue in which U.S. Latinos can connect or reconnect with the world that they may or may not have experienced, but nonetheless, as they are continually told, is a representation of Latin America and thus their heritage.
> (Dávila, 2000: 79)

At first glance this sounds like a pluralistic model in that it attempts to strengthen ethnic and cultural ties to Latin America. Dávila, however, argues that, in its effort to locate Latin America as the foci for Latinos living in the United States, Univisión ignores domestic events that are important to U.S.-based Latinos. She cites as an example Univisión's failure to cover President Clinton's 1998 State of the Union Address. In essence, Dávila claims that the Univisión model is assimilationist, but that it attempts to assimilate or perhaps re-assimilate Latinos into Latin America not into the United States. Furthermore, Dávila argues, Univisión eliminates and marginalizes the experiences and sensibilities of Cuban,

Puerto Rican and Mexican Americans in an effort to assimilate them into a larger "Pan-Hispanic" narrative.

In a subtle contrast, Dávila dissects Telemundo's "Best of Both Worlds" advertising slogan to suggest that this network has a significantly different, yet still an assimilationist vision. In Telemundo's case, the goal is to assimilate Latinos into the suburban prosperity of the American dream. Even more than with Univisión, the philosophy of Telemundo (as represented by marketing ideas such as "Two Traditions, Two Cultures, Two Languages") initially suggests a pluralistic vision. As evidence of this, Dávila reports on Telemundo's promotion of bilingual programs that show intergenerational differences in language preferences and attitudes, including a situation comedy modeled after *All in the Family*, where the Archie Bunker character is played by an equally racist Cuban bodega owner. Ultimately, however, Dávila argues that, despite some clear efforts to include Latinos living in the United States and some intra-Latino differences, the guiding focus of Telemundo is also assimilationist. She sites promotional programs that show the obvious preferred progression of Latinos from border areas to urban enclaves to suburban bliss. For Dávila, then, the central difference between Univisión and Telemundo is the goal of the assimilation process. For Telemundo, the goal is for Latinos to assimilate into the United States' middle or upper class. The goal of assimilation for Univisión is back into Latin America.

While Dávila's study examines network programming as a whole instead of just news programs, her analysis suggests that news coverage in general and election coverage specifically is likely to be significantly different on Univisión and Telemundo stations. Specifically, Dávila's analysis implies that Telemundo's more U.S. centric approach may mean that it will pay more attention to U.S. elections than Univisión. With the data we have collected we can and will explore this idea.

The specific goals of this chapter are threefold. The first is to provide a detailed description of how Spanish-language television stations as a whole cover American politics. Second, we will assess the similarities and differences in election coverage between different media markets. Third, we will describe similarities and differences between station owners. Overall, we hope to provide a comprehensive yet nuanced picture of what viewers of election news aired by Spanish-language television stations are likely to see.

## RESULTS

### Quantity of election coverage

Perhaps the most basic question is: How much coverage of U.S. elections did Spanish-language TV stations provide? Our results indicate that, at the network level, the answer depends on whether a viewer is watching Univisión or Telemundo, while at the local level the answer often depends on which media market a viewer resides in.

In terms of network coverage, election coverage comprised almost a quarter (22 percent) of all news coverage on Univisión but slightly less than one-sixth (14 percent) of Telemundo's network coverage. To put this in perspective, a typical Univisión half-hour broadcast contained six-and-one-half minutes of election coverage, while Telemundo aired just over four minutes. This is not only a statistically significant difference[10] but clearly a substantively significant difference as well given how much more information viewers can receive in an additional two-and-a-half minutes of news.

At the local news level, where race competitiveness is obviously more of a factor, the Miami stations aired substantially more coverage than either New York or Los Angeles. But, as noted above, the New York stations aired much more coverage than Los Angeles, despite having an arguably less competitive election environment. A typical half-hour local news broadcast in Miami contained just over four minutes of election news, compared with two-and-a-half minutes for a typical New York broadcast and slightly less than two minutes for a typical Los Angeles broadcast. All of these differences were statistically significant (see table 7.1). Unlike the networks, however, there are no significant within market differences between local Univisión and local Telemundo stations in terms of overall quantity of election stories.

Since viewers watch one news story at a time, it is also helpful to provide a sense of the length of an average election story. While the average length of an election story on Univisión's network was over 10 seconds longer than Telemundo's, the difference is not statistically significant. Similarly, there is no significant difference between all Univisión and Telemundo story lengths at the local level.

The results, however, show significant differences between media markets. Los Angeles had less overall election coverage than the other markets, in part because the average length of a story in Los Angeles was significantly shorter than stories in either New York or Miami. Once again, these differences are statistically significant.

In terms of ownership differences at the local level, the only significant difference occurred in New York where the Telemundo station aired longer stories on average than the Univisión station. Table 7.1 contains these results.

## What was covered

It is obvious that in a presidential election year, stories about the presidential race are likely to dominate coverage. This is especially true for

*Table 7.1* Quantity of 2004 election coverage on Spanish-language stations

| TV news outlet | % of all news time | Election coverage in a typical half hour* | Average story length** |
|---|---|---|---|
| Network news (n=205)[11] | 17.9 | 5:22 | 93 |
| Univisión (n=127) | 21.7 | 6:31 | 98 |
| Telemundo (n=78) | 13.7 | 4:06 | 86 |
| Local news (n=782) | 9.5 | 2:52 | 78 |
| All Univisión (n=395) | 9.5 | 2:51 | 77 |
| All Telemundo (n=387) | 9.6 | 2:53 | 79 |
| Local news by market[12] | | | |
| New York (n=254) | 8.7 | 2:36 | 81 |
| Los Angeles (n=191) | 6.3 | 1:54 | 67 |
| Miami (n=337) | 13.6 | 4:05 | 83 |
| Local news by market and owner[13] | | | |
| New York Univisión (n=133) | 7.6 | 2:18 | 73 |
| New York Telemundo (n=121) | 9.7 | 2:55 | 90 |
| Los Angeles Univisión (n=88) | 5.6 | 1:41 | 71 |
| Los Angeles Telemundo (n=103) | 6.3 | 1:53 | 63 |
| Miami Univisión (n=174) | 14.5 | 4:21 | 84 |
| Miami Telemundo (n=163) | 12.8 | 3:50 | 82 |

* in minutes and seconds    ** in seconds

network coverage, but is also true in local markets even if that market was not considered competitive at the presidential level. The balance between the presidential race, local races, and voting issue stories, however, provides additional detail about what viewers of local television news are likely to see.

The results show, not surprisingly, that the networks totally ignored local races. Somewhat more surprising, however, is that local Spanish-language television stations generally ignored local elections. The Univisión station in Miami devoted the most coverage to local races (10 percent of all stories). No other local station devoted more than 3 percent of its stories to local races. Both network and local news devoted many more of their stories to voting issues. Overall, slightly more than one out of ten (11 percent) network news stories focused on voting issues, while slightly more than two out of ten (21 percent) local news stories focused on voting issues.

Results at the market-level provide some insights into how local stations respond to the level of election competitiveness. To begin, given that Miami had more competitive local races to cover, we would expect that Miami's stations would cover local candidates more often than the other less competitive markets. This is clearly the case, as seen by the higher percentage of stories about local elections appearing in Miami than the other two markets. These results, not surprisingly, suggest that when their elections are competitive, stations cover local candidates.

But what happens when the stations do not have competitive races to cover? As noted above, the first response is simply to spend less time on elections. The results, however, show that the stations in Los Angeles and New York responded very differently to the lack of competitive races. In Los Angeles, the stations devoted roughly one-third (32 percent) of their stories to voting issues, significantly more than either of the other markets. In New York, the stations devoted more than three-quarters (76 percent) of their stories to the presidential race, also significantly more than the other markets. Essentially, with "nothing" to cover, the Los Angeles stations focused their election coverage on voting issues, while the New York stations focused their election coverage on the presidential race.

The results again suggest that ownership is important at the local level. As noted above, the Miami Univisión stations focused significantly more attention to local races than any other station, including its local Telemundo competitor. Correspondingly, the Miami Univisión station devoted significantly less attention to the presidential race than its Telemundo competitor. In New York, the Telemundo station devoted significantly more of its stories to voting issues than its Univisión competitor. In Los Angeles, however, there is no significant difference between the coverage provided by Univisión and Telemundo. Table 7.2 contains these results.

*Table 7.2* What was covered

| TV news outlet | % of stories about the presidential race | % of stories about local races | % of stories about voting issues |
|---|---|---|---|
| *Network news (n=205)*[14] | 80 | NA | 11 |
| Univisión (n=127) | 76 | NA | 11 |
| Telemundo (n=78) | 85 | NA | 10 |
| *Local news (n=782)* | 67 | 4 | 21 |
| All Univisión (n=395) | 65 | 6 | 21 |
| All Telemundo (n=387) | 70 | 1 | 21 |
| *Local news by market*[15] | | | |
| New York (n=254) | 76 | 2 | 19 |
| Los Angeles (n=191) | 52 | 1 | 32 |
| Miami (n=337) | 69 | 6 | 17 |
| *Local news by market and owner*[16] | | | |
| New York Univisión (n=133) | 79 | 3 | 14 |
| New York Telemundo (n=121) | 74 | 1 | 24 |
| Los Angeles Univisión (n=88) | 49 | 2 | 35 |
| Los Angeles Telemundo (n=103) | 55 | 0 | 30 |
| Miami Univisión (n=174) | 62 | 10 | 20 |
| Miami Telemundo (n=163) | 77 | 2 | 14 |

## How elections were covered

Numerous studies of campaign coverage by English-language stations show that stories tend to focus on campaign strategy and the horse race instead of substantive campaign issues (Cappella and Jamieson, 1997; Graber, 2005; Bartels, 1988 and 1993; Bennett, 2002). Our results indicate that the same generally holds true for Spanish-language television. In addition to looking at how stories were framed, we also examined how often the stations included a Latino perspective in their election stories.

At the network level, only a quarter of election stories (25 percent) focused on campaign issues while just under half (46 percent) focused on campaign strategy or the campaign horse race. The results indicate that while the Univisión network devoted more of its stories to substantive issues than Telemundo did (29 percent compared to 19 percent), the difference is only marginally significant. The Univisión network, however, was much more likely to include a Latino perspective in its network stories than Telemundo and the difference is statistically significant. Almost half of the stories on the Univisión network (44 percent) at least mentioned a Latino perspective, compared to less than a third (27 percent) of Telemundo's network stories.

At the local level, while significant market and ownership differences exist, the results suggest that they are less important than at the network level. Collectively, the local Univisión and Telemundo stations had identical breakdowns for strategy, issue and stories mentioning Latino issues. When we disaggregate the local news by market, none of the market-to-market or within market comparisons of ownership are significant in terms of percentage of stories about substantive issues. This suggests something of a ceiling in terms of issue-based coverage at the local level. The Los Angeles market, however, framed fewer stories as strategy and horse race coverage than the other markets (38 percent compared to 53 percent for New York and 62 percent for Miami). This can be partially explained by the high number of voting issue stories that appeared in Los Angeles. Voting issues tend to be counted in an "other" category since they do not directly address either issues or strategy, but the mechanics of voting. The only other significant market-to-market difference was that Los Angeles had significantly more stories that included a Latino perspective than Miami (36 percent compared to 29 percent). This difference, however, is again largely driven by the large number of Los Angeles stories about local (and hence Latino) voting issues.[17]

In terms of ownership at the local level, the results are conflicting. In New York, the Telemundo station included a Latino perspective in significantly more of its stories than its Univisión competitor, while the opposite was true in Los Angeles. The two Miami stations were virtually identical on this variable. Table 7.3 contains these results.

Table 7.3 How elections were covered

| TV news outlet | % of stories about strategy/ horserace | % of stories about substantive campaign issues | % of stories mentioning "Latino issues" |
|---|---|---|---|
| Network news (n=205)[18] | 46 | 25 | 38 |
| Univisión (n=127) | 43 | 29 | 44 |
| Telemundo (n=78) | 51 | 19 | 27 |
| Local news (n=782) | 53 | 21 | 31 |
| All Univisión (n=395) | 53 | 21 | 31 |
| All Telemundo (n=387) | 53 | 21 | 31 |
| Local news by market[19] | | | |
| New York (n=254) | 53 | 22 | 31 |
| Los Angeles (n=191) | 38 | 21 | 36 |
| Miami (n=337) | 62 | 20 | 29 |
| Local news by market and owner[20] | | | |
| New York Univisión (n=133) | 59 | 23 | 25 |
| New York Telemundo (n=121) | 47 | 22 | 37 |
| Los Angeles Univisión (n=88) | 39 | 17 | 46 |
| Los Angeles Telemundo (n=103) | 37 | 24 | 27 |
| Miami Univisión (n=174) | 57 | 22 | 28 |
| Miami Telemundo (n=163) | 67 | 17 | 29 |

## DISCUSSION AND FUTURE RESEARCH

Overall, the results of this research may, unfortunately, add new layers of complexity to the study of Latinos, the media and politics. Overall, our results clearly suggest that describing "Latino" media in some monolithic fashion is quite problematic. We found significant differences in how the Univisión and Telemundo networks cover elections and conflicting results with regard to ownership at the local level. In addition, we found often dramatic differences in local coverage between local media markets. In a very real sense, our results indicate that what viewers see about elections is dependent upon which station and in which market they are watching.

In terms of the network news, contrary to Dávila's (2000) analysis, Telemundo's election coverage was clearly not superior to that of Univisión. The Univisión network devoted more time to election coverage, focused more on substantive issues and was more likely to include a Latino perspective than the Telemundo network. Although Dávila's work looked at the networks' attempts to market themselves using different definitions of what it means to be "Latino" in America and not how this definition translates to the news and public affairs programming, it is clear that her findings do not hold up with respect to news content. Future research must take into account the fundamental differences that we present here. In many ways, these results set up the potential for a natural experiment for many of the effects questions so important to political communication scholars.

At the local level, the results show that station ownership is less important than at the network level in terms of the quantity of election coverage. On most measures of quantity, we failed to find significant differences between local stations grouped by ownership. The results, however, point to many significant differences in how local stations in the same market cover elections. Unfortunately, these differences did not follow a consistent pattern. For example, the Telemundo affiliate in New York City gave more attention to Latino issues than its Univisión counterpart. The opposite was true in Los Angeles and there was virtually no difference between the two Miami stations. On most other measures, the Univisión affiliate in Miami appeared to provide marginally better election coverage than its Telemundo counterpart; this was not the case in the other markets and even in Miami the differences were generally not significant. Clearly, the differences may not lie in station ownership but perhaps in station management. Again, future research should examine this aspect of election coverage using a larger sample of local media markets.

Part of the reason we failed to find consistent differences in ownership at the local level is because of the interesting and significant differences we found between markets. As expected, the competitiveness of elections in Miami led to more overall coverage by Miami's stations. The results, however, provide some indication that, in addition to providing less election coverage, local stations may employ different strategies when faced with an uncompetitive election environment. Our results show that the Los Angeles stations turned their attention to voting issue stories, while the New York stations chose to focus even more on the presidential race. In addition, our results show qualitative differences between markets that may or may not be related to electoral competitiveness, such as how often local stations include a Latino perspective in their stories.

In conclusion, while we found market and station variations, it is clear that the Spanish-language stations make a concerted effort to include a "Latino" perspective in their election stories. Almost four out of ten (38 percent) network election stories and just over three in ten (31 percent) local election stories included a Latino perspective. While perhaps not surprising, these results suggest that Spanish-language television has the potential to connect with and significantly influence its viewers about the U.S. elections. As the media literature indicates, a key factor in the media's ability to influence viewers is the extent to which the narrative and images portrayed connect with viewers on a personal level (DeFleur and Ball-Rokeach, 1989). The fact that Spanish-language stations clearly attempt to link their election news content to Latino issues suggests that

Spanish-language news may be quite influential in shaping the attitudes of Latino voters.

Finally, as Doris Graber argues in her seminal text, the media are "most persuasive when they involve aspects of life people only experience through the media" (Graber, 2001: 33). A sizable percentage of the audience of Spanish-language news may, in fact, only experience U.S. political campaigns through the media. This implies that Spanish-language television news has the potential to significantly influence the attitudes, political or otherwise, of its viewers. Of course, future research should attempt to test this idea as well as examine the broader question of effects in general. The results presented here, however, suggest that at least some of the conditions necessary for any media to have a significant influence on viewers' attitudes exist in the case of Spanish-language news media.

## NOTES

1 This research was supported by grants from the Pew Hispanic Center, the Norman Lear Center at the Annenberg School for Communication and the University of Wisconsin–Madison, Department of Political Science. We thank Ken Goldstein for helpful feedback.
2 Suro, 2004. See http://pewhispanic.org.
3 The individual stations and the capture rates for the news from these were as follows:

| Market (DMA) | Station call letters | Network affiliation | Video capture rate % |
| --- | --- | --- | --- |
| Los Angeles (2) | KVEA | Telemundo | 92.3 |
| Los Angeles (2) | KMEX | Univisión | 92.3 |
| Miami (15) | WSCV | Telemundo | 97.1 |
| Miami (15) | WLTV | Univisión | 98.9 |
| New York (1) | WNJU | Telemundo | 99.7 |
| New York (1) | WXTV | Univisión | 97.4 |

4 For more information, see www.commITonline.com.
5 It is, of course, possible that horse race coverage in very competitive races could help convey the importance of the race to prospective voters, which could improve turnout. In this paper, we take the more traditional approach of assuming substantive issue coverage is better for increasing voter knowledge.
6 The actual text of the question in the coding instrument reads: "Does the story discuss Latino/Hispanic interests?

    0  No
    1  Yes, Latino/Hispanic interests are mentioned but are not a primary focus
    2  Yes, Latino/Hispanic interests are a primary focus of the story"

No specific issues are labeled "Latino" or "Hispanic" in the coding instrument. The story itself must reference either Latino or Hispanic voters or issues in order to qualify as either mentioning them or focusing on them (i.e., "President Bush reached out to Latino voters today as part of his campaign stop . . .").

7 According to the 2000 U.S. Census (see http://factfinder.census.gov) Mexican Americans comprised 30.3% of all Hispanics/Latinos in the Los Angeles MSA and Cuban Americans comprised 18.1% of all Hispanics/Latinos in the Miami MSA. In comparison the largest Hispanic/Latino subgroup in the New York City MSA was Puerto Ricans at 6.3%.

8 Miami also had a highly contentious race for mayor.

9 See Cook Political Report, October 26, 2004

10 To test for statistical significance, we convert percentage of time about elections into percentages of all news stories that focus *primarily* on elections and compare them to all other news stories. We exclude stories that were secondarily but not primarily related to elections for this calculation only, since including secondarily focused election stories would artificially increase the percentage of news stories about elections in relation to stories primarily about other topics. In addition, we do not make distinctions between election stories about candidates and election stories that do not feature candidates (e.g. voting process stories, ballot initiatives, etc). It is likely that analysis using different specifications (e.g. using percentage of broadcast time and not percentage of news stories or including stories secondarily focused on elections or excluding voting process stories) might lead to different results. However, reporting these different specifications is beyond the scope of this chapter.

11 Statistical comparisons are made between percentage of all stories primarily focused on elections since many of the comparisons do not have multiple stations (e.g., network news and local market by owner). In most cases, the difference between percentage of time and stories is minimal; however, we report when significant differences appear in the two measurements. Fifteen percent of all network stories on Univisión were about elections compared to 11 percent for Telemundo. This difference was statistically significant ($t=2.566(1402)$, $p=.01$).

12 At a market-level unit of analysis, the stations in Los Angeles aired fewer stories than New York ($t=-2.527(5338)$, $p=.012$) and Miami ($t=-6.790(5018)$, $p=.000$). New York, in turn, aired fewer stories than Miami ($t=-4.295(5231)$, $p=.000$). The same pattern held in terms of average story length. Los Angeles averaged shorter stories than New York ($t=-2.442(441)$, $p=.015$) and Miami ($t=-3.021(493)$, $p=.003$). The difference in average story length between New York and Miami, however, was not statistically significant.

13 The only ownership difference that was even marginally significant at the local level was in New York on the average story length variable ($t=-1.869(252)$, $p=.063$).

14 Local Univisión stations aired fewer presidential stories than local Telemundo stations; however, the difference was only marginally significant ($t=-1.631(780)$, $p=.103$), and local Univisión stations aired significantly more local race stories ($t=3.452(570)$, $p=.001$).

15 The Los Angeles stations aired significantly fewer presidential stories than New York ($t=5.337(370)$, $p=.000$) and Miami ($3.732(370)$, $p=.000$). The New York stations aired significantly more presidential stories than Miami ($t=2.050(567)$, $p=.041$). Los Angeles also aired significantly fewer local stories than Miami ($t=-3.147(502)$, $p=.002$). The difference between Los Angeles and New York in terms of local race stories, however, was not significant. The New

York stations aired significantly fewer local stories than Miami (t=−2.695(564), p=.007). The Los Angeles stations aired significantly more voting issue stories than either market (LA vs. NYC; (t=3.336(364), p=.001); LA vs. Miami (t=3.921(328), p=.000). The difference in voting issues stories was not significantly different between New York and Miami.

16 The differences in the balance between presidential and local race stories was only significant in Miami, where the Univisión station devoted more stories to local races (t=2.854(264), p=.005) and significantly fewer stories to the presidential race (t=−3.056(333), p=.002). In terms of voting issues, the only significant difference between ownership at the local level was in New York, where the Telemundo station aired significantly more voting issues stories (t=2.127(230), p=.034).

17 In Los Angeles, 50 percent of all stories with a Latino perspective were also about voting issues. In New York the figure was 22 percent and in Miami it was just 15 percent.

18 The difference between Univisión vs. Telemundo network on percentage of stories about campaign issues was marginally significant (t=1.638(180), p=.103). The difference between the networks on percentage of stories mentioning Latino issues was significant (t=2.556(177), p=.011). To clarify, in making comparison about strategy and horserace and issue stories we (unlike our analysis of quantity of election stories) included all election stories even those coded as secondarily focused on elections. Once again, however, while we recognize that alternative specifications might lead to different results, exploring them is beyond the scope of this chapter.

19 The Los Angeles stations framed significantly fewer stories about campaign strategy than either New York (t=−3.280(415), p=.001) or Miami (t=3.415(169), p=.001). Miami framed significantly more of its stories around strategy than New York (t=2.087(537), p=.037). There were no significant differences between markets in the percentage of stories focused on campaign issues. In terms of percentage of election stories mentioning Latino issues the only significant market difference was between Los Angeles and Miami (t=1.671(375), p=.096).

20 The results show that marginally significant differences in percentage of strategy focused stories between stations occurred in New York where the Univisión station aired more strategy focused stories than Telemundo (t=1.846(252), p=.066) and in Miami where the Univisión station aired fewer strategy framed stories than Telemundo (t=−1.890(334), p=.060). There were no statistically significant differences between station owners on percentage of stories about campaign issues. In terms of percentage of election stories mentioning Latino issues the Univisión station in Los Angeles aired significantly more of these stories than the Telemundo stations (t=2.640(176), p=.009). The opposite was true in New York where the Telemundo station aired significantly more of these stories than the Univisión station (t=−2.135(242), p=.034).

# Section B

## The English-language media

# 8

# LATINO POLITICS IN GENERAL MARKET ENGLISH-LANGUAGE DAILY NEWSPAPERS: 1988–2004

*Federico A. Subervi-Vélez*

in collaboration with
*José Carlos Lozano* (1988 study)

As was stated in chapter 4, newspapers are by far the main *conveyers* of political news and information. That chapter also presented numerous characteristics of how Spanish-language dailies have covered presidential campaigns. Innumerable other writings have regularly documented how general market papers cover campaigns and politics. What has not received much attention is how general market newspapers cover Latino-related news during presidential campaigns.

In an effort to diminish that gap in the political communication literature, this chapter addresses the question: "How have the English-language daily newspapers presented political news related to Latinos during electoral campaigns?" The first section answers this question with an analysis of how five prestige daily newspapers—the *Los Angeles Times*, the *New York Times*, the *Miami Herald*, the *Chicago Tribune*, and the *San Antonio Express-News*—published headlines with Latino references during selected time periods from February through November 8, Election Day, in 1988. The second section addresses the question with a more in-depth analysis of how the *San Antonio Express-News* and the now defunct *San Antonio Light* covered the last three months of that year's campaign. The third section takes another look at Latino references in the headlines of the five aforementioned newspapers plus the headlines of the *Chicago Sun-Times* and the *New York Daily News*. The dates of the analysis of the third section are September 1 through the respective Election Day in 1992, 1996, 2000, and 2004. The chapter ends with a discussion of all these studies.

This chapter offers additional contextual information related to the political mobilization of the Hispanic community, especially regarding Latinos who have limited or no access to Spanish-language newspapers and, most importantly in this case, those who speak and read primarily English.

Numerous empirical studies of the political content of general market English-language newspapers in the United States have consistently overlooked whether and how that press covered Latinos running for office, and campaign stories and issues that could be considered of specific interest to Latinos.[1] The exception is one of our works (Schiffman and Subervi-Vélez, 2002), which analyzed selected general market media during the early campaign period in 1999. The other exception is the unpublished conference paper by Lozano (1989) based on part of the data presented here. A summary of the key findings of that analysis is presented in the second section of this chapter.

In contrast to the chapter on the Spanish-language press, omitted in this chapter are the histories of each of the studied newspapers or of the political/ideological leanings of their owners or publishers; that information has been amply discussed elsewhere.[2] Also found elsewhere are some of the stories about the rocky relationships some of these newspapers have had with minority communities in general or Latinos in particular.[3]

Nevertheless, three important issues merit reiteration. First, while the attention to Latinos has been increasing over the years, the general market media, including these newspapers, have historically lacked in the depth and attention paid to the minority communities, including Latinos, in their respective cities. Second, it is these newspapers, not necessarily the Spanish-language press, that are much more easily available to reading audiences. As was noted in chapter 3, there are few cities with Spanish-language dailies and even those few dailies are not always easily accessible to all Latinos. And, third, the English-language dailies are important for the political socialization of the population at large. This includes Latinos, especially those who speak (or read) only English or are bilingual and are interested in a fuller spectrum of the political happenings in their respective communities. What and how they cover pertaining to the political life of this component of the population may potentially affect Latinos' knowledge about, involvement in and mobilization during elections and other civic matters.

A separate yet related issue that merits attention is that the way in which the English-language media, in this case the daily newspapers, cover Latino candidates and issues may also influence how non-Latinos learn about and behave with respect to members of that group, their political candidates and concerns. Here we return to Graber's view that mass media "images are especially pervasive when they involve aspects of life that people experience only through the media" (1997: 3). Since most non-Latinos have very few opportunities to directly experience "Latino politics," it will be the English-language press (and other general market media) that will provide the mediated experience, if any at all.

In sum, the focus turns to the English-language press because it may contribute to Latinos' cognitions and actions about politics in general and about Latino politics in particular; and, also, because that press may contribute to how non-Latinos perceive political matters connected to Latinos. Studying English-language newspapers to assess if and how they cover Latino-related political news is therefore imperative for better understanding the dynamics of the American political reality that is inclusive of Latinos.

## ASSESSMENT OF THE HEADLINES IN 1988

The first section of this chapter takes a look back into history to present the key findings of a systematic and quantitative analysis of how five of the nation's elite newspapers—the *Los Angeles Times*, the *New York Times*, the *Miami Herald*, the *Chicago Tribune*, and the *San Antonio Express-News*—presented headlines with Latino references. These five were purposely selected because they are located in cities that had at the time of the study, and still have today, among the largest numbers and concentrations of Latinos. The specific focus on the headlines derives from the assumption that a Latino who is interested in politics and seeks any of these newspapers for political information will be particularly attracted to stories that have a reference to his/her ethnic background.[4] As discussed in chapters 1 and 3, Latino identity has persisted and remains vital enough for politicians and commercial marketers to target this group in distinctive ways. The headlines are the most prominent identifying part of a news item that would tell a Latino reader that such a news story is unmistakably related to his/her ethnic background.

Of course, any reader who is interested in politics is prone to read more than just the stories with headlines that have Latino references. The analysis of what the general political news stories present has been the subject of other studies and needs not be duplicated here (see, for example, Stempel and Windhauser, 1991). Also, the second section of this chapter offers a more detailed analysis of how two newspapers presented political stories with Latino content.

For this particular study, copies of the five papers published between January 1 and November 8, 1988, were coded and content analyzed following procedures similar to those used for the Spanish-language papers (see chapter 4).[5] And, as was the case in that chapter, the data analysis that follows focuses on selected findings from five distinctive time periods that were considered the most important for the campaign: the weeks around the major primaries (February 2–24 and then May 31–June 14), the weeks of the Democratic and Republican Party conventions (July 4–25 and August 1–22 respectively), and the final stretch of the campaign (September 1 through November 8, Election Day). While it is important and valuable to observe the whole campaign process, the chosen time periods adequately represent the dynamics of the 1988 elections. The units of observation were all the news stories, news-briefs, opinion columns, editorials, and editorial cartoons about or related to the 1988 campaign published during that time period.[6]

This section of the chapter presents the data about the Latino political reference in the headlines in 1988. Latino political reference implies there was a mention of Latinos, Latino candidates, Latino voters, and/or Latino organizations. Also included are headlines about issues identified as related specifically to the Hispanic community, such as the English-only ballot initiatives in various states. We also included headlines about the naming of Dr. Lauro Cavazos as Secretary of Education because most of the news stories about this historic first Hispanic member of the Presidential Cabinet alluded to the expected impact that would have on Bush receiving Hispanic votes in his own bid for the presidency. Headlines about the campaign in general, the candidates, or issues in which no mention was made about Latinos were excluded for the analysis of this chapter. Headlines about the normal duties and acts of Latino elected officials were also excluded.[7]

Table 8.1 indicates that, during the selected time periods, all five newspapers together published a total of 286 political campaign stories that had some Latino reference in the headlines. The newspaper with the most Latino-related political headlines was the San Antonio Express-News: 122. The Miami Herald published almost less than half as many: 68. The headlines in all the editions of the Los Angeles Times added up to 59. In contrast, with only 23 and 14 respectively, the New York Times and the Chicago Tribune had the fewest Latino-related political headlines.

Slightly more than half, 52 percent, of all the news were about the presidential campaign. But the distribution of presidential versus other campaigns with Latino references in the headlines varied by newspaper. The New York Times published twice as many Latino reference headlines regarding the presidential campaign than it did about other campaigns. The Los Angeles Times and the San Antonio Express-News also had more presidential Latino headline references than about other campaigns. At the Miami Herald, the opposite ratio was two of every five headlines, while at the Chicago Tribune the ratio was almost equal between the two types of story with Latino headline references.

More than just the general numbers and comparisons between newspapers, table 8.1 and the other tables from the data about the 1988 election also reveal the dismal number of Latino headline references during crucial periods of the campaign, such as the Super Tuesday primaries. At

Table 8.1 Number of news articles with distinctively Latino headlines by time period, presidential and other races, 1988

| Newspapers | Political race | Time periods 2/24 to 3/15 n | 5/31 to 6/14 n | 7/4 to 7/25 n | 8/1 to 8/22 n | 9/1/ to 11/8 n | Total n | [ n ] |
|---|---|---|---|---|---|---|---|---|
| Los Angeles Times | Presidential | 1 | 3 | 4 | 11 | 16 | 35 | [ 59 ] |
|  | Other | 1 | 4 | – | 1 | 18 | 24 |  |
| New York Times | Presidential | 2 | 2 | 2 | 6 | 3 | 15 | [ 23 ] |
|  | Other | 1 | 1 | – | – | 6 | 8 |  |
| Miami Herald | Presidential | 6 | 1 | 8 | 10 | 3 | 28 | [ 68 ] |
|  | Other | 10 | – | – | 7 | 23 | 40 |  |
| Chicago Tribune | Presidential | 1 | – | – | 3 | 2 | 6 | [ 14 ] |
|  | Other | 3 | – | – | – | 5 | 8 |  |
| San Antonio Express-News | Presidential | 4 | 3 | 21 | 16 | 21 | 65 | [ 122 ] |
|  | Other | 14 | 1 | 7 | 8 | 27 | 57 |  |
| All newspapers | Presidential | 14 | 9 | 35 | 46 | 45 | 149 | [ 286 ] |
|  | Other | 29 | 6 | 7 | 16 | 79 | 137 |  |

a time when Democratic presidential candidate Dukakis and Republican contender Bush were actively starting their courting of Latinos, especially community leaders for their respective campaigns, and during the times when Latino candidates themselves were vying for support in their local communities, these five newspapers in cities with large Hispanic populations printed very few headlines heralding the connection between those campaigns and Hispanics.

The few exceptions of this dismal headline referencing can be discerned from the coverage that the *San Antonio Express-News* provided during the convention periods for the Democratic Party, the Republican Party and then the final stretch of the campaign. In that newspaper there were also other non-presidential campaign stories with Latino-relevant headlines, such as when Latino civic and political activist, William C. Velasquez, passed away (June 15, 1988). A few stories focused on the implications that his absence from the political scenes would have on the Democratic Party's efforts to win Hispanic votes. In contrast, the *Chicago Tribune* did not publish any Latino headline references at all during the Democratic Party convention, and barely a handful during the rest of the campaign.

Another contrast in this overall analysis of the Latino-referent headlines is the disproportionate number of such headlines during the time of the Republican convention in comparison to the Democratic Party convention. Only the San Antonio newspaper had more Latino-referent headlines during the Democratic Party convention than during that of the GOP.

One of the reasons for the disparity favorable to the Republicans was President Reagan's selection in early August 1988 of Dr. Lauro Cavazos to become Secretary of Education. This "timely" selection made many headlines connecting then candidate Bush to potential Latino voters, precisely because of the courting of both Cavazos and other Latinos to be part of the GOP's "inclusion" efforts.

In the news about the presidential campaign, the main topics of the Latino-referent headlines—other than those about Cavazos—were about the candidates (including Jesse Jackson) and parties seeking the Latino vote. A parallel topic was the support that Latinos in general or a subgroup of Latinos might provide for one or the other candidates. A couple of references in the *Miami Herald* specifically mentioned Cubans' support for a candidate, i.e., Bush. One political headline in the *New York Times* alluded to Mexican Americans. All other references were the generic Hispanic or Latino; none directly mentioned Puerto Ricans. Headlines linking a presidential candidate or his party to particular Latino issues—such as immigration, employment, housing, discrimination, affirmative action, or education (other than when Cavazos was nominated and confirmed)—were also not found.

The plurality of the non-presidential race headlines with Latino references mentioned a Latino candidate's last name, his/her candidacy for a particular office, and/or the support s/he had from Latinos. For example, in the *Los Angeles Times*, Republican Gaddi Vasquez was mentioned in various headlines related to his candidacy and successful run for Orange County Supervisor. He was also mentioned for his role in the GOP convention. However, almost all of those headline mentions were printed only in the regional Orange County editions of the *Times*, not in any of the paper's other regional editions.

An important reference point of these first sets of Latino headlines vis-à-vis general campaign coverage emerges when our data are compared to the data presented by Stempel and Windhauser (1991) in their study of the coverage that 17 major newspapers gave the presidential campaign in 1988. That study included four of the five newspapers of our set, the exception being the *San Antonio Express-News*. Their table 3 (1991: 18) shows the number of presidential stories published during the last 64 days of that election period (Labor Day through the day prior to the election).

Upon calculating the proportion of the Latino-themed headlines we counted vis-à-vis the general news stories from Stempel and Windhauser's study, we observe that Latino references were less than three percent of the *Los Angeles Times'* presidential campaign stories (16 of 603), and less than half of one percent of the presidential news published by the *New York Times* (3 of 577), the *Miami Herald* (3 of 528), and the *Chicago Tribune* (2 of 401).

Presidential stories with Latino-references in the headlines were not only few, but also not featured in terms of the page locations. As shown in table 8.2, the vast majority were published on the inside pages. We also note on that table that most of the most recurrent of such headlines were about the Republicans. Three of the newspapers—the *New York Times*, the *Miami Herald*, and the *Chicago Tribune*—did not have any Democratic Party Latino-referent headlines on page 1 or on pages 2 or 3. Only the *San Antonio Express-News* and the *Los Angeles Times* offered front pages to Latino-referent headlines about both parties.

Of the few front-page Latino-related headlines, the most distinctive were about the nomination of Cavazos and references to how his appointment would affect the Hispanic vote for Bush. Dukakis' selection of Bensten for vice president did not get any Latino-referent headlines even though Bensten heralds from Texas where there are many Latino voters.[8] Non-presidential campaign stories with Latino-referent headlines were all published on inside pages. The one exception was a *New York Times'* page 1 story when Mayor Koch said he'd like a Hispanic running mate.

The arena where there were the most dismal headline references to Latinos and the presidential campaign or any other campaign issue was in

Table 8.2 Location and partisan orientation of news about the presidential campaign with Latino references, September 1–November 8, 1988

| Newspapers | Democratic Party related news | | | | Republican Party related news | | | | Both | | | |
|---|---|---|---|---|---|---|---|---|---|---|---|---|
| | page 1 | pp 2–3 | inside | total | page 1 | pp 2–3 | inside | total | page 1 | pp 2–3 | inside | total |
| Los Angeles Times | 2 | 1 | 6 | 9 | 5 | 1 | 15 | 21 | 1 | 1 | 2 | 4 |
| New York Times | – | – | 4 | 4 | 1 | – | 6 | 7 | – | – | 4 | 4 |
| Miami Herald | – | – | 10 | 10 | 3 | – | 10 | 13 | 1 | – | 3 | 4 |
| Chicago Tribune | – | – | 1 | 1 | – | 1 | 2 | 3 | – | – | 2 | 2 |
| San Antonio Express-News | 5 | 1 | 25 | 31 | 5 | 2 | 18 | 25 | 1 | – | 8 | 9 |
| All newspapers | 7 | 2 | 46 | 55 | 14 | 4 | 51 | 69 | 3 | 1 | 19 | 23 |

the opinion pages. As the almost empty table 8.3 illustrates, the editorials and opinion columns with Latino headlines, as well as the editorial cartoons with Latino references, were few and far between during the selected time periods of the 1988 election campaigns.

Once again, the San Antonio Express-News stands out as having published the most of any of the studied newspapers. English-speaking Latinos reading that newspaper would have thus found at least some direct Latino referent to the political campaign of that year. The other newspapers did not offer much in this rubric. Of particular notice for the absence of op-ed attention is the Miami Herald, which apparently defers political news and information about Latinos to its sister Spanish-language newspaper, El Nuevo Herald.

Most of the Latino-themed op-ed attention was drawn by Reagan's appointment of Cavazos. The op-ed columnists' support for Cavazos' merits was nevertheless framed in terms of the potential impact of his appointment on the Hispanic votes for Bush and the GOP. In San Antonio, Democratic Mayor Henry Cisneros' personal scandal (i.e., his extramarital affair) also brought attention as not only news but also opinion pieces focused on the consequences that could have on Democratic presidential contender Dukakis.

But the most notable op-ed Latino referents that year were about the English-only propositions in various cities and states. Such was the focus of most of the editorial and op-ed columns in the Miami Herald and the non-presidential campaign op-ed pieces in the Los Angeles Times. This received far more headline attention than the Hispanic outreach efforts and Spanish-speaking abilities of both Dukakis and Bush. Almost all the editorial comments were critical of the English-only propositions and laws. An opinion column by conservative Linda Chavez was among the exceptions in supporting those English-only propositions.

The editorial cartoon in the Los Angeles Times shows Bush in front of United States and Panamanian flags saying, "I pledge allegiance to the flag, to the United States of America, and the Republic of Panama with which we stand; Iran-Contra, through Noriega, covert aid, with cocaine and weapons for all." In the New York Times, one of the editorial cartoons lampooned the Republicans' "outreach" to Mexican Americans. It shows Reagan placing an oversized Mexican sombrero and Zapata-style mustache on Cavazos while Bush is in the background applauding. The other cartoon is critical of Dukakis' own outreach as he is shown bobbling in an M1 Tank while kissing a "Hispanic" baby. Two of the four editorial cartoons of the San Antonio Express-News, all by famed Latino cartoonist Lalo López, were critical of the GOP and Republicans. One showed the Republican candidates using sombreros to court Latino votes; another lampooned "Hispanic" delegates at the GOP convention. The other two cartoons, both published early in the campaign,

Table 8.3 Number of editorials (Ed), opinion columns (OC), and editorial cartoons (C) by time period, presidential and other races, 1988

| Newspapers | Political race | 2/24 to 3/15 Ed | OC | C | 5/31 to 6/14 Ed | OC | C | 7/4 to 7/25 Ed | OC | C | 8/1 to 8/22 Ed | OC | C | 9/1 to 11/8 Ed | OC | C | Total Ed | OC | C |
|---|---|---|---|---|---|---|---|---|---|---|---|---|---|---|---|---|---|---|---|
| Los Angeles Times | Presidential | – | – | – | – | 1 | – | – | 2 | – | – | – | – | – | 1 | – | – | 4 | – |
|  | Other | – | – | – | – | – | – | – | 2 | – | – | – | – | – | 4 | – | – | 6 | – |
| New York Times | Presidential | – | – | – | – | – | – | – | – | – | – | – | 1 | 1 | 1 | 1 | 1 | 1 | 2 |
|  | Other | – | – | – | – | – | – | – | – | – | – | – | – | 1 | – | – | 1 | – | – |
| Miami Herald | Presidential | – | – | – | – | – | – | – | – | – | – | – | – | – | – | – | – | – | – |
|  | Other | – | 1 | – | – | – | – | – | – | – | – | – | – | 1 | 4 | – | 1 | 5 | – |
| Chicago Tribune | Presidential | – | – | – | – | – | – | – | – | – | 1 | 1 | – | – | 1 | – | 1 | 2 | – |
|  | Other | – | – | – | – | – | – | – | – | – | – | – | – | – | – | – | – | – | – |
| San Antonio Express-News | Presidential | – | 1 | 2 | – | 1 | – | – | 2 | – | 1 | 6 | 2 | 2 | – | – | 3 | 10 | 4 |
|  | Other | – | – | – | – | 1 | – | – | – | – | – | – | – | 1 | 6 | – | 1 | 7 | – |
| All newspapers | Presidential | – | 1 | 2 | – | 2 | – | – | 4 | – | 2 | 7 | 3 | 3 | 3 | 1 | 5 | 17 | 4 |
|  | Other | – | 1 | – | – | 1 | – | – | 2 | – | – | – | – | 3 | 14 | – | 3 | 18 | – |

were critical of politicians in general for their lack of understanding of Latinos.

Overall, during the 1988 campaign, the elite newspapers in the five major metropolitan cities with large Latino populations did not feature many headlines in the news or the opinion pages connecting the presidential or other campaigns with Latinos or with issues we could identify as distinctively Latino. This limited attention to Latinos and Latino issues is a direct reflection of the few stories on such matters. However, it does not mean that there were no references to Latinos in political news stories that did not have Latino headlines. We know first hand that there were stories that, as part of the text, alluded to Latinos and Latino issues. The point is that evidently this population, and issues distinctively relevant to them, were either not the main topic of the stories or were not recurrently highlighted in the headlines. Part of the reason for the limited focus on Latinos and Latino issues in the headlines may lie in the respective candidates or their media managers who did not emphasize Latinos or Latino issues. Yet it also may be the result of editorial policies that gear those headlines more to generic topics than to particular ethnic populations or references. Latinos seeking ethnic-references to inform and mobilize them to vote would not have easily found those, at least not in the headlines of most of the studied papers.

## FOCUS ON THE SAN ANTONIO NEWSPAPERS IN 1988

While some of the U.S. cities with larger Latino populations have one or more daily Spanish-language newspapers, in 1988 San Antonio did not have any; nor did it have any Hispanic-owned English-language newspaper catering for the informational needs of the local Latino community, most of whom speak English (89 percent according to the 1986 *Hispanic Almanac*). At the time, Mexican Americans[9] in that city had to rely on the two English-language dailies—the *San Antonio Express-News* and the *San Antonio Light*[10]—to receive information about the issues and candidates important to them. The lack of alternative newspapers covering the 1988 election from Hispanic angles on a daily basis made the Latino community more dependent on those two newspapers and even amplified the importance of these as the main political forum for Latino candidates and issues.[11]

While the question of the actual role of these papers in shaping the political attitudes and perceptions of Mexican Americans was not addressed, this section provides basic information about the extent and nature of the news coverage relevant to the San Antonio Latino community. If one considers the role of the press in a given community to be a public forum where all major groups obtain access and express their concerns and viewpoints, then it would be expected from the two newspapers to provide substantial coverage of issues and candidates relevant to 41 percent of their city's total population. The lack of access to and information about this ethnic group, on the other hand, would elicit serious doubts about how fair and representative those dailies were in the political process.

Using the same data set from which the headline study was derived—but concentrating only on the final election period (September through November)—this section of the chapter assesses all the political messages with at least a passing mention of Hispanic topics or candidates in all issues of the *Express-News* and the *Light*.[12] No attempt was made to define *a priori* which would be the most relevant Hispanic issues. A list of them was compiled according to the particular topics mentioned by candidates (either Latinos or Anglos), journalists or any other source in the political messages with Latino mentions. Hispanic candidates were mostly identified by their surnames and/or ethnic references in the political messages.

News about Hispanic politicians acting as public officials and not as candidates was not included for analysis. For example, news about Henry Cisneros' performance as mayor of San Antonio with no references to electoral issues or activities was not included. Neither were news stories included about the activities of Albert Bustamante or Henry B. Gonzalez as Congressmen, unless in the context of their re-election campaigns or other electoral issues such as endorsing candidates or criticizing Republican candidates. News messages about Anglo candidates were included in the study only when they made explicit references to Hispanic topics or candidates. General political messages about Anglo candidates or issues with no mentions to Latino topics or candidates were not included in the analysis.

In cases where the political message was not devoted completely to Latino topics or candidates (i.e., if 80 percent of it was devoted to Anglo candidates and issues, and only 20 percent referred to Hispanic issues or candidates), the news story as a whole continued to be the unit of analysis for all variables, with the exception of the topic and the size of the Latino mention. For determining the topic and size of mention, the unit of analysis was the specific sentence or sentences referring to Hispanic issues or candidates. Thus, if 60 percent of a news story was devoted to Anglo candidates or issues, and 40 percent was devoted to Latino candidates or issues, the latter 40 percent was the unit of analysis for determining the topic and the mention's size.

## General patterns of coverage

Overall, the *San Antonio Light* and the *San Antonio Express-News* had similar patterns in their campaign coverage of topics and issues relevant to the Mexican American/Latino community. The kind of Latino topics that were mentioned most often in both newspapers were primarily related to "campaign activities" (e.g., debates, endorsements of candidates, appeals to Hispanic voters, and fundraising, rallies), and the "horse race" (e.g., Latino candidates' places vis-à-vis other non-Latino or Latino candidates, results indicated by polling organizations, and speculation about possible candidacy by a politician), with occasional personality profiles of Mexican American candidates by opinion columnists.

This pattern was consistent—whether the news was about the presidential campaign or about the local and regional campaigns in San Antonio and Texas. In the presidential coverage, references about Latinos in news articles about the Bush–Dukakis race were made in the context of campaign activities (e.g., Dukakis speaking to a Mexican American audience), or results of polls predicting Hispanic votes for each candidate. Many of these messages about campaign activities mentioned Hispanics only briefly.

In fact, the profiles by opinion columnists of Latino local and state candidates were more frequent than the discussion of issues of either the local or national races. Discussion of Latino issues like education, employment, discrimination, economic development opportunities, and housing was not predominant in the news items: only 15 percent of all *Express'* messages and 6 percent of the *Light'*s dealt with issues relevant to the Mexican American community. These issues were not presented frequently in any type of message, not even in opinion columns or editorials.[13]

However, the *San Antonio Light* provided more *analytical* and interpretative coverage of electoral races or issues relevant to Mexican Americans than the *San Antonio Express-News* because it discussed Latino issues or candidates in opinion columns and editorials. While 25 of the *Light's* total number of political messages were opinion columns, the *Express* included only 14 opinion columns in the same period. Similarly, the *Light* published 9 editorials while the *Express* included only 3.

Less than a handful of editorials in both newspapers dealt sympathetically and sensitively with fundamental Latino issues. For example, in a September 15 editorial the *Express* referred to the GOP courting of the Latino vote, and raised doubts about that party's sincerity in its task force recommendations to tackle the most pressing problems relevant to the Hispanic community. After blasting Texas Republicans for their endorsement of the "ethnocentric, xenophobic" Official English proposal earlier in the year, the editorial praised Bush's position against that movement and the nomination of Dr. Lauro Cavazos as Education Secretary. Another example is from the *Light*, where an op-ed piece by Jesse Treviño, a columnist and member of the editorial board of the *Austin American-Statesman*,[14] stressed that issues like the environment, education, and AIDS were essential both to Hispanics and to average working Americans. Unfortunately, according to Treviño, neither Bush nor Dukakis were addressing these issues in their campaigns.

## Information about Hispanic candidates

As in the case of the presidential candidates' coverage, both papers con-centrated on reporting the Latino candidates' campaign activities and their place vis-à-vis other candidates; there was minimal or no informa-tion at all about their points of view on the most important issues for the Latino community. While the *Express* tended to provide slightly more information about the stand of Hispanic candidates running for sheriff, mayor, and U.S. representative on different issues, the percentage was still very low. In their Latino electoral coverage, neither daily seemed to redress the traditional neglect of general issues in the U.S. press coverage of any electoral processes.

For example, although U.S. representatives Henry B. Gonzalez and Albert Bustamante made the news many times during the three-month period, they were not covered as candidates stating their position on issues, or performing specific campaign activities. Rather, they made the news as politicians who endorse other candidates, or as public officials performing their job. In the whole period, there was no news story about Jerome L. Gonzalez, the Mexican American Republican opponent of Bustamante, or about the campaigns of the then incumbent state repre-sentatives Orlando Garcia, Gregory Luna, Ciro Rodriguez, and Dan Morales. Perhaps because these candidates were not running against Republican candidates but against Libertarians, the papers decided they were not newsworthy. Consequently, Latino readers of both newspapers did not receive information about the incumbents' recent agenda, position on issues, or campaign activities.

## Anglo candidates in Latino political messages

Finally, Anglo candidates were as likely as Latino contestants to get into the political messages with Latino references. Almost half the candidates about whom the news had some Latino reference in the text of the news were Anglos. However, more than 90 percent of these political mes-sages (Anglo candidates talking about Latino topics) were about the presidential hopefuls, Bush–Quayle and Dukakis–Bentsen, not about state or local Anglo candidates. The presidential contenders and Mexican American office-seekers, thus, seemed to have similar access in both newspapers to express their points of view to Latino voters or inform them about their campaign activities.

No political messages printed in either newspaper about the 56 state and local Anglo candidates (Democrats and Republicans) included even passing mentions of Hispanic topics. This finding implies either that the vast majority of state and local Anglo candidates were not addressing topics or issues relevant to the Latino community, or that both papers' reporters failed to mention these candidates' concerns about Hispanics.

## National coverage of Latino politics

The campaign coverage of Latino topics or candidates outside Texas was almost non-existent. Mexican American or other Latino readers of both papers were not able to know what was going on in other regions with large Latino populations, such as California, Florida, Illinois, and New York. Only three stories in the *Express* and four in the *Light* had datelines in other parts of the country outside Texas. Only Washington was somewhat present in the *Express* coverage as a result of opinion columns sent by its own correspondent Bruce Davidson, who wrote op-ed pieces regularly about either the presidential race or the Texan incumbent candidates to the U.S. Congress (Henry B. Gonzalez and Albert Bustamante). It could be said that both newspapers did a poor job as sources of information for the San Antonio Latino community regarding the political participation and development of Latinos in other parts of the country.

This does not imply that readers of the *San Antonio Express-News* or the *San Antonio Light* were only able to obtain information about Anglo or general issues. Many studies have consistently found that issues— either ethnic or non-ethnic—are very frequently left out from electoral coverage. Thus, while quantitatively news messages about issues relevant to Latinos were not abundant in either newspaper, references to them did indeed exist and sympathy for them expressed.

One of the conclusions that can be drawn from this in-depth analysis of these two San Antonio newspapers is that, even in a city where practically half of the population is Hispanic, the political coverage of Latino candidates and issues was, at best, lackluster even during the final months of the 1988 campaign. Whether this was a reflection of few Latino candidates, the limited attention to Latino issues offered by non-Latino candidates, or the newspapers' own editorial policies, it remains the case that Latinos seeking ethnic references to inform and mobilize them to vote would not easily have found them in San Antonio that year.

## ASSESSMENT OF HEADLINES DURING THE 1992–2004 CAMPAIGNS

The assessment of the English-language newspapers during the 1988 election was a historic first in revealing the patterns of the coverage of news with Latino references during an election year. Still, how typical were those patterns in subsequent elections? This section provides a partial answer with an assessment of the headlines of seven English-language newspapers during four additional campaign periods: September 1 through the corresponding election days: November 3, 1992; November 5, 1996; November 7, 2000, and November 2, 2004. The focus here is the same five prestige dailies studied for section one, plus two tabloids: the *Chicago Sun-Times* and the *New York Daily News*.[15] These two newspapers were added to the study because they are tabloids that have large readerships among Latinos.[16]

For this part of the study, only the electronic archives of these newspapers were scrutinized.[17] The first step was searching for all the stories that within the aforementioned time frames included the terms "Hispanic OR Latino," the terms "Hispanic OR Latino AND vote," the terms "Cuban AND vote," or "Mexican American AND vote."[18] Then, all the headlines and abstracts[19] of the stories that the respective archives listed upon searching for these terms were read to identify all the news related to the presidential campaigns of those years, and for stories about other political campaigns, including referendums taking place in the state or city. Only political stories that had headlines that referred to Latinos were categorized and analyzed as indicated below.

Table 8.4 shows the consistent scarcity of political headlines with Latino references during the final months of the four studied elections. While few definitive patterns can be discerned from that data, it can be noted that the newspapers in Miami, Los Angeles, and San Antonio offer their readers more stories with the Latino references than is the case for the newspapers in New York or Chicago.

The higher number of Latino referent headlines in the *Miami Herald* reflects the coverage given to Democratic mayoral candidate Alex Peneles in the elections in 1996 and 2000, and the mayoral and Senate races in 2004. The Republican victor of that latter race, Mel Martínez, became the first Latino federal senator from Florida. Also, during the presidential elections, there were at least a handful of headlines alluding in some way to how the local Cuban community supported or opposed one or both of the presidential candidates and these candidates' stands with respect to some issues (usually how to deal with Castro's Cuba) that were of interest to the city's Cubans.

In the *San Antonio Express-News*, the relevant headlines also alluded to how the local Latinos supported one or the other presidential candidates or the efforts of these candidates to reach (sometimes in Spanish) to Latinos. Mexican Americans running for local office were also featured in headlines in 1992 and 1996, but the archival search did not reveal similar headlines in 2000 or 2004.

The Latino references in the *Los Angeles Times* reflected particularly the coverage given to the efforts to register Latinos in 1992, 1996, 2000, and

Table 8.4 Number of political news stories (including editorials and opinion columns) with distinctively Latino headlines: Sept 1–Nov 1, 1992; Sept 1–Nov 5, 1996; Sept 1–Nov 7, 2000; and Sept 1–Nov 2, 2004

| Newspapers | Political race | 1992 | | | 1996 | | | 2000 | | | 2004 | | | Total | | |
|---|---|---|---|---|---|---|---|---|---|---|---|---|---|---|---|---|
| | | D | R | D/R | D | R | D/R | D | R | D/R | D | R | D/R | D | R | D/R |
| Los Angeles Times | Presidential | 2 | | 1 | | | | 1 | 1 | 1 | 1 | 2 | 2 | 3 | 3 | 4 |
| | Other | 2 | | 8 | 1 | | 8 | | 2 | 13 | | | | 3 | 2 | 29 |
| New York Times | Presidential | | | | | 1 | | | 2 | 1 | | | 1 | | 3 | 2 |
| | Other | 3 | 1 | 5 | | | 2 | | | 2 | | | | 3 | 1 | 9 |
| New York Daily News | Presidential | | NA | | | NA | | 1 | | 1 | 1 | 1 | 1 | 1 | 1 | 2 |
| | Other | | NA | | | NA | | | | 1 | | | 2 | | | 3 |
| Miami Herald | Presidential | | 3 | | 3 | 2 | 1 | 3 | 3 | 2 | 2 | 5 | 6 | 8 | 13 | 9 |
| | Other | 1 | 1 | 1 | 5 | | 10 | 5 | 2 | 3 | 3 | 6 | 11 | 14 | 9 | 25 |
| Chicago Tribune | Presidential | | | | 1 | 2 | | | 2 | 1 | 1 | | 2 | 2 | 4 | 3 |
| | Other | | | 2 | 1 | | 2 | 1 | | | | | 3 | 2 | | 7 |
| Chicago Sun Times | Presidential | 1 | 1 | 2 | 1 | | | | 1 | | | | | 2 | 2 | 2 |
| | Other | 1 | | 2 | | | 1 | | | | | | | 1 | | 3 |
| San Antonio Express-News | Presidential | 3 | 8 | 1 | 1 | | 1 | 4 | 2 | 3 | | | 2 | 8 | 10 | 7 |
| | Other | | | 4 | 5 | | 3 | | | | | 1 | 1 | 5 | 1 | 8 |
| All | Presidential | 6 | 12 | 4 | 6 | 5 | 2 | 7 | 11 | 9 | 5 | 8 | 14 | 24 | 36 | 29 |
| | Other | 7 | 3 | 22 | 12 | | 26 | 6 | 4 | 19 | 3 | 6 | 17 | 28 | 13 | 84 |

D = Democratic Party/candidate; R = Republican Party/candidate; D/R = Both parties/candidates or other issues; NA = Not available in electronic archives

2004, the debates regarding proposition 209 in 1996, and the GOP's efforts to win Latino votes in 2000 and 2004.

The GOP's Latino outreach efforts also received headlines in other newspapers in 2000 and 2004. Latino outreach efforts, especially with Spanish-language advertisements, were given headlines in other years, too. However, of particular notice was the story with the headline "Bush Understands Needs of Hispanics," published in the Chicago Sun-Times on November 3, 2000. The byline of that story—which might have been an opinion column[20]—was by Roberto de Posada, a Hispanic who for years has been promoting Republican causes from within the Republican National Committee and/or other conservative organizations (see Santillán and Subervi-Vélez, 1991). In that paper, not a single other headline discernable via our search procedure alluded to Latinos and politics.

One final note about the Latino references in the headlines in these four election periods: 90 percent were published in the inside pages of their respective newspapers. Only the Miami Herald regularly offered page A1 stories with Latino referent headlines. Six of the thirteen page A1 stories of this type were about Peneles' mayoral campaign and election; the others were about the presidential campaigns. Two of the three headlines connecting the Republican presidential candidates and Latinos were on page A1 in 2000; that same year none of the three stories connecting the Democratic presidential candidates and Latinos were on page A1. In 2004, five additional Latino-referent political headlines appeared on page A1 of this paper. Three of those headlines were about the presidential campaign; two of these referred to the efforts by both Kerry and Bush to woo Latinos, the other mentioned Kerry's lead among Latinos in national polls.

Only two other newspapers published page A1 stories with Latino references. The San Antonio Express-News had three page A1 stories (one regarding Hispanics' involvement with the GOP in 1992, and two about the potential impact of the Hispanic vote in 1996 and then again in 2000). The Chicago Tribune had one A1 story in 1996, and that was regarding Victor Morales "Quixotic" campaign in Texas for the U.S. Senate. In the Los Angeles Times one Latino-referent political headline in 2004 made the front page; the rest that year and previous years were on inside pages. And in the San Antonio Express-News there were no page A1 Latino-referent political headlines, although various such headlines were published on page B1 or Metro 1, as was the case in the Los Angeles Times. Still, the most common location of most of the Latino-referent political headlines in practically all the newspapers was the inside pages.

## DISCUSSION

The findings of these various studies, limited as they may be, offer some important perspectives about the characteristics of the political news presented in the English-language daily newspapers in the five metropolitan cities with the largest Latino populations in the country, and especially with respect to San Antonio, Texas.

The first general finding that merits being stressed is the scant number of political news with Latino references in the headlines. Latino or non-Latino readers of the studied newspapers would find it hard to know from just scanning through the headlines of those papers that there are stories pertaining to Latinos in the context of national or local political campaigns.

Second, the vast majority of the stories with Latino references are placed on the inside pages of their respective papers. Only the *Miami Herald* stands out—relative to the other papers—with more frequent page A1 stories with Latino references in the headlines. In that newspaper and in most of the others, Republicans have an edge in the more favorable page A1 placement of stories that connect them to Latinos. That said, both the *Miami Herald* and the *Los Angeles Times* occasionally did place Latino-referent stories (especially about local elections and Latino candidates) on the first pages of their respective metro or neighborhood sections.

Third, the headlines' references to Latinos were hardly ever about distinctively "Latino issues" such as immigration, employment, housing, discrimination, affirmative action, or education. If in the actual texts of the news these issues were addressed, they were mentioned in hardly any headline. The exceptions again were the less than a handful of stories about Republican presidential candidates' efforts to win Latino (i.e., Cuban) votes in Florida.

In quantitative terms, the detailed analysis of the two English-language newspapers in San Antonio in 1988 also revealed the inadequacy of the coverage of political stories related to Latinos. In fact, while the two dailies in that city at the time were printing an average of 10 political messages per day, only 1.6 out of that number included at least a passing mention of Latino topics or candidates. This means that in a city where Latinos constituted 41 percent of the total population in 1988, there should have been more coverage of the electoral process including Latino perspectives.

The assessment of the coverage of the presidential race, in particular, showed that Latino topics were mentioned primarily in the context of the horse race or campaign activities; there seemed to be only scant coverage of Hispanic issues in political messages about the presidential race. The stories reflected the presidential candidates' lack of concern for the discussion of the issues as well as the newspapers' failure to include the issues in the news. A similar pattern was observed in the coverage of local Latino candidates in San Antonio. Those stories focused primarily on their campaign activities or on the horse race they faced. Out of 20 Mexican American Democratic and two Republican candidates running in the November 1988 election, only four Democrats and one Republican were the subject of specific political messages. The neglect of the other Hispanic hopefuls may have had more to do with the general indifference of the press toward minor political races (or toward those races of incumbents without opponents), than with a specific "discriminatory" neglect of Latino candidates because of their ethnic background. Nevertheless, the findings suggest that the readers of *San Antonio Light* and the *San Antonio Express-News* in 1988 were more likely to find information about debates, endorsements, fundraising activities, and results of polls, than about social, political or economic issues relevant to their own Hispanic community.

Very similar patterns were observed while reading through the abstracts of the stories of the other newspapers assessed in 1992, 1996, 2000 and 2004. Even though only the stories with relevant headlines were categorized and briefly analyzed for this chapter, it was repeatedly evident from the abstracts that stories about Latinos/Hispanics and politics did not focus much at all on issues. The abstracts also suggest that even fewer stories were about political matters related to Latinos in cities or states outside the local area covered by the papers.

The most positive finding stemming from the detailed analysis of the two San Antonio newspapers is that, although the quantity of political messages devoted to the discussion of Hispanic issues was low, there was occasional genuine interest in addressing several issues relevant to the papers' Mexican American readers. For example, the *San Antonio Light* quoted Hispanic political activists' criticisms of the lack of issues in the electoral campaigns, and provided a forum for issues put forward by Mexican American women. The *Express-News* criticized Republicans for advocating an English-only proposal, and for their lack of sensitivity towards Hispanics in Texas. Regular opinion articles by Hispanic columnists, such as Jesse Treviño, Richard Estrada, Kathy Sosa, and Fernando Piñón, in the op-ed section of both newspapers also reflected some consistent editorial policies geared towards taking into account Latino perspectives in the political coverage. For example, Lynnell Burkett, editor of the *Light*'s op-ed section, devoted several of her columns to praise Hispanic activists such as Andy Hernández, who at the time was director of the Southwest Voter Registration and Education Project, and Maria Berriozabal, a Mexican American who was serving as councilwoman in San Antonio.

Lacking the more in-depth analysis of all the English-language newspapers during these and other election campaigns, we cannot address whether or not these papers provided their readers with the same or better attention to Latino political issues than is evident from the analysis of just the headlines and the reading of the abstracts of the stories yielded by the searches of the electronic archives. But if across these and subsequent election periods the patterns revealed by the headlines, the abstracts, and the critical in-depth analysis of the San Antonio newspapers are the norm, then we can affirm that the coverage—with or without headlines with Latino references—is still very lackluster and inadequate.

Of course, information about the horse race and campaign activities fulfills important roles in any political process. What is being argued here is not that these topics should have been replaced by political messages about Latino issues, but that the readers of these major English-language dailies should also receive more regularly during political campaigns information about the most important issues being faced by Latinos and their respective communities. If we can assume that the patterns observed in the San Antonio papers in 1988 apply to other papers in other years, we would conclude that the vast majority of news stories and op-ed pieces were not necessarily about education, employment, housing, and discrimination, or about the candidates' position on them. While other studies about political communication in the mainstream media have found a similar neglect of issues in general U.S. electoral processes (e.g., Graber, 1984), the severe problems still facing Latinos (e.g., poverty, lack of decent housing, discrimination, and unemployment) accentuate that neglect.

We are the first to acknowledge that each of these English-language newspapers certainly published political campaign stories that did not have references to Latinos in the headlines, yet addressed issues about Latinos. Still, the need for better Latino political communication coverage cannot be overstated. In 1988, English-speaking Mexican Americans in San Antonio had no other printed medium—aside from the two aforementioned newspapers—for obtaining on a daily basis information about the candidates and issues relevant to their community. Nowadays, it is only one such English-language medium—the *Express-News*. In Chicago, neither the *Tribune* or the *Sun-Times* seem to have dedicated much space to Latino-related stories during campaigns; the same applies to the two studied newspapers from New York.

For English speaking Latinos in those cities, as is the case for all other English speaking Latinos across the county, being properly informed about politics, especially from a vantage point of their Latino community, is crucial for their political mobilization and participation and even more essential for democratic processes at the national, state, and local levels. Furthermore, it could be contended that Anglo readers also need to have information about the political perspectives and actions of such a vital segment of the population. After all, Latinos residing in the five sites studied and all across the country are constantly exposed through all mainstream media to issues and candidates that may or may not be of particular relevance to them.

Many questions remain unanswered about the quantity and quality that English-language newspapers provide about political communication news and information related to Latinos. The following chapter offers another analysis that confirms part of what was observed with the three studies summarized here. Still, many more contemporary studies are needed about the actual impact of English-language media's political communication on Latino audiences.

## NOTES

1 Little attention has also been paid to how the general market press covers African Americans or, for that matter, members of other ethnic minority groups, running for office.

2 The history, political economy and additional background information about the main U.S. newspapers and other media are also easily found in other sources; see Altschull (1984, 1995), Bagdikian (2004), Bennett (1992, 2001), Gans (1979), Herman and Chomsky (2002), Schudson (1978, 1995). Also omitted, because of the ample discussion elsewhere, are the axioms, theories, and justifications that validate performing content analysis of politics in the press in general; see, for example, Hofstetter (1981), and Stempel and Windhauser (1991).

3 See, for example, de Uriarte (1996), Santa Ana (2002), Subervi-Vélez et al. (1994), Wilson and Gutiérrez (1995), Wilson, Gutiérrez, and Chao (2003).

4 This section of the chapter was written in 2004, long after the data had been originally collected in 1988. Because of various transfers of data from different computer systems and other problems, there was a loss of valuable components of the data set that would have allowed for a more extensive analysis of more than just the headlines—such as is presented for two papers in section 2 of this chapter—for all five of these newspapers.

5 The coding instrument allowed for notations of, among other things: (a) newspaper, (b) date, (c) section, (d) page, (e) location on page, (f) headline size and rank, (g) text size and rank, (h) number of photos, (i) article type, (j) news source of article, (k) geographic location of news, (l) type of political race, (m) candidate or party, (n) candidate's ethnicity, (o) topic of the political message, and (p) specific ethnic (e.g., Latino) topic of the story and the proportionate amount of space (relative to the rest of the story) dedicated to the Latino angle. In addition, the headlines were copied and entered into computer data files for subsequent analysis.

6 All the coding, not just of the headlines but of the complete articles of all of the 1988 newspapers, was done by the same team of research assistants who helped with the coding of the Spanish-language dailies: Rosa Acero, Lisa Acosta, Suzanne Avellano, Lorena Castellanos, María Denney, Daniel Escalzo, Karen Gavin, Tony Ozuna, Prisi Quijada, and Susana Quintero, who at the time were students at the University of California at Santa Barbara. I reiterate

my gratitude to them for their work, especially to Ms. Quintero who took on supervisory responsibilities during the time I was in Brazil on a Fulbright Research grant.

7  Headlines referring to the candidates' functions as public officials and not as candidates running for office, even if these individuals were Latinos, were also excluded from the analysis.

8  The two page 1 headlines in the *Los Angeles Times* referred to (a) Dukakis lauding immigrants upon his visit to Ellis Island during a campaign stop, and (b) Jackson's critique of Bush's racism.

9  Because the Latino community of San Antonio is predominantly of Mexican heritage, for this section of the chapter we interchangeably use the terms Latino, Hispanic, and Mexican American.

10  The *San Antonio Light* was an afternoon daily. It ceased publication on October 6, 1992. For a brief history of this paper, see the Texas State Historical Association's web site at http://www.tsha.utexas.edu/handbook/online/articles/view/SS/ees5.html. For a brief history of the *San Antonio Express-News*, see http://www.tsha.utexas.edu/handbook/online/articles/view/SS/ees3.html.

11  Points of discussion mentioned specifically by candidates, journalists or other sources in the political message as relevant to the Latino community, such as education, housing, employment, health, abortion, human rights and so on.

12  The same research team mentioned in note 6 did the coding of these two newspapers. The analysis and unpublished paper upon which this section is derived was written in 1989 when the data sets for these newspapers were complete and had not been damaged (see note 4 above). At the time, the *San Antonio Light* was also still in circulation and a very important source of news and information in that city.

13  Again, this neglect of issues is in tune with the general lack of attention on the part of newspapers to issues in general campaigns detected by other scholars. Since this study did not look at non-Latino political messages, it is difficult to determine whether the neglect of Hispanic issues corresponded with a neglect of issues in general in either of the San Antonio newspapers.

14  Both the *Light* and the *Express* published Treviño's articles frequently. Also, the *Light* included in its op-ed pages articles by other Hispanic columnists, like Richard Estrada, an editorial staff writer and columnist for the *Dallas Morning News*, and Kathy Sosa, a local Hispanic media consultant. The *Express* had also some other Latino columnists, like Fernando Piñón.

15  The electronic archives of *New York Daily News* start in 1997. Thus, only data for the year 2000 and 2004 are shown for this paper.

16  There are no comparable tabloids in Miami or San Antonio. Following the procedures listed elsewhere in this section, a search of the electronic archives of the *Los Angeles Daily News* did not produce a single relevant story.

17  This particular study was done by searching only the electronic archives of the newspapers during the specific dates indicated above: September 1 through the corresponding Election Day in 1992, 1996, 2000 and 2004. Each particular archive has its own different search options that yield different amounts of information. For example, the *San Antonio Express-News* electronic archive allows for searches of headlines, headlines and lead, or full text—a feature not available in any other paper. Some archives but not all of them allow for specifying which section of the paper is searched: news, opinion, classified, etc. The search engine of the *Miami Herald* does not indicate whether or not an item that fits the search parameters is a news item, an opinion column, or an editorial. That distinction is also not evident in the stories identified by the

search engine of the *San Antonio Express-News*, the *New York Daily News* or the two Chicago newspapers.

18 The specific procedure varied depending on the search options of each newspaper's electronic archives. But, for all newspapers, the headlines and abstracts that were generated with the search of these terms were read in order to identify stories with headlines that included any possible reference to Latinos and the political campaigns of the corresponding year.

19 Each newspaper also has a different terminology for what is provided—e.g., summary, abstract, or excerpt—and these vary in length and format. Some are the lead sentences or paragraph; others are summaries of the story, while some are truncated sentences of the news item. Full texts are available for a fee of approximately $2.95 per story. Lacking time, human and financial resources, full stories could not be purchased to do more extensive content analysis.

20 The abstracts of the *Chicago Sun-Times* do not indicate if the news items are news, opinion columns, editorials, etc.

# 9

# COVERAGE OF LATINO POLITICAL ISSUES IN 40 GENERAL MARKET DAILY NEWSPAPERS NATIONWIDE: 1989

## Louis DeSipio and James R. Henson

How have Latino political issues been covered by general market English-language daily newspapers in other cities with substantial Latino concentrations? The findings from the content analysis of newspapers in 40 United States cities in 1989 help answer this question. Data were collected as part of the Latino National Political Survey (LNPS)[1]

This particular newspaper study was designed with two goals: first, to develop a sense of how much coverage the press in high-concentration Latino areas dedicates to the news of the Latino communities; and, second, to examine the types of issue covered in articles that mentioned Latinos or Latino national-origin groups. While the data set was designed for use as a "control variable" for that survey, it also offered an unprecedented opportunity to examine the characteristics of news coverage of Latinos over a considerable period of time and in a wide geographical area.

The selected newspapers were the ones with the largest daily circulation in each of 40 cities included in the "parent" LNPS study.[2] At the time of that study, the population in each of these cities was already at least 10 percent Latino (García, García, Falcón, and de la Garza, 1989: 850). Given the geographical diversity of the newspapers, a sampling scheme randomly selected each paper two days per week for review. The days chosen for each newspaper changed from week to week in order to assemble a sufficiently varied sample of each paper without incurring the costs of coding 275 newspapers per week (several of the papers under review publish combined Saturday and Sunday "Weekend" editions).[3] Between August and December 1989, a total of 1,774 newspapers were reviewed, with each of the 40 papers sampled on at least 34 days. Table 9.1 shows the total number of issues reviewed for each paper, the first issue reviewed, and the last issue reviewed.[4]

*Table 9.1* English-language newspapers analyzed

| Newspaper | No. of papers coded | Date of first paper coded | Date of last paper coded |
|---|---|---|---|
| *Albuquerque Journal* | 44 | 7/25/89 | 12/19/89 |
| *Arizona* (Phoenix) *Republic* | 47 | 7/25/89 | 12/29/89 |
| *Austin American-Statesman* | 51 | 7/11/89 | 12/31/89 |
| *Bakersfield Californian* | 41 | 7/23/89 | 12/7/89 |
| *Boston Globe* | 43 | 7/22/89 | 12/18/89 |
| *Brownsville Herald* | 47 | 7/18/89 | 12/29/89 |
| *Carlsbad Current Argus* | 45 | 7/18/89 | 12/18/89 |
| *Central New Jersey Home News* | 42 | 7/24/89 | 12/12/89 |
| *Chicago Tribune* | 43 | 7/12/89 | 12/29/89 |
| *Corpus Christi Caller Times* | 40 | 7/19/89 | 12/10/89 |
| *Dallas Morning News* | 51 | 7/13/89 | 12/25/89 |
| *El Paso Times* | 49 | 7/13/89 | 12/18/89 |
| *Fresno Bee* | 46 | 7/25/89 | 12/25/89 |
| *Ft. Lauderdale Sun Sentinel* | 35 | 8/2/89 | 11/26/89 |
| *Gary Post Tribune* | 44 | 7/20/89 | 12/15/89 |
| *Hartford Courant* | 48 | 7/19/89 | 12/26/89 |
| *Houston Chronicle* | 49 | 7/14/89 | 12/28/89 |
| *Jersey City Journal* | 43 | 7/31/89 | 12/30/89 |
| *Kansas City Times* | 48 | 7/19/89 | 12/27/89 |
| *Las Vegas Review Journal* | 40 | 7/24/89 | 12/5/89 |
| *Long Island Newsday* | 42 | 7/23/89 | 12/13/89 |
| *Los Angeles Times* | 42 | 7/22/89 | 12/6/89 |
| *Lubbock Avalanche Journal* | 42 | 7/22/89 | 12/15/89 |
| *McAllen Monitor* | 44 | 7/21/89 | 12/17/89 |
| *Miami Herald* | 43 | 7/27/89 | 12/17/89 |
| *New York Daily News* | 52 | 7/12/89 | 12/20/20 |
| *Newark Star Ledger* | 44 | 8/3/89 | 12/26/89 |
| *North Jersey News* | 47 | 7/26/89 | 12/27/89 |
| *Orange County Register* | 49 | 7/29/89 | 12/26/89 |
| *Philadelphia Inquirer* | 40 | 7/25/89 | 12/20/89 |
| *Portland Oregonian* | 36 | 7/23/89 | 11/25/89 |
| *Riverside Press Enterprise* | 46 | 7/26/89 | 12/26/89 |
| *Rocky Mountain* (Denver) *News* | 46 | 7/11/89 | 12/12/89 |
| *Sacramento Bee* | 47 | 7/27/89 | 12/21/89 |
| *San Antonio Express-News* | 51 | 7/11/89 | 12/30/89 |
| *San Diego Union* | 36 | 8/3/89 | 11/26/89 |
| *San Francisco Chronicle* | 46 | 7/26/89 | 12/29/89 |
| *San Jose Mercury News* | 45 | 7/28/89 | 12/26/89 |
| *Santa Cruz Sentinel* | 46 | 7/25/89 | 12/29/89 |
| *Tampa Tribune* | 34 | 8/1/89 | 11/22/89 |
| Nationwide | 1,774 | | |

Coding protocols were designed to capture reporting of Latino *political* issues. Consequently, sections of the paper not likely to contain relatively explicit political coverage were excluded from the sample. In practice, this typically meant that we reviewed the news, state and local, and op-ed sections and excluded from our review sports, entertainment, announcements, and business sections. Op-ed pages (or sections) were coded regardless of where they appeared in the newspaper.[5]

Articles were coded if they explicitly contained references to Latinos (or any other variant of a pan-ethnic identifier such as "Hispanic" or "Spanish-origin"), to a Latino national-origin group (e.g., to Puerto Ricans, Mexican Americans, Cuban Americans), or a Latino-surnamed individual in the context of electoral politics. The purpose of this approach was to capture articles in which political content was explicitly linked to Latinos. The study followed the model of the LNPS in limiting examination of Latino national-origin groups to Cubans, Mexican Americans, and Puerto Ricans. The methodological reasoning for this decision in the LNPS is examined in García, García, Falcón, and de la Garza (1989) and de la Garza et al. (1992).

To derive sufficient data to address the aforementioned goals, a 25-item coding guide was developed.[6] Separate coding sheets with the responses to those items were completed for each article with Latino coverage. When a paper was reviewed and found to have no coverage, a coding sheet was also completed, but for the whole paper.

For articles with relevant news items or the paper without any Latino articles, the coding sheet captured basic information about the newspaper and its publication date. For newspapers with relevant articles, the coding included: location of the article within the newspaper; number and content of any photos associated with the article; type of article (news reporting, op-ed, editorial, etc.); source of the article and the ethnicity of the author (with surname used as a surrogate for Latino authors); and place within the article that Latinos or Latino national-origin groups were mentioned. The headlines of the selected articles were also transcribed, and the coding was supplemented with information on the subject of the article, the location where the reported events took place, and whether Latino organizations were mentioned in the article.[7]

## FINDINGS

At the inception of this project, we were not sure how much coverage we would find on explicitly Latino topics. On the one hand, the areas included in the sample comprise the cities with the highest Latino populations nationwide (although not necessarily those 40 cities with the *highest* concentrations of Latinos). On the other hand, personal experience suggested that coverage of Latinos was rare. Nevertheless, it was surprising how few stories explicitly mentioned Latinos or Latino national-origin groups.

Overall, approximately 57 percent of the paper/days reviewed had no coverage at all that met the coding protocol. Of the remaining 43 percent, the average paper contained 1.55 articles. Nationally, then, in these 40 cities, the chance of randomly picking up a paper and finding a story meeting our coding protocols was approximately 0.662. In other words, one would see approximately two articles over every three days.[8] This scarcity prevailed despite our rather liberal coding protocol, which allowed inclusions of articles that had: (1) a mention of Latinos or one of the Latino national-origin groups in the headline or the first three paragraphs; (2) a reference to a Spanish-surnamed candidate for elective office; or (3) a discussion of one of the broader themes. This latter protocol allowed us to follow an article through to its conclusion and, within the article, find a reference to Latinos or to one of the Latino national-origin groups.

Viewing this as a national phenomenon obscures significant local variations in the coverage of Latino issues. The *Miami Herald*, for example, averaged 2.5 articles each day. At the other extreme, the *Gary Post-Tribune* and the *Arizona Republic* averaged just 0.159 and 0.191 articles each day, respectively (or one approximately every five to six days). The average number of daily articles in each of the papers appears in table 9.2. Overall, just six of the 40 papers averaged one or more articles per day—the *Miami Herald*, the *Corpus Christi Caller Times*, the *San Antonio Express-News*, the *El Paso Times*, the *Albuquerque Journal*, and the *San Jose Mercury News*. Three times as many papers (18) averaged less than one article every two days.

The level of coverage by individual papers obscures a larger phenomenon. Consistent regional variation appears in the level of coverage of Latino issues. To examine regional patterns of coverage of Latino issues, we divided the nation into six regions. In the three papers from Florida, just 38 percent of the observations contain no Latino coverage (an experience driven in large part by the high level of Latino coverage in the *Miami Herald*). In the Midwest, on the other hand, more than 76 percent of the newspapers had no Latino political coverage on a randomly selected day. Table 9.3 highlights these regional variations.

These results should be viewed with some caution. This regionally based study was limited by the different number of papers and observations in each of the regions.[9] Among the six regions, many fewer papers were reviewed in the Midwest, the South, and the Mountain West than in the Northeast, South Central, and the West. The smaller regions had many fewer observations.

*Table 9.2* Level of coverage for sampled newspapers by region

| Region/newspaper | Number of articles per day | National rank[10] |
|---|---|---|
| **South** | | |
| Miami Herald | 2.512 | 1 |
| Ft. Lauderdale Sun Sentinel | 0.543 | 21 |
| Tampa Tribune | 0.441 | 24 |
| **South Central** | | |
| Corpus Christi Caller Times | 1.300 | 2 |
| San Antonio Express-News | 1.294 | 3 |
| Austin American-Statesman | 0.980 | 7 |
| Dallas Morning News | 0.941 | 8 |
| Brownsville Herald | 0.809 | 11 |
| McAllen Monitor | 0.795 | 20 |
| Houston Chronicle | 0.694 | 15 |
| Lubbock Avalanche Journal | 0.310 | 33 |
| **Mountain West** | | |
| El Paso Times | 1.224 | 4 |
| Albuquerque Journal | 1.068 | 5 |
| Rocky Mountain (Denver) News | 0.717 | 13 |
| Carlsbad Current Argus | 0.622 | 17 |
| **West** | | |
| San Jose Mercury News | 1.000 | 6 |
| Fresno Bee | 0.935 | 9 |
| Los Angeles Times | 0.881 | 10 |
| Arizona (Phoenix) Republic | 0.191 | 39 |
| San Diego Union | 0.806 | 12 |
| Orange County Register | 0.714 | 14 |
| Santa Cruz Sentinel | 0.630 | 16 |
| Sacramento Bee | 0.574 | 19 |
| San Francisco Chronicle | 0.457 | 23 |
| Riverside Press Enterprise | 0.413 | 27 |
| Bakersfield Californian | 0.366 | 30 |
| Las Vegas Review Journal | 0.325 | 32 |
| Portland Oregonian | 0.278 | 35 |
| **Midwest** | | |
| Chicago Tribune | 0.372 | 29 |
| Kansas City Times | 0.271 | 37 |
| Gary Post Tribune | 0.159 | 40 |
| **Northeast** | | |
| New York Daily News | 0.577 | 18 |
| Hartford Courant | 0.542 | 22 |
| Philadelphia Inquirer | 0.425 | 25 |
| Jersey City Journal | 0.419 | 26 |
| Newark Star Ledger | 0.409 | 28 |
| Central New Jersey Home News | 0.333 | 31 |
| North Jersey News | 0.298 | 34 |
| Boston Globe | 0.279 | 36 |
| Long Island Newsday | 0.262 | 38 |

*Table 9.3* Newspaper coverage of Latinos by region

| Region | Total papers | Number of articles | Papers with no articles number | (%) |
|---|---|---|---|---|
| South (Florida) | 112 | 142 | 43 | (38.4) |
| South Central | 375 | 336 | 179 | (47.7) |
| Mountain West | 184 | 168 | 78 | (42.4) |
| West | 567 | 332 | 337 | (59.4) |
| Midwest | 135 | 36 | 103 | (76.2) |
| Northeast | 401 | 160 | 276 | (68.8) |
| National | 1,774 | 1,174 | 1,016 | (57.2) |

## "National" coverage of Latino issues

A second question about the absolute level of Latino coverage needs to be addressed—is there "national" Latino coverage? In other words, are there some stories or some issues that are central enough to each of these communities to receive space in all the newspapers? Clearly, since coders did not read all 40 newspapers each day, the question cannot be conclusively answered. With this limitation in mind, the sample indicates that the answer is no.

Of the approximately 120 days covered in this sample among all of the papers (August through November) and the 60 days with varying degrees of partial coverage (July and December), 23 days generated 12 or more articles.[11] The study focused on these 23 days with higher than average levels of coverage to determine evidence of "national" Latino coverage—coverage of the same Latino story throughout the country.

Between 10 and 18 papers reviewed yielded a range of 15 to 30 observations each of those 23 days (see table 9.4). On none of these 23 days do all papers in the subsample have coverage of Latino issues. The number of papers with no Latino coverage on these days with higher than average coverage ranged from 1 to 10; the number of papers with Latino coverage ranged from 5 to 13.

Among the papers that do have coverage, few cover the same stories. Table 9.4 highlights the common stories, noting the exceptions. As this table also indicates, none of these days had universal coverage of the same Latino issue. Instead, while there was some consistency across states or across the country, local coverage was always more common than coverage of national news. In addition to coverage of local news stories, some patterns of statewide coverage of particular stories emerged in three states: Texas, California, and Florida. This finding suggests the absence of explicitly Latino issues that editors uniformly recognize as meeting their papers' criterion for "national" news; Latinos do, however, shape the creation of state-level news in several states with large Latino populations. Hence, the

*Table 9.4* Days with 12 or more article observations during 1989

| Date | A | B | C | Major story or stories of the date |
|------|---|---|---|------------------------------------|
| 8/2 | 8 | 7 | 24 | (1) Florida: Elections; (2) Other: Local issues |
| 8/13 | 4 | 8 | 17 | None |
| 8/16 | 3 | 7 | 16 | (1) Primary election in Florida; (2) Local issues |
| 8/25 | 7 | 8 | 21 | (1) Release of 1990 census data and promise of new Hispanic Congressional seats; (2) Local issues |
| 8/27 | 4 | 8 | 22 | (1) Miami Congressional race; (2) Local issues |
| 8/29 | 6 | 8 | 18 | (1) East: High turnout expected in FL Congressional race; (2) Texas: Mexican American Democrats meeting; (3) Others: Local issues |
| 8/31 | 6 | 8 | 19 | (1) Results of Florida Congressional election; (2) Scandal at LULAC; (3) Local issues |
| 9/7 | 1 | 10 | 15 | (1) Ileana Ros-Lehtinen sworn in to Congress; (2) California: State Senator Torres arrested for drunk-driving; (3) Other: Local issues |
| 9/14 | 5 | 0 | 18 | (1) Report on elderly Hispanics; (2) Local issues |
| 9/17 | 5 | 9 | 21 | (1) Mass naturalization ceremony on Mexican Independence day; (2) Local issues |
| 9/19 | 10 | 6 | 23 | (1) Texas: Immigration policy; (2) Texas: Judicial selection; (3) New York: Trial of ex-Representative Robert García; (4) Other: Local issues |
| 10/12 | 5 | 8 | 20 | (1) Census estimate of the size of the Latino population; (2) Debate over counting undocumented immigrants in 1990 Census; (3) Trial of ex-Representative Robert García; (4) Local issues |
| 10/21 | 1 | 13 | 19 | (1) Conviction of ex-Representative García |
| 10/22 | 7 | 11 | 30 | (1) Concerns about trial of Hispanic police officer in Miami; (2) Local issues |
| 11/2 | 3 | 13 | 21 | (1) Antonia Novello named Surgeon General; (2) Local issues |
| 11/15 | 6 | 9 | 21 | None |
| 12/6 | 6 | 5 | 18 | (1) California: redistricting; (2) Local issues |
| 12/7 | 4 | 9 | 23 | (1) Trial of Miami police officer; (2) Creation of presidential panel on Hispanic illiteracy; (3) Local issues |
| 12/8 | 0 | 11 | 28 | (1) Conviction of Miami police officer; (2) Study finds Hispanics are overweight |
| 12/9 | 6 | 6 | 18 | None |
| 12/10 | 8 | 6 | 20 | (1) Support for convicted Miami police officer; (2) Local issues |
| 12/14 | 4 | 5 | 18 | (1) Various redistrictings; (2) Local issues |
| 12/16 | 3 | 6 | 15 | (1) Report on Hispanic poverty; (2) Local issues |

*For key see overleaf.*

*Table 9.4* continued

Key:
A: Number of newspapers with no Latino coverage
B: Number of newspapers with Latino coverage
C: Total observations
None: There is no clear pattern. Some papers cover local issues. Others cover national issues, but there is no overlap between papers.
Local issues: Newspapers with coverage cover local Latino issues.
State or region mentioned: There is consistent coverage on the issue in the papers reviewed that day from throughout the area mentioned.

overwhelming majority of Latino political content stories covered in newspapers are local or regional in nature.

## Topical content of Latino political news

Of those stories with Latino-relevant political content, the modal category was social issues, into which 46.1 percent of the coded articles fell. Electoral politics was the next most frequently recurring category (33.0 percent), followed at some distance by Latino ethnic identity (11.3 percent). Economic issues and foreign relations/foreign policy issues received scant coverage, respectively comprising 4.3 percent and 2.9 percent of the stories coded.

Events that occurred during the research period influenced the specific issues addressed in surveyed articles. The most frequent topics, for example, were elections and voter registration (17.2 percent of stories coded), Latino elected officials and corruption (7.3 percent), discrimination and racism (5.0 percent), redistricting (4.9 percent), and judicial process (4.2 percent). Two of these topics resulted from major and widely covered Latino political content stories—the trial of Miami police officer William Lozano led to stories about the judicial process, the trial of former New York U.S. Representative Robert García for bribery, and the arrest of California State Senator Art Torres on drunk driving charges led to stories about Latino elected officials and corruption. Elections throughout the country, including a highly covered race in Miami, generated stories about elections and voter registration. Preparation for the 1990 census led to many discussions of the redistricting process. No single story or set of stories generated articles about discrimination and racism. Thus, these stories represent a plethora of individual events with a common theme.

## Prominence of coverage

Our coding captured two primary indicators of the prominence of Latino political issue coverage—the location of articles in the newspaper and the level at which Latino content within the article was mentioned. Articles receiving the most prominent coverage on both dimensions were few. Most Latino-content articles, for example, did not appear on the front page or on the front page of interior sections. Twelve percent of the coded articles were on the newspaper's front page; approximately half of these articles that featured Latino coverage were above the fold (5.5 percent) on the front page. An additional 14 percent of articles with Latino coverage were on the front page of an interior section. Of the remaining Latino-content stories, 49 percent appeared in the interior of the front section and 26 percent in the interior of other sections.

The next indicator we used to measure the level of prominence of Latino coverage was where the Latino coverage appeared within the article. We designed the coding protocols to be sensitive to the visibility of the Latino content of stories rather than to pinpoint where Latinos were mentioned in the coded articles. We found a relatively large share of articles with the Latino mention in the headlines and/or leads (43 percent). This finding may be slightly skewed by coding protocols oriented to registering high visibility coverage.[12] The next most common level of mention was more than two sentences within the body of the article (see table 9.5).

The overall pattern of issue coverage recurs when examining the placement of articles and the level of mention of Latino content. Of the articles located on the front page of the front section, 54 percent covered social issues, 26 percent covered electoral politics, 11 percent covered economic issues, 4 percent covered Latino or ethnic group identity, and 2 percent covered foreign relations issues with a connection to the Latino community.

Within topic categories, the prominence of stories varied widely. Of the articles coded as covering electoral politics, 45 percent displayed the Latino content of the stories in the headline or lead. Corresponding figures in other categories were 36 percent for social issues, 34 percent for economic issues, 53 percent for foreign relations, and 65 percent for stories related to Latino identity.

*Table 9.5* Location of Latino coverage within articles[13]

| Location | Number of articles | (%) |
|---|---|---|
| Headline and lead | 499 | (42.5) |
| Headline and more than two sentences | 48 | (4.1) |
| Lead and more than two sentences | 184 | (15.7) |
| Lead and less than two sentences | 60 | (5.1) |
| More than two sentences | 243 | (20.7) |
| Less than two sentences | 140 | (11.9) |
| Total | 1,174 | |

## Group focus of coverage

Among the stories identified to have Latino content, approximately half identified the subject matter with the terms Latino, Hispanic, Latin American, or some other pan-ethnic identity term. Approximately 35 percent mentioned a specific national-origin group or some combination of national-origin group(s) and one of the pan-ethnic terms. Among the articles mentioning specific national-origin groups, approximately 7 percent mentioned Cuban Americans, 6 percent Mexican Americans, and 3 percent Puerto Ricans. Since 19 percent of the articles mentioned a combination of group names, the percentages reported here slightly underestimate the actual number of mentions of each ethnic identifier (see table 9.6).

The topic areas varied widely in the degree to which issue areas were explicitly linked to Latinos *as* members of ethnic groups, as the coding variable identifying how the Latino content was indicated in articles demonstrates. In one of the largest categories—electoral politics—mention of Latinos was limited to the inclusion of a Latino surname in 43 percent of the coded articles in that category. In contrast, 63 percent of articles addressing social issues and 57 percent of articles concerning Latino ethnic identity used a pan-ethnic identity term (e.g., Latino, Hispanic). Few articles, regardless of story content, used national-origin-focused identifiers such as Mexican American, Puerto Rican, or Cuban American. As national-origin-focused identifiers are the preferred identity terms of most Latinos (de la Garza et al., 1992: 40), this finding is quite surprising and indicates a disconnection between how news organizations cover Latinos and how Latinos perceive themselves.

The dominant use of the terms Latino or Hispanic as ethnic identifiers is consistent across the country with the exception of Florida, where Cuban (or Cuban American) is the identity term most often used. While approximately half of the articles in other regions refer only to Latinos or Hispanics, over one-third of the articles in Florida papers used Cuban (or Cuban American) as the chosen ethnic identifier. In comparison, just

*Table* 9.6 Latino referent within article

| Referent | Number of articles | (%) |
| --- | --- | --- |
| Latino, Hispanic, or pan-ethnic reference | 591 | (50.3) |
| Mexican American | 67 | (5.7) |
| Puerto Rican | 32 | (2.7) |
| Cuban American | 85 | (7.2) |
| More than one referent | 217 | (18.5) |
| Latino surname only | 182 | (15.5) |
| Total | 1,174 | |

26 percent of Florida papers used a pan-ethnic identifier. Florida also saw a high level of mixed mentions. Of the articles in Florida papers, 25 percent used both a pan-ethnic identifier *and* a national-origin specific identifier.

## Latino political organizations

Scholars of political participation in the United States have long seen a connection between the diversity and strength of community organizations and other forms of political activity (Verba and Nie, 1972). Thus, coding protocols collected information on the mention of Latino political organizations in the selected articles. Of the articles coded, 71 percent mentioned no Latino political organizations. Nine percent of articles mentioned state or local organizations, 14 percent mentioned national or regional Latino organizations, and 6 percent mentioned multiple organizations.

The League of United Latin American Citizens (LULAC) received the most mentions. With 6 percent of the coded articles mentioning this organization, it far exceeds any others in terms of press mentions.[14] However, because articles mentioning two or more national organizations were assigned a generic code, the frequencies of the mentions of specific groups in most cases are slight underestimates.

Topical coverage exhibited somewhat more variation in the tendency toward references to Latino organizations. The share of articles in the electoral politics categories that lacked any mention of Latino organizations (80 percent) was substantially larger than the figure for the overall sample average (71 percent). The articles dealing with both Latino identity and foreign policy mentioned Latino organizations much more frequently: 59 percent of the Latino identity codings and 53 percent of the foreign policy codings had references to Latino organizations. These findings should be viewed with some caution because of the small overall number of articles about these topics.

## Article and author characteristics

The final characteristics of newspaper coverage of Latino political topics are structural. Without comparative data for non-Latino coverage, the goal here is to present descriptive data on the types of articles with Latino coverage, the media source of these articles, and the ethnicity of the authors. Table 9.7 summarizes these characteristics.

Almost 70 percent of articles with Latino political coverage were news stories. The next largest categories—opinion columns and news briefs—accounted for an additional 10 percent each. Five percent of the articles coded were letters to the editor. The remaining types of story—photo

*Table 9.7* Article and author characteristics of news stories with Latino political content

| Type of article | Number of articles | (%) |
| --- | --- | --- |
| News/current event | 821 | (69.9) |
| News brief | 114 | (9.7) |
| Graphic/photo story | 4 | (0.3) |
| Opinion column | 118 | (10.1) |
| Opinion column by regular Latino columnist | 23 | (2.0) |
| Editorial | 28 | (2.4) |
| Special report | 8 | (0.7) |
| Letter to the editor | 57 | (4.9) |
| Other | 1 | (0.9) |
| Total | 1,174 | |
| *Media source of article* | | |
| Paper staff | 576 | (49.1) |
| Wire services | 377 | (32.1) |
| Hispanic Link | 28 | (2.4) |
| Guest author | 82 | (7.0) |
| Combined sources | 4 | (0.3) |
| Cannot be determined | 107 | |
| Total | 1,174 | |
| *Author ethnicity (by surname)* | | |
| Author not identified | 432 | (36.8) |
| Latino surname | 212 | (18.1) |
| Non-Latino surname | 519 | (44.2) |
| Latino and non-Latino surnames | 11 | (0.9) |
| Total | 1,174 | |

stories, opinion columns by regular Latino columns, editorials, and special reports—made up the final 5 percent of articles.

The newspapers' staff wrote slightly less than half of the Latino content stories. Wire services supplied just less than one-third of articles. Other sources—guest authors, the Hispanic Link news service, and combined sources—accounted for the remaining stories.

Many articles (approximately 37 percent of the sample) did not have a byline, so it was not possible to ascertain the author's ethnicity. Of the remaining stories, reporters with non-Latino surnames wrote the majority (70 percent of those with named authors). Approximately 20 percent of Latinos do not have Latino surnames, so this is not an exact measure. Nevertheless, these findings indicate that the majority of Latino content stories were not written by Latinos.

The descriptive characteristics of Latino content articles tell us how newspapers disseminate information about the Latino community. The average article takes the form of a news story written by the paper's staff, most often by either an unnamed author or a non-Latino-surnamed reporter. Wire services also provide a significant share of news. Thus, the lesson of these findings from 1989 is that, for Latino issues to have been covered in these major newspapers, the entry point was local, through individual newspapers, and because of national sources or national events. At the time, newspapers were covering the Latino community in local, not national, terms. It remains to be seen if that is still the case today for the regular coverage of the Latino community, particularly during presidential elections.

## CONCLUSIONS

This study identified no nationally consistent coverage of issues clearly identified as being of special interest to Latinos (or to Latino national-origin groups). Instead, newspaper reporting that explicitly mentions Latinos and the Latino community varies significantly from city to city. No single topic or issue assures coverage across these cities. As a result, future analysis must focus on local and regional coverage patterns.

Despite the finding that local coverage dominated newspapers' articles on Latinos and Latino community issues, it cannot be said that there are no Latino issues or that coverage focuses *solely* on Latino national-origin groups. We find a consistent cross-regional pattern of Latino issues falling within the broader category of social issues. More often than not, with the exception of newspapers in Florida, coverage focuses on Latino or Hispanic as an ethnic identifier instead of a specific national-origin group. Thus, the lack of uniformity of coverage and the concomitant lack of clearly recognized issues that would be of interest to a Latino readership should not suggest that there are no national explicit Latino-content issues in the print media.

The sparseness of the coverage may be, in part, a function of the timing of our study (which was conducted simultaneously with the Latino National Political Survey in 1989). The days with the highest levels of explicit Latino coverage occurred just before and after elections (approximately from two weeks before to a few days after the election). In areas with Latino candidates, as many as eight observations were recorded from a single newspaper in one day. The importance of campaigns to news coverage with Latino salience transcended the local community in which the event occurred. Two among the few stories that could be considered possibly of "national" Latino-content involved elections. One was the election of Ileana Ros Lehtinen as the first Cuban American member of the United States Congress; the other was the first election in Watsonville, California, after a court-ordered conversion to single-member city council districts. Only one other news item clearly merited consideration as a "national" story—the trial and conviction of Miami police officer William Lozano for the shooting to death of an African American motorcyclist. Although Officer Lozano is Colombian-born, the story was often presented as a conflict between Miami's largely Cuban American Hispanic community and its black community.

At the most general level, the results of this study echo earlier analyses, which pointed out the wide variation in press attention to Hispanics and Hispanic issues. As Greenberg et al. noted, "Newspapers varied markedly in their coverage of Mexican Americans across the sites studied and across the different types of news items . . . Some newspapers reflect Mexican Americans prominently and substantially in most or all content areas; others definitely do not" (Greenberg et al., 1983b: 676). The political focus of the study, however, nullifies close comparative comments between these findings and other findings concerned with the overall volume of coverage. Nevertheless, our findings lead us to question studies (e.g., see Turk et al., 1989) that find a close to proportionate ratio of coverage of Latino issues to Latino share of population. It is possible that the coding of Latino-related stories in sports, announcements, bulletins, soft news, and features could substantially inflate the measurement of *substantive* Latino-relevant content. That would be an important distortion of the position of Latinos if one's concern is the presentation of Latino issues in the political discourse of the community.

The characteristics of coverage in the sample suggest that Latino political issues are still covered inconsistently and, with important exceptions (e.g., coverage of Cuban Americans, especially in Florida), minimally. This infrequent coverage is evident in the proportion of the observations in the sample—almost half—that report a daily newspaper with no Latino political coverage.

These results point out the need to reconsider assumptions about pluralist democracy in the United States, which implicitly color policy recommendations, political strategies, and academic analyses. The absence of any mention of Latino political organizations in more than two-thirds of the coded articles suggests that somewhere in the process of collective action and group representation Latino organizations are not being featured in the public political discourse. This gap would be understandable within the conventional logic of pluralism if Latinos were new to, or newly organized within, the political system; they are neither. That restricted visibility, together with the overall lack of coverage of Latino political issues, indicates the limited success of political strategies based on pluralist assumptions about the political system, and of the explanatory value of pluralist theory in understanding the position of Latino groups in the United States.

An alternate—or, more likely, complementary—explanation is that Latinos have simply failed to effectively learn and play by the rules of political competition in the United States. To completely reject such an explanation would be to attribute the limits of Latino political success on a variety of fronts wholly to structural factors, an unduly reductionist conclusion. But the fact remains that Latinos have by and large played "by the rules" in the political system. The persistent difficulties Latinos still seem to have in their efforts to penetrate the news media—a conduit to the public agenda—suggests that a more critical attitude toward the rules of the political system may be called for. This is not to suggest that coalitional and interest group strategies should be renounced as hopeless; rather, we suggest that coalitional strategies that incorporate a critique of the mechanics of the democratic process would be more politically effective, and would be more likely to get Latino community issues into print.

## NOTES

1 We would like to express our appreciation to the co-principal investigators of the Latino National Political Survey—Rodolfo O. de la Garza, F. Chris García, John A. García, and Angelo Falcón—for the opportunity to conduct this research. For a full discussion of the development and scope of the LNPS, see chapter 1 of their 1992 book.

2 The LNPS sampling design divided the nation into primary sampling units of cities that included at least 90 percent of the Cuban-origin, Puerto Rican-origin, or Mexican-origin populations. From these, 40 primary sampling units were selected at random.

3 A matrix was constructed with consecutive weeks on the horizontal axis and individual newspapers represented on the vertical axis. Each paper was randomly assigned two numbers between one and seven, to signify days on which that newspaper would be coded during the first week. Subsequent weeks were assigned coding days based on a sequential progression starting from the initial random assignment. For example, if we assigned the *Rocky Mountain News* an initial random coding designation of 2 (Monday) and 5 (Thursday) for the first week of the study, the designation for the following week's sample would be the next numbers in sequence, i.e., 3 (Tuesday) and 6 (Friday).

4 The selection and review of the 40 newspapers took place during the fieldwork period for the LNPS. We began reviewing each city's newspapers between the second week of July and the first week of August 1989. Initially, the LNPS was to end in November 1989. After the start of the newspapers project, this date was extended; our reviews for most of the newspapers continued into December 1989.

5 To further reduce the labor costs associated with the coding process, coders initially limited their review to the headline, photograph captions (if any), and first three paragraphs of each story in the covered sections of the newspaper. To be selected for detailed coding, these parts of the article had to explicitly refer to Latinos, Latino national-origin groups, or Latino-surnamed individuals seeking or holding elective office. It soon became evident, however, that this process caused many articles with significant Latino content to be missed. As a result, supplementary coding protocols were developed to allow reviewers to read beyond the third paragraph of a story. Discussion of "minorities," "race,"

"immigrants," "immigration," "aliens," "poverty," "education," or "elections" allowed a complete read of the article. After this change in strategy, coders re-examined all previously reviewed newspapers to ensure that the entire study followed the same protocols.

6 We express our appreciation to Federico Subervi-Vélez for sharing his insights and the coding guide used for his content analysis on this subject (see chapters 4 and 8 of this book). The variables coded (with explanations when not self-explanatory) for the study presented in this chapter were as follows:

1 Newspaper
2 Month
3 Day
4 Day of week (a numerical code to verify that the random selection protocol was being followed)
5 Section
6 Page (the front page of all subsequent sections were coded as page one regardless of whether the paper treated it as a continuation of the front page)
7 Fold (for articles on the front page of any section to identify the prominence of the article on the page)
8 Headline (this variable included all the text in the headline)
9 Headline status (this variable compared the headline of the article being coded to other headlines on the page)
10 Columns across (a measurement of the percentage of the page occupied by the headline of the article being coded)
11 Number of photos
12 Content of photos
13 Kicker on front page (a notice on the front page that the coded article appears in the interior of the paper)
14 Front page photo kicker (a photo on the front page advising that the article being coded is in the interior of the paper)
15 Jump headline (evaluates the presence of explicit Latino content in the headline on the continuation of the article)
16 Article type (distinguishes between articles, news briefs, letters to the editor, editorials, opinion articles and opinion columns by (regular) Latino columnists)
17 Media source of article (distinguishes locally generated material from wire service reporting)
18 Ethnicity of author (by surname)
19 Location of the reported event
20 Dateline of article (reports the source of the story as opposed to the location of the event; for example, stories about Latino poverty nationwide might have come from the Census Bureau and have the dateline of Washington)
21 Topic (a broad distinction between economic, social, electoral, foreign policy, and Latino ethnic identity issues)
22 Latino subtopic (a list of approximately 80 specific story topics categorized into the five general topics in variable 21)
23 Latino or Latino national-origin group mentioned
24 Organization(s) mentioned
25 Level of mention (location in the article of the Latino or Latino national-origin group mentioned).

7 To ensure that the two coders were capturing the same information, coder interreliability checks were conducted twice—once at the beginning of the study and once in the middle. Both checks produced satisfactory results. In the initial test of 99 codings, reliability across all items was 90.5 percent. The interreliability ranged from 100 percent on story structure variables to 89 percent on the most connotative, the story content items. On the second check of 228 codings, reliability increased on all variables, to 97 percent on the content items and 97.7 percent overall.

8 The average number of articles per day used here and in table 9.2 is calculated by dividing the total number of observed articles by the total number of days reviewed. Of the 2,190 observations, 1,016 represent findings of no coverage. The remaining 1,174 observations represent articles from 758 newspaper days. Hence, the average finding among those papers that have coverage is 1.55 articles. Among the papers reviewed, none had more than 8 articles (observed once).

9 An observation refers to each individual examination of a newspaper. The finding of no coverage represents an observation. Each article also represents an observation. Thus, a paper with three articles is counted as three observations. We had 2,190 observations. Of these, 1,174 represent articles and 1,106 represent a finding of no coverage.

10 The rank presented in table 9.2 is derived from the relative number of articles per day for each of the papers. In an effort to factor Latino population density of the cities into the ranking, we tried to deflate by raw number of articles per day by the local Latino population density. This produced results that wildly inflated the rankings of the low-density cities and resulted in an unrepresentative ranking. Nevertheless, we recognize that the raw ranking presented in this table biases the results to cities with large and active Latino populations. As a result, we recommend that it be used with caution more as a tool for developing aggregate differences (such as top quarter versus bottom quarter) rather than specific relative standing.

11 If the review of papers were evenly distributed across the week and the presence and absence of articles were distributed evenly at present levels in a random manner, we would review 11.4 papers each day and have 14.1 daily observations. Of the 14.1, 6.5 would represent the absence of articles and 7.6 would be articles from 4.9 papers. Clearly, the presence of articles will cluster around certain days when events occur, news is made, or information is released.

12 Since the primary purpose of monitoring newspaper coverage was to provide a control variable for the analysis of survey data, it was deemed efficient at the outset of the newspaper analysis to use guidelines that would limit the time spent by coders reading articles without prominent Latino content. Consequently, articles that mentioned Latinos late in the article in the context of subjects not generally associated with Latinos were likely not coded. The number of such cases is likely to be small.

13 The coding protocols were designed to capture explicit Latino content early in stories except in those about specific topics: "minorities," "race," "immigrants," "immigration," "aliens," "poverty," "education," or "elections." These results, then, overestimate the share of Latino references appearing early in the articles.

14 The other organizations to which we assigned a specific code, and the percentage of the total coded articles in which they were singularly mentioned, were: the Mexican American Legal Defense and Education Fund (MALDEF) (2.7%),

National Association of Latino Elected and Appointed Officials (NALEO) (1.2%), Southwest Voter Registration Institute (0.6%), National Council of La Raza (0.9%), Cuban American National Foundation (0.8%), Impacto 2000 (0.6%), Congressional Hispanic Caucus (0.4%), and the Institute for Puerto Rican Policy (0.1%).

# 10

# TELEVISION NEWS, CHARACTER ISSUES AND LATINO IMAGES IN U.S. NATIONAL ELECTIONS OF 1988, 1992 AND 1996

*Kenton T. Wilkinson*

A confluence of developments changed electoral politics in the United States during the final two decades of the twentieth century. As television reinforced its primacy as a communication medium, news coverage emphasized character issues surrounding candidates. Meanwhile, the U.S. population became more ethnically and racially diverse, and political parties devoted increasing attention and resources to reaching specific segments of the electorate. Although most discussion of character issues by media pundits and academic experts has focused on the credibility, and therefore the electability of candidates for public office, this chapter broadens the concept in arguing that character is a multifaceted construction, and that the media, especially television, act as key arbiters in the negotiation of character perceptions among groups engaged in politics. Character issues are treated in two ways on the following pages: as conduits to evaluate representations of the trustworthiness of Latinos as a voting bloc during three presidential elections, and to compare English- and Spanish-language television news coverage of a potentially volatile inter-ethnic news story. A number of problems emerge which are likely to transform U.S. electoral politics and political communication in the twenty-first century.

As other chapters in this volume clearly demonstrate, the Democratic and Republican Parties actively solicited Latino votes in national elections from the 1970s through the first decade of this century. Concurrent with such appeals were occasional television news reports aired in 1988, 1992 and 1996 which emphasized the potential influence of the Latino vote on U.S. politics and governance. Of course, these reports were interspersed with non-election-related news stories focusing on Latinos and their involvement in U.S. society. The election-related reports are considered in conjunction with the general news concerning Latinos in order to discern the composite portrayals of Latinos constructed by television newscasts. The portrayals that emerge raise this question: Are Latinos presented to mainstream television audiences as being worthy of the political power they potentially command?

## TELEVISION AND THE CHARACTER ISSUE

Television plays a central role in two collective processes that increase in salience as the country's demographic profile continues to change. First, many scholars agree that television has surpassed the print media as the principal source of political information for most voters. Increasingly, the effectiveness of a political campaign depends on a candidate's (and her/ his managers') skill at using televised news coverage and political advertising to enhance the candidate's image and position vis-à-vis opponents (Jamieson and Waldman, 2003). Second, intercultural relations among racial, ethnic, and linguistic groups are influenced by television programming—be it information, entertainment, or "infotainment" oriented. Television provides the codes we use to structure our beliefs about who we are, who others are, and how well the political system accommodates our interests versus others' (Campbell, 1995; Gandy, 1998).

Television's primacy in the electoral politics of a culturally diverse society like the U.S. leads parties and candidates to cultivate their images carefully for broad appeal, and thereby complicates the long-standing character issue (Graber, 2005). Candidates' characters have been at issue in U.S. political reporting since colonial times. Early in the nineteenth century, Alexis de Tocqueville wrote, "the characteristics of the American journalist consist in an open and coarse appeal to the passions of his readers; he abandons principles to assail the characters of individuals, to track them into private life and disclose all their weaknesses and vices" (cited in Sabato, 1991: 25). Although exaggerated by Tocqueville, the preoccupation of reporters with character has persisted through shifts in political climates, changing journalistic practices and advances in media technology.

Early in the television age, political conditions encouraged journalists to turn a blind eye to candidates' indiscretions so long as they appeared not to impinge on their public performance (Ansolabehere, Behr and Iyengar, 1993). But journalistic laissez faire did not mean that the voting public was disinterested—a study of factors influencing presidential voting decisions from 1952 to 1972 found "character traits and characteristics of candidates" most persuasive (Just et al., 1996: 8). The Watergate debacle convinced journalists that politicians' personal weaknesses *could* have political significance, and scrutiny of their character increased, reaching a fever pitch in 1987 when Democratic presidential hopeful Gary Hart was caught in an extramarital affair.[1] The intense scrutiny showed no signs of subsiding more than a decade later when President Bill Clinton was tried (and acquitted) in the United States Senate for high crimes and misdemeanors related to his denials, under oath, of having had sexual relations with the White House intern, Monica Lewinsky.

Public reaction to character issues has been fickle. In 1988 the public cited character traits as more important than issue positions as relevant qualifications for the president (Buchanan, 1991: table 5.3). Yet, as the Clinton–Lewinsky affair unraveled between January 1998 and February 1999, the president maintained consistently high job approval ratings and in the Gallup organization's annual poll was identified by the largest percentage of respondents, 18 percent, as the person they most admired (Saad, 1998). Such contradictions underscore the importance of contextual factors in influencing public reactions to character issue reporting. The public is concerned about candidates' character attributes, especially their integrity and competence (Ansolabehere, Behr & Iyengar, 1993: 172; Denton, 1994: 179), but is also sensitive to "attack politics" practiced by opposing political parties or the media. The candidates' goal, of course, is to respond to character issue challenges by emphasizing her/his integrity or competence, and in some cases by calling into question their accuser's possession of those attributes. When diverse subgroups of the electorate having competing political, economic and social agendas is factored in, the confluence of forces and interests becomes very complicated indeed. As we will see in the case of George H. W. Bush, a deft response to character questions in an inter-ethnic controversy can yield political gain (even as it diverts voters' attention from the conflict).

This abbreviated overview of character issues has revealed two blind spots at the intersection of political science and communication studies. While lip service is paid to the diversity of the electorate, too many experts continue to treat it as an undifferentiated mass, and pay little attention to the news media's influence on subgroup relations.[2] We know television influences viewers' perceptions of cultural groups within U.S. society, but the political dimensions of that influence have not been adequately explored at the collective level. The roles of media in political competition and intergroup relations merits more sustained attention. A second blind spot concerns the narrow construal of the character issue. Given the structure of the U.S. electoral system, the public's impression of its government representatives is key, and heavily dependent on the press. We must keep in mind that political communication, albeit emphasizing character issues and the horse race aspects of campaigns, also influences voters' impressions of political actors at all levels of social organization (Neighbor & Villarreal, 1991: 27). This chapter argues that television viewers' judgments of character apply beyond the candidates to cultural groups and institutions as well. The finding by Samuel Popkin (1991) that voters use "cognitive shortcuts" in assessing the character of candidates may be combined with Dahlgren and Chakrapani's (1982) compelling argument that television news offers its viewers concrete "ways of seeing" other ethnic groups to suggest that the actions and trustworthiness of other cultural groups are also under scrutiny by viewers. The question arises: What ways of seeing Latinos did network television news programs offer the viewing and voting public during three election years?

## ELECTION YEAR NETWORK NEWSCASTS

The study used the on-line Vanderbilt Television Index (http://tvnews.vanderbilt.edu) to retrieve abstracts of the nightly newscasts on ABC, NBC and CBS, which mentioned Latinos and/or Latino-related issues. Keyword searches of Latino and election-related terms[3] were conducted for January 1 through Election Day—the first Tuesday of November—for 1988, 1992 and 1996.[4] For each year studied, the abstracts were categorized according to two criteria: the centrality of Latinos and/or Latino-related issues as principal actors or focuses, and the reports' inclusion of election-related or non-election-related issues. I make two assumptions in my interpretations: reports in which Latinos play a central role are more influential in shaping viewers' perceptions of Latinos than are reports in which they play minor roles, and the non-election-related reports influence audience members' perceptions of the trustworthiness of Latinos as a voting bloc.

The findings of this study should be prefaced with a few caveats regarding data gathering and categorization. The Vanderbilt Television Abstracts provide useful sketches of news reports and their contents, but should not be assumed to represent fully the audiovisual richness or persuasive nuances of those reports. Keyword searches uncovered the principal Latino-related stories, but not all stories appearing on every network. For example, a 1992 news event concerning Lena Guerrero, a candidate for Texas Railroad Commissioner, was reported on all three networks; this study only captured NBC's report because it contained the word "Hispanic" whereas the other two abstracts did not include keyword terms (see table 10.3 and note 3). Furthermore, distinguishing whether Latinos and/or Latino-related issues carried a central or minor focus was challenging for several reports, and is based on textual analysis of the abstracts. Given the polysemic nature of many audiovisual news reports, audience interpretations likely varied. In spite of the limitations noted, this data-gathering method serves the general purposes of this study.

As table 10.1 demonstrates, the number of Latino-related reports

*Table 10.1* Summary of findings: Latino-related television news reports aired by the ABC, CBS and NBC networks in 1988, 1992, 1996*

| Focus of news reports | 1988 | 1992 | 1996 | Total |
|---|---|---|---|---|
| **Central** | | | | |
| Latinos/Latino issues | 21 | 9 | 7 | 37 |
| The Latino vote | 5 | 1 | 1 | 7 |
| Candidates'/parties' appeals to Latinos | 2 | 0 | 0 | 2 |
| **Minor** | | | | |
| Latinos/Latino issues | 18 | 11 | 5 | 34 |
| The Latino vote | 0 | 1 | 0 | 1 |
| Candidates'/parties' appeals to Latinos | 3 | 0 | 1 | 4 |
| Total number of stories | 49 | 22 | 14 | 85 |

* CNN was included for 1996 and aired three of the 12 stories found (see Table 10.4)

appearing on the networks' evening news programs diminished with each presidential election year. While the decline occurred in all categories, it was most pronounced in two: stories regarding the potential size and impact of the Latino vote, and presidential candidates' efforts to reach Latino voters. The following overviews of news report content reveal that negative reports consistently outnumbered positive ones.

## 1988 news reports

During the final presidential election year of the "Decade of the Hispanic," news programs dedicated five reports to the Latino vote (three of them focused on Texas), and mentioned appeals by candidates to Latino voters in five others. The strong emphasis on Latinos may be attributed in part to the language abilities of Democratic candidates Michael Dukakis and Lloyd Bentsen, both of whom appeared on network newscasts speaking Spanish. Another contributing factor was that Republican presidential candidate George H. W. Bush's son Jeb—who served as governor of Florida from 1998 to 2007—is married to a native of Mexico (as will be discussed further). Texas attracted attention not only for its weight in the Electoral College and large population of Latinos, but also as the home state of both George H. W. Bush and Lloyd Bentsen who had run against one another in a 1970 U.S. Senate election, which Bentsen won.

The non-election-specific reports concerning Latinos fit three general categories: legal, demographic, and social/cultural. We must keep in mind that the categories are not mutually exclusive, and most reports carry political and/or economic undertones. Discrimination suits brought by Latino (and other minority) officers against law enforcement agencies were a major focus of legal reports. Immigration and the federal

*Table 10.2* Summary of Latino-related news reports aired in 1988

| Topic and focus of story | No. of reports | Weekday and date of report | Length of report* | Network |
|---|---|---|---|---|
| **Central focus on Latinos** | | | | |
| FBI discrimination vs. Latino agents | 4 | T, 3/1 | 4:30 | NBC |
| | | F, 8/26 | 4:40 | CBS |
| | | F, 9/30 | 0:30 | NBC |
| | | F, 9/30 | 1:30 | ABC |
| Latino voting power in Texas | 3 | T, 3/1 | 2:40 | CBS |
| | | Sa, 8/7 | 3:20 | NBC |
| | | F, 10/28 | 2:50 | ABC |
| Discrimination against minorities in Chicago police department | 1 | M, 3/28 | 0:20 | ABC |
| Extended amnesty deadline for illegal aliens? | 1 | T, 4/26 | 4:10 | ABC |
| *Avance* parenting program in San Antonio | 1 | Sa, 5/28 | 3:10 | ABC |
| Latino vote special report | 2 | Su, 5/5 | 4:40 | NBC |
| | | M, 9/12 | 4:00 | NBC |
| Increased interest in Latino media audiences/La Bamba | 1 | W, 6/15 | 3:00 | ABC |
| George Bush courts Latino voters | 1 | W, 7/6 | 0:20 | ABC |
| Latinos comprise new wave of immigration | 1 | Sa, 7/23 | 2:20 | NBC |
| Lloyd Bentsen courts Latino vote in Texas | 1 | Sa, 8/6 | 2:00 | CBS |
| Lauro Cavazos appointed to Cabinet | 2 | T, 8/9 | 0:30 | ABC |
| | | T, 8/9 | 0:20 | CBS |
| U.S. Census Bureau report on Latino population growth | 3 | T, 9/6 | 0:20 | CBS |
| | | T, 9/6 | 0:30 | ABC |
| | | T, 9/6 | 0:20 | NBC |
| **Minor focus on Latinos** | | | | |
| "White flight" in Chicago (Blacks and Latinos moving in) | 1 | Th, 3/24 | 2:30 | ABC |
| Chicago Latinos live in a gang "war zone" | 1 | T, 3/29 | 6:20 | NBC |
| Program to address high Latino school drop-out rates | 1 | Sa, 4/24 | 4:00 | NBC |
| Reagan endorses Bush; challenges to Bush in CA | 1 | W, 5/11 | 2:50 | CBS |
| Report on AIDS: Blacks and Latinos threatened | 1 | Su, 6/12 | 8:00 | CBS |
| Republican Party courts Hispanic voters | 1 | W, 6/29 | 1:55 | ABC |

| Topic and focus of story | No. of reports | Weekday and date of report | Length of report* | Network |
|---|---|---|---|---|
| Latino school drop-out rates and economic issues | 1 | W, 7/6 | 4:10 | CBS |
| Jesse Jackson addresses Latino voters | 1 | F, 7/8 | 2:00 | ABC |
| "Barrio Scenario" political strategy outlined | 1 | Sa, 8/6 | 4:10 | CBS |
| Bush points out his Mexican American grandchildren | 2 | T, 8/16<br>T, 8/16 | 4:30<br>2:10 | CBS<br>NBC |
| Bush retorts press question regarding grandchildren | 2 | W, 8/17<br>W, 8/17 | 3:00<br>3:40 | CBS<br>NBC |
| FBI discrimination vs. Latino agents (part of longer report) | 1 | M, 8/29 | 4:30 | ABC |
| Bush celebrates with Latino voters | 1 | M, 9/12 | 4:30 | CBS |
| Dukakis appeals to Black and Latino voters | 1 | Sa, 10/15 | 4:10 | CBS |
| Four Latino law enforcement organizations endorse Dukakis | 1 | Sa, 10/15 | 4:10 | NBC |
| Report on English-only propositions | 1 | Sa, 11/5 | 2:10 | CBS |

* In minutes and seconds

government's amnesty program for undocumented aliens also were emphasized—this theme recurs powerfully in 1996. Brief stories were reported on the Latino population growth related to the immigration issue, and on the expansion of Spanish-language media and advertising industries in the U.S. One menacing report concerned a demographic shift likely to alarm some mainstream viewers: the "White flight" from Chicago neighborhoods as Black and Latino residents moved in. Most, but not all reports on social issues contained negative elements. Latinos were portrayed as living amidst gang wars, dropping out of school in high numbers, and as especially threatened by the spread of AIDS. Two positive reports concerned the *Avance* parenting program in San Antonio, and Lauro Cavazos' appointment as Secretary of Education.

## 1992 news reports

In 1992, the number of network news reports on the Latino vote and the candidates' efforts to attract it diminished considerably from the level in 1988. Two reports focused on the Latino vote, but none reported George H. W. Bush's or Bill Clinton's efforts to woo Latino voters. Whereas Texas was the principal geographic focus of the 1988 reports, in 1992

243

California, New Mexico and the South were highlighted. Latino/Latina politicians figured more prominently in news reports. Positive reports included San Antonio mayor Henry Cisneros' prediction of strong Latino support for Clinton–Gore, and an increased number of Latinos running for U.S. Congress. A negative report revealed that the Democratic candidate for Texas Railroad Commissioner, Lena Guerrero, made false claims about her academic record.

The non-election-specific reports concerning Latinos in 1992 fit the same general categories identified for 1988, but with some telling differences. Except for a report about a Latino juror in the trial of Anglo Los Angeles police officers accused of beating a Black man, Rodney King, all reports with a legal theme emphasized crime. In one report a Latino journalist was a murder victim; three others identified Latinos as criminals during the riots following announcement of the police officers' acquittal in the Rodney King case. The demographic reports aired in 1992 had a distinct economic disposition. (The reader is reminded of Bill Clinton's credo, "It's the economy, stupid.") A report examining Latino market growth was aired too early in the year, on January 2, to have had much impact on voters' judgments or behaviors in the November election.

Two other reports, also appearing early in the year, focused on high unemployment among Latinos and Blacks. Thus Blacks, who were presented to news audiences as Latinos' partners in crime during the Los Angeles riots, were depicted as sharing other problems as well. A report concerning the incidence of HIV and AIDS among the two groups appeared in March, and the sole report on a Latino community examined South Central Los Angeles, an area that is commonly identified with Blacks in mainstream America's consciousness and popular culture. Given this close association by network newscasts, one wonders about the impact of a later report which explained that many Latinos are caught between the Anglo and Hispanic cultures. This implies that association with Blacks brings other groups down whereas the Anglo culture is something to aspire to. It also is strong evidence of race bias in U.S. television news (Campbell, 1995; Wilson, Gutiérrez and Chao, 2003).

The major themes of 1992 were all present in a CBS report aired on May 28. Following the riots, presidential candidates Bush and Clinton visited Los Angeles to survey the damage, discuss rebuilding as well as job-creation efforts, and, of course, to seek votes through news coverage. The candidates, in cautiously negotiating a political minefield, touched on economics, justice and social harmony in an effort to establish rapport with minority groups without alienating the mainstream voting public. The report included critical and skeptical comments from six Black and Latino residents and political representatives regarding the rebuilding effort. Most of them questioned the motives behind the presidential candidates' visits. We may assume that the tensions reflected in the report

*Table 10.3* Summary of Latino-related news reports aired in 1992

| Topic and focus of story | No. of reports | Weekday and date of report | Length of report* | Network |
|---|---|---|---|---|
| **Central focus on Latinos** | | | | |
| Growth of Latino market in U.S. | 1 | T, 1/2 | 2:20 | NBC |
| Latino investigative reporter murdered in New York City | 1 | Th, 3/12 | 2:40 | CBS |
| Latino community in South Central Los Angeles | 1 | W, 5/27 | 4:30 | ABC |
| Latinos played a prominent role in Los Angeles riots | 2 | Th, 6/18 F, 6/19 | 2:40 2:20 | CBS CBS |
| Importance of Latino vote in elections | 1 | Su, 8/9 | 3:00 | CBS |
| Latinos caught between two cultures | 1 | T, 9/8 | 4:10 | CBS |
| Lena Guerrero (TX) misrepresented her academic record | 1 | F, 9/18 | 2:10 | NBC |
| Controversy amid Hallmark's sale of Univisión Network | 1 | Su, 10/4 | 3:00 | CBS |
| **Minor focus on Latinos** | | | | |
| Head Start funding, increased numbers of Black, Latino workers | 1 | T, 1/21 | 5:00 | NBC |
| Unemployment among Latinos, others outlined | 1 | F, 2/7 | 2:30 | CBS |
| Incidence of HIV/AIDS among Latinos and Blacks | 1 | Th, 3/5 | 4:00 | ABC |
| Latinos in South support Clinton on Super Tuesday | 1 | T, 3/10 | 7:00 | ABC |
| Gang truce following Los Angeles riots | 1 | T, 5/5 | 8:00 | CBS |
| Lone Latino on R. King police jury favored guilty verdict | 1 | W, 5/6 | 7:50 | CBS |
| Los Angeles riots, rebuilding, presidential candidates' visits | 1 | Th, 5/28 | 5:30 | CBS |
| Latinos potentially hold swing vote in CA | 1 | Sa, 8/15 | 2:30 | NBC |
| Henry Cisneros predicts high Latino vote for Clinton | 1 | W, 9/23 | 8:40 | NBC |
| Latino leader comments on vote in New Mexico | 1 | Th, 10/22 | 2:30 | CBS |
| Increased number of Latinos run for U.S. Congress | 1 | Su, 11/1 | 4:00 | NBC |

* In minutes and seconds

will continue to challenge U.S. politics and political communication so long as the population diversifies and voters' confidence in their elected officials remains low.

## 1996 news reports

For 1996, the number of news report abstracts appearing in the Vanderbilt Television Index and containing the terms "Hispanic" and "Latino" declined to 12 from a high of 39 in 1988 and a midrange of 20 in 1992. The trend toward fewer reports on Latinos' influence in U.S. elections continued, as did the geographic focus on states having numerous Electoral College votes and large Latino populations. Texas and Florida were highlighted in a report (September 27, ABC), which mentioned Latinos' booing of Republican vice presidential candidate Jack Kemp, who had reversed his position on affirmative action (Kahlenberg, 1996).

Legal issues in 1996 emphasized immigration and abuses by law enforcement officers. Passage of California's Proposition 187—to limit illegal aliens' access to government-funded services such as education and health care—brought immigration to the forefront of public debate in the 1994 congressional and gubernatorial elections. In 1996, Proposition 209 prohibited affirmative action in government hiring and college admissions at California's public universities. ABC aired a report concerning the economic, linguistic, and cultural assimilation aspects of immigration. NBC and CNN covered the Latino and Immigrants' Rights March on Washington D.C. to protest anti-immigration legislation and reductions in government aid programs to legal immigrants. (The NBC report included brief commentary on the relationship between citizenship and Latino voters' participation in elections.) A report on Pat Buchanan's presidential candidacy included video coverage of a Latino man publicly challenging Buchanan's views on immigration.

The reports concerning abuses by law enforcement officers were probably associated, in many viewers' minds, with the beating of Rodney King and the riots in Los Angeles following the acquittal of his attackers. A television news crew videotaped police officers beating two Mexican nationals on a roadside in El Monte, California. Latinos also were mentioned as targets of profiling by police in a report focused mostly on Blacks.

Latinos again were grouped with Blacks—and mentioned only briefly—in two other 1996 news reports. One story focused on computer literacy and employability in future job markets; another reported the increased interest among Black and Latino youths in ice hockey, a sport that historically has seen little participation by non-Anglos. Other social/cultural stories concerning Latinos focused on girls' participation in gangs, and remembrances of the Tejano singer Selena on the first anniversary of her murder in 1995.

*Table 10.4* Summary of Latino-related news reports aired in 1996

| Topic and focus of story | No. of reports | Weekday and date of report | Length of report* | Network |
|---|---|---|---|---|
| **Central focus on Latinos** | | | | |
| Selena remembered on first anniversary of her death | 1 | Sa, 3/31 | 2:40 | CBS |
| Mexicans beaten on roadside by CA police | 1 | T, 4/2 | 1:10 | CNN |
| Focus on immigration (language, assimilation, economics) | 1 | Th, 5/16 | 7:40 | ABC |
| Latino vote: parties' efforts to reach and voter registration | 1 | Sa, 6/29 | 2:10 | ABC |
| Gangs and girls | 1 | W, 9/4 | 4:20 | CBS |
| Latinos in capital to protest immigration/welfare reform | 2 | Sa, 10/12<br>Sa, 10/12 | 3:10<br>1:10 | NBC<br>CNN |
| **Minor focus on Latinos** | | | | |
| Latinos, like Blacks, will fall behind without computer skills | 1 | F, 1/5 | 3:50 | CBS |
| Latino man challenges Pat Buchanan on immigration | 1 | F, 2/23 | 7:40 | CNN |
| Latinos and other minorities beginning to play ice hockey | 1 | Sa, 3/30 | 3:10 | ABC |
| Latinos, like Blacks, harassed through police "profiling" | 1 | W, 5/22 | 4:00 | CBS |
| Presidential campaign in TX and FL | 1 | F, 9/27 | 5:50 | ABC |

* In minutes and seconds

## Latinos and the character issue

The network newscasts' diminishing emphasis on the Latino vote over the three election years contradicts the opening statement of *Pursuing Power: Latinos and the Political System*:

> If the 1980s were the "Decade of the Hispanic," the 1990s appear to be the decade of Hispanic "recognition and diversity." The major institutions of American society—governments, businesses, schools, the media, and others—as well as much of the general populace, finally recognize the presence and major impact of Latinos.
>
> (Garcia, 1997: 1)

On network news programs, Latinos' political clout received more recognition in 1988 than in 1992 or 1996, years marked by reports on the Los Angeles riots and the negative consequences of immigration. Coverage in 1988 appears to be influenced by the novelty of the "Decade of the Hispanic" and some of the candidates' personal attributes, which brought Latinos within closer range of the cameras trained on those candidates. Here I refer to the Spanish speaking abilities of Democratic candidates Michael Dukakis and Lloyd Bentsen, and Republican George H.W. Bush's Mexican daughter-in-law and half-Mexican grandchildren. While the size and influence of the Latino electorate increased during the 1990s, candidates Bill Clinton, Ross Perot and Bob Dole had fewer personal ties to Latinos, and the novelty of the Decade of the Hispanic apparently wore off for news organizations. (Latinos regained press attention during the Latin Boom of the late 1990s and early 2000s—such cyclical popular interest and its attendant news reporting merits further investigation.)

The multiple implications of news coverage joining Latinos with Blacks in reports on social and economic problems deserve fuller attention than I can provide here (see Ríos & Mohamed, 2003). In his book, *Black and Brown in America*, Bill Piatt underscores the complexity of the groups' relationship and television's tendency to "offer soundbites or videoclips . . . of minority youths who throw rocks at one another or exchange gun fire" rather than "presenting the stories of successful peacemakers" (Piatt, 1997: 10). The news reports garnered by this study tended to present Latinos and Blacks as partners in problems, not as rivals, but, given the negative nature of the reports, they were unlikely to bolster mainstream viewers' confidence in their trustworthiness as citizens or voters in either case. As experts on politics, the media, and ethnic relations have noted, power and class are the principal underlying issues in these news reports (Wilson, Gutiérrez and Chao, 2003; Heider, 2000). In the triangular relationship between politicians, the press and the public, the first two command the greatest influence over the content of political information reaching voters. The public's power to influence news content is limited (except on Election Day), a problem that is exacerbated for disadvantaged minority groups. An election year case with ethnic undertones clearly demonstrates this skewed power dynamic.

## THE "LITTLE BROWN ONES" INCIDENT

On August 16, 1988, presidential candidate George H. W. Bush and members of his family arrived in New Orleans, site of the Republican National Convention. As political protocol dictates, President Ronald Reagan and his wife, Nancy, were departing the convention so as not to overshadow the Bushes. In order to emphasize the symbolic changing of the guard, and to bolster Bush's presidential image, a photo opportunity was arranged on the tarmac in front of Air Force One. Each candidate gave a short speech to a crowd of spectators and numerous journalists. At one point during the event, Barbara Bush motioned her grandchildren toward her to introduce them to the Reagans. As she did so, microphones on the nearby podium amplified George Bush's comment to the Reagans: "That's Jebbie's kids from Florida, the little brown ones." The children have darker complexions than other members of the Bush family because their mother, Columba, is from Mexico.

Bush's comment was broadcast on evening news programs and widely reported the following day. The question arose whether his use of "little brown ones" was pejorative, a slur on the children's ethnic heritage; normative, intended to differentiate the Mexican Americans from other children in the vicinity; or perhaps affectionate, a term of endearment. How the American public interpreted Bush's remark could affect his ability to attract the Latino vote on Election Day, and was a potential indicator of character for voters in a variety of cultural groups, not only Latinos. A comparison of how three English- and two U.S. Spanish-language television networks covered the story provides insight into the salience of character issues in U.S. campaign politics, and reveals how distinct sectors of the media "spin" campaign-related news.

## English-language television coverage

English-language networks provided brief coverage of Bush's remark on August 16, the day he uttered it. Sound-bites of the comment were included as segments of longer news packages concerning the Republican convention and the Bush campaign—reporters used only six seconds to introduce the 3.5-second sound-bite within news reports of two minutes (NBC), and 4.5 minutes (CBS). Only the most attentive viewers were likely to have deciphered Bush's comment. The following day's coverage was more extensive and provocative. Since it was the first Bush–Quayle news conference, most reporters' questions concerned vice presidential candidate Dan Quayle's relative inexperience in national politics, his rumored affair with Paula Parkinson, and his National Guard service during the Vietnam War (i.e., character issues). In the closing moments of the news conference, Bush was asked about the reference to his grandchildren as "little brown ones." Here is how the different networks introduced and reported Bush's retort.

> BRIT HUME (ABC): Finally there was a question to Bush about the flap caused by his reference yesterday to his half-Mexican grandchildren as "little brown ones." He replied with a rare display of emotion.

BUSH: Those grandchildren are my pride and joy. And when I say pride I mean it. And for anyone to suggest that that comment was anything other than what it was, I find it personally offensive. And this is my family and I'm going to protect them.

BRIT HUME: That was said in anger but was an indication of the energy that George Bush showed all day. Ronald Reagan is gone, he is now the party's standard bearer. He has made his choice—a surprise choice—he seems delighted with it and for today at least he was a new man. [43 seconds]

* * * * *

BOB SCHEIFFER (CBS): Then when Bush got a personal question, reporters got a glimpse of a side of him that is seldom seen. Told an incident at the airport yesterday had offended some Hispanics because he referred to three of his grandchildren— who are Mexican American—as "the little brown ones," Bush replied with a controlled anger.

BUSH: Those grandchildren are my pride and joy. And when I say pride I mean it. And for anyone to suggest that that comment was anything other than what it was, I find it personally offensive. And P.S., I don't want to see these kids hurt. This heart knows nothing but pride and love for those three children and you're going to see them with me every inch of the way.

BOB SCHIEFFER: Bush's intensity sent a spark of electricity through a fairly routine news conference, and his advisors couldn't have been more pleased. It's a side of George Bush they've been trying to get him to show for years. [49 seconds]

* * * * *

DENNIS MURPHY (NBC): And he displayed a flash of anger that Hispanics might take as a slur his reference yesterday to his three Mexican American grandchildren as "the little brown ones."

BUSH: P.S. I don't want to see these kids hurt. And they weren't hurt by what I said. And if they're hurt by misinterpretation that isn't fair, and I don't like it, and this is my family, and I'm going to protect . . . [21 seconds]

These transcriptions reflect the news reports' emphasis on Bush's political skills in diffusing a potentially damaging issue, his mettle as a leader, and his loyalty and love of family. The focus on political skills aided Bush's efforts in overcoming the "wimp factor" which dogged him earlier in the campaign.[5] The English-language newscasts absolved Bush of racial bias or a limited commitment to diversity—the very questions evoking strong reactions to his comment by some Latinos. No specifics were offered as to who had reacted to the comment, or how they had interpreted it. The reports inferred that Bush's show of strength would gain him votes, but the possibility was not raised that he might alienate Latino voters who, we recall, were relatively conspicuous on the television news agenda in 1988.

## U.S. Spanish-language television coverage

The national newscasts of neither Telemundo nor Univisión reported Bush's remark on the day it was spoken. The following day, August 17, both networks broadcast statements by the children's father, Jeb Bush, a fluent Spanish speaker. It should be noted that the two news programs examined here represent an important source of information on this issue for Spanish-speakers in the U.S. Like the English-language networks, Telemundo's coverage consisted of a short segment (24 seconds) at the end of a news package concerning George Bush's selection of Dan Quayle as his running mate.[6] Jeb Bush's statement followed commentary by the reporter Magdalena Fernández (my translation).

> FERNÁNDEZ: But speaking of alienating possible voters, Bush emphatically denied that he had again stuck his foot in his mouth. Yesterday, when introducing his grandchildren to President Reagan, he said, "here are the little brown ones." Bush explicitly denied insinuations that he had referred to them in a pejorative manner.
>
> JEB BUSH: I'll tell you one thing—my father's love for my children is so strong that he would never say something to hurt them or to offend a group in this country that is as big and important as . . . [cut to Fernández speaking from the convention floor].

The Telemundo report differed from English-language coverage by questioning the comment's potential impact on Bush's efforts to win the Latino vote.

Univisión's coverage of the incident was the most extensive (2 minutes, 3 seconds) and was presented in a distinct format, an interview with Jeb Bush by co-anchors Maria Elena Salinas and Jorge Ramos in a temporary studio located above the convention floor (my translation).

> SALINAS: Jeb, first an issue that's somewhat sensitive for the Bush family, which is the comment that your father made

251

yesterday that many people have taken as an insult. Your father referred to your children as "the little brown ones." What exactly happened?

BUSH: Well, I wasn't there, but I can tell you that my father's relationship with my children is so sacred, so important to him that never, never would he say something to hurt the children he adores. He adores my children and is proud of their heritage. That is, my father is so innocent and so decent in all of this that I think the problem is that there are a lot of journalists here with nothing to do, and it could be that when there's nothing to do, their imaginations run a bit.

SALINAS: You think it's the fault of journalists who misinterpreted your father's meaning?

BUSH: Of course, because my father would never feel something, would never say something negative about my children's race.

SALINAS: Then he said it with affection?

BUSH: Yes, and love.

RAMOS: A final question on this issue. What can you say to all of the people who have taken offense at the comment?

BUSH: I can only say that my father is a man who not only loves my children, but is proud of their Hispanic heritage. That's the final truth, and I believe that the response that George Bush, my father, gave at the press conference says it all. [The interview continues with discussion of Dan Quayle and other campaign issues.]

Although Univisión provided lengthier coverage of the issue than did Telemundo, it too offered the Bush campaign an opportunity to drive home its point—that the candidate's words were misconstrued—from a credible source speaking the audience's vernacular. The Univisión anchorpersons alluded twice to the comment's possible alienation of Latino voters, but did not specify who had taken offense. The interview also permitted Jeb Bush to question the character of journalists in fanning the flames of the misunderstanding, and to call attention to his father's spirited reply during the press conference.

Some intriguing manifestations of the character issue emerge from analysis of the "little brown ones" incident. The English-language networks presented the controversy as a character issue, but placed it in the context of the stories they were prepared to cover—the Republican National Convention and the transfer of party leadership (and possibly the presidency) from Ronald Reagan to George H. W. Bush. The Latinos who the remark had offended called into question Bush's moral qualities and commitment to ethnic and racial diversity, but were not seen or heard directly. The English-language networks put their own spin, as influenced by Bush and his handlers, on the character issue. For their part, the Spanish-language networks raised the character issue in the context of inter-ethnic relations, but did so in a lopsided fashion. Jeb Bush was granted airtime to defend his father, but those who had taken offense at the remark remained silent and anonymous. As Quiroga (1997) points out, this is a recurring problem in news coverage of Latino-related issues.

## CONCLUSION

Unfortunately, this study may be counted as part of what Louis DeSipio identifies as "a growing body of literature [which] demonstrates that sheer numbers alone do not ensure that Latino communities will become central to the American political process" (1996: 29). It is a disturbing tendency. In the penultimate year of the Decade of the Hispanic, television news highlighted the increased presence, spending power and potential political clout of Latinos, inferring that this slumbering giant, once awakened, would change U.S. political, economic, and cultural life. Subsequent news coverage emphasized social problems, and the giant was shown looting in 1992 and sneaking over the border to pilfer public services in 1996.[7] Although it would be a stretch to claim that mainstream news audiences recall specifics of Latino-related stories from election year to election year—or even from January to Election Day—the general tenor of characterizations are likely to stick. In response to the question posed at the outset, most viewers of the reports discussed here would probably conclude that Latinos are unworthy stewards of the political power they potentially command. This bodes poorly for developing an electoral system that will equitably serve an increasingly diverse U.S. society in future years.

It would be easy, yet misguided, to place all blame for this problem and responsibility for its resolution on television news or the media in general. If positive change is to occur it must derive from a variety of sources. Television news departments need to review their methods, motives, and responsibilities in reporting the news with greater balance and deference to political and cultural pluralism. Rather than lay short-term plans for candidates in select races, political parties should engage longer-term efforts to assess the needs and interests of the electorate's subgroups and to determine, then develop, contact points with their own goals and platforms. Political scientists need a fuller understanding of the complex dynamics of character perceptions among politicians, the press, and voters as well as other actors in political processes. Communication researchers should pay closer attention to how media portrayals intersect with political processes and ethnic group relations among a diverse electorate. As the number of media technologies and outlets multiplies, more research is needed concerning the similarities and differences in the political coverage of news sources. For their part, Latino voters require a stronger voice and more decisive proactive conduct in their relations with political parties, politicians, and the media if they are to foster more and better coverage of their communities' significant contributions to U.S. society. Two gubernatorial elections in 1998 suggested possible change in the dynamics this chapter has revealed, but came under clouds of uncertainty with the 2000 presidential elections and President George W. Bush's response to the attacks of September 11, 2001.

In 1998, George W. Bush was re-elected governor of Texas and his brother Jeb, father of the "little brown ones," won the governorship of Florida. Both attracted Latino votes through careful handling of Latino-related issues and speaking Spanish in public appearances and campaign advertising.[8] Two years later, in the 2000 presidential election, the Bush brothers' relationship became a central issue in the legal struggle over disputed votes cast in Florida which eventually allowed George W. Bush to defeat the Democratic candidate, Al Gore. Florida's Latinos voted in similar percentages to other voters in the state as well as to the nation at large: 49 percent for Bush versus 48 percent for Gore (Glanton, 2000). Many Latinos were encouraged when Bush warmed to President Vicente Fox and made Mexico the first international destination of his presidency. One journalist wrote in May 2001, "President Bush is wooing Hispanics with all the passion of mariachis beneath the window of that special señorita" (Kiefer, 2001). However, the September 11, 2001 terrorist attacks pushed immigration reform, border concerns and other Mexico-related issues to the back burner as domestic security and the War on Terror came to dominate the Bush administration's agenda.

As other contributors to this volume have noted, the 2004 presidential elections saw a shift in Latino voting favoring the Republican Party. Although much of the 2004 electoral data was still under analysis as this chapter was completed, I advocate for the extension of studies along the lines of this chapter to future election periods. Technological innovations have made sources of information about politics and social groups more accessible than ever. Latinos have gained increasing attention in the 2000s as the so-called "Latin Boom" infused popular culture; Latinos became the United States' largest minority group, and their substantial buying power became more broadly recognized (and coveted). As regards political communication, researchers and the public alike may benefit from more thorough assessments of the collective portrayal of Latinos in the mainstream media. Latino voters and political leaders must take note of how faithfully their interests and actions are being represented and act accordingly.

## NOTES

1 Ansolabehere, Behr and Iyengar (1993: 62) cite these additional reasons for journalists' increased emphasis of the character issue beginning in the 1970s: journalism's "locker room atmosphere" changed as more women entered the profession; the volume and intensity of campaign coverage increased; the competition for audience share increased the pressure on journalists to report racier stories more quickly.

2 The terms "Latino" and "Hispanic" appear in the indexes of few books and in few reference databases covering electoral politics and the media. In sources where the term does appear, the treatments are typically quite limited.

3 For each of the years studied, the terms "Hispanic" and "Latino" were employed by themselves to gather all news reports mentioning that population group. Subsequently, "Hispanic" and "Latino" were sought in combination with the terms "vote," "campaign," "election," "politic*," and the principal presidential candidates' last names to garner election-related reports.

4 CNN was included for 1996 and aired three of the 12 stories found (see table 10.4).

5 Political pundits agreed that Bush's heated exchange with CBS's Dan Rather during an interview broadcast on January 25, 1988 was intended to dispel the wimp image and increase his presidential stature (Ansolabehere, Behr and Iyengar, 1993: 63).

6 The similarity in news packaging may have derived in part from Telemundo's arrangement with Cable News Network to co-produce the news program, *Noticiero Telemundo-CNN*.

7 This trend in simplistic, negative coverage of Latinos and Latino issues by English-language networks has now been well documented in the annual *Brownout Reports* published by the National Association of Hispanic Journalists. See, for example, Subervi (2004) and the 10-year compendium report, Subervi (2005).

8 George W. Bush won 46 percent of the Latino vote in Texas (up from 25 percent in 1994) while Jeb won 61 percent of Florida's Latino vote (down from 71 percent in his unsuccessful 1994 campaign).

# 11

# LA MALA EDUCACIÓN OF NETWORK MEDIA AND NATIONAL POLITICS

A content analysis of the education issue in the 2000 presidential election

*Amy G. Langenkamp* and *Federico A. Subervi-Vélez*

Beginning with the Civil Rights Movement in the 1960s and the introduction of the Bilingual Education Act of 1968, the education of racial, ethnic, and language minorities has been a centerpiece of political conversations in the United States (Keller and Van Hooft, 1982; Lyons, 1990). During the 2000 presidential campaign, the issues surrounding the educational system in the United States came to the foreground as one of the most important banners for the candidates and voters. Consequently, the media repeatedly brought the issue of education, including multicultural and multilingual education, to the forefront of campaign coverage.[1]

As the presidential candidates' education platforms were mentioned and discussed in the news, political analysts paid close attention to Latinos because they were being courted by Democrats and Republicans, both parties considered this ethnic group as having the potential to influence the outcome of the election (Figueroa and Sonia, 2000). Like the rest of the nation, Latinos stated education as among their most important issues in the 2000 election (NCLR, 2000). Not surprisingly, during the campaign, Latinos were at the center of the candidates' education speeches that focused on public school choice, affirmative action, and the achievement gap.

Given the importance of the education issue that year and the heightened attention given to Latinos, we explored how information regarding education, as a political issue, was being presented in the news. To that end, we first studied the education platforms of Al Gore and George W. Bush. Then we conducted a content analysis of the major television network news coverage to assess how the education issue was covered during the

256

last nine weeks of the campaign—the period when most potential voters, especially independent and swing voters, increase their attention to news about the elections. We also assessed whether or not the TV news coverage provided attention to education issues as pertaining to and relevant to Latinos.

Latinos are not a monolithic social, economic, cultural, or political block. Opinion surveys have shown that there are national, generational, socio-economic status, and regional differences regarding Hispanics' views on issues such as abortion, international affairs, immigration, the death penalty, and even affirmative action (de la Garza et al., 1992).[2] This has made them even more attractive to politicians of both parties who seek to exploit the particular issues with which they may capitalize their respective outreach efforts.

Latinos, however, do share a common and heightened interest in the issue of education because it is considered the most important road to success and achieving the "American dream." Thus, for politicians of any party, this issue is also most certain to strike a common chord across the country among Latinos of all national origins.

Reaching out via the mass media is a large part of any modern campaign strategy. Politicians and their campaign managers regularly incorporate the ubiquitous media in their efforts to frame the most salient issues (Esser and D'Angelo, 2003; Iyengar, 1991). It could thus be expected that the media, particularly television, would be a major avenue used by the presidential candidates to reach Latinos and point out how the educational policies of their respective parties are relevant and attuned to Latinos' own interests.

Television was the focus of this study because it is a major source through which people gather information about political candidates, particularly at the national level. Network national news has traditionally held the largest and most consistent audience in the U.S., making it the most pervasive and uniform source for political news (Graber, 1997). Graber also notes the importance of television in the construction of political issues. Through polls and repeated focus on certain aspects of an issue, television has considerable control over candidates' platforms and the components highlighted to the voting public (Graber, 1997; Iyengar, 1991).[3]

If such is the case, there is significant value in analyzing how those networks cover political news. Assessing how key campaign issues, such as education, were presented on ABC, CBS, and NBC would be revealing of the information about these issues available to the general public. Moreover, network television news has a large audience, and the news presented has the potential to influence voters' behavior. Thus, a content analysis of the political information presented by the networks would help understand the information deemed to be important by the networks and provide some valuable insights into what may have contributed to the voters' decision to support one contender over another.

As discussed in chapter 3 of this book, Spanish-language television—especially Univisión and Telemundo—serves as an important source of political information for Latinos. However, it is also true that a very large percentage of Hispanics use English-language television for their political information. In fact, viewing English news media is a principal source of information particularly among Latinos who are registered to vote (de la Garza et al., 1992). Hence, the analysis of the issue of education in the English-language network news is certainly justified.

Literature widely covers the issues of Latino educational achievement, both in the historical and theoretical contexts (Delpit, 1993; Roscigno and James, 1999), the political importance of Latinos and the role of the mass media in politics (see chapters 1–3 and the sources cited therein). However, no previous research has connected that literature with the educational content of news stories during a campaign. Looking at the manner in which the networks presented this issue, and then comparing it to the candidates' actual policy plans, links previously disparate areas of research concerning Latinos, the educational policies proposed by presidential candidates, and political communication.

## METHODOLOGY[4]

### The education policies of the presidential candidates

To contextualize the analysis of the representation of education as a campaign issue, we began with an assessment of the education platforms of Al Gore and George W. Bush. Information about those education platforms was obtained through each candidate's respective web site. The Republican Party and the Democratic Party campaign headquarters were also contacted in order to confirm that the outlined policy on the web sites was a complete source of information on the education issue. However, to maintain equity in the quantity of information representing each candidate, the analysis focused on what was stated with respect to the future education policy. Therefore, town hall meetings, speeches, and notes about each candidate's records are not part of the analysis.

### Data collection of network television news

The analysis of media coverage of the three major networks—ABC, CBS, and NBC—was conducted over the last nine weeks of the campaign: September 4, 2000, Labor Day and the "official" opening of the presidential campaign, to November 7, 2000, Election Day. To this end, the corresponding transcripts for each of the newscasts were analyzed for relevant stories. The transcripts were located by using the search engine Lexis-Nexis, which contains such data for practically all the major English-language news media in the United States. The sample studied consists of all the news segments from each of the three networks that contained references to the topic of education.

In addition, transcripts of relevant special news shows related to the campaign, such as the televised presidential debates and the immediate discussions following the debates offered by each network, were also included in the analysis. Although not part of the network news programs, the debates are essential for inclusion because they represent a widespread access to information for voters. In addition, the presidential debates are included under the title of news according to the Lexis-Nexis search engine and were analyzed for additional information regarding the candidates' education policy.

In order to obtain the sample of news stories relating to the issue of education, Lexis-Nexis was searched on a weekly basis using both a variety of terms and various combinations of those terms. In addition, search strategies specific to Lexis-Nexis were utilized to create a more comprehensive investigation of the database.[5] Altogether, 72 stories (including repeats) relating to education and the election were coded and analyzed. Of those, 23 news stories (including repeats) contained specific information on Latinos and educational policy.

The network news transcripts were examined for policy information with respect to the issue of education. Information regarding opinions about the other candidate, the current administration, and the candidates' past record were not included in the final analysis. In other words, analysis focused entirely on the stated policy of the candidate. Exceptions to the adherence of policy analysis were made in two instances, both driven by the type and style of network media coverage. First, networks often reported on the "horse race," i.e., who was ahead in the campaign. Such coverage is included because of its potential influence on the news consumer, the voter. In those cases, however, the general "horse race" was not included, but rather polls which indicate who is ahead with voters on the issue of education and opinions about certain aspects of education, such as the issue of school vouchers. Second, each network ran various stories about the state of education in the United States as a direct result of the stated importance of the education issue by the candidates and the voters. Those stories are included, as the networks used them to construct the issue of education and illustrate its importance in the context of the election.

## FINDINGS

### The education platforms

During the 2000 campaign, both George W. Bush and Al Gore developed education policy platforms and touted them as key elements to their agenda if elected president.[6] Rather than reiterating each tenet of those platforms, the focus of this analysis concentrates on the candidates' attention to education issues pertaining to Latinos and the closing of the educational achievement gap. While much of each platform was dedicated to reforming education and improving the educational system, certain policies target Latinos more than others. Because of the complexity of issues facing Latinos in the public schools, certain policies, although not explicitly stating Latinos as their targeted population, would benefit Latinos nonetheless. For example, policies directed at closing the existing gap between White and minority students were particularly relevant to Latinos, as were policies directed towards low-income families. Given that Latinos are overwhelmingly enrolled in city public schools as a population, policies addressing inner city schools were also highly relevant to Latinos.

### George W. Bush's education platform

In his education platform Bush dedicated a number of policies towards minority students including Latinos and students from low-income families. The three themes that dominated his platform were accountability, school choice, and higher education. The first of these was threaded into various aspects of the GOP candidate's tenets. He proposed giving bonuses in federal funds to states that closed the achievement gap and to spend $5 billion over five years to ensure that every disadvantaged child can read. High standards for all students while "leaving no child behind" became one of his often used slogans, as was reminding voters of his record with the public school system in Texas and its accountability structure as an example of education policy he would forward as president.

Bush's greatest attention to Latinos and other minorities pertained to school choice initiatives. He proposed that in schools identified as failing for three consecutive years, parents would be given the option of transferring their child *or* use their share of federal funding to pay for another option of their choice. This other option included tutoring, charter schools, and the highly controversial choice of non-public schools. He also proposed offering certificates to low-income parents to aid in payment for after-school programs, including faith-based programs.

Regarding higher education, the Republican presidential candidate's platform promoted an increase in funding for Hispanic Serving Institutions and an increase of $4,000 in individual Pell grants for low-income students. Both of these policies would certainly be directly beneficial to Latinos.[7]

### Al Gore's education platform

In Gore's education platform, the three themes identified which deal with Latinos as disadvantaged students were failing schools, dropouts, and government support. The main theme Gore returned to repeatedly was the issue of failing schools, which usually have high minority populations. Under Gore's plan, states would have been required to identify and close all failing schools, which would have subsequently been reopened as charter schools or under new leadership. While the school was being turned around, parents would have been given the option to transfer their child to an alternative public school. In terms of reduction in the achievement gap, incentives and rewards would be provided for states to reduce the gap. In states that did not succeed in reducing the achievement gap, funds would be withdrawn and filtered into individual schools instead. In order to attract teachers to high-need areas, signing bonuses were to be offered to teachers and principals as well as loan forgiveness to college students willing to accept the challenge of working in these areas.

The second theme of Gore's platform addressed the problem of dropouts. Gore proposed providing matching federal grants to states that raise their compulsory school age to 18 in an attempt to keep students from dropping out before graduation from high school. Furthermore, school districts making significant progress in reducing the dropout rate would receive monetary bonuses for helping students who have become alienated from the school system and are considered to be at risk of dropping out altogether.

Finally, Gore's platform focused on governmental support. Gore proposed a number of policies aimed at giving additional help to certain populations. The plan targeted populations at risk of failure, such as children with special education needs and language-minority children. This government support also targeted additional educational support for low-income children. This policy was based on research indicating that low-income parents often cannot afford the extra help their child needs to be successful in school, such as pre-school attendance, after-school programs, and time off from their job to become more involved at school (Roscigno and James, 1999). Several of Gore's policies targeted at-risk and low-income youth. For example, most of Gore's spending was planned towards making voluntary pre-school universally affordable. This included expanding funding for pre-school programs such as Head Start and Early Head Start to help pay for childcare. In addition, after-school programs were to be made universally available to students at a failing school, although Gore would not have allocated money for faith-based after-school programs. An expansion in the Family and Medical Leave Act would have allowed parents to attend parent–teacher conferences and other school functions during the day. Lastly, a funding increase in special education was proposed to target early identification and intervention. This relates to non-English speakers, regardless of the bilingual policies of the school district, because of the special help that non-English-speaking students need upon entering the school system. In Gore's plan, additional funding was allotted for Limited English Proficient children to ensure appropriate language assessments, which directly impacts upon Spanish-speaking Latino children.

Overall, Gore's education platform included more direct policies to assist Latino children in the school system. The most notable difference between the two platforms was in the amount of assistance to be given by the federal government while the reformation of the education system is taking place. Bush stressed the importance of accountability for students, schools, and states. Beyond refocusing Head Start towards literacy, he proposed implementing any policy to bring up accountability and reduce the dropout rate of Latinos. Gore designed his program around federal assistance given to Latinos who are in failing schools. Bush, on the other hand, proposed giving the choice to individual families. Distinguishing the similarities and differences of Gore and Bush and their respective programs required an in-depth reading of each platform. Another way to get such information, and the manner in which many voting citizens learned about the candidates, was through the network news. While both candidates' platforms either dealt directly with educating Latino children or issues in education which directly impact Latinos, this type of coverage was almost non-existent in network news stories concerning the education issue.

## Education in the network news

In the evening news programs—ABC's *World News Tonight*, CBS's *Evening News*, and NBC's *Nightly News*—all three networks aired the same number of stories, nine each, which mentioned the issue of education as part of the presidential campaign. In the morning news programs, ABC's *Good Morning America* had notably more reports (13) than did NBC's *The Today Show* (9), or CBS's *The Early Show* (4). Two pre-dawn news programs, ABC's *World News This Morning* and CBS's *Morning News*, also had two stories each. In the in-depth news programs, ABC's *Nightline* and CBS's *60-Minutes* each network broadcast two stories on the issue of education as part of campaign 2000. And in the Sunday morning news and interview shows, there was one discussion of this issue on CBS's *Face the Nation* and another on NBC's *Meet the Press*.

With the exception of the greater emphasis on ABC's *Good Morning*

*America*, the networks did not differ much in the context of stories dedicated to education as a campaign issue. Overall, there were three types of education stories. As analyzed in more detail below, about half of the reports by each network did not deal with policy information. Instead, the networks either mentioned the importance of education as an issue with voters, reported on the "horse race," or showed the candidates touting their education message. However, each network had at least two feature stories on this topic during the last nine weeks of the campaign. Although not specifically addressing educational policy, those stories featured education as an important issue facing the country. The other stories offered brief outlines of education policies proposed by Gore and Bush.

In discussions of the "horse race," the networks reported consistently that education was the number one voter concern in the 2000 presidential election. Also consistent were the reports that Gore led Bush in voter polls when it came to the education issue. For example, ABC (10/17) ran a story about a poll which found that on the issue of education 48 percent of voters favored Gore versus 41 percent favored Bush (Gershon, 2000e). Similarly, among voters whose number one issue was education, CBS (10/29) reported that 48 percent would vote for Gore and 38 percent would vote for Bush (Murphy, 2000c). Interestingly, however, in an earlier news item after the second debate ABC (10/11) reported that Bush had surpassed Gore's lead on this issue, although the network provided no polling information to support that claim (Gershon, 2000c).

On the specific issue of school vouchers that would allow parents to send their child to a different school, the networks did note the stark contrast between Gore and Bush but presented conflicting polling reports. For example, CBS (9/18) reported a widespread acceptance of vouchers with 55% African-American, 58% Hispanic, and 45% Whites in support of that policy (Pitts, 2000a). A month later, ABC (10/17) reported that 40% of people were in favor of vouchers as long as it didn't take away from public school money (Gershon, 2000e). Generally, NBC avoided coverage of the "horse race" regarding the issue of education, with very little polling information on who was ahead when it came to that issue. NBC (10/25) did cover a RAND study that challenged Bush's "education miracle" in Texas (Gerbasi, 2000b). In fact, during the week before the election, NBC reported exclusively on the RAND study when dealing with the education issue.

## News about education in general

The analysis revealed that there were no major differences in content or depth among the networks that highlighted similar themes. According to all three networks, both candidates proclaimed that education was a major campaign issue, that it was a major problem facing the nation today, and thus a major focus of attention of their forthcoming presidential agenda (Gershon, 2000b; Capus, 2000a; Pitts, 2000a). The three networks also reported that each candidate proposed increasing spending on education in the national budget. For example, Gore was quoted on ABC (9/26) saying that he would increase spending on education (Simpson, 2000). CBS (10/30) focused more on the dollar amounts each candidate would spend, with Gore at $115 billion and Bush at $47 billion (Pitts, 2000a). NBC (10/17) on the other hand, mentioned several times the candidates' proposals for an expanded role of the government in education, the amount of money to be spent *and* future policies towards education.

Aside from actual statements of policy, both candidates emerged with themes regarding education. These were catch phrases that the candidates and news reporters repeated continually throughout the campaign. For example, in an ABC (9/25) story, Bush's trademark comments regarding education involved addressing what he called "the education recession" in the United States and the need to reform the system through high standards, local school control, and strong accountability (Simpson, 2000). In a subsequent ABC story (9/29), Gore pushed the need to boost teacher quality, stressed accountability for all with rewards and consequences, and called for an expansion in the federal government's role in education (Jones, 2000c). The candidates' education themes, similar to those found in the platforms, dominated the content of the coverage by the networks.

Although the networks' presentation of the candidates' ideas were relatively clear, the news reports about the cost of the presidential candidates' education plans were seemingly inconsistent. Each network indicated different figures throughout the campaign. In part, this could have been driven by a lack of clarity from the candidates themselves. By the end of the campaign, however, the networks came more or less to a consensus as to the cost of each education plan. CBS (10/30) reported that Gore's education policy involved a $115 billion education plan over 10 years, representing an increase in 50 percent in the current budget (Pitts, 2000a). CBS had already indicated (9/18) that half of this money would have gone towards making pre-school available for all children and expanding Head Start to service those children (Pitts, 2000a). According to a story by CBS (10/29), the main focus of Gore's education plan involved recruitment of new teachers, raising teacher's salaries, testing new teachers, teacher training and professional development (Murphy, 2000c). That same story reported that Gore would eventually spend a total of $170 billion to build new schools, modernize school buildings, and hire 100,000 new teachers. In addition, all three networks (ABC 9/29, CBS 10/29, and NBC 10/3) pointed out that Gore's plan on making higher education more affordable would have come in the form of a $10,000 tax cut for college education (Jones, 2000c; Murphy, 2000c; Capus, 2000b).

The price of Bush's education plan, on the other hand, was more difficult to determine based on the networks' reporting. Essentially, all networks (ABC 9/25, CBS 10/29, NBC 9/25) reported on Bush's proposed spending of $47–48 billion over 10 years, targeting literacy for all students and in the implementation of a voucher program (Jones, 2000a; Murphy, 2000c; Gerbasi, 2000a). According to a CBS (9/25) story, Bush's main focus for his spending revolved around a voucher program, early literacy programs, mandatory testing for grades 3–8, and additional money for safe school programs and after school programs (Murphy, 2000b). That CBS story also quoted Bush as proposing to spend $25 billion on early reading programs and $13.5 billion over five years with one third going towards literacy reform and that some of his spending would go towards expanding money for college scholarships and grants for low-income students for their first year of college.

Beyond the price of the education plans, throughout the campaign voters learned from the networks about the general education plans of each candidate. Gore was reported on ABC (9/4) as proposing to make pre-school universal for all children by 2004 (Gershon, 2000a). Another ABC (9/29) story also stated that Gore indicated that all money for public schools should stay in the public school system and that he did not support public school vouchers for private school attendance (Jones, 2000c). That same news item indicated that Gore instead opted for public school choice in the form of adding more charter schools to the public school system so that if a school was labeled as a failing school, the state and school districts would be required to invest in reforming that school; if, after two years, the school had not made substantial enough improvements, it would be closed and subsequently reopened under new leadership (Jones, 2000c).

On a CBS (10/30) story, Bush's education plan was reported as involving higher standards, accountability, and literacy—a policy requiring the testing of children each year in grades 3–8 (Pitts, 2000b). That news item also pointed out that, according to Bush, Head Start should reform its curriculum to accommodate these goals and focus more on literacy. In an earlier story on ABC (10/17), Bush was reported as stating that failing schools would have three years in which to turn around and if improvements were not made in that time, federal aid would be cut to those public school districts, and that those districts would then be required to give $1500 to each family of a child in the school in the form of a voucher that could be used for private school education, tutoring, or another public school (Gershon, 2000e).

## The education issue during presidential debates

The presidential debates garnered additional information regarding the education proposals of Bush and Gore. Each candidate presented some more details regarding his previously proposed plans, but did not forward any controversial new information or policy. Bush focused primarily on reading, calling literacy the "new civil right." He saw phonics as integral to curriculum, the creation of reading laboratories, and teacher retraining. Bush also stressed accountability, with a plan to post the testing results of each school on the Internet and allow parents to use vouchers to help remove their children from failing schools. Gore, on the other hand, emphasized signing bonuses for the recruitment of new teachers, money for school districts to build new schools and modernize existing schools, and reduction of class sizes to allow students more one-on-one time with teachers (NBC 10/3, Capus, 2000b; NBC 10/11, Capus, 2000c; NBC 10/17, Capus, 2000d).

## Latinos in the news about education

Practically absent in the networks' regular campaign news, as well as in the debates, was the distinctive focus on Latinos. Not a single regular story on the candidates' educational policies focused specifically on this group. Beyond the brief allusion to Latinos in an ABC (9/26) story that had as part of its backdrop a visual of an elementary school in Los Angeles (Jones, 2000b), the networks seem to have reflected centrist strategy in an attempt to appeal to the broadest possible electorate.

The candidates' platforms, especially Gore's, dealt with issues confronting students challenged by low-income, the achievement gap, and faltering public schools, all of which are relevant to Latinos. However, during the 2000 campaign, the networks barely touched on those particular topics, much less was there any focus on Latinos and how those platform proposals could influence the Latino vote. Likewise, the presidential candidates (as well as the vice-presidential candidates) failed to mention Latinos distinctively when they discussed the issue of education during the debates.

The most notable attention to Latinos in campaign news about education was observed in *special* stories that focused exclusively on the subject of education. The topics of those stories included the perceived importance that voters gave to the issue of education, and more specifically the concerns about minority education and the achievement gap. And while Hispanics were mentioned in those special stories, there was no emphasis on how that might affect the Latino vote.

For example, an approximately 15-minute in-depth investigative report aired on CBS's *60-Minutes* (9/10) focused on the achievement gap of minority groups in light of the Texas Assessment and Accountability Test (TAAS) (Hewitt, 2000a). That story pointed out that the Bush campaign claimed that, as an outcome of policies implemented under Bush's administration as governor of Texas, TAAS scores had climbed significantly, especially for Hispanics and other minorities. However, the report also indicated that experts arrived at different conclusions regarding mandatory testing. Educational researchers interviewed by *60-Minutes* stated that evidence was skewed because record numbers of Hispanics had dropped out of school, did not take the test, and were then excluded in the analyses conducted by the school system administrators. The implications on Latinos regarding the accountability and testing in Texas under Governor Bush was also picked up in ABC's *Good Morning America* (9/25), (Jones, 2000a). And NBC's *The Today Show* (11/4) featured one story on English-only initiatives in Arizona, dealing with the concern that Latinos are not learning English in their bilingual classrooms (Gerbasi, 2000d).

Other education stories in which some attention, albeit more briefly, was given to Latinos dealt with the shortage of teachers in New York City public schools (CBS *The Early Show*, 10/30) (Pitts, 2000b), and in a story on affirmative action in higher education (CBS *60-Minutes*, 10/29) (Hewitt, 2000b).

The most noteworthy special interest story involved school choice. Vouchers, considered a controversial part of each candidate's education campaign, were the focus of at least one report by each network (ABC 9/25, Jones, 2000a; NBC 10/26, Gerbasi, 2000c; CBS 9/23, Murphy, 2000a). The reason behind the coverage on this topic could have arisen because voters could draw a clear line between the candidates' positions on the issue of vouchers: Bush favored vouchers; Gore opposed them. Each story presented scenes or segments from a struggling inner city public school. The reports showed parents, including Latinos, willing to try anything other than maintaining the current bleak situation. Of special note was the CBS report on a special vote in California on school vouchers scheduled for November 8, Election Day, 2000. This CBS (9/23) story reported that vouchers are not working for Latinos in New York City and raised concern for a policy affecting the Latino population in a state such as California, where there is a large Latino student population.

## DISCUSSION

During the 2000 presidential campaign, voters and the two main candidates for the nation's top office considered education a very important issue. This issue was also particularly important for U.S. Latinos, regardless of their national background. Given that Latinos were perceived as an emerging and important voting force, we expected that the presidential candidates and the news media, specifically the national network news, would have not only made the issue of education very salient throughout the campaign, but also focus assiduously on Latinos. At a minimum, we were hopeful that various news reports would present and maybe even critically discuss how the proposed education policies of Al Gore and George W. Bush might affect Latinos, and how potential voters of this ethnic background would react and consider voting for their candidate based on that important issue.

The assumptions and expectations did not hold true, at least not in the network news during the final stretch of the campaign, September 4 through November 7. The focus on Latinos was also notably absent in the brief mentions of and discussions about education during the presidential (and vice-presidential) debates. We do not know if prior to the studied dates there was more in-depth analysis of this issue and how the policies of the presidential candidates were expected to affect Latinos.

It would seem that the candidates and the national television networks, in their respective efforts to appeal to broad constituencies and audiences, chose to focus on generic centrist messages related more to the cost of the program than to actual reform. They also did not elaborate on details or angles of particular relevance to Latinos.

The campaign did begin with discussions of the Latino voting power and the candidates' courting the Latino vote (NCLR, 2000), and the recognition of education as an important issue for this ethnic group. However, as the race neared Election Day and Gore and Bush remained virtually tied in the polls, little or nothing was reported on how the candidates' educational policies could affect Latinos or how those policies could influence the Latino vote. More often than not, English-language news about education during the final stretch of that year's campaign overlooked Latinos—and other minorities and the poor. Much of this neglect could be a consequence of vote pandering occurring as Election Day approached as a result of the unprecedented tight race for president in 2000.

Limited coverage concerning the candidates' educational platforms and the absence of critical evaluation of the educational policies—in particular, who would benefit from them or be most negatively affected by them—was the norm. Also noticeably absent in the Democrat's and the Republican's education platform, as well as the media coverage of education, was attention to one of the most important concerns for Latinos: bilingual education. Perhaps because of the controversial nature of this issue, bilingual education remained untouched by the candidates and thus not raised independently by the network news either. Yet, within the education system, issues such as dual language instruction and dropout rates are paramount for Latinos. Other than in special news reports, the overall coverage of education during campaign 2000 was limited and lacking in analysis of what would happen to a child, much less a Latino child, under each candidate's educational plan.

Of course, the networks alone are not to blame as they primarily covered the well-orchestrated words and actions of the candidates. It is the presidential candidates and their media campaign managers who are responsible for not emphasizing Latinos in their educational policies and in the media messages during the campaign. However, the networks' reporters, news directors, and other decision-makers also did not consider Latino angles to the coverage of the issue of education worthy of more critical and in-depth analysis, disregarding the policy contained in candidates' platforms almost entirely.

Latinos continue to be negatively affected by many of the ongoing educational policies, and reform initiatives must urgently be targeted towards this population. Given the television networks' capacity to reach so many voters, including Latinos, these media in particular could potentially bring such issues to the forefront of future political campaigns and discussions.

Future research on Latino political communication should prioritize evaluating the link between news coverage and actual voting behavior, continuing to make connections between the media, political issues, and the interests of minority groups. Research on how issues considered important for Latinos or any other minority group are played during a presidential campaign would benefit from analyzing the primary period, when narrower constituencies are addressed by the contending candidates. The research might also benefit from analysis of *local* news media in communities were large segments of the Latino population (or other minority group of interest) reside. Perhaps then we can more accurately assess whether politicians and the media remain focused on generic news and mainstream voter appeals or whether they address more centrally issues that affect Latino children living within the school system, attending failing inner city schools every day, and trying to overcome *la mala educación*.

## NOTES

1  See, for example, ABC *World News Tonight* (September 7, 2000); CBS *The Early Show* (September 18, 2000); NBC *Nightly News* (September 8, 2000).

2  See also the most recent opinion polls conducted by the Pew Hispanic Center, available on line at www.pewhispanic.org.

3  While in the 2004 election the Internet became a pervasive tool for political candidates, this was not yet the case in 2000.

4  The textual analysis of the platforms, the Lexis-Nexis searches, and textual analysis of the news was conducted by the first author in collaboration with the second author at the University of Texas at Austin.

5  Search terms used on Lexis-Nexis Academic Universe: Gore OR Bush + education; Gore OR Bush + Latino*; Gore OR Bush + Hispanic*; Latino OR

Hispanic + education; Latino OR Hispanic + campaign; Latino OR Hispanic + vote; Bilingual + education; Campaign OR vote + education; Mexican* + education; Puerto Rican* + education; Cuban* + education. The asterisks indicate the use of the exclamation point "!" in the search term. Lexis-Nexis will search a word ending with an exclamation point with all relevant suffices. For example, a search with the term "Latin!" implies the words Latino, Latinos, Latina, Latinas. This results in more comprehensive results.

6　Information for Bush's education platform was found at www.Bush2000.com and Gore's education platform was found at www.algore.com.

7　Hispanic Serving Institutions refers to colleges and universities at which at least 25 percent of the students are Latino. Pell grants are the funds made available by Congress for low-income students who are seeking their first undergraduate college degree; this type of grant does not have to be repaid.

Part III

# CAMPAIGN STRATEGIES, POLITICAL ADVERTISEMENTS, SURVEYS

# 12

# DEMOCRATIC AND REPUBLICAN MASS COMMUNICATION CAMPAIGN STRATEGIES

## Historical overview

*Federico A. Subervi-Vélez* and *Stacey L. Connaughton*

*Figure 12.1* Courtesy of TMS/MCT Reprints

Two things are most evident in the Democratic and Republican Parties' mass communication campaign strategies directed at Latinos in the United States. First, for over half a century, Latinos have been a clearly identified and targeted group in presidential elections. Second, during each national election period, the Democrats and Republicans have had different and distinct strategies with respect to the organizational efforts and the money spent on media to get the Latino vote, and regarding the types of message developed to try to persuade that particular ethnic electorate.

These general observations stem from studies conducted since 1984 by the first author and his colleagues (i.e., Subervi-Vélez, Herrera, and Begay, 1987; Santillán and Subervi-Vélez, 1991; Subervi-Vélez, 1992; and Subervi-Vélez and Connaughton, 1999) and by the second author and her colleagues since 2000 (Connaughton, 2002; Connaughton and Jarvis, 2004; and Connaughton, 2005). This chapter brings together and

*Figure 12.2* Candorville cartoon strip, dated April 17, 2007
*Source:* Darrin Bell

*Figure 12.3* Candorville cartoon strip, dated April 18, 2007
*Source:* Darrin Bell

summarizes those works in order to present the major common threads and unique aspects of various Latino-oriented mass communication campaign strategies dating from the presidential elections half a century ago to modern times.

Before delving into the main topics of that historical overview—the organizational efforts and media expenditures, and the characteristics of the media messages directed to Latinos—it is important to reiterate some observations that offer context to the analyses that follow.

First, political candidates and parties develop their election campaigns with numerous assumptions about what it takes to win. Regardless of the degree to which the candidates or their supporting strategists believe that the media have direct cognitive, attitudinal, and/or behavioral effects on the electorate, all major campaigns in modern times are evidently run with significant attention to the media. In presidential elections, millions of dollars are spent on the infrastructures and personnel that produce earned (free) media exposure as well as paid media (ads) in the press, radio, and especially television. The Internet is now also an integral component of the strategies to disseminate campaign information to voters, including Latinos (see Len-Rios, 2002; Barbarena, 2005). While some of the messages produced across the different media are aimed at reaching the public—i.e., potential voters at large—many are directed at particular segments of the population. Targeted campaigning, especially via the media, is an essential corollary of modern elections. In the United States electoral processes, Latinos have not been exempted from targeted campaign efforts via the mass media or the Internet.

Second, Latinos are not a monolithic group in their sense of identity or in their political orientations. Latinos' sense of identity or adherence to particular indicators related to ethnic identity (e.g., language, music, family traditions) will vary by social class and the heritage related to the national origin of the individual and/or his or her ancestry, e.g., Puerto Rico, Mexico, Cuba, etc. (see Subervi and Ríos, 2005). Generally, similarities among Latinos increase as the size of the geographic region and subgroup decreases. However, as alluded to in chapter 3, Latinos also hold varying degrees of sociopolitical affiliations; some are stronger, others are weaker depending on the community in which they live and the particular issues, problems, and goals faced in a determined moment of their lives.

Third, as has also been alluded to in previous chapters, a special factor that characterizes the Latino population in the United States is that in almost every community where they reside there are various Latino-oriented media—in both Spanish and/or English. Campaigns that specifically target Hispanics for selling a product—be it a consumable good or a political candidate—must take the above factors into consideration if they are to win the Latino market in a particular locality, state, or the nation. Thus, national campaigns require, for example, themes, sounds, and/or images that serve as common denominators among various Hispanic groups. Meanwhile, statewide or local campaigns should instead try to strike a chord of relevance to the predominant Latino group(s) in the region. Even then, the fact that there are millions of Latinos who are not United States citizens or legal residents of this country has bearings on Latino-related political communication. The political news and the paid political messages directed at Latinos who are legally able to vote undoubtedly also reach those who, for whatever reason, cannot. It is very probable that the interpersonal communication and interactions between Latinos who vote and those who cannot have some influence on Latinos' political mobilization or lack thereof.

Fourth, the cumulative research over time has further documented how both parties have integrated Latinos into their party organization and campaign strategy including their communication outreach strategies (see particularly Connaughton, 2005, for the most recent documentation on this topic). Thus, Latinos have been appointed to positions in the party organization; Latino elected and appointed officials have served as surrogates for the parties' major candidates; and the parties have begun to learn the nuances of Latino-oriented media and Latinos' use of those sources and general market media. That organizational inclusion is now being institutionalized and a Latino "flavor and rhythm" has spread throughout the parties' internal operations and has been communicated in their campaign messages.

These observations frame the historical overview of the organizational efforts and media expenditures, and of the characteristics of the media messages directed to Latinos by the Democratic and Republican Parties.

************

In the first exploratory research conducted in 1984, at a time when there were no previous empirical or academic works on the subject of this chapter, Subervi-Vélez, Herrera, and Begay (1987) considered two contending propositions about the Democratic and Republican Parties' strategies toward Latinos via the mass media. They stated,

> On the one hand, it could be hypothesized that the media efforts of the Democratic Party would be greater than the Republican Party's because the former would need and seek to maintain the traditionally pro-Democratic Party Latino vote. On the other hand, a hypothesis could also be made that the Republican Party's would be greater because, aware of their limited support among Latinos, they would have to try harder in making inroads among that population. The greater efforts of the Republicans could also be due to the substantially greater size of their campaign coffers.
>
> (Subervi-Vélez, Herrara, and Begay, 1987: 187)

The data gathered about the 1984 elections supported the second proposition. The same was the case with respect to the 1988 elections, when Republicans continued to significantly outspend Democrats in all phases of the campaign, including the mass communication efforts to reach Latinos. Only in 1996 was a different pattern observed, when the Democratic National Committee and the Clinton–Gore campaign made more concerted and better-financed efforts to win Latino votes.[1] In the following pages we compare and contrast the distinct mass communication strategies historically taken by each party when dealing with the Latino electorate, the funds expended, and the messages crafted to get the Latino vote. The two chapters that follow document how those strategies remained divergent in the 2000 and 2004 elections when the GOP's Latino-oriented organizational efforts and communication expenditures continued to outpace those of the Democratic Party.

## THE REPUBLICAN PARTY

The Republican Party's outreach to Latinos is not a recent phenomenon. There was a time at the turn of the twentieth century and up to the early 1930s when "the GOP was considered more socially progressive than the Southern-based Democratic Party on the issues of civil rights, electoral reform, women's suffrage, and regard for family-oriented farms and small businesses" (Santillán and Subervi-Vélez, 1991: 287). The GOP's drastic economic and immigration policies during the Great Depression (1929–32) were very detrimental to Mexican Americans, who overwhelmingly gave their support to President Roosevelt and the Democratic Party. However, starting in 1952, moderate Republicans launched systematic and concerted efforts to regain Latino votes (Santillán and Subervi-Vélez, 1991). Following the blueprints laid out in the 1966 "Southwest Strategy" and the "Hispanic Victory Initiative '84," the GOP has persistently advanced its Latino communication strategies, which include developing the organizational and media efforts to *specifically* target Latinos.[2]

The GOP's "Southwest Strategy" was launched in 1966 to take advantage of the Democrats' perceived neglect of Latinos during the Kennedy and the Johnson administrations. At the time, "the Republican leadership theorized that as Mexican Americans moved upward on the economic ladder, they would most likely identify with the economic views of the

*Figure 12.4* Courtesy of Lalo Alcaraz

GOP because of their higher social status" (Santillán and Subervi-Vélez, 1991: 293). Thus began a more concerted effort to reach out particularly to Mexican American white-collar professionals and business owners. That year, in speeches, rallies, meetings with Mexican American civic organizations, and in media messages directed to this group, top Republican candidates for office, such as Ronald Reagan seeking the governorship of California and John Towers running for re-election as U.S. Senator from Texas, repeatedly touted and praised the entrepreneurial spirit and conservative values of Mexican Americans. The electoral victory of these two Republicans, each of whom garnered approximately 30 percent of the Mexican American vote, served as an incentive to boost the outreach efforts to this population. Those efforts then helped Richard Nixon with his narrow victory for president over Democrat Hubert Humphrey in 1968.

While the GOP's communication targeted specifically toward Latinos continued, the support for Republicans fell drastically owing to the debacles of the Vietnam war, the Watergate scandal, the impeachment of President Nixon, and then President Ford's neglect of Hispanics during his administration. It was candidate, and then president, Reagan who reinvigorated the Latino outreach in 1980 and even more so in 1984. And so emerged the GOP's most concerted communication effort to regain the support from Latino voters as laid out in the Republican National Committee's "Hispanic Victory Initiative '84: A proposed strategy for the Reagan–Bush '84 Hispanic campaign."

That document laid out specific plans for advertising, public relations, and publicity, as well as the importance of using the mass media, particularly the Spanish-language print and broadcast media, as vehicles in which to present and herald the GOP's candidates and messages to Latinos across the country. The use of the media was so central in that 66-page blueprint that it states: "In summary, let the Democrats register all the Hispanics they want. The battle for the hearts and minds of Hispanic voters will be fought in the media" (p. 51). Moreover, Spanish-language media were also key instruments for that outreach, as the document also points out that: "you may be able to reach them [Latinos] in English, but you have to convince them in Spanish" (p. 51).

That 1984 blueprint, which was integral to the Reagan–Bush re-election campaign, was accompanied by a budget of at least $4.850 million divided approximately as follows: $2.162 million for television, $1.295 million for radio, $.226 million for newspapers, $.108 million for magazines, $.203 million for outdoor promotions, $100,000 for campaign literature, and $450,000 for direct mail.[3] Of the funds designated for television, approximately 75 percent was used for English-language advertisements on the general market television networks, while the remainder was used for Spanish-language promotions on Spanish-language television.

278

A major architect of the development of targeted campaigns in Spanish as well as in English was Lionel Sosa.[4] At the time, he was president of his advertising company in San Antonio and since the 1960s had been instrumental in producing the advertising messages that had helped John Tower's bid for senator and Ronald Reagan's campaign for president. Applying the lessons of his commercial advertising expertise, a key tool of his approach was the classification and then targeting of Hispanics based on their level of acculturation. This implied assessing the language (Spanish, English, or both) and culture (Latino, "Anglo," or both) in which the Latinos felt most comfortable, and then using this knowledge, along with other demographic data, to carefully craft the distinctive messages and select the particular media channels for these in the cities/states targeted for campaigns (see Subervi-Vélez, Herrera and Begay, 1987: 190). To complement that data, the GOP also commissioned survey research that would help determine, among other things, the media uses and preferences of Latinos and thus know where and when to place the political information, advertising and related propaganda. Those tactics have undoubtedly been used and significantly augmented in subsequent years.

For instance, although no exact figure was publicly disclosed, it can be inferred that during the 1988 presidential campaign the Republican Party spent even more funds nationwide in its efforts to win Latino votes as the GOP continued making major inroads in its media-based information and propaganda endeavors. Among the many distinctions of that year's activities it is important to highlight that the Republican National Committee's Hispanic outreach operatives produced and disseminated dozens of propaganda pieces that Latino-oriented media across the nation printed or broadcast as legitimate "news" without attributing those pieces to the RNC or its Republican media operatives. Among these were 22 "Radio Actualidades" shows produced between August 31 and October 25, 1988, and over 30 "news stories" and "opinion columns" generated during the last three months of the campaign.

Of particular notice was that identical editions of many of the latter items were sent with different bylines to many Spanish-language newspapers. A distinctive example to illustrate that practice is the stinging anti-Dukakis opinion column that was published in New York's daily newspaper El Diario-La Prensa (9/21/88) showing a byline by President George Bush, while the exact same piece, word for word, was printed as a news article in the Salinas, California weekly El Sol (9/30/88) but under the byline of José Martínez. At the time, Martínez held a prominent position in the Bush administration, but that was not stated in the "news article." There were many other such "news" stories and "opinion columns" that year and most probably during many years prior to and after that campaign. The details of this strategy, including the extent to which it has been continued in subsequent elections and its influence on

Latinos' political opinions and mobilization, have yet to be the subject of any political communication research.

In this historical overview of the GOP's communication strategy it is also important to highlight that, throughout various decades, this party has promoted and stuck to two complementary themes in its Latino-oriented advertising messages during presidential elections. The first theme has been that the Republican Party and its candidates for office are best for Latinos to achieve the "American dream." The second theme has been the depiction of Hispanics as equals, as Americans first; not as stereotypes.[5] The Latino-oriented political advertisements, especially the television spots produced by the GOP from the earliest years of our analysis through the 1988 campaign, not only reiterate these messages in some form or fashion, but do so with words, sounds and images that appeal primarily to the recipients' affective senses.[6] As Sosa himself has stated, what is necessary to succeed in this arena is that "an emotional nerve be touched" (Sosa as quoted in Subervi-Vélez, Herrera, and Begay, 1987: 193).

Thus, the Republican candidates or their spokespersons featured in the television ads have been presented in settings of soft hues or patriotic colors along with pleasant background sounds, while the voices of the speakers or the voiceovers deliver the pitch in very amenable yet confident tones. In the Spanish-language versions of the spots, the Latino characters speak in pan-Hispanic Spanish, with no distinguishable accent or other visual cues that could place them as being specifically from Mexico, Puerto Rico, Cuba or any one Latin American country. Likewise, the characters in the English-language versions talk with impeccable command of that language and are semi-formally dressed as would be any typical American middle-class person. Again, no specific "ethnic" indicator is overtly evident other than the slightly darker (brown/bronze) color of the skin and some facial features that do show they are not white or Caucasian.

The focus on those themes has conversely meant the omission of Latino-oriented advertisements that bring forth problems faced by Latinos, or address controversial issues such as housing, immigration, and health care. Likewise absent, until the last two presidential election periods, were negative advertisements against the Democratic Party or its presidential candidates. In essence, the pattern has been the featuring of ads that make the observer, be s/he Latino or non-Latino, feel comfortable and good about the Republican Party and its candidates. As discussed in the section that follows, the Democratic Party's communication strategy has indeed been different and distinct from that of the GOP.

Figure 12.5 Courtesy of Lalo Alcaraz

## THE DEMOCRATIC PARTY

The history of the Democratic Party's outreach to Latinos also has deep roots. For many decades, at least the progressive leaders of this party have embraced and promoted causes and issues relevant to large segments of this population, such as civil rights and social justice in housing, immigration, and education. However, in contrast to the Republican Party, we have not identified any specific document dated prior to 1988 in which any distinguishing communication strategy was laid out. Moreover, the Latino-oriented media-based information and propaganda expenditures have been much less than those of the GOP, while over the years the theme of the advertising message has been less cohesive. The production quality of many of the television spots has also been far from superior.

Any discussion of the Democratic Party's Latino-oriented communication strategy must begin by recognizing that, throughout the twentieth century, the majority of the Latino votes during presidential elections have been cast for the Democratic candidates. This holds true in practically every state, too; the exception being Florida where, since the mid-1960s, Cubans have favored the Republican presidential candidates. The fact that this pattern has held so steadily implies at a minimum two things: first, that there has been at least a perception that the Democratic

Party's policies are more responsive to most Latinos' socio-economic interests and needs, however these are defined, and, second, that messages to that effect have been conveyed in some form or fashion to Latinos prior to and during election campaigns.

The absence of blueprints laying out the early stages of Latino-oriented communication tactics does not therefore imply the lack of activities in that arena. However, with or without written strategic plans, when compared to the patterns followed by the GOP, the Democratic Party's outreach has been different in terms of targeted constituencies, more limited in the advertising expenditures, and scattered in the themes of the advertised message content.

Santillán and Subervi-Vélez observed that the approach that both the Republicans and the Democrats usually have followed to reach Latinos has been mainly the mobilization of grass root and civic organizations and whatever interpersonal and local communication output these could produce. Yet a distinctive approach by the Democratic Party's Latino outreach during the Kennedy and Johnson campaigns of the early 1960s was that the efforts were developed nationwide instead of in just a few states in the Southwest (1991: 292). Even so, the Democratic Party's outreach was directed primarily to the grass root activists and not necessarily or especially to the middle-class and business-owning Latinos.

Also, given the persistent support of the vast majority of Latino voters, financial and other resources were apparently not considered needed or expendable for major media and propaganda efforts directed to this group. This was clearly the case during the 1984 presidential campaign when the amount of funds specifically designated for Latino-oriented communication expenditures to promote the Democratic presidential candidate, Walter Mondale, was dismal—barely $120,000 nationwide—in contrast to the GOP's $4 million-plus (Subervi-Vélez, Herrera and Begay, 1987). In a complementary study of that campaign period, it was also found that, for all candidates for all offices, the Democratic Party invested a scant $94,742 altogether in Spanish-language radio and television in the five major metropolitan cities with Latinos (Los Angeles, New York, San Antonio, Chicago, and Miami). In comparison, the GOP spent $217,925 for its Spanish-language radio and TV spots in the same locations (Santillán and Subervi-Vélez, 1991: 312).

The data gathered and interviews conducted about the 1984 elections did not reveal whether the Democratic Party's decisions on how and where to invest in such propaganda were based on systematic research about Latinos' language preference and use of the media in Spanish and/ or English. But it was clear that the paid advertising was disseminated primarily (if not exclusively) via Spanish-language media. Moreover, the few ads that were produced were aired a maximum of 10 days prior to

Election Day, not months or weeks in advance to inform and mobilize Latinos throughout the duration of the campaign period.

In 1984, the themes of the spots were diverse: one emphasized the Democratic Party's stance on the Simpson-Mazzoli immigration bill, which was being debated in Congress that year. The other theme was endorsements by prominent Hispanic leaders promoting the Democratic Party candidates. Neither set of advertisements offered a unified theme for Latinos across the country. The immigration bill was of little interest to Puerto Ricans (all of whom are U.S. citizens by birth), to Cubans (all of whom are given preferential status), or to third and fourth generation Mexican Americans. Likewise, the leadership spots would be most relevant only for the local communities where the leaders reside or are best known.

The 1988 presidential campaign brought about some of the same patterns already alluded to, as well as some new approaches in the Democratic Party's Latino-oriented communication strategy (see Subervi-Vélez, 1992). During the primaries, when none of the many presidential candidates had the clear support of the majority of Democratic Party followers, Latino voters were highly sought, especially in Texas and California. Dukakis' early inroads with Latino grass roots and community leaders made a difference in his winning the delegates needed for the nomination. But after the nomination and convention in Atlanta in July, and up to the final weeks of the campaign, the party's major goal was to win back the unconverted and the eroding votes of white, middle-class voters, especially the "Reagan Democrats" who had deserted the party in 1984. When that failed, the focus returned to the loyalists, including Latino activists. It seemed that the Democratic National Committee did not have in process a long-term, consistent and systematic communication effort to connect to Latino voters in general or the middle-class business owners and professionals in particular.

Nevertheless, a number of Latino Democrats did manage to develop some communication strategies to win Hispanic votes. This is most evident in the document titled "Viva Dukakis 1988 Victory Strategy" dated June 27, 1988, and prepared by Richard Ybarra, who served as Dukakis' California campaign director. Various sections of that six-page document clearly reveal the important role of mass communication, including free media and political advertising, especially on Spanish-language television, for the party's outreach to Latinos that year. Although much larger than what was designated in 1984, the proposed budget was merely $325,000, excluding funds for media advertising.

As Subervi-Vélez (1992) pointed out, there were other documents that attested to the Democrats' enhanced media efforts to win Latino votes in 1988. Those efforts explicitly recognized the value of reaching out to the Latino-oriented media, while integrating those efforts to the general market press operations. One outcome of the DNC's Latino-communication strategy was that ample coverage was obtained for Dukakis with the Spanish-language media. His fluency in Spanish—the first presidential candidate who could fully understand and interact directly with Spanish-speaking reporters—certainly contributed to that coverage. Absent from those documents was the creation of radio or print propaganda to be passed on as "legitimate" news to any Latino media.

In 1988, the development of an effective monitoring system was also considered essential to the success of the Democrats' Latino media strategy. The strategy documents did not indicate whether the monitoring system was implemented. But the interviews with the DNC representatives did not reveal any acknowledgment of or outcry regarding the RNC's propaganda in the form of "Radio Actualidades" or "news and opinion" stories.

With respect to the advertising component of that year's communication strategy, the Democratic Party once again did not deliver major funds. The *total* budget allocated for the combined production of television and radio spots to be directed to Latinos across the country was a meager $45,000.[7] Even the production using those funds became cumbersome because Dukakis' campaign directors in Boston insisted on reviewing all ideas and copy prior to the approval and development of any advertisement. That process, which required repeated translations, caused delays and misunderstandings that undermined the ultimate production and dissemination of the broadcast as well as some print advertisements (Subervi-Vélez, 1992).

The process of selecting the themes for the messages that year was tortuous as were the actual pitches themselves. For example, the New York, San Antonio, and Los Angeles teams of Latino advertisers held divergent views on key words for the Dukakis slogans. Of particular concern for the New York team was the use of the words "con Dukakis nos entendemos" (with Dukakis we understand each other). According to the East Coast team, for Puerto Ricans that might convey an unintended sexual connotation. Of the five 30-second TV spots that were eventually produced, the two that aired in the New York area excluded that particular slogan. But the slogan was kept for the three TV spots for the Southwest and for the national print promotions.

In terms of the topics addressed in the spots, the common denominator was the focus on problems and issues faced by Hispanics. These were addressed in attack ads that blamed Republicans for problems related to housing, low wages, lack of health care, immigration, and drugs in schools. Two of the spots featured a head shot of Dukakis speaking in Spanish and addressing these issues. The other two had mock scenes that alluded to some of those problems. The fifth ad was different as it was designed to show parallels between Dukakis and his family and Latino families. Yet for all five spots, which were aired only very late in the campaign, the quality of the images, sound, and delivery of the messages was very limited and nowhere close to those produced by the GOP. A similar critique can be made about the Spanish-language radio spots, all of which were also attack ads, about issues, and critical of the Republicans. Two of those spots were produced from the audio portions of the TV commercials. Only one radio spot, based on a "corrido" (ballad), was distinct and original.

This brief historical overview of the Democrats' 1984 Latino-oriented communication strategy closes with a mention of four English-language print advertisements directed at Hispanics that year. These promotions, paid for by the Dukakis/Bentsen Committee, Inc., were also attack ads against Republicans and focused on issues faced by Latinos: the need for better jobs, wages, health insurance, education, and drug-free schools. All four full-page ads were published in October 1988, but only in *Vista*, a mostly English-language magazine that focuses on Hispanic Americans.[8] These four promotions in English seem to be the major national propaganda effort that the Democratic Party directed toward English-speaking Latinos during the presidential campaign in 1988.

The Democratic Party's Latino communication strategy was not documented in 1992, the year Bill Clinton campaigned and wrestled the presidency from incumbent George Bush. Thus, we cannot discuss what changes, if any, took place in that year's communication outreach directed to Latinos.[9] However, his 1996 re-election campaign not only brought a quantum leap in such efforts, but also an abundance of records about how the media were used to win Latino votes that year. Of the numerous details about those efforts and the records analyzed by Subervi-Vélez and Connaughton (1999), various points merit mention in this summary overview.

Of foremost importance is the fact that that year's Latino communication strategy was developed following a "blueprint" as well as numerous directives (in the form of various memoranda) detailing specific steps and actions to take to reach out to Latinos via the Spanish-language and English-language mass media. The blueprint was a document titled "Latino Communications Strategy, 1994–1996," authored by Andy Hernández, who had been appointed by Clinton to serve as the DNC's Director of the Office of Latino Outreach (OLO) when the office was established in 1994. In fact, the establishment of the OLO marked a distinct approach in the organizational structure of the DNC, which had typically reached out to Latinos and other minorities by way of other overarching branches of the organization. Hernández also authored many other memos guiding the OLO's staff on maintaining lists and professional ties with Spanish-language media, preparing press releases for those media, including translations of documents, materials, and press releases from the DNC's office. For Hernández and his staff—including the advertising groups brought in that year—the media were considered powerful tools that had to be used more effectively in English and Spanish to mobilize Latino voters.

To carry out this strategy for the presidential campaign, the DNC allocated to the OLO $1.5 million dollars, the largest amount for Latino communication efforts in the history of the party. Although still less than the funds spent by the GOP in any previous campaign year since 1988, this amount, according to Mr. Hernández, was 10 times more than the amount allocated by the DNC for Latino efforts in 1992. The presence of two Latinos in Clinton's top administration—Henry Cisneros (Secretary of Housing) and Federico Peña (Secretary of Transportation)—was instrumental in obtaining these funds and pushing the DNC to enhance its Latino communication efforts.

With more money at hand, the OLO did engage in significantly more sophisticated communication strategies to reach out to Latinos. In addition to the activities alluded to above, other key tactics of that campaign included the conducting of polls and focus groups on Latino voting behavior, media uses, and candidate preferences. Queries were also made about Latinos' perceptions of the Republican Party's policies, as well as about Democratic proposals deemed to be of importance to Latinos such as affirmative action, bilingual education, welfare reform, increasing the minimum wage, student loan programs, and immigration reform. With data from that research and queries at hand, the OLO developed a cohesive set of Latino-oriented images and arguments to be disseminated via both earned (free) and advertised (paid) media initiatives. As outlined in one of Hernández's memos, the four components of the messages were: "(1) They [the Democrats] know us [Latinos]; (2) they are with us; (3) they will fight for us; and (4) they have won for us" (quoted in Subervi-Vélez and Connaughton, 1999: 56).

Putting into use the data gathered on the specific and diverse Latino-oriented media across the country, the OLO developed good working relations with those media, including the scheduling of press briefings, conferences, and interviews at which they made available the Democratic Party candidates and/or Latino community leaders who could speak on their behalf. The OLO also distributed photos of President Clinton with Latinos and Latino leaders, feature articles in Spanish and in English that included bylines of prominent Democrats, arranged for a spokesperson from that office to participate in weekly interviews with Latino broadcast and print outlets, and even created press releases and one- to two-minute radio messages that were made available for Latino media to use as part of their "news."[10] Moreover, that office produced on a monthly basis the *Latino Democrat* and *Dole Watch* newsletters. The first was distributed among Latino Democratic activists and community leaders, while the latter was also circulated among that group as well as to Latino media in

286

order to highlight the differences between Clinton and his Republican rival. The specific themes and issues highlighted in all the media outreach and related propaganda were selected in coordination with the DNC so as to adhere to a cohesive Democratic Party message. An underlying theme in the outreach to Hispanics was "When Republicans win, Latinos lose."

While there was unity and coordination in the selection of cohesive issues and themes to be disseminated in the earned media as well as in the messages produced for the advertisements, the development of that propaganda was not hierarchal and bureaucratically centralized as had been the case in 1988. Instead, two teams were hired: one to create complementary distinct advertisements for the predominantly Puerto Rican voters in the East Coast, and another for the predominantly Mexican American constituents in the Southwest. Without going into the details of the paid messages, a few highlights must be pointed out.

First, the messages, as in previous campaigns, focused on issues that affected Latinos. The difference in 1996 was that the messages showcased the Clinton administration's work to solve those issues such as increasing jobs and having drug-free schools, thus reaffirming the earned media messages that Democrats do care about Latinos.

Second, applying the OLO's research about Latinos' use of the media, Latino-themed spots were produced and aired for both Spanish and English-language media, thus recognizing that Hispanics had to be reached via general market media and via Latino-oriented media in both languages, too. Given that research showed that even Latinos who were not totally fluent in Spanish tuned into Spanish-language radio, spots were produced for this medium and aired in selected Latino communities across the country. Likewise, the OLO placed advertisements in Spanish, English and also in bilingual format in general market and Latino-oriented media. The main theme of these focused positively on the president's record with Latinos. But in addition to the positive Democratic propaganda, the OLO also produced anti-Republican and, in particular, anti-Dole adverts in Spanish and English for print and radio.

Third, another indicator of the OLO's use of research was observed in the strategic targeting of Latinos and Latino-oriented media to be reached out to. Seventeen states with the largest Latino populations were selected for intense campaigning, and one in particular, Florida (specifically, central Florida) was the most focused on because it was considered winnable with the support of the mostly Puerto Rican population. The strategy was successful that year in many states, including Florida, which despite its mostly Republican Cuban population was won by Clinton.

Finally, the OLO's media efforts were not restricted to the last few weeks of the campaign. The activities summarized in these paragraphs (and those presented with more details in Subervi-Vélez and Connaughton, 1999), were developed and implemented throughout that campaign year.

In sum, 1996 marked the first year in which the Democratic Party had a specialized unit—the Office of Latino Outreach—and then developed a Latino-oriented communication strategy that was funded, researched, and implemented with free and paid efforts in both Spanish-language and English media directed at Spanish-speaking and English-speaking Hispanics.

## CONCLUSION

This historical overview of the Democratic and Republican Parties' mass communication campaign strategies directed at Latinos in the United States demonstrates the two main points set forth in the introduction of this chapter. First, both parties have identified, targeted and wooed Latinos during presidential elections dating back to the last century. Second, during each national election period, the Democrats and Republicans have developed different and distinct strategies with respect to the organizational efforts and the money spent on media to get the Latino vote, and regarding the types of message developed to try to persuade that particular ethnic electorate.

*Figure 12.6* Courtesy of Lalo Alcaraz

The documents and interviews upon which the communication strategies have been ascertained clearly suggest that the Republican Party has invested a lot more funds, targeted primarily business and professional Latinos, systematically used free and paid media in English and Spanish to carry its messages long before the actual Election Days, and repeatedly promoted a central theme based on the Republican Party being a conduit for Hispanics to achieve the American Dream. The data also suggest that the Democratic Party has invested little funding (as compared to the GOP) and, until the 1996 campaign, primarily targeted Spanish-speaking Latinos, via a few Spanish-language advertisements in that type of media late in the campaign, with a disparity of messages focusing on problematic socio-economic issues.

Up to the 1988 elections, there was little evidence of a correlation between the vast funds the Republican Party spent or those not spent by the Democratic Party, and the number of votes they respectively received from Latinos. Mexican Americans and Puerto Ricans usually voted overwhelmingly Democrat, while Cubans invariably voted primarily Republican.

However, the Republican Party's communication strategy may have been a significant if not crucial factor in the inroads it has made among Hispanic business owners and professionals—in effect, the middle-class Latinos most inclined to get involved in politics and vote. On the other hand, the Democratic Party's inconsistent and usually poorly funded communication outreach efforts may have limited its ability to continuously mobilize its formerly loyal Latino constituents.

Of course, many other factors have contributed to the issue of for whom Latinos vote, among them the economy, real or perceived job opportunities, existing and proposed policies on health, education, welfare, and even the conflicts in the Middle East and elsewhere. Yet, for each of these issues and others that become prominent before, during and after election campaign periods, mass communication comes into play. At every turn, the media become major conduits by which the political parties, the candidates running for office, and/or their surrogates present their interpretations and spins favorable to their own side and negative to the opposition.

It is therefore not surprising to note that both political parties and their respective candidates have increased and improved their strategies and budgets to reach Latinos via the mass media. The next two chapters bear testimony to how that was indeed the case during the 2000 and 2004 elections. This pattern is most likely to continue in upcoming elections. Contributing to that will be not only the growth of the Latino population in states with large electoral colleges, but also the expansion of the Latino-oriented media all across the nation. Research to assess how each party uses mass communication strategies to gain major inroads with Latino voters awaits to be done.

## NOTES

1 We did not gather data on the 1992 elections, nor have we come across any research on the Latino-oriented communication expenditures for that election year.

2 For details about the Republican Party's communication efforts with Latinos during the 1950s to 1980s, see Santillán and Subervi-Vélez (1991: 307–315). For detailed assessments of the 1984 and 1988 campaigns, see Subervi-Vélez (1992) and Subervi-Vélez and Connaughton (1999).

3 The actual amount designated for Latino outreach may have been more than what was indicated in the 1984 blueprint document. See Subervi-Vélez, Herrera and Begay (1987: 189).

4 For an understanding of his background and ideological frame of reference, see the books authored by Sosa: *The Americano dream: How Latinos can achieve success in business and in life* (1998), *El sueño americano: Cómo los Latinos pueden triunfar en Estados Unidos* (1998), and *Think and grow rich: A Latino choice* (2006).

5 This was stated by Sosa during an interview conducted by University of Texas graduate student, Oscar Zambrano, in 1993.

6 The first author has an extensive personal collection of Latino-oriented political spots. He is working on obtaining copies of other spots and making all the transcripts and images of those available via the Latinos and Media Project web site, www.latinosandmedia.org.

7 Interviews with DNC Latino operatives in 1988 suggest that up to one million dollars were assigned for Latino communication efforts, but that many funds went unspent because of the disagreements on the strategies and messages to be produced.

8 *Vista* magazine is a free supplement in the Sunday editions of various general market English-language newspapers across the country. Their combined circulation in October 1988 was 1,375,200.

9 While conducting the interviews regarding the Democratic Party's Latino communication outreach during the 1996 presidential campaign, various sources listed numerous complaints about that party's lack of efforts specifically directed to Latinos. If the DNC or the Clinton/Gore headquarters had any specific Latino communication strategies, the documentation to that effect was not available to this researcher or his student assistants.

10 This practice is similar to the GOP's strategy of distributing "opinion columns," and also the making available of "radio actualidades" as if they were actual "news" pieces. Unknown, however, is whether the DNC's OLO indicated different authors on identical opinion pieces, or how the radio stations that received the tapings aired the stories, i.e., as stemming from the OLO and thus identifying them as such, or as "legitimate" news without source attribution.

# 13

# PLURALISM EXAMINED

Party television expenditures focused on the
Latino vote in presidential elections

*Zachary W. Oberfield* and *Adam J. Segal*

This chapter has two goals. The first is to conduct an in-depth investigation into the strategies used by the two major parties and their candidates to court Latino voters in the 2000 and 2004 presidential elections. The data for this analysis were drawn from a comprehensive database of national political campaign television advertisements, network and affiliate political files, as well as interviews with elite members of each political party and campaign. The second goal is to situate these elections historically to understand appeals made to Latinos in presidential elections and to suggest a strategy for Latinos to attract party attention. Meeting this second goal requires us to understand the ways in which the two parties have responded to the relative diffusion and concentration of Latino voters. If attracting campaign appeals in a democracy influences policy outcomes (Frymer 1999), what is the optimal voting strategy for Latinos?

Traditional pluralists would argue that Latinos should bind together, consolidate resources, and speak as one voice (Dahl 1956; 1961). DeSipio, de la Garza, and Setzler (1999) and Guerra (1992) favor this strategy arguing that, since Latino voter turnout remains low compared to other ethnic groups, Latinos can best attract attention from the parties by voting as a cohesive bloc. Other strategists would argue that if Latinos consolidate behind one party, they will reduce the competition for their votes and do themselves considerable harm (Downs 1957; Bartels 1998). For instance, Bartels (1998) argues that a group with a low turnout percentage that is concentrated in one party risks decreasing its own electoral power because group members are no longer seen as "up-for-grabs." Groups perceived as committed are less likely to be competed for by both parties. The second part of this chapter presents evidence to resolve this puzzle by investigating appeals made to Hispanics in seven presidential election cycles. Though our findings should be treated as tentative, we find that when Hispanics split their votes, or when there is a widespread public perception that they did, they attract more political attention in the subsequent presidential election.

## METHODOLOGY

The core material we use to study the 2000 election is television advertising data compiled by the Wisconsin Advertising Project (WiscAds) at the University of Wisconsin–Madison throughout the 2000 campaign.[1] WiscAds received raw data from the Campaign Media Analysis Group (CMAG), a private commercial firm that used satellite technology to monitor political advertising. During the campaign CMAG monitored the major national broadcast television networks and affiliates and 25 leading cable networks in the 75 largest media markets (which reached over 80 percent of the American population). CMAG records the date, time, television station and length of each ad. CMAG also reports the estimated cost of the ad for the average time slot in which it aired. It is important to note that this process captures the cost of the media buy, not the amount spent on production or placement.[2] WiscAds maintains a database of advertisements that records each ad's sponsor, assigned title, channel/network/affiliate on which it aired, market, and estimated cost. In addition to this information, coders[3] selected the three top campaign issues discussed in each advertisement.

In 2000 CMAG did not pursue data from any of the television markets beyond the top 75. As a result, CMAG did not have any data from some markets critical to this research, such as Orlando and Tampa. These two cities are important because they have high concentrations of Latinos, especially Puerto Ricans and Cubans. Therefore, it was important to supplement the CMAG data with other research to fill in the gaps. To that end, Segal filed requests for spending data by the presidential candidates and their parties with the Univision and Telemundo networks and with affiliate stations in Florida, New Mexico, Nevada, Pennsylvania, Wisconsin and other important states, including New York where one notable ad ran briefly. This effort yielded critical data that confirmed and complemented the CMAG data and enabled the development of a comprehensive picture of Spanish-language television advertising during the 2000 campaign. Segal obtained additional complementary information upon interviewing top campaign strategists, officials, and consultants from both parties. Using qualitative analysis of the data, both authors examined each of the Spanish advertisements aired by the candidates with an eye toward issue content and image arrangement.

In 2004 Segal filed requests for copies of all network and affiliate political files where the campaigns reported airing ads. Upon completing the process, Segal compared these data to the 2004 data supplied by the University of Wisconsin Advertising Project to verify their accuracy. In addition, Segal conducted an analysis of the content of 2004 ads, which uncovered interesting changes in strategy for the parties and campaigns.

To situate the 2000 and 2004 elections historically, Oberfield (2003) examined and consolidated prior published reports on Spanish advertising over six presidential election cycles. Most of these data were collected by elections and communications scholars through conversations with party and campaign elites. These spending data are compared with national Latino turnout data to illustrate the relationship between the relative concentration of Latino voters and party appeals.

## THE 2000 PRESIDENTIAL ELECTION

### Spanish-language advertisements

Republicans and Democrats aired more than 275,000 presidential political advertising spots in the nation's top 75 media markets in 2000. Of this total, nearly 3,900, or 1.4 percent, were Spanish-language or bilingual advertisements.[4] The parties and candidates spent the majority of their Spanish-language television advertising dollars in the same few targeted states. The Bush campaign spent at least $810,000 on Spanish-language television ads during the 2000 campaign. The RNC and affiliated groups spent at least $1.5 million nationally in support of Bush on Spanish-language television ads. The Gore campaign spent at least $490,000 on Spanish-language ads nationally. The DNC spent at least $475,000 nationally on these efforts. As a result, the Bush campaign and the RNC outspent the Gore campaign and the DNC by more than a 2–1 ($2,310,000–$965,000) margin on Spanish-language television stations nationally.[5] However, a large part of this difference is accounted for in GOP advertising in California which Bush was never expected to win.

The Bush campaign fielded a large Hispanic media team to ensure that the candidate was equipped to reach Latino voters: The Maverick Media group, based in Austin, Texas, comprised veteran Republican consultant Lionel Sosa, former Democratic strategist Mark McKinnon, San Antonio-based ad-maker Luis Garcia, Bush pollster Matthew Dowd, consultant Stuart Stevens, and Kathy Sosa. Lionel Sosa and the rest of the team were in direct communication with chief strategist Karl Rove throughout the campaign. This gave the Latino strategists involved with the campaign's communications effort an influential role in overall campaign decision making. The campaign team concentrated its Spanish-language advertising strategy during the general election on winning New Mexico, Florida, and Colorado, according to Sosa. Data suggests the campaign decided to redirect resources it had allocated to Colorado to other states because the Gore campaign removed Colorado from its list of battleground targets.

Under the "Victory 2000" program, RNC chairman Jim Nicholson, Chief of Staff Tom Cole, and Deputy Press Secretary Leslie Sanchez were the staff officials responsible for the organization's paid Spanish-language advertising and earned media strategies. Sanchez assembled a group of the Republican Party's top consultants to advise the RNC on its Hispanic[6] strategy and to produce ads. Lionel and Kathy Sosa, ad-maker Frank Guerra, pollster Lance Terrance, former California Republican Party political director Mike Madrid, and the RNC officials participated in this effort.[7] The RNC focused funds on ad buys in California, Florida, and New Mexico.[8] Though technically separate, many of the same people that were advising the RNC on its communications strategy were advising the Bush campaign on its efforts.

The Bush and RNC advertisements in 2000, with mostly positive tones and few contrasts with the opponent, often spoke of the "Latino blood" in the Bush family and included dominant themes such as Bush's candidacy as a "new day" for Latinos and the candidate's commitment to helping Latinos achieve the "American dream." Family values, education and school reform, diversity, prescription drugs for senior citizens, and Bush's record as governor of Texas were common issues in the paid advertising.

The Gore campaign was top-heavy with non-Latino Democratic advertising executives. Chief strategist and ad-maker Carter Eskew oversaw all advertising operations from within the Gore campaign headquarters in Nashville, Tennessee. Eskew brought in presidential campaign veterans Harrison Hickman and Bill Knapp to work with him to produce the majority of the campaign's advertisements. It was Knapp who solicited two primary vendors for the campaign's Spanish-language advertising efforts. Knapp essentially reported to Eskew, Hickman, and Bob Shrum, the campaign's top consultants who spent a great deal of time in Nashville.[9] The Gore campaign contracted with Maryland-based EMM Creative and the client account was handled by Jim Learned and Pablo Izquierdo, now partners in Elevation, a firm tied to Knapp. Armando Gutierrez, a long-time Democratic operative and presidential campaign veteran, was hired to produce the DNC's Spanish-language spots and some of the Gore campaign's spots early in the cycle (and returned, briefly in 2004, to produce a controversial ad for John Kerry's campaign). The DNC's chairman at the time, Joe Andrew, was not as involved with the party's Spanish-language television efforts as his counterparts at the RNC, though the DNC developed its own earned-media and grassroots efforts.[10]

The Gore ads, all positive in tone, and DNC ads, often negative in tone, focused on issues like health care, social security, Medicare, and tax deductions for college education.[11] Sharply negative ads challenged Bush's record and used images and interviews with "average" Latinos in

Texas to attack Bush's record as governor. One DNC ad featured Latinos living in squalor in Texas under Bush's watch.

The only special interest group or third party organization that aired a significant amount of Spanish-language television ads during the presidential campaign was the Sierra Club. The national environmental organization assisted the Gore campaign's Spanish-language television strategy by airing tens of thousands of dollars in negative ads attacking Bush. In one of the spots, viewers were told, "As governor, George W. Bush ignored the air pollution problems in Texas" (Braverman, 2000). The ads were produced by Haddow Communications and totaled more than $270,000. They ran in Los Angeles ($64,000), Miami ($44,000), Orlando ($50,000), Albuquerque ($77,000), Denver ($24,000), and Chicago ($12,000).[12] The ads, which featured industrial scenes from Texas, questioned Bush's commitment to the environment and detailed air and water pollution in his home state. The ads also highlighted Gore's support for pollution restrictions. While not telling voters to choose Gore, they asked them to visit the Sierra Club web site to learn more about the candidates before voting.

### The primaries

Both candidates used Spanish-language television and radio commercials during the 2000 primaries and caucuses. Gore ran his early Spanish-language television ads in New York ($90,000) and California ($190,000).[13] Gore's primary opponent, Bill Bradley, was the only other major party presidential candidate to air Spanish-language television ads in the primaries. Bradley spent $73,000 on the Univisión and Telemundo stations in Los Angeles.[14] The impact of these ads was limited, especially because the nomination was essentially locked up before these contests, and Gore easily defeated Bradley among Latinos in the California Democratic primary.

Bush launched his primary and caucus campaign's paid media efforts in October 1999. This effort included what the GOP team reported to be the first Spanish-language advertisements in Iowa and Arizona. For the Iowa Caucus, the campaign created a 60-second Spanish-language radio ad that said, "Once again, the spotlight is on Iowa. And for the first time it's shining on the Latino community. We're voters too, and George W. Bush believes that all Iowans should help elect a president. In this presidential election you will see a fresh start, the beginning of a new day for Latinos" (York, 1999). The ad was produced by Lionel and Kathy Sosa (Associated Press, 1999). The television advertising process began in early 2000 when the Bush campaign reported that it became the first to air a Spanish-language television advertisement in the Arizona presidential primary. At the time, Bush was in a potentially close race against Arizona senator

John McCain, who had soundly defeated him in the New Hampshire Republican primary.[15]

## The general election

### Florida

With a rising statewide Latino population, among the largest in the nation, Florida is at the center of the demographic shifts taking place nationally. The state's 2,750,000 Latinos accounted for nearly 17 percent of the state's population. During the campaign, strategist Bill Knapp and other Gore advisers argued that spending large sums on television in Miami to influence Cuban voters was "wildly inefficient" especially in a state with competitive media markets where television advertising is "terribly expensive." Knapp said the campaign made the decision to spend heavily in the Orlando and Tampa markets, which had larger populations of more sympathetic Latino voters.[16] In effect, the Gore campaign all but conceded the Miami Hispanic vote to Bush, a departure from the 1996 Clinton–Gore campaign. Some of Gore's Latino advertising consultants called this choice a fateful decision.

The Bush campaign employed a different strategy. Bush and the RNC actively courted the community throughout the election, spending an astonishing $785,000 on Spanish-language television advertisements in Miami. According to the WiscAds final report from 2000, total Republican spending in the Miami media market was more than $6 million. Total Democratic spending was $3.4 million.[17] Republican spending on Spanish-language advertising in Miami was more than ten times the rate spent by the Bush campaign and the RNC in Orlando or Tampa.[18]

Republicans never took the Cuban vote for granted despite the constant media description of the community as a consistent Republican voting bloc. Sanchez noted that past electoral voting histories in Miami's predominantly Cuban population had created a strong Republican base and set political precedence. The RNC's Sanchez explained that demographers and pollsters indicated that Latino voters were quickly changing the demographic make-up of Florida, and noted evidence of new Latino demographics in Miami that show an increasingly diverse non-Cuban population.[19] Even the Cuban population is changing. Sosa observed that "The Cuban is still, of course, a very conservative Republican, but is becoming more independent. Second-generation voters are not necessarily as conservative."[20]

Most of the Bush campaign's strategists said they recognized the shifting political leanings of the Latino community in Miami and the rest of the state and identified it as one of the most important aspects of a Republican strategy to win the state. "Miami is only 50% Cuban, whereas eight years ago it was 85% Cuban," added Sosa. "What has happened is the more liberal Hispanic is having more influence. It's not the slam-dunk it was four years ago . . . We knew that Florida was the key state. We had hoped to turn New Mexico around as well," said Sosa. "Florida is where we decided 'if we are going to spend our money in one place it should be there'." Sosa maintains that Bush received 6,500 more Latino votes than Gore in Florida, a fact not disputed by available exit poll numbers.[21]

Frank Guerra, an RNC advertising consultant, explained that the Bush message to Latinos was not stratified. "The overall goal was to communicate to Hispanic voters, no matter where they were in Florida, the issues that are important to Hispanics in any community," Guerra said. "This was the reverse of Gore. I think what it shows was a lack of commitment to communicate to Hispanics. For a long time the Democratic Party has taken Hispanics for granted. They have just wrongly assumed that all Hispanics are liberal and will tow the Democratic line. I think that what it reflects, what the last five, ten election cycles reflect, is a wrong assumption by the Democratic Party that they own the Hispanic vote. I am making that as an absolute judgment about the lack of attention to Hispanics."[22]

In a game of priorities the Gore campaign chose not to compete in the expensive Miami media market. The EMM Creative team, creators of Gore's advertisements, strongly disagreed with the campaign's decision to concede Miami. It was their core disagreement with the senior campaign strategists. "They wanted to concede the Miami Latino-Cuban vote because they felt that Miami was majority Cuban and meaning also majority Republican, and they felt that they wanted to also basically concede that market and focus elsewhere in Tampa and Orlando," said Pablo Izquierdo, a part of the EMM Creative team. "But we argued that the demographics of Miami had changed, no longer were the Cubans dominant, and within the Cubans themselves, second generation Cubans were not giving Republicans votes and were more moderate. And there were newer populations flowing into Miami from Central and South America that no longer made it a monolithic Cuban market. We won that argument about two weeks away from Election Day, and they let us buy Miami for two weeks, but by then it was too little too late. It was going to be more like a $50,000 buy, I am guessing here. Twenty-five grand a week would be a significant buy."[23]

EMM's Jim Learned argues that had more money been spent in Florida things could have been different for Gore. "With true 20–20 hindsight, I'm sure it would have made a big difference," he said. "My sense is the Democrats could have done a lot more. It wouldn't be done again." His business colleague is blunter. "It was the key losing factor," said Izquierdo. "We think that if we had been stronger in Miami we would have won Florida. We could have picked up those thousand votes very easily."[24]

## Orlando and Tampa

With thriving Latino communities, the Orlando and Tampa markets accounted for the bulk of the Gore–DNC spending in Florida. It was also a significant portion of the Bush–RNC buys. With rapidly growing new immigrant communities in Central and South Florida, these two areas gave the candidates the potential to tap into a new, diverse generation of voters. The two campaigns nearly matched each other dollar-for-dollar between the two cities. Gore and the DNC spent $68,000 in Orlando and $61,000 in Tampa. Bush and the RNC spent $57,000 in Orlando and $82,000 in Tampa.[25]

## New Mexico

In the close presidential race in New Mexico, where Gore defeated Bush by a razor-thin 366-vote margin (286,783 to 286,417, each earned 48 percent of the vote), the Gore campaign's aggressive advertising and grassroots strategy paid off handsomely (Barone, 2000). The Gore campaign and the DNC outspent the Bush campaign and the RNC $204,000 to $73,000, almost 3–1, on Spanish-language television advertising in the Albuquerque/Santa Fe media markets, the largest in the state. With significant spending by the Sierra Club on advertisements attacking Bush ($77,000), Gore's margin of spending on supportive advertising over Bush reached 4–1.[26]

In addition to the paid media strategies, both campaigns devoted very significant resources to earned media efforts in the state, arranging interviews for campaign surrogates. Personal contact with voters, through phone calls and door-to-door canvassing, added to a historic level of voter contact. During the final stretch of the election the Gore team had surrogates visit the state on a weekly basis. They included virtually all of the Clinton administration's cabinet officials, Gore, his running mate Senator Joe Lieberman, and Gore's daughter Kristen.[27] Henry Cisneros and Gore campaign outreach director Janet Murguia conducted live satellite media interviews on Albuquerque English-language television stations. The campaign and the DNC arranged interviews on Spanish-language radio stations across New Mexico for Lieberman and a group of Latino Democratic leaders.[28] These efforts complemented the high level of paid advertising in New Mexico, the Gore campaign's most significant Spanish-language ad buys outside of the California primary.[29]

Staffers who directed efforts in New Mexico for both candidates explained that the paid and earned media efforts in New Mexico played an important part in all statewide campaign strategies. They noted that, unlike every other state in the nation where Latinos are viewed as a minority constituency group, in New Mexico candidates and parties treat Latinos as the majority. This means that outreach efforts are primarily aimed at Latino voters.

Bill Knapp praised Armando Gutierrez's strategy in New Mexico and the role it played in giving Gore the edge on Election Day. "I would give him almost total credit for New Mexico," said Knapp. He explained that in addition to extensive Spanish-language advertising in the state, the Democrats sponsored English ads and media tours that were geared toward Hispanics. "It was a blue island in a red sea," Gutierrez said referring to the GOP victories in neighboring states in the Southwestern U.S.[30]

### California

Following the major primaries, the presidential campaigns and the media began to focus on potential battleground states in the general election. While the media included California in the list of states that were potentially in-play during the general election, the two campaigns had different perspectives on the status of the state. Bush and the RNC poured in more than $10 million worth of television advertising, including more than $1 million in Spanish-language television spots, only to lose the state by a significant margin. The Gore campaign did not sponsor any television advertisements in California during the general election, preserving limited resources for close battleground states.[31]

Bush campaign strategists argued that it was a responsible decision to spend so much money on advertising in California. Frank Guerra, whose firm placed millions of dollars of RNC ads in the state, defended the buys as a down payment on long-term Latino support.

Lionel Sosa agreed, "That's two things. An investment in the future and a showing of appreciation to the volunteers who worked so hard, poured their hearts out. We needed to show that we wouldn't leave them hanging in the wings. A lot of that money was raised in California, to do the job there. They were working hard, and thought they could win, though we knew we couldn't." As a result the campaign was compelled to spend a significant amount of money raised in California on advertising in California, he said.[32] The Gore campaign's chief strategist said he was not surprised by the Bush campaign's decision to spend millions of dollars in the state, and noted that the spending was relatively minor when viewed as a part of the campaign's enormous spending total.[33]

Another perspective on the GOP spending in California is that it was an attempt to draw the Democrats into spending precious resources in a state they considered safe. During the 1992 election, Clinton campaign manager James Carville had utilized such a strategy in Florida. As the

Democrats poured money and resources into appeals to Latinos in Florida, the Bush campaign changed its perspective on Florida from safe to contested (Debenport and Dahl, 1992). Carville essentially forced Bush to meet this challenge and spend significant amounts of money to ensure Florida voted for the Republican. While Bush held onto Florida in the general election, Carville's strategy had effectively diverted GOP money from other important battleground states. If this was the underlying motive of the Republicans, it drew little response from Gore who spent meagerly in California.

### Nevada

Hoping to repeat Clinton's 1996 victory, which drew significant support from Nevada's rapidly growing Latino community, the Gore and DNC team outspent the Bush and RNC efforts $186,000 to $45,000 on Spanish-language television advertisements statewide.[34] Despite the 4–1 television spending advantage, Gore lost the state to Bush by 4 percent of the vote. President Clinton had beaten Republican Senator Bob Dole in the state by 1 percent of the vote in 1996. In the final weeks of the election, the Gore campaign strategists saw just how close the election was going to be and wagered on high spending in Nevada. The decision cost Gore in other states; the campaign spent 30% more money on Spanish-language television advertising in Nevada than in Florida.

## English-language advertisements in Latino markets

In addition to examining Spanish-language advertising, we sought to understand how candidates and parties reach out to Latinos with English-language advertisements. In the dawn of Latino political recruitment the parties used Spanish advertising, believing that "U.S. Hispanics are most receptive to media content in the Spanish language. Spanish programming elicits an emotional response from the Hispanic audience that is missing in English-language media" (Guernica, 1982: 5). In 1983, de la Garza, Brischetto and Vaughan found that Spanish language ads were trusted sources of political and community news for Latinos who were monolingual (de la Garza, Brischetto, and Vaughan, 1983). Taking this approach, the 1984 Reagan–Bush Hispanic Victory Initiative spelled out: "you may be able to reach them [Latinos] in English, but you have to convince them in Spanish" (Subervi-Vélez, 1992: 27).

In more recent years, studies have shown that Latinos who are monolingual (who are likely to be older, female, or of a lower socio-economic status) are more apt to tune in to Spanish-language programming, and less likely to vote, while bilinguals are likely to have extensive contact with English media and are more likely to vote (Subervi-Vélez, Herrera and

Begay, 1987: 191). While Spanish advertising appeals continue to be an important aspect of Latino voter recruitment, it is worth analyzing appeals to Latinos in English.

Oberfield analyzed the issues that the candidates addressed in English-language ads to determine whether the parties were addressing Latino issues with those types of advertisement at a higher rate in cities with large Latino populations. He looked at English-language ads in six markets where the parties spent significant money on Spanish-language advertisements as well as two markets where they did not: Chicago and Detroit. Table 13.1 shows the number of Latinos in these nine large markets as a percentage of the population.

Based upon DeSipio (1996), Oberfield chose abortion, crime, civil rights, education, the environment, health care, immigration, and moral values as Latino issues that the candidates could be expected to address in advertising targeting Hispanic voters.

The density of the Latino population in a market caused no discernable difference in the issues addressed by the candidates in the English-language advertising. A few factors help explain this result. Broadly speaking, the issues candidates chose to speak to most Americans about are also Latino issues. The size of a city's overall minority population and the electoral value and competitiveness of each state were additional factors. It is interesting to note that the Republicans outspent the Democrats on "Latino issue" English-language ads in four of the key markets: Phoenix, San Diego, Los Angeles, and Miami. The primary issue areas that they addressed were education and health care. The environment and civil rights issues were secondary foci. Democrats spent more on "Latino issues" in New York, though these buys were made during the primaries.

*Table 13.1* Percent Hispanic Population in Selected Cities in 2000

| City | % |
| --- | --- |
| Albuquerque | 39.9 |
| Chicago | 26.0 |
| Detroit | 5.0 |
| Los Angeles | 46.5 |
| Miami | 65.8 |
| New York | 27.0 |
| Philadelphia | 8.5 |
| Phoenix | 34.1 |
| San Diego | 25.4 |

*Source*: Statistical Abstract of the United States (Valdés, 2000)

301

## English-language advertisements nationwide

Looking at "Latino issue" advertisements nationwide, it is clear that the parties attempted to change voters' popular perceptions of them. Democrats, interested in combating perceptions that they were soft on crime, outspent Republicans by five million dollars on this issue. They also invested heavily in ads about the environment and health care. The Republicans devoted far more attention to education than to any other issue. In addition, they invested heavily in health care and challenging Gore's environmental advantage. It is notable that both parties ignored immigration in their advertising agendas. The Republicans spent over $25 million more than the Democrats addressing "Latino issues" in English ads. Republicans spent nearly as much on education ads ($57.5 million) as the Democrats spent on all their English-language Latino-issue ads ($59.1 million).

Table 13.2 shows the sum of advertising dollars spent by each party nationally. Note that sums include the general election and primary contests and that the cost was not apportioned between issues where the ad addressed multiple issue areas.

## Outcomes: Spanish-language ads and Latino rate of support

What was the effect of Spanish-language advertising on Latino support at the polls? The spending totals by state (see table 13.3) show that the Democrats invested heavily in Nevada and New Mexico with significant investment in Illinois. The Republicans chose California and Florida for their Spanish advertising campaigns. They also spent limited sums (relative to their total) in New Mexico and Nevada. Table 13.3 also shows the percentages won by each candidate by state.

*Table 13.2* National spending on "Latino issue" advertisements, 2000

| Topics | Democrats Total per topic | Republicans Total per topic |
|---|---|---|
| Abortion | $227,410 | $394,318 |
| Crime | $5,630,659 | $0 |
| Civil rights | $964,746 | $24,792 |
| Education | $10,999,852 | $57,542,568 |
| Environment | $12,806,562 | $3,078,008 |
| Health care | $28,513,659 | $23,792,843 |
| Immigration | $0 | $0 |
| Moral values | $0 | $391,153 |
| Grand total | $59,142,888 | $85,223,682 |

Table 13.3 Total expenditures and percent of Latino vote won by state, 2000

| | Bush | | Gore | |
| --- | --- | --- | --- | --- |
| | Total expenditures | % of Latino vote | Total expenditures | % of Latino vote |
| Arizona | $42,000 | 34 | $0 | 65 |
| California | $1,155,000 | 29 | $205,000 | 68 |
| Colorado | N/A | 25 | N/A | 68 |
| Florida | $924,000 | 49 | $129,000 | 48 |
| New Mexico | $73,000 | 32 | $204,000 | 66 |
| New York | $118,000 | 18 | $2,000 | 80 |

Bush performed well in his home state of Texas and in Florida while drawing nearly a third of all Latinos in Arizona and New Mexico. Gore consistently won higher percentages of Latinos and did especially well in New York and, considering the Bush campaign's tremendous advertising advantage, performed quite well in California. Gore performed worst in Bush's strongest states, Texas and Florida. Based solely upon Spanish-language advertising spending it seems that the Democrats spent wisely in New Mexico (where a high percentage of Latinos helped them narrowly win the state) and the Republicans were smart to invest in Florida (where a narrow advantage in the Latino vote helped win the state).

## THE 2004 ELECTION

In 2004 both parties significantly increased the amount of money devoted to Spanish-language political television ads in the presidential race between President Bush and John Kerry, reaching a combined spending record of about $9 million. As table 13.4 indicates, the Bush campaign spent $3,282,000; the Kerry campaign spent $1,354,000; the DNC's Independent Expenditure (a 527 organization) spent $1,398,000; the New Democrat Network's 527 organization spent $2,304,000; and the conservative 527 organization, Progress for America, spent $476,000.

Segal finds that in 2004 the Republican advertising effort was more aggressive, more negative, contained more contrasts with the Democrats, and involved more religious issues than in 2000. Also, at a higher rate than general English television advertisements, abortion and gay marriage were central issues in both Bush and RNC ads on television, radio, in print ads and in flyers and other materials.

In Segal's post-election interviews with top campaign strategists, Segal confirmed these perceptions and learned that they were, in part, influenced by interviews conducted by the Bush team with focus groups

Table 13.4 Total Spanish-language TV spending by market, 2004 presidential election

| | Florida | | | New Mexico/Texas | | Arizona | Colorado | | Nevada | | Ohio | PA | WA | NC | Totals by campaign organization |
|---|---|---|---|---|---|---|---|---|---|---|---|---|---|---|---|
| | Miami | Orlando | Tampa | Albuquerque Santa Fe | El Paso Las Cruces | Tucson Phoenix | Col. Springs Denver | Pueblo | Las Vegas | Reno | Clevlnd. | Phil. | Yakima | Raleigh Durham | |
| Kerry | $ 197,000 | $ 185,000 | $ 153,000 | $ 197,000 | $ 8,000 | $ 189,000 | $ 80,000 | $ 15,000 | $ 171,000 | $ 31,000 | $ 30,000 | $ 85,000 | $ 4,000 | $ 9,000 | $ 1,354,000 |
| DNC | 744,000 | 53,000 | 57,000 | 101,000 | 128,000 | 105,000 | 51,000 | 43,000 | 101,000 | 15,000 | | | | | 1,398,000 |
| NDN | 488,000 | 382,000 | 203,000 | 177,000 | 95,000 | 481,000 | 151,000 | 52,000 | 246,000 | 29,000 | | | | | 2,304,000 |
| Democratic per city | 1,429 | 620,000 | 413,000 | 475,000 | 231,000 | 775,000 | 282,000 | 110,000 | 518,000 | 75,000 | 30,000 | 85,000 | 4,000 | 9,000 | Total Democratic 5,056,000 |
| Bush | 1,459,000 | 229,000 | 200,000 | 297,000 | 211,000 | 365,000 | 173,000 | 33,000 | 258,000 | 57,000 | | | | | 3,282,000 |
| PFA | 270,000 | 56,000 | 52,000 | 83,000 | 15,000 | | | | | | | | | | 476,000 |
| Republican per city | 1,729,000 | 285,000 | 252,000 | 380,000 | 226,000 | 365,000 | 173,000 | 33,000 | 258,000 | 57,000 | | | | | Total Republican 3,758,000 / Grand total 8,814,000 |

Key: DNC Democratic National Committee, NDN New Democratic Network, PFA Progress for America

among Spanish-speaking Latino voters.[35] Bush's victory in New Mexico in 2004 is one indication of the potential success of the changed strategy his team chose in 2004.

## Situating the 2000 and 2004 elections historically

Returning to the theoretical question posed at the chapter's outset: do Latinos draw more attention when their votes are concentrated with one party in the previous election? Figure 13.1 shows the percentage of Latino votes won by each of the major parties in the past six elections.

This figure illustrates that Latinos have shown some significant variation over the past 20 years but never voted less than 50 percent for the Democratic candidate and rarely over 90 percent for the Republican candidate. Pluralists would expect the Democrats to spend heavily on Spanish-language advertising in 1992 and 2000 after elections in which Latinos voted for Democrats near or above 70 percent. Non-pluralists would expect that the closer the Latino vote was to 50/50, the greater combined party investment would be in the next election. How have the parties and respective candidates responded to these changes? Figure 13.2 illustrates the amount of dollars spent on Spanish advertising over this period.

Though the evidence is somewhat ambiguous, there are three instances in which the non-pluralist position is supported empirically. First, in 2004, after the 2000 election in which Republicans made inroads on the

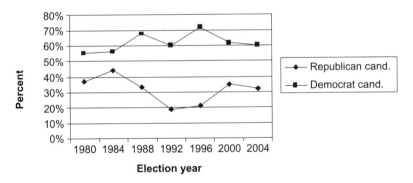

*Figure 13.1* Percent of Latino vote won

*Note:* In 1988 one estimate suggested that 66% of Latinos chose Dukakis while the USHL estimated that 70% chose Dukakis. In this analysis the middle value (68%) is used. In 2004, though many exit polls showed Bush won 44% of the Latino vote, a careful analysis by Leal et al. (2005) shows that the more accurate figure was 32%.

*Source:* Isabel Valdès, In-Culture Marketing, 1996–2006, IVC, www.isabelvaldes.com

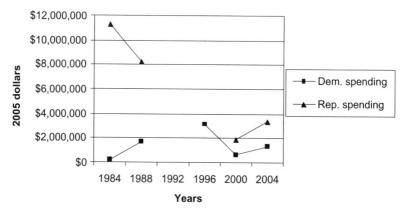

*Figure 13.2* Aggregate spending in 2005 dollars

*Note:* All figures are in 2005 dollars. This chart should be interpreted with caution. The data from 1984–1996 were anecdotally gathered and come from different sources. The sum for these years represents total outreach to Latino voters. The data from 2000 and 2004 elections come from the WiscAds data and only measure Spanish-language advertising.

Democrats' success in 1996, we see an increase in spending by both parties. Second, when Latino support goes above 70 percent in the 1996 election, both Democrats and Republicans spend relatively little in 2000. Third, in the 1988 election, after Latinos had voted nearly 50 percent for Ronald Reagan in 1984, Democrats spent significantly on courting the Latino vote. Though it is inappropriate to use this evidence to proclaim that Latinos should discard pluralist strategies, these data suggest that the parties court Latinos after elections in which they are perceived as "up for grabs." Future work should attempt to verify these findings and build a model that includes many variables that might predict party expenditures. Essentially this chapter argues for the inclusion of an independent variable that gauges the difference between the amount of votes won by each party in the previous election. Also, it is important for future work to detail the percentage of party appeals spent on Latino appeals so that differences in fundraising do not cloud our understanding of party out reach!

## CONCLUSIONS

This chapter has made two contributions. First, it has chronicled how the parties courted the Latino vote through television advertising in the 2000 and 2004 presidential elections. Latino voters have rocketed to new heights of political importance, though their influence on national elections remains limited to competitive elections in battleground states. With rapidly growing numbers, they are actively courted by both Republicans and Democrats. Latinos continue to be underrepresented at the polls, contributing fewer votes to national elections than African Americans in spite of outnumbering them. As DeSipio, de la Garza, and Setzler (1999) remind us, the percentage of turnout among Latinos has not changed greatly despite this group's population explosion and newfound attention by the political parties. A growth in turnout percentage and number will mean greater political results for this diverse community.

The historical part of our analysis suggests that when the Latino vote is split between the parties they may attract greater party expenditures in the subsequent presidential election. In recent years the majority of Latinos have voted for Democratic candidates. However, when exit polls show Latinos voting closer to 50/50, they appear to be rewarded in the next election with enhanced appeals. This finding suggests that pluralist strategies may not be useful for Hispanic leaders aiming generally to attract party attention. A more fruitful strategy may be to develop consensual Latino issue positions and to encourage attention from both parties. Being perceived as "committed" to the Democrats does not appear to win enhanced appeals from either party.

## NOTES

1 The data were obtained from a joint project of the Brennan Center for Justice at New York University School of Law and Professor Kenneth Goldstein of the University of Wisconsin–Madison, and include media tracking data from the Campaign Media Analysis Group in Washington, D.C. The Brennan Center-Wisconsin project was sponsored by a grant from The Pew Charitable Trusts. The opinions expressed in this chapter are those of the authors and do not necessarily reflect the views of the Brennan Center, Professor Goldstein, CMAG, or The Pew Charitable Trusts.

2 Brennan Center for Justice. http://www.brennancenter.org. Multiple press releases during the 2000 campaign.

3 WiscAds coders are graduate and undergraduate students at the University of Wisconsin–Madison.

4 WiscAds coders classified Spanish advertisements as any ads containing Spanish, including those with equal amounts of Spanish and English content. Segal notes the leading presidential campaigns aired English, Spanish, and bilingual advertisements all aimed at various segments of the Hispanic electorate during the 2000 election.

5 Segal, 2003: 32–33 (http://www.jhu.edu/advanced/government/hvp). Data was compiled from Wisconsin Advertising Project/CMAG and Univisión and Telemundo stations.

6 While for this book the term "Latino" is preferred, the RNC uses the term "Hispanic" in most of its internal operations and some, but not all, public communication regarding this ethnic group.

7 Segal's interview with Leslie Sanchez; September 18, 2002. Also, York, (November 1999).

8 Segal's interview with Lionel Sosa; 2002.

9 Segal, 2003: 32–33.

10 Segal's interview with Armando Gutierrez; 2002.

11 It is common for candidates to attempt to avoid being perceived as "going negative" in advertisements produced by their own campaign—in this case, the Gore–Edwards campaign. Instead, the negative propaganda emerges primarily from the party or PAC attack advertisements.

12 Segal, 2003: 26. Wisconsin Advertising Project/CMAG and Univisión and Telemundo stations.

13 Segal, 2003: 26. Wisconsin Advertising Project/CMAG and Univisión and Telemundo stations.

14 Segal, 2003: 32–33. Wisconsin Advertising Project/CMAG and Univisión and Telemundo stations.

15 White House, 2000.

16 Segal's interview with Bill Knapp; 2002.

17 Final report by the Wisconsin Advertising Project and Brennan Center. Monday, December 11, 2000.

18 Wisconsin Advertising Project/CMAG and Univisión and Telemundo stations.

19 Segal's interview with Leslie Sanchez; 2002.

20 Segal's interview with Lionel Sosa; 2002.

21 Segal's interview with Lionel Sosa; 2002.

22 Segal's interview with Frank Guerra; 2002.

23 Segal's interview with Pablo Izquierdo; 2002.

24 Segal's interviews with Jim Learned and Pablo Izquierdo; 2002.

25 Segal, 2003. Wisconsin Advertising Project/CMAG and Univisión and Telemundo stations.

26 Wisconsin Advertising Project/CMAG and Univisión and Telemundo stations.

27 Segal's interview with Andres Gonzalez, former Gore campaign New Mexico state director in 2000 and former executive director of the DNC's Hispanic Outreach Project; October 18, 2002.

28 "DNC 2000 Media Report: Hispanic Satellite Media Tours" and "DNC 2000 Media Report: Radio"—QRS Newmedia report.

29 Segal, 2003. Wisconsin Advertising Project/CMAG and Univisión and Telemundo stations.

30 Segal's interviews with Bill Knapp and Armando Gutierrez; 2002.

31 Segal, 2003. Wisconsin Advertising Project/CMAG and Univisión and Telemundo stations.

32 Segal's interview with Lionel Sosa; 2002.

33 Segal's interview with Carter Eskew; 2002.

34 Segal, 2003. Wisconsin Advertising Project/CMAG and Univisión and Telemundo stations.

35 Segal's interviews with Sosa, Guerra, and the RNC's Raul Damas; 2004.

# 14

# TALK ABOUT ISSUES

## Policy considerations in campaign 2004 Latino-oriented presidential spots

*Stacey L. Connaughton, Dina Nekrassova* and *Katie Lever*[1]

> Focus on issues. That's how I believe you get to Latino voters.
> (*Armando Gutierrez, founder of Gutierrez & Associates;*
> *created and produced Latino-oriented advertising for*
> *DNC, Clinton 1996 campaign; Gore 2000 campaign*)[2]

Issues have long been associated with presidential campaign discourse (Benoit, 2001; Hansen and Benoit, 2002; Jamieson and Campbell, 1997; Johnston and Kaid, 2002; Kaid, 2004; Petrocik, 1996; Pfau, Holbert, Szabo and Kaminski, 2002). As Armando Gutierrez suggests in the above quotation, talking about issues is considered by some political strategists to be a primary way in which to inspire voters' attachments to candidates and/ or parties. Scholars have supported this claim with evidence that voters do consider candidates' issue positions when making judgments about presidential candidates (Iyengar and Kinder, 1987; Petrocik, 1996). Indeed, issues are an integral part of presidential campaign discourse.

When examining the role of issues in campaigns, some scholars have argued that issues are "owned" by parties (Petrocik, 1996; Petrocik, Benoit and Hansen, 2003–04; Damore, 2004). This philosophy is espoused in the theory of issue ownership (Petrocik, 1996), which suggests that one party may have a reputation among constituents as being more credible when it comes to certain issues than other parties. In the United States, the Democratic Party, for instance, has been granted greater credibility on social welfare issues (i.e., education, environment, jobs) and intergroup relationships than its Republican counterpart, whereas the GOP has been awarded more credibility on taxes and defense (see Petrocik, 1996; Petrocik et al., 2003–04). The theory holds that this reputation is developed over time as parties discuss and attend to certain issues, and that decisions about what issues to discuss are based on the nature of the party's constituencies. When candidates talk about those issues that their party

"owns," constituents are more likely to receive those issues, and the candidate who espouses them, favorably (Ansolabehere and Iyengar, 1994).
Moreover, when a party's issues are high on the public agenda, and that
party publicly discusses them, the party might have electoral advantage
(Petrocik et al., 2003–04).

Researchers have examined issue ownership within the context of
general market presidential campaigns (Petrocik, 1996; Petrocik et al.,
2003–04; Damore, 2004) and congressional campaigns (Brasher, 2003); yet
the theory has received less attention with regard to the aspects of those
campaigns that are designed specifically for niche voters, such as Latinos.
Although the theory is not meant to be constituency-specific per se, one
wonders how it might play out with campaign messages intended for specific populations, and whose issues are perceived by some as differing
somewhat from those of the larger citizenry (see DeSipio, 1996, for this
discussion).

Although not explicitly utilized in studies of Latino-oriented campaign
discourse, some tenets of the theory of issue ownership have been
touched on in this literature. For instance, scholars have documented how
the Democratic Party historically has been considered "home" to some
Latinos, including Mexican Americans and Puerto Ricans, among others
(Connaughton and Jarvis, 2004; Connaughton, 2005; Subervi-Vélez,
1992). From that literature, and in the spirit of issue ownership theory,
one could argue that the Democratic Party grew a reputation among some
Latinos over time as being more responsive to their interests and policy
preferences. The strength of the Democratic Party's relationship with
Latinos has come into question in recent years, however (Connaughton,
2005). Since 1980, for instance, the GOP has systematically and actively
courted Latinos both during campaigns (Subervi-Vélez, 1992; Subervi-
Vélez and Connaughton, 1999) and between campaigns (Connaughton,
2005), and has spent more money on political advertisements than the
Democrats have. Although effects of these political ads have yet to be
examined, scholars have amassed empirical evidence that the GOP has
made inroads with Latinos in the 2000 and 2004 presidential campaigns
(Kenski and Tisinger, 2006). Thus, questions about how each party con-
structs issues for Latino voters, and which issues they spend time talking
about, merit investigation.

Scholars who have studied Latino-oriented political campaign communication have pointed out that some issues are constructed as specifically
"Latino" issues by another source—the mass media. This line of research
complements discussions about the agenda-setting effects of the mass
media in campaigns with various constituencies (see Iyengar and Kinder,
1987; McCombs and Shaw, 1972). Scholars have argued that the mass
media play a significant role in the political life of Latinos (Subervi-Vélez,
Herrera and Begay, 1987) and have suggested that the mass media often

construct certain issues as "Latino issues" (e.g., bilingual education and immigration).[3]

In this study, we are not interested in testing which source (parties or media) influences voters more, nor do we seek to examine aspects of issue ownership theory in the Latino context (e.g., potential discrepancies between the issue agenda of the campaigns and the media's report of issues emphasized by the candidates; see Petrocik et al. (2003–04) for a study that does so with general market ads). Rather, we are interested in *which* issues the parties have constructed as salient to Latino voters and *how* they have done so in campaign discourse. It is our contention that the issues which the parties choose to talk about in discourse that is designed specifically for Latinos, as well as the ways in which the parties talk about those issues, says a lot about (a) how the parties perceive this U.S. subpopulation, and (b) how they seek to inspire their attachments and influence their voting behavior. Thus, we examine Latino-oriented party campaign discourse and ask: *What issues do the Democratic and Republican Parties construct as Latino-oriented issues in Campaign 2004?*

This question is important for a host of reasons. First, it allows us to get a sense of what issues the parties deemed salient to Latinos during one presidential campaign. In this regard, this descriptive study serves as a point of departure for future investigations that might seek to test relationships among issues in Latino-oriented discourse and other aspects of Campaign 2004. Second, unearthing what are constructed as salient issues for Latino voters is of consequence to Latinos. As a constituency that has been characterized as "up for grabs" in presidential campaigns over time (see Connaughton, 2005; Subervi-Vélez, 1992), the two major parties have competed for Latinos' affinities, at least during presidential campaigns. Revealing how the parties construct issues of concern to Latinos will not only capture how the parties sought to invite Latinos to their camps in this campaign, but also might enable future scholars to shed light on how Latinos see *themselves* vis-à-vis the U.S. political campaign process and dominant U.S. political parties. Third, what is discussed in campaign discourse, and how it is discussed, matters to the U.S. democratic process. Campaigns are a crucial part of democracy (Hart, 2000). Discussion about issues allows citizens to gather data necessary to make decisions about which party/candidate is most closely aligned with their interests and policy preferences. Indeed, democratic theory suggests that a candidate's discussion of issues during campaigns should inspire connections between citizens and government. How citizens' attachments to parties are inspired says a great deal about the functioning of American democracy (during elections) and the perceived relationship between party organizations and citizens.

How Latino issues are constructed in campaign discourse also warrants further investigation because the very notion of a set of "Latino" issues has been an ongoing topic of debate in academic and public policy circles. DeSipio (1996) presents an excellent discussion of how Latinos' public policy issues have been characterized in multiple ways by various sources. According to DeSipio, early scholars of Latino politics considered Latinos to be concerned primarily with immigration policy and their countries of origin. Additionally, Latino organizations such as MALDEF, NALEO, and NCLR often frame Latino issues as civil rights issues and those on the U.S. domestic social welfare agenda (i.e., bilingual education, primary and secondary education, health care, immigration and naturalization). In the 1980s and 1990s, scholars of Latino politics often considered Latinos to be concerned primarily with the local needs of the communities in which Latinos are concentrated (Hero, 1987, 1992; de la Garza, Menchaca and DeSipio, 1994). These local issues are varied depending on the nature of the communities, but themes like education, poverty, crime, drugs, and gangs are often cited (see DeSipio, 1996, for further discussion). DeSipio contends that in articulating which issues are supposedly salient to Latinos, previous work has ignored key subgroup differences among this diverse population (i.e., Mexican Americans, Cuban Americans, Dominicans, etc.). Drawing on national data from the Latino National Political Survey, he concludes that Latinos' primary policy concerns "focus on social issues to the exclusion of economic, moral, foreign policy, or ethnic issues" (DeSipio, 1996: 57). As this brief review reveals, there is much debate about what constitute Latino policy concerns. The current study seeks to contribute to this ongoing conversation by showcasing how the Democratic and Republican Parties cast, and thus construct, "Latino" issues in Campaign 2004.

To begin addressing our research question, we examined one genre of presidential campaign discourse: televised Spanish-language political advertisements produced by the Kerry–Edwards and Bush–Cheney 2004 campaigns. We selected televised presidential campaign ads because the parties employed decentralized methods with their radio and print ads, making these messages difficult to record and investigate. We chose to examine Spanish-language ads because research has suggested that Latinos who are Spanish-language monolinguals constitute a considerable portion of the U.S. citizenry. These individuals are more apt to tune in to Spanish-language media (not English-language media) and are less likely to vote (Subervi-Vélez et al., 1987). We opted to examine televised political ads because, as the next section reveals, spots serve several functions in campaigns and have been utilized as a predominant way in which parties have sought to connect with voters, both general market and Latino.

## PRESIDENTIAL CAMPAIGN TELEVISION
## ADVERTISEMENTS AND LATINO VOTERS

Political ads are a prevalent genre of presidential campaign discourse. Advertisements, in print and televised forms, serve several functions in campaigns. They may educate citizens by providing information about issues (Brians and Wattenberg, 1996; Kern, 1989; Patterson and McClure, 1976). They have also been found to foster learning about politics (Just, Crigler and Wallach, 1990). And, they influence potential voters regardless of the strength of the individual's partisan attachment (Ansolabehere and Iyengar, 1995).

Political communication researchers have examined issues in campaign discourse in various ways, often at times in conjunction with candidate images. Considering issues and images as distinct types of content, scholars such as Kaid and Johnston (2000), Jamieson, Waldman and Sherr (2000), and West (1997) have investigated the extent to which general market spots discuss issues or images. In reviewing the empirical findings from these studies, Benoit (2001) contends that the jury is still out on which content type, issues or images, is more prevalent in presidential spots. What he perceived as mixed results prompted him to analyze thematic units found in general market spots from 1952 to 2000, looking for issues (which he defines as policy issues) and candidate images (character) in these ads. In doing so, he advanced several hypotheses and research questions, two of which revealed statistically significant findings that are particularly relevant to the current project: (a) policies (issues) are discussed more frequently than character (image) in presidential television spots (61% policy; 39% character); and, (b) Republican presidential television spots contained more messages stressing character than Democrats (42% versus 36%) whereas Democratic ads contained more messages emphasizing policy than Republican spots (64% versus 58%).

In addition to investigating issues and image in presidential spots, scholars have examined the content of advertisements created specifically for niche audiences. Indeed, Latinos are one of those niche audiences for whom the two major parties have designed ads. The Democratic and Republican Parties have devoted considerable resources to courting Latinos via political spots in both English and Spanish languages since 1980 (Connaughton, 2005; Subervi-Vélez, 1992; Subervi-Vélez and Connaughton, 1999). Although the GOP has outpaced their Democratic counterparts in terms of spending (see Oberfield and Segal, chapter 13 of this volume; Subervi-Vélez, 1992), both parties now regularly develop separate divisions of their National Committees during presidential campaigns whose charge it is to court Latino voters and develop advertisements and other messages to do so (see Connaughton, 2005, for variations in the two parties' organizational structures and processes over time).

Previous studies of Latino-oriented television spots have contributed to understandings of these efforts in various ways. Scholars have (a) described the relationship of Latino-oriented ads to overall strategies to court Latinos (Subervi-Vélez, 1992; Subervi-Velez and Connaughton, 1999); (b) noted discursive features of Latino-oriented ads over time (1984–2000) that seek to inspire identification (Connaughton, 2005; Connaughton and Jarvis, 2004); and (c) chronicled the Democratic and Republican Parties' Latino-oriented advertising strategies in various media markets (Oberfield and Segal, chapter 13 of this volume). Yet scholars have yet to discern what issues are portrayed as being of concern to Latinos in Latino-oriented presidential spots. By investigating this question in the 2004 campaign, it is hoped that a larger conversation about the role of issues in Latino political campaign communication will be inspired.

## METHOD

In this study, we examined 18 Spanish-language television advertisements (spots) produced by the Bush–Cheney (n=11) and Kerry–Edwards (n=7) campaigns. The ads were collected from several sources: the Stanford University Political Communication lab web site,[4] the Hispanic Voter Project at Johns Hopkins University and director, Adam J. Segal,[5] and newspaper coverage that printed complete transcriptions of Latino-oriented ads. Spots from both the general and primary campaigns were included in our sample. Spots on the Stanford University web site were available in Spanish in audio form and were transcribed verbatim by a native Spanish speaker. Ads from the other sources were available in textual form. Although English translations of most ads were available online, we opted to ensure the accuracy of the translations that we used. Thus, all ads were first translated from Spanish to English by two native Spanish speakers. The first author (fluent in Spanish) then compared the translations and made minor adjustments.

Because we were concerned with the ways in which issues were talked about, we chose to utilize two units of analysis in the study: (a) message unit and (b) entire advertisement. Following Connaughton and Jarvis (2004), a message unit was conceived of as a complete thought, and each ad was divided into message units before the coding process began. The coding scheme was based on that which was used by Connaughton (2005) and was modified slightly to include topics on the national stage during Campaign 2004 (e.g., stem cell research). Two members of the research team then coded each message unit for issues. In line with Benoit, *issue* was defined as utterances that "concern governmental action (past, current, or future) and problems amenable to governmental action" (Benoit, 2001: 116). The research team members coded message units individually;

codes were then compared and agreement was reached. Afterwards, each advertisement was also considered as a unit of analysis to determine if one issue or more than one issue was discussed in the ad.

Descriptive and non-parametric statistics/analyses were run on the data. In addition to these descriptive statistics, our study was enriched by a discursive analysis of the texts themselves. In doing so, we attended to (a) the number of issues presented in each ad/message unit; (b) how the issues were framed; and (c) what discursive forms were used in the texts (e.g., narrative). Thus, to answer our research question, we combined descriptive statistics with rich description of the ads themselves.

## ISSUE TALK IN CAMPAIGN 2004
## SPANISH-LANGUAGE SPOTS

The data revealed that domestic issues were the most prevalent issue references in the Spanish-language television advertisements in Campaign 2004. When ads from the two candidate campaigns were analyzed together, the economy (which includes jobs) emerged as the most often mentioned issue in the message units (n=20; 15.9%). Health care (n=12; 9.5%) and education (n=9; 7.1%) were the next two most frequently noted issues. Table 14.1 reveals all results.

Although our limited sample does not allow us to run chi-square analyses to note significant differences between the advertisements of the two candidate campaigns, our data do point to some modest distinctions revealed in the descriptive statistical analyses. The Bush–Cheney campaign talked most often about the economy, an issue discussed in 27 percent of their ads' message units (n=20). It should be noted that the Bush–Cheney campaign was the only one to mention the economy in their Spanish-language ads; the Kerry–Edwards campaign did not. This is

*Table 14.1* Issue frequency in Campaign 2004 Latino-oriented spots

| Issue | Combined ads (both campaigns) |
| --- | --- |
| Defense | 1 |
| Economy | 20 |
| Education | 9 |
| Health care | 12 |
| Immigration | 1 |
| National security | 4 |
| Social security | 3 |
| Terrorism | 2 |
| Several issues mentioned | 2 |

Note: The message unit is the unit of analysis reported here

particularly noteworthy in that jobs are often included among social welfare issues and among those that the Democratic Party is purported to "own" (see Petrocik et al., 2003–04). The GOP candidate campaign also mentioned health care in 12.2 percent of their ads' message units (n=9) and education in 8.1 percent (n=6). Table 14.2 summarizes issues discussed in these Democratic and Republican spots.

The message units in the Kerry–Edwards ads were, curiously, often void of issues. Indeed, in 44 out of the 52 message units, no issues were mentioned. When issues were mentioned, they included health care (n=3; 5.8%) and education (n=3; 5.8%). And, in one message unit, several issues—health care, education, and (implicitly) the economy (in terms of "opportunity")—were noted. Surprisingly, the Kerry–Edwards campaign brought up a policy issue not often discussed in political advertisements— immigration. This issue appeared in one of the Democrats' Spanish-language advertising message units (1.9%). Curiously, however, explicit references to the economy (and jobs) are absent in these Democratic ads (see table 14.2).

The Bush–Cheney spots covered a wider range of policy issues. Out of all issues mentioned in the ads of both candidate campaigns, Bush–Cheney talked about all of them except immigration (see tables 14.1 and 14.2). That is, the GOP candidates' ads mentioned the economy, health care, education, terrorism, national security, social security, and defense spending. The Kerry–Edwards campaign, on the other hand, appears to have been more selective; the Democratic candidates talked only about education, health care, and immigration, and made one mention of "opportunity" which contextually could be interpreted as referring to jobs (economy). And, again, 44 out of the 52 Kerry–Edwards message units did not contain reference to issues at all.

Here, it is important to note that the Bush–Cheney spots contained a

Table 14.2 Issue frequency in Republican and Democratic Campaign 2004 Latino-oriented spots

| Issue | Bush–Cheney ads n = 74 | Kerry–Edwards ads n = 52 |
|---|---|---|
| Defense | 1 | 0 |
| Economy | 20 | 0 |
| Education | 6 | 3 |
| Health care | 9 | 3 |
| Immigration | 0 | 1 |
| National security | 4 | 0 |
| Social security | 3 | 0 |
| Terrorism | 2 | 0 |
| Several issues mentioned | 1 | 1 |

Note: The message unit is the unit of analysis reported here

greater total number of message units (n=74) than the Kerry–Edwards campaign (n=52). These data make sense given that our sample included 11 Bush–Cheney ads and 7 Kerry–Edwards spots. The range of total message units within a given ad varied. One Kerry–Edwards ad, for instance, contained 12 message units while another had 4 (mean length = 7.50 message units). The Bush–Cheney ads ranged from 5 to 10 message units with the mean length approximating 7 per ad (mean length = 6.73). Regardless of this slight variation among the two parties, it is noteworthy that Bush–Cheney spots covered a greater range of topics than Kerry–Edwards ads.

Not only do the Bush–Cheney advertisements speak to more issues, they are also denser in that they pack several issues into a single ad. Consider one GOP spot entitled "Agenda Nacional."[6] Notice how, in this one ad, three message units attend to the economy (and jobs), one to education, and three to health care:

> NARRATOR: President George Bush and our leaders in Congress have a plan.
> To strengthen our *economy*.
> To create more *jobs*.
> To train more *workers*.
> To invest in *education*.
> To help small businesses provide *health insurance* to their employees.
> To give *health insurance* to all poor communities.
> To *create a central hospital* in all poor communities.
> Read the plan that will improve your life. [emphasis added]

In this spot, the Bush–Cheney ad creators borrowed a strategy used by the Democratic Latino-oriented ad team in previous years: that is, they strung issue after issue together, in a bullet point format, within a single ad (see Connaughton, 2005, for a discussion of this strategy). When a viewer listens to this spot, and when we analyze the spot as an entire unit, more than one issue emerges as being touched on in the ad. This strategy appeared in several Bush–Cheney spots (see also "Tus Opciónes," "Nuestro País, Nuestro Presidente," and "Diferencias")[7]. In a similar amount of space (5–10 message units) and within a similar time frame (a 30-second spot) as their Democratic competitors, the Bush–Cheney campaign appears to have covered more ground in terms of issues, and did so concisely—merely mentioning multiple issues in one ad.

Although the descriptive statistics share an interesting story themselves, the content of the spots reveal some other distinctions among the parties. One begins to note differences when attending to *who is speaking in the ads*. Two of the Kerry–Edwards spots utilized vignettes within which Latinos speak; that is, these ads incorporated stories that cast Latinos as characters in a drama that unfolds before the viewer's eyes. One vignette showcased a Latino family—father, mother, and a female high school graduate—on the daughter's graduation day. The Latino family members have speaking roles in the ad, as does a narrator who integrates the Kerry–Edwards campaign's promise to "open the doors of college education to all of our children and to improve public education" ("Graduación"). Another Kerry–Edwards spot followed a similar vignette structure, opening with a young boy and his father in a physician's office. The drama begins with the boy, excited to return home, greeting his father and the physician asking to speak to the father alone. The father learns that his health insurance will not cover the boy's expenses. As in the previous ad, the narrator weaves the issue—health care—into the ad, indicating that "John Kerry wants all children to have access to health insurance." Two out of the seven Kerry–Edwards ads examined in our study adopted this story-telling structure. In four spots, only the narrator spoke and in one ad, only Kerry spoke (talking head ad).

Like the Kerry–Edwards spots, a narrator talked throughout the majority of the Bush–Cheney advertisements (in nine out of 11 spots). Yet the Bush–Cheney ads incorporated the Latino citizen as speaker in a slightly different way. In one ad, the Bush–Cheney spot incorporates citizen testimonials. In this ad, entitled "Impuestos" ("Taxes"), the narrator begins by saying: "Latinos all over are tired of higher taxes." At that moment, a mature Latino male laments: "It always is 'Raise taxes'." A young Latino and a young Latina also add testimonials later in the spot. In contrast to the Kerry–Edwards ads described above, Latinos in this GOP spot articulated opinions about policy issues.

The GOP utilized another tactic as well—silence. One advertisement consisted of only visual graphics (no voices) and showed statements about the issue (in this case, the economy) on the television screen. The ad, "Más seguro, más fuerte" ("Safer, stronger"), begins with a message unit that does not contain explicit reference to a specific issue, but then incorporates several issue message units that appear line by line across the screen:

An economy in recession.
The stock market in decline.
The dot.com boom in bankruptcy.

All three message units refer to the economy, and the entire ad is purely visual.

Another lens through which to note potential discursive differences between the parties is to consider *how* the two candidate campaigns talk about these issues. Examining the language used in these ads enables us to make a couple of general observations: (a) the Kerry–Edwards spots positioned almost every issue they talk about in terms of the family unit; (b) the Bush–Cheney ads often positioned the issues they touched on in terms of John Kerry and "the Liberals in Congress." Both points will be discussed further in the next few paragraphs.

Regardless of whether or not an ad talked about a specific issue, family was a theme evident in almost every Kerry–Edwards ad. Indeed, an explicit reference to "family" or "children" was made in seven of the nine Democratic candidate spots. And often, family was discursively tied to an issue presented in the ad. For instance, one advertisement entitled "Fé" ("Faith") discussed immigration. Notice how the ad connects the policy stance (reforming immigration policy) with Latino families:

> NARRATOR: Faith is one of the cornerstones of our culture. We need a leader who is guided by those values. And who delivers on his promise to help others. *In his first 100 days as President, John Kerry will present a plan to reform immigration and help reunify families* [emphasis added]. We have faith in John Kerry because he has faith in us. John Kerry, our hope for a better future.

In this advertisement, reforming immigration is presented as a means through which Latino families can be united again. Family is an integral part of Latino culture; thus, it is not surprising that the parties mention it and utilize it to make policy preferences sound more palatable. What is surprising is that the *Democratic* candidates utilized family references so consistently in these ads. In a study of advertising strategies employed to court Latino voters, Connaughton (2005) interviewed several strategists and ad creators from both parties and found that the Democrats tended to favor courting Latinos on issues, whereas it was the GOP that historically sought to convince Latinos that they had two values in common: faith and love of family (both values appear in the above Democratic spot). Yet in these 2004 Spanish-language ads, it is the Democratic Party that emphasized family consistently.

Another observation can be made from these ads: the GOP explicitly named its opponent whereas the Democrats did not. The Bush–Cheney spots often positioned the issues they touched on in terms of John Kerry and "the Liberals in Congress." This is a noteworthy finding, for studies of presidential campaign discourse have noted that it is often the challenger who is more likely to attack the incumbent (see Benoit, 2001). In the advertisements examined in this study, however, it is the incumbent spots, those from Bush–Cheney, that make explicit reference to their opponent and his allies. An ad called "Inteligencia" provides an example of this tactic. Notice how the Bush–Cheney national security plan is not mentioned in this ad, but rather Kerry's voting record is:

NARRATOR: Now, John Kerry promises to reform the intelligence system. But when he was a member of the Intelligence Committee, Kerry missed 76% of the meetings. The year after the first attack on the twin towers, Kerry missed all the meetings on terrorism. And that same year, Kerry proposed to cut the Intelligence budget by $6 billion. What Kerry promises is different from what Kerry does.

Kerry is mentioned (often more than once) in eight out of the 11 Bush–Cheney ads in this study. Of those eight GOP ads, Bush is explicitly mentioned by name in only three ads. Conversely, in the seven Kerry–Edwards spots, Bush is not named. The challenger's ads do imply that social and economic conditions are in need of improvement, a set of circumstances that the viewer may then attribute to the Bush administration. Yet Bush's name does not appear in the Kerry–Edwards Spanish-language ads.

## DISCUSSION

This study has examined which issues were constructed in Campaign 2004 as being salient to Latino voters, and has discussed some of the ways in which these issues were presented. The analyses reveal some curious findings. For one, the GOP ads presented the economy (including jobs) as a salient issue for Spanish-speakers whereas the Democratic ads did not. This is an interesting finding, especially with regard to jobs, in that previous research has suggested that the Democratic Party tends to own social welfare issues such as jobs (although the economy more broadly defined is considered a performance issue, not owned by either party; see Petrocik et al., 2003–04). Second, the GOP mentioned a greater number of issues in its ads. The only issue that the Republican candidate did not mention is immigration, a policy issue that advertising strategists have considered a taboo topic within the advertisement genre (see Connaughton, 2005) yet one which the Democrats talked about in one ad. In discussing more issues, the Republican ads utilized a denser structure in the sense that they incorporated several issues into a single message unit and into a singular ad. Interestingly, the majority of Democratic ads did not have an issue mention in them (n=44 out of 52). With regard to the ways in which the parties constructed issues, the Democratic ads couched them within values—family and faith; the Republican Party often utilized the bullet point structure of quickly introducing issue after issue after issue.

In reflecting on these findings, one could interpret them in various ways. For instance, one might question the extent to which, in courting Spanish-speaking Latinos, the parties adhere to issues that they are perceived to "own." Indeed, in these advertisements, the GOP appeared to talk about issues on which it has been granted credibility (i.e., taxes, military spending) *as well as* issues that have been entrusted to the Democratic Party (i.e., jobs, health care, education). Although the Democrats do talk about health care and education in their ads, it seems that the GOP cast a broader net in courting Spanish-speaking Latinos, and engaged in what Damore (2004) and others have called "issue trespassing." One can imagine a couple reasons why the GOP might do so: (a) its historically shaky relationship with some Latinos, such as Mexican Americans and Puerto Ricans (see Connaughton, 2005; Subervi-Vélez, 1992); and (b) the desire to entice swing voters (particularly given the nature of Campaign 2004). Still, it is interesting that, among this particular subset of the Latino constituency, Spanish-speaking Latinos, the GOP adopted what some might argue is a risky strategy in articulating issues that they have not been perceived to own.

Furthermore, the candidates' strategies in talking about issues are reminiscent of some of Cheney's (1983) techniques for fostering identification with an organization (party). Specifically, by couching issues within the context of enhancing the lives of Latino families, the Kerry–Edwards campaign utilized what Cheney calls a common ground tactic. That is, the importance of family in Latinos' lives (a value) was raised in these spots as a way to articulate that the Democratic Party recognizes the significance of, and shares, the family values of Latino voters. By establishing this common ground, it is hoped that Latino voters will develop or enhance their attachments to the Democratic Party and its candidates. Bush–Cheney spots, on the other hand, appear to have employed another identification tactic: the construction of a common enemy. Indeed, in many of the Bush–Cheney spots, Kerry is repeatedly accused of missing many important meetings implying that he is an agent of existing problems that adversely affect the nation and its citizens. In other words, Kerry and the "Liberals in Congress" are constructed as a common enemy, an enemy both of the GOP and of Latino voters. Through an identification lens, one can interpret such negative portrayals of Kerry as attempts to clearly distinguish the president from his opponent, creating an "us" (GOP and Latinos) and a "them" (Democrats), in attempts to foster Latinos' identification with the Republican Party. Whether these Democratic and Republican tactics actually did foster identification and/or influence behaviors is an area for future research.

One might also examine these findings in light of previous research and note that it appears the parties have flip-flopped strategies for courting Latino voters. In an examination of Democratic and Republican Latino-oriented communication campaign strategies over time, Connaughton (2005) argued that the Democratic Party has sought to connect with Latinos via issues (policy) whereas the GOP has attempted to do so via values (family and faith). Curiously, in the current study, the *Democratic* ads raised family as a value, sometimes while talking about policy issues (i.e., the family vignette on education discussed earlier in this chapter), and the *GOP* ads spoke to issue after issue, often times within the same ad. Perhaps it was the nature of this particular campaign (the campaign of the swing voter) that prompted strategists to break from historical patterns in courting this constituency; or, perhaps our findings are linked to the fact that we examined only Spanish-language advertisements. Perhaps if English language spots had been included in our sample as well we would have found similar patterns to those uncovered in previous work. These are issues for future research to investigate.

In general, findings from this study encourage future scholars to continue to investigate what and how issues are constructed for Spanish-speaking populations. In a sense, findings from this study encourage scholars to examine issue ownership theory among specific subpopulations of the citizenry. This could be an important move, for it has been shown that Latino-oriented campaign discourse and that of general market campaigns, over time, have been somewhat distinct (see Connaughton and Jarvis, 2004). Along these lines, one wonders if issues the citizenry at large perceives to be "owned" by Republicans and Democrats necessarily are the same for Spanish-speaking Latinos. That remains a query for future empirical study.

## NOTES

1  The authors with to thank the Stanford University Political Communication Lab as well as Adam J. Segal and the Hispanic Voter Project at Johns Hopkins University for making their collections of Spanish-language advertisements accessible to them. The authors also wish to thank Federico A. Subervi-Vélez for his helpful comments on this manuscript and for giving them the opportunity to contribute to this volume.
2  Interview with first author; July 10, 2001.
3  Brasher (2003) brings these two lines of argument together by pointing out that both parties and media play a role: candidates will talk about those issues the mass media construct as important *and* those which the parties are purported to "own" during campaigns, although for different reasons (see Brasher, 2003: 458 for more details).
4  See http://pcl.stanford.edu/campaigns/campaign2004/archive.html.
5  See http://advanced.jhu.edu/government/hvp/hvp_2004_Interim_Report.pdf.
6  The text for this spot was obtained from http://advanced.jhu.edu/academic/government/hvp/hvp_2004_Interim_Report.pdf.
7  Texts for the spot "Tus Opciónes" was obtained from http://pcl.stanford.edu/campaigns/campaign2004/archive.html; and texts for "Nuestro País, Nuestro Presidente," and "Diferencias" were obtained from http://advanced.jhu.edu/academic/government/hvp/hvp_2004_Interim_Report.pdf.

# 15

# LATINOS' USE OF MEDIA AND THE MEDIA'S INFLUENCE ON POLITICAL KNOWLEDGE AND PARTICIPATION

Findings from the 1989 Latino National
Political Survey

*Federico A. Subervi-Vélez*

in collaboration with
*Victor Menayang*

The belief that mass media influence the political dynamics of the elect-orates is probably as old as the first newspapers themselves. Research assessing the impact of the media on American politics also has a long history (Nimmo and Sanders, 1981; Kaid, 2004). While the results of the numerous studies conducted throughout the decades on the subject of media effects on politics are not always very conclusive, there is neverthe-less merit to the proposition that media can be influential (see works cited in chapters 2–3).

The evidence, however, is primarily based on research of the Anglo European segments of the U.S. population. With the exception of the works cited in chapter 3 (e.g., Allen & Chaffee, 1979; Jeffres, 1999, 2000; Kennamer, 1987; McCombs, 1968), very few scholars have assessed the role of media in the political life of members of this country's ethnic minority groups. While minority group politics have been of increasing interest in academia, the same cannot be said for the study of political communication related to these populations. And, as noted in the third section of chapter 2, less than a dozen studies have analyzed statistical relationships between *Latinos'* media use or exposure, and their political knowledge, attitudes, or behaviors. The last publication was dated in 1985.

The Latino National Political Survey (LNPS)[1] allows for a more contemporary assessment of potential effects of the media on Latinos' political life. This is possible because the survey contained a number of questions related to media as well as politics. And even though the LNPS did not include the best questions for assessing in a comprehensive and detailed way the connections between these variables, the findings discussed below nevertheless shed some new light on how media have potential influence on some Latinos' political orientations.

This chapter presents key findings from our analysis of the LNPS data on both media and politics. The primary questions we sought to answer were the following: Are there any significant relationships between patterns of exposure to and use of the mass media, and the political knowledge and behaviors of Latinos? And, are there significant variations in the media relationships to politics among subgroups of Latinos, i.e., Mexican Americans, Puerto Ricans, and Cuban Americans?

## TOWARD A PARTIAL AND INTERIM MODEL

The most comprehensive statistical assessments of Latino political participation point out the predictive value of a number of factors. Those analyses, based on the same LNPS data used in this chapter, suggest time and again the positive influence of basic socio-economic variables such as age, education, and income. Ethnic origin, organizational membership, perception of discrimination, and mobilization are among a few other variables that provide insights into the intricacies of Latinos' voting and non-voting political dynamics. The frameworks in which the aforementioned variables are discussed allude to theories and/or present models related to assimilation, mobilization, ethnic resilience, ethnic politics, "ghettoization," minority group oppression or experiences, and generational or immigrant group experiences, among others (see DeSipio, 1996; Espino, 2003, and the articles in the special issue of the *Hispanic Journal of Behavioral Sciences* edited by García, Falcón, and de la Garza, 1996). Interestingly, *not even one* of those works brings forth any discussion whatsoever about the potential influence of, or interplay between, the mass media and any of the studied variables.

Building on our past studies in this area, on the research experience and findings discussed in chapters 2 and 3 of this book, and on Jeffres' (1999) work, we can assertively propose that media can and do make a difference in the political knowledge and behaviors of ethnic groups, including Latinos. What is also clear, however, is that the media do not stand alone, nor are they necessarily the most important factor in this process. Instead, media are, so to speak, mediating variables that may—under the right circumstances—enhance knowledge and participation in politics.

The model proposed and tested with the data at hand is partial and interim. It is partial because it includes only some of the multiple variables that should be analyzed for better understanding and predicting the political communication dynamics of Latinos. It is interim until more precise measures of politically related media uses are made available for scrutiny. What is proposed, then, is a limited test of the media's potential role in Latinos' political knowledge and participation.

## Hypotheses

Our assumption that media do make a difference requires hypotheses that affirm media influence above and beyond the traditional demographic variables. Thus, the first hypothesis tested with these data proposes that, even after controlling for demographic and SES variables, the greater the exposure to the mass media, the greater the *political knowledge* of Latinos. However, not all media can be expected to have equal influence on that knowledge. As has been amply documented in other studies, and as alluded to in chapters 4 and 8, newspapers generally carry more political content than television or radio.[2] Thus, it is also hypothesized that exposure to newspapers will have a greater influence on political knowledge than will exposure to television.

Using the same rationale proposed above, the second set of hypotheses of this study is that, even after controlling for demographic and SES variables, the greater the exposure to the mass media, the greater the *political participation* of Latinos. Again, the role of the press is assumed to be greater than that of broadcast media. It then follows that exposure to newspapers will have a greater influence on political participation than will exposure to television.

Direct influence will be assessed between media exposure and the two sets of political variables. But, because in the process the paths between media, knowledge, and participation will also be calculated, it will be the relationship between the first and second set of hypotheses that will be most revealing of the potential role of the media on participation. These will show if the influence is direct or mostly mediating via knowledge gains.

The third and final set of hypotheses builds on the assumption that there are differences in the political status and experiences of the various Latino groups in the U.S. Thus, it is proposed that there will be significant differences in the relationships between media exposure, political knowledge, and political participation of Puerto Ricans vis-à-vis Mexican Americans vis-à-vis Cubans. In other words, separate sets of data analysis testing the aforementioned hypotheses will reveal different sets of results for each group. Even if the general paths hold true for Latinos as a whole, as expected, and even for each group individually, as is also anticipated, the strengths of the relationships between the variables are foreseen to yield significant variations across each ethnic group.

In the process of testing these hypotheses and thus answering this main question of this study—Are there any significant relationships between patterns of exposure to and use of the mass media, and the political knowledge and behaviors of Latinos?—we begin the findings by presenting data on the respondents' patterns of use of the media and how these patterns are related to traditional variables such as gender, age, education, income, proportion of years in the U.S., language proficiency in Spanish and English, and the respondents' country of origin (i.e., Mexico, Puerto Rico, Cuba). The final section of the findings will then focus on the relationship between these aforementioned variables and political knowledge and participation.

## Caveats

Before turning to the data analysis, four important caveats should be kept in mind. As already mentioned, the media questions utilized here are not the ideal for assessing potential media influences. One of the lessons of the more sophisticated research on the relationships between exposure to the media and political orientations is the need for specificity. General questions about either media behaviors or about political orientations typically may not yield significant statistical associations among those variables. Asking specific questions, as we would have liked to see done when the LNPS was conducted, would have been preferable to assess the impact of media exposure on Latino politics.[3] Lacking the options, at this time we can only recognize the limitation this poses on the conclusiveness of confirming or rejecting our hypotheses. Nevertheless, the results shown below are encouraging for the next generation of research in this arena. Suggestions for future research with the specific factors, such as the availability, language and quality of Latino-oriented media in the community, are thus proposed at the end of this chapter and again in the concluding chapter of the book.

A second caveat is that, in the case of Latinos, any assessment of the potential role of the mass media has to take into consideration a factor that is not usually part of the study of most populations. That factor is the subject's use of, or exposure to, *Latino-oriented* media. As discussed in previous chapters and elsewhere (Subervi-Vélez et. al, 1994; Subervi and Eusebio, 2005; Subervi-Vélez, 2006), in most major metropolitan areas in the U.S., Latinos have available to them a vast array of Spanish-language and some English-language media that are primarily aimed at this group. These media, in addition to the general market media, may be contributing forces in the political socialization of this population. However, many Latinos also live in communities with few, if any, Latino-oriented media.

If they live in small rural communities they may have, at best, access to some Spanish-language radio programming.

The third caveat is that Latino-oriented media may be local or national. Spanish-language dailies are available primarily at the *local* level; there is no Latino-oriented newspaper in Spanish or English similar to *USA Today*, *The Wall Street Journal*, or the national edition of *The New York Times*. In fact, in large metropolitan areas, some local periodicals are often found in selected neighborhoods only. The most national of the print media are major magazines such as *Hispanic*, *Hispanic Business*, *Vista*, and *Latina*. But there are some statewide or regional publications as well. Most magazines are available by subscription, and also in selected supermarkets and other stores in cities with large concentrations of Hispanics.

With few exceptions, Latino-oriented radio, practically all of which is broadcast in Spanish, is also local. Some exceptions would be if the radio stations are part of the Radio Bilingüe Network, or, as of 2004, part of new networks such as Univisión Radio or the Border Media Partner networks. (From 1998 to 2003, there was also another commercial radio network, Radio Unica, but that network closed operations in October 2003.) National *news* programming on radio would otherwise stem from subscriptions to commercial syndicated news/information services (such as CNN en Español Radio, or the Associated Press in Spanish), or to noncommercial news/information services (such as Radio Bilingüe's *noticiero*, or the English-language Latino USA weekly program of news and culture).

Latino-oriented television, most of which is broadcast in Spanish, is both national and local. Networks such as Univisión and Telemundo offer national programs, including their evening newscasts that are similar in format and some of their content to the general market network news. However, many of the local affiliates of these networks also broadcast some of their own productions, including public affairs programs and local news.

The final caveat is that, as with any study of Latinos, it should be kept in mind that this population is not monolithic. This can be discerned from many of the political writings about Latinos already cited in previous chapters, as well as in numerous sociological writings (Fox, 1996; Padilla, 1994a; Tienda and Mitchell, 2006; Weyr, 1988). Moreover, there are differences within each of these groups that stem from various factors such as having a predominantly urban or rural background, the length of years of residing in the U.S., and of course the primary cultural milieu in which they live in the U.S. Thus, as can be expected, the sample of Latinos selected for this study, which consists of Latinos who have Mexican, Puerto Rican, and Cuban roots, share similarities as well as differences in immigration patterns, cultural practices and traditions, and also in their political histories and experiences. Any or all of those factors may contribute to variations in the interpretations given by the various Latino subgroups to political information gathering and mobilization in the U.S. Likewise, those factors may also influence how the Latinos respond differently to political surveys, including the LNPS.

Given these considerations, the experiences of Latinos with the media, be these general market or Spanish-language Latino-oriented, may be more diverse than is the case for the Anglo population. This again speaks to the importance of the inclusion of specific questions in survey research on such maters. Thus, our findings and conclusions about media influences are not based on the assumption of a national common experience in exposure to Latino-oriented media or any other media. Nevertheless, just as it is understood that for the population at large there are variations in the content of the media, so it is the case for the Latinos studied here. What still holds firm is the proposition of the mediating potential of the media on the subjects' political dynamics.

## VARIABLES SELECTED AND ANALYTICAL PROCEDURES

As stated above, this chapter makes use of data collected in the Latino National Political Survey. We focus primarily on the relationship between exposure to and use of the media (which constitute our mediating variables), and political knowledge and participation (which are the dependent variables). Some of the traditional background factors were also included as independent variables in the analysis, in order to account for their contributions to the dependent variables.

The media variables analyzed include primary source for political and public affairs news (media preferred), language of the primary media attended, and the frequency of media attendance.[4]

Political variables, the dependent variables in this analysis, are political knowledge and political participation. The first was constructed from questions asking respondents about five factual political figures and the position they held[5] plus one question about the make-up of the U.S. House of Representatives.[6] The participation scale was constructed from five questions regarding actual participation in voter registration and voting.[7]

The other specifying variables are gender, age, proportion of years in the U.S.,[8] educational level, household income, and also Spanish language and English language preferences and ability (constructed from two questions[9]).

Variable selection reduced the number of subjects used in this analysis. In the first step, because we are using measures of political participation in the form of voting, we decided to analyze only those who were U.S. citizens, which brought down the potential sample to 2,339 subjects out of the total sample of 3,415. We further narrowed the analysis to those with a valid answer in terms of their origins—that is, Mexicans, Puerto Ricans, and Cubans—resulting in a sample size of 1,776 respondents. Mexicans constitute the largest proportion of this analyzed sample (49.4 percent), followed by Puerto Ricans (33 percent), and Cubans (15.5 percent). Only TV viewers and newspaper readers are included in the analysis because "frequency" questions only dealt with these types of audience.

The main statistical procedure utilized for assessing the relationships between the background variables and the media variables, and then between these and the dependent variables, was hierarchical regression. This allows for "distinguishing the variance explained by the different independent variables" (cf. Subervi-Vélez, 1984: 96] along the proposed path analysis of variables relationship.

Using the forced inclusion procedures,[10] we entered one block of variables at a time. Sex and age are in the first block. Proportion of years in the U.S., educational level, and household income are in the second block. Spanish language ability and English language ability constitute the third block.

These were selected as predictors of two of the media use variables, which subsequently were entered as the fourth block as mediating variables to help explain political knowledge and political participation. Political knowledge was in turn a mediating variable when it was entered in the fifth block as a predictor of political participation.

Following our theoretical model, gender and age are entered in the equation with each variable in the second block as the dependent variable. All the variables in the first and second blocks were then entered into an equation in which each variable in the third block turned into a dependent variable, and so on, until the political variables are entered in the analysis. For each equation, we observed the standardized regression coefficient, the significance of the part correlation, and the proportion of variance accounted for by entering the specific variable.

Table 15.1 shows the frequency distributions of the main variables that are the focus of the analysis to assess the relationship between media exposure and politics. Detailed analysis that compare Latinos with respect to the background variables, other media measures, or that assess the relationships between the background variables and media variables are excluded in this table.[11] For additional analysis and discussions of the findings from the LNPS data, see de la Garza, DeSipio, García, García, and Falcón (1992); García, Falcón, and de la Garza (1996), and Oberfield (2003).

*Table 15.1* Frequencies, means, and (standard deviations) of selected independent, mediating, and dependent variables

| Variables* | All Latinos[12] | Mexican Americans | Puerto Ricans | Cuban Americans |
|---|---|---|---|---|
| | n=1,776 | n=878 | n=587 | n=312 |
| Male | 45% | 46% | 44% | 45% |
| Female | 55% | 54% | 56% | 55% |
| Age | 39.8 (16.4)** | 39.0 (16.1) | 38.3 (15.1) | 44.9 (18.2) |
| % of years in the U.S. | .83  (.25) | .96  (.12) | .73  (.28) | .68  (.27) |
| Education | 10.6  (3.8) | 10.5  (3.7) | 10.0  (3.8) | 12.0  (3.7) |
| Income[13] | 7.4  (4.1) | 7.8  (3.9) | 5.9  (3.9) | 8.9  (4.1) |
| Spanish language ability | 3.8  (1.8) | 3.2  (1.8) | 4.1  (1.5) | 4.8  (1.5) |
| English language ability | 5.7  (2.0) | 6.3  (1.8) | 5.3  (2.1) | 4.8  (1.8) |
| Read newspaper | 2.9  (2.7) | 2.8  (2.8) | 2.8  (2.6) | 3.5  (3.0) |
| Watch TV news | 4.5  (2.5) | 4.1  (2.5) | 4.7  (2.3) | 5.2  (2.3) |
| Political knowledge | 2.5  (2.0) | 2.3  (1.8) | 2.0  (1.9) | 4.1  (1.9) |
| Political participation | 2.7  (1.9) | 2.7  (1.9) | 2.5  (1.9) | 3.3  (1.9) |
| Voting turnout*** | 53.2% (.5) | 49.9% (.5) | 50.4% (.5) | 67.5% (.47) |

\* See text and corresponding endnotes for definitions of variables
\*\* Numbers in parenthesis represent standard deviations
\*\*\* Based on 1989 data; presented for contextual and comparative purposes only

## FINDINGS

The patterns that emerge from the data are divided into two broad categories: (1) media use for news and political and public affairs, and (2) the relationships between news media exposure and political knowledge and participation.

## Media use

When it comes to seeking political and public affairs news, Latinos—in this case Mexican Americans, Puerto Ricans, and Cubans who are U.S. citizens—turn more to television than to print media. Approximately 75 percent of the sample (n=1,776) stated that they primarily rely on television as their first choice for political and public affairs news, while only 16 percent turn first to newspapers. Radio and magazines lag far behind with 7 percent and 0.6 percent respectively.

This is not surprising given that they spend more time with television than with newspapers. To the question "How many days during the past week did you watch national network news on TV?," at least 62 percent of the sample stated 4 or more days; the average was 4.5 days. In contrast, to the question "How many days during the past week did you read about politics and public affairs in a daily newspaper?," only 37 percent indicated 4 or more days, the average being 2.9 days. In fact, 32 percent said they had not spent any days reading such matters in the press; only 11 percent said the same with respect to television.

Even though television is the medium used by most, the press is still an important source for political and public affairs news and receives added attention among those who prefer this medium. To the question of what *other* medium is used for such purpose, 45 percent of those who responded to this item (n=1,772) mentioned newspapers, and 29 percent indicated radio; television was mentioned by 22 percent. Only 5 percent of the respondents mentioned magazines. Also, among those who turn first to newspapers, the average almost doubles to 5.7 days with respect to weekly attention to this medium. In fact, among that group, 77 percent read about politics and public affairs in the press at least four days a week. Among Latinos who stated they turn first to TV, the average number days of viewing that medium is practically unchanged (to 4.7), as is the percentage of respondents who watch it four or more days a week (66%).

Within this first rubric of data, there were a number of significant differences across the Latinos groups. For example, the average number of days Cubans watched TV (5.2) was higher than the average for Puerto Rican (4.7) who, in turn, had a higher average than Mexican Americans (4.1). Based on analysis of variance, all the differences among the groups were significant at $p<.001$; likewise, the average number of days Cubans read newspapers (3.5) was significantly ($p<.05$) higher than that of both Mexicans and Puerto Ricans who, at 2.8 days, were similar to each other.

The differences among the groups is evident in other ways as well. While Latinos of all three national origins are similar in the primary media they rely on for political and public affairs news, they vary in the language of the media chosen as a primary source, and in the language preferred for the additional media mentioned. For those who turn first to TV (n=1,339), English was preferred by 70 percent of the Mexican Americans, but by only 40 percent of the Puerto Ricans and 45 percent of the Cubans. For people who rely primarily on newspapers (n=288), the corresponding figures are 85 percent among Mexican Americans, 52 percent among Puerto Ricans, and 49 percent among Cubans. And for those who rely on radio (n=20), English is used by 60 percent of the Mexican Americans, in contrast to 38 percent of the Puerto Ricans and 46 percent of the Cubans.

Latino group differences were again evident in the additional media used for political and public affairs news. Among Latinos who responded and stated that their secondary source is television (n=375), English was preferred by 74 percent of the Mexican Americans, but by only 42 percent of the Puerto Ricans and 56 percent of the Cubans. For those who rely on newspapers as a second source (n=766), the corresponding figures are 86 percent among Mexican Americans, 48 percent among Puerto Ricans, and 59 percent among Cubans. For the respondents who stated radio is their second source (n=501), English is preferred by 57 percent of the Mexican Americans, but only by 28 percent of the Puerto Ricans and by 30 percent of the Cubans.

Other distinctions among Latinos are the use of media in both languages and the use of Spanish. For the Puerto Ricans and Cubans who rely most on TV or newspapers, over 35 percent use these media in English *and* in Spanish; the figure is significantly lower among Mexican Americans (26 percent). And among the few members of both of these groups who rely primarily on radio, Spanish is preferred by 39 percent of the Puerto Ricans and 42 percent of the Cubans; the same is true for only 8 percent of Mexican Americans. Group variations surface again with respect to the *additional* media the members of each group turn to for political and public affairs news. In this respect there is a greater use of Spanish-language media, especially radio, among Puerto Ricans and Cubans, than is the case among Mexican Americans.

A more telling set of variations among Latino groups stems from the analyses of the background variables, including language abilities, as predictors of media used for news about political and public affairs (see table 15.2 and figures 15.1a–d[14]). First, age (i.e., being older) has a positive influence on reading newspapers *and* on watching television news among

*Table 15.2* Standardized path regression coefficients of independent variables on media selected for political and public affairs news

| Dependent variables/ Groups | Independent variables | | | | | | | |
| --- | --- | --- | --- | --- | --- | --- | --- | --- |
| | Sex | Age | % years in US | Education | Income | Spanish ability | English ability | $R^2$ |
| Read newspaper | | | | | | | | |
| All Latinos | .15** | .19** | .05 | .31** | .01 | .06* | .02 | .11 |
| Mexicans | .10** | .25** | .02 | .41** | −.04 | .06 | −.03 | .13 |
| Puerto Ricans | .19** | .16** | .02 | .19** | .07 | .01 | .13** | .11 |
| Cubans | .23** | .18* | .19** | .24** | .05 | .07 | −.04 | .12 |
| Watch TV news | | | | | | | | |
| All Latinos | .05* | .18** | −.11** | .12** | −.01* | .09* | .03 | .06 |
| Mexicans | .01 | .22** | −.03 | .12** | .01 | −.03 | −.02 | .04 |
| Puerto Ricans | .12** | .16** | −.02 | .07 | .03 | .17** | .12* | .06 |
| Cubans | .01 | .16* | −.16* | .06 | −.09 | .14* | .04 | .10 |

*: $p < .05$, **: $p < .01$

all Latinos. The same is true for gender (being male) and (higher) education, but among all respondents, these latter two variables only influence the exposure to the press. More Puerto Rican men than women watch TV news; but there is no gender difference in that exposure between Mexican Americans and Cubans. Also, education positively influences Mexican Americans' exposure to the news on television, yet that variable yields no significant influence among the other two groups' exposure to this medium. Table 15.2 further shows that English language ability positively influences Puerto Ricans' exposure to both newspapers and TV news. And, Spanish language ability has a similar effect on Puerto Ricans' and Cubans' exposure to TV news but has no influence on either group's exposure to the press. Interestingly, income makes practically no difference on the level of exposure to these two media.

Before discussing some of our interpretations of these data, the next section presents the data linking media use to political knowledge and to political participation.

## MEDIA CONNECTIONS TO POLITICAL KNOWLEDGE AND PARTICIPATION

The previous data contribute to better explain how Mexican Americans, Puerto Ricans, and Cubans are similar and different in their use of media for political and public affairs news, and some of the factors that contribute to those media use patterns. However, the two key questions of the chapter remain to be answered: (1) Are there any significant relationships between patterns of use of the mass media, and the political knowledge and behaviors of Latinos? And, (2) are there significant variations in the media relationships to politics among subgroups of Latinos? Tables 15.3 and 15.4a–d suggest that the answer to both is *definitively* yes. As mentioned above, only television viewers and newspaper readers were included in the analysis that follows because a measure of *frequency* of media use variable is only available from these two media.

The first table shows that, in addition to the traditional background variables, exposure to newspapers and to television does contribute to Latinos' political knowledge, but that the influence of these media varies across groups. For all Latinos as a group, gender (being male), higher levels of education, and older age are the most important factors associated with political knowledge. In fact, the contribution of each of these three variables has different weight but overall does not diminish when the Latinos subgroups are looked at separately. The same holds true with respect to reading the press for political and public affairs news.

One of the most revealing analyses pertains to income. For the sample as a whole, it has a negative influence on political knowledge. Thus, the

Table 15.3 Standardized path regression coefficients of independent variables on political knowledge

| Groups | Independent variables | | | | | | | | | |
|---|---|---|---|---|---|---|---|---|---|---|
| | Sex | Age | % years in US | Educ | Income | Spanish ability | English ability | Read paper | Watch news | $R^2$ |
| All Latinos | .15** | .34** | .06 | .44** | −.04* | .02 | −.01 | .15** | .07** | .29 |
| Mexicans | .19** | .34** | −.04 | .40** | −.05 | −.08 | .03 | .12** | .09** | .28 |
| Puerto Ricans | .14** | .40** | .26** | .35** | −.04 | −.00 | .02 | .20** | .05 | .33 |
| Cubans | .12* | .20** | .04 | .36** | −.03 | .06 | −.02 | .15** | −.04 | .18 |

*: p < .05, **: p < .01

Table 15.4a Standardized path regression coefficients of independent variables on political participation: all Latinos

| Dependent variable | Independent variables | | | | | | | | | | |
|---|---|---|---|---|---|---|---|---|---|---|---|
| | Sex | Age | % years in US | Education | Income | Spanish ability | English ability | Read paper | Watch news | Political knowledge | $R^2$ |
| Political participation | −.00 | .26** | | | | | | | | | .07 |
| | −.01 | .41** | .08** | .29** | −.02 | | | | | | .14 |
| | −.01 | .41** | .10** | .30** | −.02 | .03 | −.01 | | | | .15 |
| | −.03 | .39** | .09** | .26** | −.01 | .03 | −.00 | .13** | −.03 | | .17 |
| | −.07** | .33** | .08** | .17** | −.00 | .02 | −.00 | .10** | −.05* | .22** | .20 |

*: $p < .05$, **: $p < .01$

Table 15.4b Standardized path regression coefficients of independent variables on political participation: Mexican American subsample

| Dependent variable | Independent variables | | | | | | | | | | |
|---|---|---|---|---|---|---|---|---|---|---|---|
| | Sex | Age | % years in US | Education | Income | Spanish ability | English ability | Read paper | Watch news | Political knowledge | $R^2$ |
| Political | -.03 | .28** | | | | | | | | | .08 |
| participation | -.01 | .45** | .06 | .32** | -.02 | | | | | | .17 |
| | -.01 | .45** | .08* | .35** | -.02 | -.00 | -.06 | | | | .17 |
| | -.04 | .44** | .08* | .31** | .01 | -.00 | -.06 | .11** | -.04 | | .19 |
| | -.09 | .34** | .09** | .19** | .03 | .03 | -.06 | .07* | -.07* | .29** | .26 |

*: p < .05, **: p < .01

Table 15.4c  Standardized path regression coefficients of independent variables on political participation: Puerto Rican subsample

| Dependent variables | Independent variables | | | | | | | | | | |
|---|---|---|---|---|---|---|---|---|---|---|---|
| | Sex | Age | % years in US | Education | Income | Spanish ability | English ability | Read paper | Watch news | Political knowledge | $R^2$ |
| Political participation | .04 | .16** | | | | | | | | | .03 |
| | .01 | .32** | .14** | .22** | .01 | | | | | | .09 |
| | .00 | .33** | .12* | .20** | .01 | .04 | .11* | | | | .10 |
| | -.01 | .31** | .12* | .18** | .00 | .05 | .10 | .10* | -.01 | | .11 |
| | -.03 | .26** | .08 | .13* | .01 | .04 | .09 | .07 | -.02 | .15** | .12 |

*: $p < .05$, **: $p < .01$

Table 15.4d Standardized path regression coefficients of independent variables on political participation: Cuban subsample

| Dependent variables | Independent variables | | | | | | | | | | R² |
|---|---|---|---|---|---|---|---|---|---|---|---|
| | Sex | Age | % years in US | Education | Income | Spanish ability | English ability | Read paper | Watch news | Political knowledge | |
| Political participation | -.05 | .27** | -.00 | | | | | | | | .07 |
| | -.06 | .35** | .02 | .21** | -.11 | | | | | | .12 |
| | -.05 | .35** | -.02 | .22** | -.12* | -.03 | -.10 | | | | .12 |
| | -.10 | .32** | -.03 | .17** | -.12* | -.01 | -.09 | .21** | -.13* | | .18 |
| | -.11 | .31** | | .15* | -.12* | -.02 | -.08 | .20** | -.13* | .08 | .18 |

*: p < .05, **: p < .01

lower the income level, the less political knowledge. But this variable has no statistically significant bearing on Cubans' political knowledge. Moreover, while it does have a significant influence for Mexican Americans and for Puerto Ricans, it does not after the media use variables are brought into the equation.[15] In other words, the effect that low income has on the political knowledge of these latter two groups is overridden if they read the press. And for Mexican Americans, watching TV news also helps overcome the negative influence of income.

Another finding exclusive for Mexican Americans is that the negative effect that Spanish language has on their political knowledge is also washed out when they read the press and watch television news. Yet, for Puerto Ricans and Cubans, there is no significant influence of language ability or of watching TV news on their political knowledge.

One additional observation merits attention in explaining the political knowledge of Puerto Ricans. For that group only, the greater the proportion of years residing in the U.S., the greater their knowledge in this arena. And it may be possible that the press is a contributing factor in this socialization process for Puerto Ricans. Also, it may be a factor that contributes to diminish the differences between males and females of this group.[16]

Tables 15.4a–d show the coefficients when political participation is the dependent variable. Once again, for all Latinos and for the individual groups assessed separately, education and age are constant positive factors—a finding consistent with past research. These data also point out that the negative impact of gender (being female) on political participation is not significant when the data are analyzed separately for each group. But there are numerous differences with respect to the influence of the media variables as well as with other background variables, and even on how political knowledge contributes to participation. The similarities and the differences are best illustrated with figures 15.1a–d.

For Mexican Americans, participation is most strongly predicted by age, followed by political knowledge. Proportion of years in the U.S., contrary to its null effect on knowledge, does contribute to the rates of participation among this group. In contrast, while the watching of TV news had a positive influence on political knowledge, it is a negative factor for participation. The picture emerging for this group is that, aside from the expected contribution of education and age, political socialization in the form of knowledge—which in part stems from exposure to news media—helps Mexican Americans who have lived longer in the U.S. participate as voters. But for this type of political behavior, reading newspapers slightly enhances the involvement while, on the other hand, watching more of the news on television may contribute to diminish that activity. Could this reflect a sense such as: if I read the press I'll know

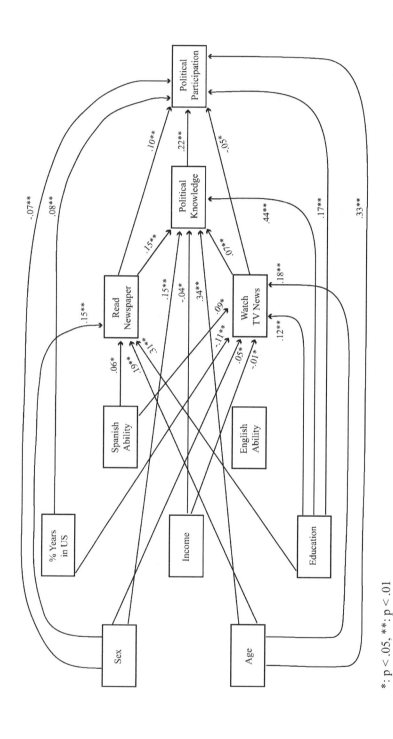

*: p < .05, **: p < .01

*Figure 15.1a* Selected coefficients of path model explaining media exposure, political knowledge and participation: all Latinos

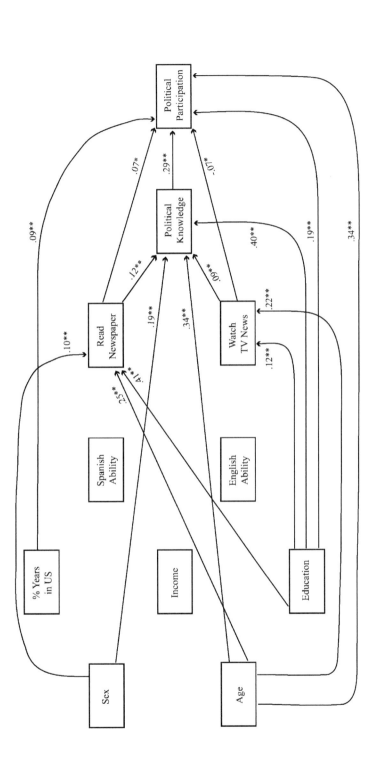

*: p < .05, **: p < .01

Figure 15.1b Selected coefficients of path model related to media exposure, political knowledge and participation: Mexican American subsample

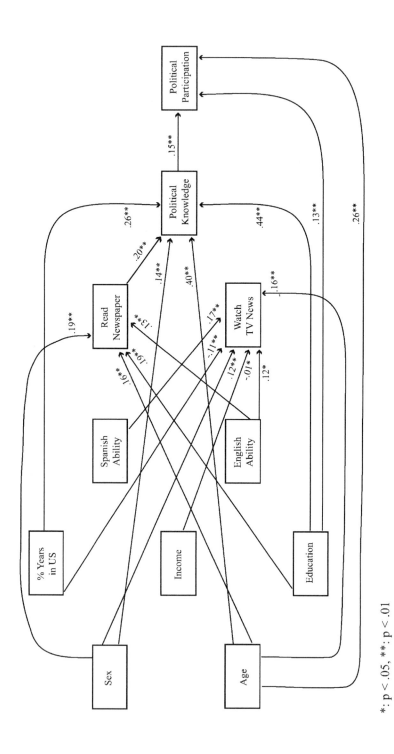

*: p < .05, **: p < .01

*Figure 15.1c* Selected coefficients of path model related to media exposure, political knowledge and participation: Puerto Rican subsample

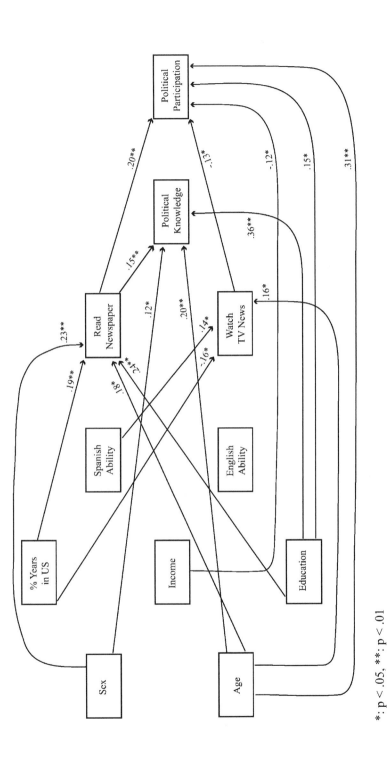

*: p < .05, **: p < .01

*Figure 15.1d* Selected coefficients of path model related to media exposure, political knowledge and participation: Cuban subsample

more and thus participate more, but if I watch TV news, I may know more but not be inclined or induced to vote?

For Puerto Ricans, age and education are key contributors to their political participation, as is political knowledge. Two factors that play a role on this latter variable—proportion of years in the U.S. and reading newspapers—are not significant on participation once the knowledge comes into the equation. Thus, for this group, the older people who know more about the political process do get involved and vote regardless of the time they have spent in the U.S. or the amount of news they consume via the newspapers or television. Here, the importance of the media, but specifically newspapers, is indirect, i.e., by enhancing participation by way of the political knowledge.

A different picture emerges for Cubans. Aside from the expected positive impact of age and education, their political participation is negatively influenced by income. For this group, the factor that seems to be more influential than income is reading newspapers and, in a negative way, watching the news on television. Also, for Cubans only, political knowledge is not statistically significant for predicting their participation, at least within the context of this set of variables.

## DISCUSSION

The data analyzed, first with respect to media use patterns, and then regarding the relationship between media use on political knowledge and participation, offers evidence of both some degree of acculturation as well as the continued pluralism among Latinos.[17] Most importantly, it definitively supports the proposition that media are important factors in the political dynamics of Latinos in the United States.

Starting with the media use patterns, the data clearly suggest that most Latinos do use media for political and public affairs news. The majority of the respondents indicated turning to more than one medium for news while only a small percentage reported not watching television news or reading the newspapers for such purposes.

The fact that most Latinos indicated they use English-language media for political news and information could readily be a reflection of their acculturation to the U.S. This is especially the case when that preference stems from the subjects' language abilities. Mexican Americans, apparently having been more socialized in English, prefer their news media in that language. But, for a large number of Puerto Ricans and Cubans, the use of media in Spanish, especially as a second source for news, was nevertheless quite strong.

Before it can be concluded that Latinos are "acculturated" when it comes to media use for political news, two other points require attention.

These pertain to accessibility of the various media and to the specificity of the question regarding the media use. First, as discussed earlier in this chapter, Spanish-language news media, especially daily newspapers, are not as readily available in all communities where Latinos live in the U.S. Thus, aside from the language factor, Spanish-language media may simply not be there for Latinos—at least those who speak Spanish—to be able to turn to them for political news or public affairs information.[18] And, second, it should be recalled that the survey instrument did not inquire, for example, which medium Latinos turn to in order to learn about political news and public affairs *that pertain to their respective (Mexican, Puerto Rican, Cuban) community* in the U.S. It is therefore possible that for bilingual or Spanish speakers, the medium preferred for news may not have been predominantly in English.

The data also show that while there are some factors, such as age and education, that influence all Latinos' exposure to the news media, there are other factors, such as gender and language skills, that contribute differently to how members of each group use the various media. Given these data and contexts, what can thus be reaffirmed is that Latinos' use of media for political news and public affairs is strong, and also reflective of an acculturation process, especially among Mexican Americans. It would seem, nonetheless, that for this population as a whole, both English-language and Spanish-language media are important news sources, which in turn may contribute to their political socialization.

The influence of the news media on Latinos' political socialization is especially evident regarding political knowledge, but also pertaining to political participation. With respect to knowledge, the data are conclusive in pointing out that this is positively related to education, age and gender (being male). Most importantly, however, the data also affirm the value of the press even after controlling for these and other background variables. What was most revealing, at least with respect to Mexican Americans and Puerto Ricans, is how reading the press is not only significant for higher levels of political knowledge, but that it can reduce the influence that lower levels of income may have on that knowledge. Additionally, for Mexican Americans, both the reading of newspapers and watching TV news also diminishes the negative impact that may stem from being more fluent in Spanish than in English. Meanwhile, for Puerto Ricans, reading newspapers complements the political socialization that builds with the increased time spent living in the U.S.

The influence of exposure to print and television news on Latinos' political participation is also evident even though it allows fewer generalizations across the three groups. The first generalization that merits attention is that when the groups are studied separately, there is no impact of gender on participation. The weak negative coefficients that suggest that females participate less are not statistically significant. And while age and education are again strong common denominators for Latinos as a whole and for each group in particular, other explanatory variables are not.

Mexican Americans' political participation is additionally explained by political knowledge, greater proportion of years in the U.S., and also positively by reading newspapers but negatively by watching TV news. For Puerto Ricans, the positive influence that is contributed by reading newspapers and by having spent increased proportions of their life in the U.S. is washed out by political knowledge. For this group, for which exposure to the press has a significant contribution on knowledge, the media effect on participation is indirect. But, for Cubans, participation is directly and positively related to reading newspapers while negatively related to watching TV news. Also, for this group only, lower income negatively affects their participation, an activity they will engage in regardless of their political knowledge.

Finally, the fact that exposure to Spanish-language media is related to the political knowledge and/or participation of at least some of the studied Latinos implies that such media do not necessarily separate Latinos from partaking in American politics. On the contrary, for some Latinos, exposure to such media helps them acculturate, i.e., learn more about and get involved in U.S. politics. Concomitantly, the fact that some politically active Latinos do use Latino media suggests that they are pluralistic (i.e., distinct in comparison to non-Latinos) upon simultaneously using such media and nonetheless becoming knowledgeable of, or participants in, U.S. politics.

To conclude, this particular analysis of the Latino National Political Survey data offers new insights into the value and importance of assessing the role of the media for better understanding the political dynamics of Latinos in the United States. It is clear that Mexican Americans, Puerto Ricans, and Cubans do use the news media for political news and public affairs. And even though the first choice in language for such media is English, it is also true that many Latinos also seek Spanish-language news media. Finally, either directly or indirectly, exposure to the press is a significant contributor to Latinos' knowledge about American politics and to their participation in electoral matters. In the concluding chapter, suggestions are outlined for improving future assessments of the role the media in Latino political communication processes.

## NOTES

1 For a full discussion of the development and scope of the LNPS, including the sampling methods, measurements, and parameters related to that survey, please see chapter 1 and appendix 2 of the book by de la Garza, DeSipio, García, García, and Falcón (1992). Some key points related to the survey:

the subjects included in the study were Hispanics of three targeted groups—Mexicans (1,546), Puerto Ricans (589), and Cubans (682)—who were 18 years of age or older; s/he, one parent, or two grandparents were of that ancestry; and resided in 40 Standard Metropolitan Statistical Areas. The subjects, interviewed in person between August 1989 and April 1990, were selected on the basis of a multistage area probability sample based on data from the 1980 census. Sixty percent of the Latino subjects were interviewed in Spanish. For the analysis of the data, the principal investigators "generated weights that reflect selection probabilities and incorporate adjustments for nonresponse and poststratification" (de la Garza et al., 1992: 220). The analysis of data for this chapter also followed the weighting procedure.

2 Of course, some television and radio programs may carry more political content than some newspapers. But, given the brief format of news programs of most these media, we can hold our assumption that newspapers could provide more political news and thus may have a greater influence at least in terms of helping increase the knowledge about political developments. Besides, the LNPS questionnaire did not include queries regarding respondents' exposure to particular political news media. It is those specific types of questions that could allow more accurate predictive assessments of the relationship between use of those media and political knowledge or behaviors.

3 In 1988, when the questionnaire for the LNPS was being developed, the first author of this chapter was able to convey this issue to the principal investigators of the national study. Although not as specific and focused as we would have liked, the questions included in the survey at least provide some information on how respondents use the mass media. See note below.

4 The media questions and their corresponding number in the questionnaire are: "In general, which, if any, do you rely on *most*, for news about politics and public affairs: television, newspapers, magazines, or radio?" (Q.48); "Is that in English, in Spanish, or both?" (Q.49); "How many days during the past week did you watch *national* network news on TV?" (Q.52); "How many days during the past week did you read about politics and public affairs in a daily newspaper?" (Q.53).

5 The wording and number of this question was: "Now we have some questions concerning various political figures. What job or political office does Dan Quayle hold now? How about William Rehnquist? What job or political office does he hold now? How about (each of the following persons: Cesar Chavez, Robert "Bobby" Garcia, Xavier Suárez)? What position does he hold now?" (Q.131, correct answers were coded as 1, otherwise 0).

6 The wording and number of this question was: "Which party has the most members in the U.S. House of Representatives? Republican, Democrat, Other?" (Q.132, a correct answer was coded as 1, otherwise 0).

7 The wording and corresponding numbers of these questions were: "Have you ever been registered to vote in the U.S.?" Yes, No, Don't Know, Refused (Q.74); "Are you currently registered to vote in the U.S.?" Yes, No (Q.75, coded as Yes=1, No=0); "When we talk to people about elections, we find that a lot of people were not able to vote because they weren't old enough, they weren't registered, they weren't interested, they were sick, or they just didn't have time. How about you, did you vote in the elections in November 1988?" Yes, No, Don't Know, Refused (Q.78, coded as Yes=1, otherwise 0); "For whom did you vote for President in 1988?" (Q.83, coded as 1=vote for any of the candidates, and 0=did not vote); and "Did you vote in the U.S. House of Representatives elections of 1986?" Yes, No, Don't Know, Refused (Q.84, coded as Yes=1, otherwise 0). From the responses to the questions listed in this and the

preceding endnotes, two scales were constructed. The knowledge scale ranged from 0–5; the participation scale also ranged from 0–5.

8  This variable is constructed by dividing the number of years residing in the United States by the respondent's age.

9  "What language do you usually speak at home: only Spanish, more Spanish than English, both languages equally, more English than Spanish, or only English?"; "Considering your abilities in understanding, speaking, reading, and writing English, which of these statements best describes your abilities in Spanish? Would you say that you: don't know Spanish, are much better in English, are better in English, are no different in either language, are better in Spanish, or are much better in Spanish?"

10  That is, the "ENTER" method in the SPSS package used for this analysis.

11  Statistical tests for differences among the three main Latino groups are shown in the regression analyses in the other tables of this chapter.

12  The discrepancy between this number (1,776) and the sum of the n's for the three groups (1,777) is due to the weighting of the samples. This process "added" an extra female to the Cuban sample.

13  The income numbers correspond to income categories of which the following are relevant to the figures on this table: 5=$13,000 to 14,999; 6=$15,000 to 16,999; 7=$17,000 to 19,999; 8=$20,000 to 24,999; and 9=$25,000 to 29,999.

14  For the construction of the path diagrams, special thanks are extended to Dr. Douglas Barrett, postdoctoral researcher at the Department of Psychology, University of Texas.

15  Based on the stepwise regression analysis, which showed that income had negative statistically significant coefficients but insignificant coefficients after the last two variables (read newspaper and watch TV news) were entered into the equation.

16  When the media variables are included in the equation, the gender coefficient is reduced from 0.19 to 0.14. Although both coefficients are significant, the 0.14 is evidently less that the 0.20 stemming from the use of the press.

17  For a discussion on Latino acculturation and pluralism from a mass communication perspective, see Subervi and Ríos (2005). It should be clear that, in the context of this work, acculturation is used to imply the process of taking on characteristics typically associated with the dominant society, while not necessarily forgetting or abandoning characteristics related to the original culture of the country or ethnic group of origin. Pluralism has a similar implication in the sense of showing evidence of maintaining an original culture, but also with respect of being distinct vis-à-vis the dominant population.

18  Another possibility for the respondents' preference for English may also be the *limited access* to Spanish-language media, especially newspapers. As discussed earlier in this chapter, at the time of the LNPS in 1989, Spanish-language dailies were published in only three metropolitan areas in the U.S. (New York, Los Angeles, and Miami). In other communities, Spanish-language newspapers were at the time published only on monthly or weekly bases. And though a few more cities may have dailies now, many Latino communities do not have any Spanish-language or even English-language *Latino-oriented* press at all. In fact, some of the existing Latino-oriented publications are small and are at best advertising pages for local business; they contain little or no news and information about politics and/or public affairs. And, as was observed by Subervi-Vélez (1988), the political content of the Spanish-language daily press in the U.S. is limited in its presentation of Latino-oriented news and opinion columns. The exceptions to this characteristic were the Spanish-language dailies published in Miami, which have strong conservative and pro-Cuban

partisan perspectives in the news and opinion pages. Moreover, Spanish-language television potentially does reach over 90 percent of the U.S. Latino population. But, often, access to this medium requires subscription to cable at a cost not easily afforded by many Latinos. The political and public affairs content of this medium may be more evident, but—as noted by Constantakis-Valdéz (1993) (see also chapters 5–7)—coverage of presidential campaigns is limited; the diversity of such fare is certainly not as ample as in English-language TV. Spanish-language radio, on the other hand, is widely available in almost every community where over a few hundred Latinos reside. However, while there is no cost for access to this medium, very few radio stations have been found to air anything other than numerous paid political advertisements and occasional newsbreaks to keep their audiences informed about political and public affairs (see Santillán and Subervi-Vélez, 1991).

# 16

# LATINO AGENDA-SETTING EFFECT ON THE 2004 PRESIDENTIAL ELECTION

## María Flores and Maxwell E. McCombs[1]

During the 2004 presidential election, a Latino—Peter Miguel Camejo—ran as a candidate for the office of vice president of the United States. Ralph Nader, the Independent Party's presidential contender, nominated him for that role on Monday, June 21, 2004. Camejo is a first generation Venezuelan American who was born in New York in 1939. He is a political activist, environmentalist, businessperson, and financier. In 1987, Camejo founded Progressive Asset Management of California, an investment firm that conducts socially responsible investments. Nader shared his concepts of social justice and economic policies, noting that "his [Camejo's] work in advancing socially responsible investment shows his understanding of how we can work within our economic system to advance social justice" (Nader for President 2004: 1).

Camejo has run for office several times—most recently, as a Green Party candidate in the gubernatorial recall election in his home state of California.[2] A Latino running for the vice presidency, albeit from a third party, offered a unique opportunity to measure and test the ethnic component of the Agenda-Setting Theory, and to do so within the Spanish-language media, i.e., the news broadcast by the Univisión and Telemundo networks.

As discussed in previous chapters of this book, Latino-oriented media play very distinct informative roles in U.S. electoral campaigns. Moreover, Spanish-language television—the focus of this study—informs and also produces news stories that connect with Latino culture. Just as important, the networks provide guidance for their immigrant audiences across the nation by helping them understand the dynamics of United States politics in general and election processes in particular.

Roberto Suro, director of the Pew Hispanic Center, affirms that "getting a handle on the extent and quality of political coverage on Spanish

TV is important . . . not only because these broadcasts reach a number of voters, but also because a great many immigrants are learning about our political culture and getting to know our political leaders through these news shows" (Univisión Network, 2005: 2). And even though immigrant audiences who are not U.S. citizens have a limited direct participation in U.S. elections, they may participate indirectly because they are relatives or friends of U.S. citizens who can vote. Given that family is a very important agent when it comes to voting decisions, immigrants might influence their relatives' political knowledge and/or orientations, too.

In order to assess some of the potential influences of Spanish-language television on Latinos during the 2004 presidential campaign, we examined the public issues covered by these networks in their election news stories and asked two questions about this news coverage. First, to what extent did these news organizations present similar patterns of coverage? Because of the influence of traditional journalistic routines for news gathering and professional news norms, there typically is a high degree of correspondence among the public issue agendas of news organizations. Was this the case for the national Spanish-language TV networks in 2004? Second, to what extent did the public issues considered most important among Latino voters reflect the pattern of news coverage in Spanish-language TV? In other words, what was the agenda-setting effect of Spanish-language network news among Latino voters during the 2004 presidential campaign?

In answering these questions, we also assess if the presence of a Latino candidate for high office made a difference in campaign coverage and Latinos' perceptions of that year's elections. Our study found that Univisión and Telemundo covered Bush 54%, Kerry 44%, and Nader 2%. Camejo was silent on the main Spanish television networks. Since the only major Latino candidate was silent, this study focused on public issues exclusively. On the date of Camejo's presentation as candidate for vice president, María Elena Salinas, Univisión's major female news anchor, interviewed him about his nomination. This was the only news story Univisión (or Telemundo) presented about the Independent vice presidential nominee.

## AGENDA-SETTING THEORY

Every society has enumerable public issues and problems to address at any point in time. However, it is impossible for members of a society to act upon or even to acknowledge all of its concerns at once. This raises the question of how particular public issues come to be known and capture society's attention. Agenda-Setting Theory serves as a framework to discuss the attention that the media and Latino audiences gave to Latino issues during the 2004 presidential campaign. The value of this theory is that it addresses how various social sectors, and the media in particular, make known and prioritize public issues (McCombs and Shaw, 1972). Agenda-Setting Theory encourages the careful examination of the process whereby issues are discussed, in a specific order, according to their perceived significance, albeit the order of significance will change over time. McCombs explains that, "for all news media, the repetition of a topic day after day is the most powerful message of all about its importance" (2004: 2). It thus becomes useful for this line of research to identify who has set the social agenda that is in place during a particular period of time. To that end, Agenda-Setting Theory focuses on the key components of the political triangle: the public, news media, and policy makers.

Regarding our first research question about the extent to which news organizations present similar patterns of coverage, previous research presents strong evidence of a high degree of homogeneity in the media agenda. This pattern holds for a wide variety of situations: (a) a mix of nine local and national news media in the original Chapel Hill study (McCombs and Shaw, 1972); (b) local newspapers and television during a municipal election in Spain (Lopez-Escobar, Llamas, McCombs and Lennon, 1998); and (c) in a non-election setting, two major national newspapers in Japan (Takeshita, 2002).

There also is little doubt that people rely on these media agendas for information about their social and political environment. McCombs elaborates, "for nearly all of the concerns on the public agenda, citizens deal with a second-hand reality, a reality that is structured by journalists' reports about these events and situations" (2004: 1). Nonetheless, "the media [do] not reflect reality [fully], but select certain aspects for coverage. They cover some stories and ignore others giving greater attention to some issues rather than to others and decide how to interpret and frame the issues that they cover" (Perloff, 1998: 210).

This selection process of deciding which public issues are most important is how the media agenda develops. Fundamentally, the media act as gatekeepers, holding a list of topics that they believe are the top priority for citizens. It is those topics that usually receive more coverage over a certain period of time. As Perloff suggests, "The news [do] not inject viewers with perspectives; [they suggest] that certain issues are more important than others, and people (some more than others) come to accept these interpretations and adjust their political priorities accordingly" (1998: 219). This characteristic of the mass media helps shape public impressions and opinions regarding a specific public issue.

According to McCombs, "Agenda-Setting Theory evolved from a description and explanation of the influence that mass communication has on public opinion about the issues of the day" (2004: xii). As Severin and Tankard (2001) indicate, the media shape what is news at a particular time and date and thus establish a public issue's priority by the presentation of what is deemed the most important problem that a city, state, or nation is facing. Concomitantly, the absence of coverage is also significant by building a particular silent agenda. Overall, Agenda-Setting Theory establishes that the media do not tell people what to think, but instead they do tell the public what to think about. The core of Agenda-Setting Theory establishes that "the media agenda influences the public agenda with the competing causal hypothesis that the public agenda influences the media agenda" (McCombs, 2004: 10).

## Ethnic agenda-setting

While the predominant research using agenda-setting propositions has been conducted regarding general market media and non-minority audiences, there is some evidence of the applicability of this theory for analyzing ethnic minority audiences and media, too. Ethnic agenda-setting research implies that a study will observe a particular ethnic group and its own ethnic media.

For example, Miller and Wanta proposed that demographic variables such as race could play a significant function in the agenda-setting effect dynamics. For their study, they considered that when "the [mainstream] media [cover] issues that are important to whites [from a white male perspective], perhaps minority populations will be less susceptible to agenda-setting effects since the press is not covering issues that are important to them" (1996: 915). Building on their content analysis of the *Tampa Tribune* (Florida), the *Eugene Register-Guard* (Oregon), the local TV news for both cities, and ABC's *World News Tonight* during a selected time period in early 1994, followed by telephone interviews with 577 respondents in the target cities, the authors hypothesized that whites would display stronger agenda-setting effects than minority respondents.[3] While the findings suggest "that whites and minority groups did not have different issue agendas, nor did the groups differ on the magnitude of agenda-setting effects" (Miller and Wanta, 1996: 913), the authors also found a significant difference when they compared issues that received little or no coverage. In the authors' words: "the minorities in Tampa demonstrated a higher level of concern with the low-coverage issues than the whites in Tampa" (1996: 920).

Miller and Wanta, who had also hypothesized that the agenda-setting effect would be different across ethnic groups and cities, did not observe such variations. Instead, they found that "minorities in Eugene did not acculturate themselves into the white population more closely in Eugene than the minorities in Tampa did. Again, minorities in both sites showed similar tendencies toward agenda-setting influences" and that "the issue agendas of minorities and whites were very similar in both Eugene [r= +.59] and Tampa [r= +.60]" (1996: 921). The authors thus conclude that, "minorities and whites appear to have processed issue salience cues transmitted through the news media at extremely similar degrees" (1996: 921).

However, Miller and Wanta also observed that "one area in which the sites did differ is on concern with issues that received little coverage in the news media. Minorities in Tampa thought issues that received little coverage were more important than the white population thought they were. Possibly this finding is due to the fact that Tampa has several alternative media sources that serve minority populations" (1996: 922). This led Miller and Wanta to consider that ethnic media could create their own media agenda, which in turn might influence minority populations in particular because exposure to the ethnic media "may have given respondents an agenda of issues for their discussions that differed from the mainstream news media agenda. Thus, the interpersonal communication of minority respondents may have conflicted with the coverage of issues in the mainstream news media" (1996: 922).

We can discern from these insights that it is important to study the agenda-setting dynamics within the ethnic community and its own ethnic media because the issues and attributes such media offer might differ significantly from the mainstream media's agenda as well as the general public's agenda. Another example of an agenda-setting study that considered minority populations and both general market and ethnic media was conducted in McAllen, Texas,[4] during spring 1997, by Ghanem and Wanta (2001). They examined how Spanish-language media effects might differ between the local Hispanic and non-Hispanic population, and probed whether or not the agenda-setting functions of the English-language media were the same as the Spanish-language media. To this end, Ghanem and Wanta did a content analysis of news aired on Univisión, ABC, and CBS, and gathered data from a telephone survey. Respondents' media language preference was inferred by their Spanish media usage, but their ethnicity was based on the respondent's own self-concept.

Ghanem and Wanta found that "exposure to Spanish cable news, as expected, was positively associated with the Spanish agenda-setting effects score (r=.13, p< .05). However, exposure to the English-language network news was not related to the English agenda-setting effects score. In other words, exposure to the news was associated with agenda-setting effects only for Spanish cable news" (2001: 285). The authors attribute the lack of agenda-setting effect of the English television networks to the media availability; "English speakers in McAllen were using a wide variety of news media, while Spanish speakers, because of limited news options, demonstrated a much more narrow pattern of news usage, focusing almost entirely on Spanish cable news" (Ghanem and Wanta, 2001: 286). This study also affirms the importance of observing the role of the

354

ethnic media for better understanding potential agenda-setting effects of media on a specific ethnic population.

One of the first political agenda-setting effects studies focusing on minorities was conducted by Waisath (2002) during the primary elections for Texas governor in 2002, which involved only three major candidates: Republican Rick Perry, who ran unopposed for the GOP nomination, and Democrats Dan Morales (former State Attorney General) and Tony Sanchez (a wealthy businessman from Laredo). This election was notable in that two Hispanic candidates competed against each other for their party's nomination. Waisath investigated the extent to which the descriptions of the three candidates in the *Austin American Statesman* (the local general market daily newspaper) impacted upon Latinos' perceptions of these candidates. Theoretically, these are called second-level agenda-setting effects (McCombs, 2004, chapter 5). Basic agenda-setting effects at the first level compare the salience of objects (public issues, candidates or other topics) on the media and public agenda. In turn, these objects have attributes. When the media and the public describe political candidates, for example, they place varying degrees of emphasis on the attributes of these candidates. Waisath used a content analysis of the newspaper[5] and a survey of 286 randomly selected Austin respondents to determine the media and public agenda of attributes. Her comparison of these data revealed a second level agenda-setting effect: a significant correlation between the attribute agendas of Austin residents and the local newspaper for Tony Sanchez (+0.94), but a nonsignificant correlation for those variables with respect to Perry (−0.08) and Morales (−0.08).

According to Waisath, the outcome may be explained by the fact that Perry and Morales had already had substantial history in office and the campaign trail, and the media may have thus offered less attention to them. In contrast, more media attention fell upon Sanchez, a relative political novice and unknown candidate who nonetheless spent millions of dollars of his own wealth to make himself known, especially via numerous ads on English-language and Spanish-language television. However, the media did not focus their attention on race. The coverage of Morales and Sanchez de-emphasized the race attribute and instead focused on "more discernable specific issue positions, qualifications, or character similarities or differences among candidates" (Waisath, 2002: 24).

While the findings of these studies are mixed, they nevertheless point to the merit of giving distinct consideration to ethnic groups and their media in agenda-setting research. Such is the goal of the current study that focuses on the agenda-setting effect of Spanish-language television network news on Latinos' public opinion during the 2004 presidential election campaign.

## Additional contexts: religion and media use

Before turning to the methodology and findings of this study, some add-itional contextual information about religion and Latinos' use of news media is necessary. In our agenda-setting research, we first examined what public issues were important for the Latino community, and what issues were made most prominent in the Spanish-language television net-work news. According to several poll projections during the 2004 cam-paign period, religion was considered to be a key factor for President Bush's success with Hispanic voters. For example, the Pew Hispanic Center's public opinion surveys of 2000, as well as those in 2004, com-bined with the Edison/Mitofsky National Election exit polls in 2004, showed that the Protestant segment of the Latino electorate "tilted more heavily for Bush in 2004 giving him 56 percent of their votes compared to 44 percent in 2000. Thus, Hispanic Protestants were both a growing and increasingly pro-Republican constituency between the two elections. Meanwhile, Bush's share of the Hispanic Catholic vote held steady at 33 percent in the [50] state exit polls" (Suro, Fry, and Jeffrey, 2005: 14).

A contrasting perspective was offered by Leal, Barreto, Lee, and de la Garza (2005) who pointed out that "if Bush indeed garnered 44% of the Latino vote, Latino religious conservatives should have supported the president in disproportionately large numbers. No other particular seg-ment of Latino voters—with the exception of Cuban Americans and Republicans—seemed to rally behind the president" (2005: 14). This group of researchers analyzed the *Washington Post*/Univisión/TRPI National Survey of Latino Voters of October 2004, which indicated that "non-Catholic Christians were more likely than Latino Catholics or seculars to identify with the Republican Party. For the Republicans, appealing to Latino evangelicals and other non-catholic Christians may be the key to making (small) inroads to the Latino electorate, while Latino Catholics would be an important part of a future winning coalition for the Demo-crats" (Leal, Barreto, Lee, and de la Garza, 2005: 46).

One additional study that also reveals the power of religion in Latino politics can be discerned from a survey conducted by the William C. Velasquez Institute (WCVI), which showed that the religious group from which Bush gained the majority of his votes was from Latino Muslims (66.7 percent), followed by Latino Protestants (53.3 percent). That same poll showed there was less support from Latino Jews (33.3 percent) and Latino Catholics (31.3 percent). Moreover, 100 percent of Latino Muslim voters indicated their political affiliation as Republican; the same affili-ation was indicated by 66.7 percent of first-time voters, 66.7 percent of female, and by 50 percent of voters between 18 and 24 years old and those 65 years or older (Flores, 2004: 3). Considering these survey find-ings, for the content analysis part of our agenda-setting study we decided to assess whether or not religion was featured in the political news broadcast by Telemundo and Univisión.

Other important contextual information for our study is that television continues to be a major source of news for Hispanic voters, regardless of their language preference. In fact, according to a Pew Hispanic Center Survey, among Latinos, network television news is the preferred media source for political and governmental news (Suro, 2004). These survey results are based on multiple responses: "any respondent who reported using more than one language in any media or who reported using different languages in different media was counted as someone who gets some of their news in both languages. Respondents who reported using only English or only Spanish for all their news media choices were put in the English and Spanish categories" (Suro, 2004: 3). Almost half (47 percent) of the respondents to that survey indicate watching Spanish-language network TV while 41 percent said they watch the network news in English; 44 percent do so in both languages. Local news in Spanish-language TV was a source mentioned by 36 percent of Latinos while only 13 percent mentioned watching local English-language news; 26 percent stated they watch local news in both languages. Newspapers were less central as sources for political and governmental news. In this case, 19 percent of the respondents to the Pew survey mentioned the English-language press, 6 percent indicated using Spanish-language papers, while 11 percent read newspapers in both languages. There was less use of the radio (10% English, 5% Spanish, 4% bilingual); and even fewer Latinos used the Internet (17% English, 2% Spanish, 11% bilingual) for political and governmental news.

While the Pew Hispanic Center's data point to a very high and consistent use of television, including Spanish-language TV, for political and governmental news, how Spanish-language TV affects voters' behavior is less certain. According to the WCVI data, the media source that Latino voters used the most to obtain information about the 2004 elections was English-language television (35%), followed by English-language newspapers (13.3%), Spanish-language television (12.8%), Spanish-language newspapers (5.7%), English-language radio (5.3%), Spanish-language radio (3.6%), and Spanish and English Internet (1.7%) (Flores, 2004: 2).

Nevertheless, language undoubtedly plays a critical factor in the pattern of Latinos' media consumption and their perception of the value of the news. According to Suro, "for Hispanics, choices in news media are more complex than for the general population because so many can access news in two languages" (2004: 1). A multilingual person has access to a variety of media choices opening the window to a completely new media spectrum for exposure and consumption. The Pew Hispanic public opinion poll (Suro, 2004) also indicated that Latinos rated Spanish-language news coverage regarding public issues that are significantly relevant to Hispanics in the United States as excellent/good (76%).

In sum, the focused attention on television, in particular Spanish-language TV, is justified, especially given that television is the primary medium for political campaign communication. As Luis Miranda, Director of Miranda y Más, Inc., has pointed out, "in any campaign, anywhere in this country television continues to be the most important way to communicate and where you spend 70% of all of your available dollars" (Univisión, The Hispanic Vote, 2004).

## METHODOLOGY

Two data sets were analyzed in order to respond to the two research questions of this study: (1) How similar are the news agendas of Univisión and Telemundo?, and (2) What was the agenda-setting effect of Spanish-language television network news on Latinos during the 2004 presidential election? To assess the election agenda of Univisión and Telemundo, the 5:30 to 6:00 p.m. national evening news from October 1 to November 7, 2004, was content analyzed.[6] The units of analysis were the general election topics and issues reported during each election news story. Coders carefully reviewed each newscast looking for election stories and focused on a story's central theme. This yielded a total of 196 election stories: 139 by Univisión and 57 by Telemundo, indicating that Univisión devoted more airtime to cover the election campaign (a finding that corroborates the results discussed in chapter 13 of this book).

To establish Spanish-language television's agenda, these 196 news items were classified into 21 distinct topics—8 general election news categories and 13 issue categories (these 21 topics are listed in the tables). This was done separately for the two television networks. Based on the number of stories about each of these topics, the 21 categories were ranked from high to low, again separately for each television network (see table 16.1 for a comparison of the two television networks). Spearman's rank-order correlation (rho) was used to determine the degree of similarity between the two television networks' agendas. A correlation of +1.0 would indicate perfect agreement; a correlation of 0.0, no agreement whatsoever.

To assess the agenda-setting effects of Spanish-language news coverage on Latino voters, table 16.2 displays the rank-order of the 13 issues for Spanish-language television and for Latino voters. The voter data analyzed for this study was the William C. Velazquez Institute's 2004 National Latino Election Day Exit Poll conducted by Flores (2004), which measured public opinion among Hispanics. To ascertain the issue agenda of Latino voters, this survey asked "Which one issue mattered most in deciding how you voted for president?" Conducted on November 2, 2004, the survey was based on a proportional-stratified-random sample of 943 Latino voters who were interviewed after casting their ballots. The sample was collected through 41 precincts located across 11 states in which more than 80 percent of all national Hispanic registered voters reside.

According to Flores, the "WCVI Latino sample was younger than the national government's estimate, about as college educated as the Pew Center's estimate of registered Latino voters, possessed less than the U.S. Bureau of the Census' estimate of people of Mexican ancestry, was more Democratic than the Pew estimate but was also more Republican" (2004: 3).

## Comparing media agendas

In order to understand the media's agenda in more detail, it is necessary to observe each Spanish-language television network in particular. In general, a network news department decides what is newsworthy the day the newscast airs. During the 2004 presidential election, our research identified 18 topics on Univisión's election agenda, and 13 topics on Telemundo's election agenda. In terms of public issues, Univisión reported on 10 issues and Telemundo, 7 issues.

Voting procedures, discussion of the Latino vote, and polls were at the top of Univisión's agenda. The top issues on Univisión's agenda were Iraq, terrorism, and the economy and jobs. Dominating the top of Telemundo's agenda were voting procedures and discussion of the Latino vote. And the dominant issue was terrorism. As we move deeper into each medium's agenda, there are divergences, but an overall pattern of agreement already is apparent in these top of the agenda topics. The correlation between Univisión's and Telemundo's election agendas was strong (+ 0.75), a finding that replicates the homogeneity of media agendas found in many other settings, both election settings and non-election settings.

In order to further understand why the category "voting procedures" ranked at the top of the news agenda, we examined Telemundo's 2004 press releases and Univisión's partnership with National Association of Latino Elected Officials (NALEO). For Telemundo, whose agenda was dominated by stories about voting procedures, there were a total of six press releases related to the 2004 presidential election. Three of them announced special programming information about the presidential debates. A press release on October 13, 2004, announced "the 90-minute debate will be [was] simultaneously translated into Spanish by three independent translators: one assigned to President Bush, one to Senator Kerry, and one to moderator Bob Schieffer of CBS News" (Telemundo Continues its Commitment, 2004: 1). On October 20, 2004, Telemundo announced President Bush's exclusive interview with Pedro Sevcec (5:30 p.m. newscast anchor) at the White House (Aviso a los Medios, 2004: 1).

*Table 16.1* Comparison of campaign coverage on Univisión and Telemundo

| | Univisión n=139 | | Telemundo n=57 | |
|---|---|---|---|---|
| | *% of stories* | *(rank)* | *% of stories* | *(rank)* |
| **General election coverage** | | | | |
| Voting procedures | 15.7 | (1) | 47.0 | (1) |
| Latino vote | 9.9 | (2.5) | 21.0 | (2) |
| Polls | 9.9 | (2.5) | 3.2 | (5.5) |
| Debates | 6.5 | (6) | – | (17.5) |
| Candidates' campaigns | 5.0 | (9.5) | 3.2 | (5.5) |
| 2000 Election | 5.0 | (9.5) | 3.2 | (5.5) |
| Ethnicity | 1.7 | (16) | – | (17.5) |
| Voter education | 1.7 | (16) | 1.4 | (10) |
| *Sub-total* | 55.4 | | 79.0 | |
| **Issue Coverage** | | | | |
| War in Iraq | 8.3 | (4.5) | 1.4 | (10) |
| Terrorism | 8.3 | (4.5) | 11.0 | (3) |
| Economy and jobs | 5.7 | (7) | 3.4 | (5.5) |
| Health care, Medicare | 5.0 | (9.5) | – | (17.5) |
| Religion/moral values | 5.0 | (9.5) | 1.4 | (10) |
| Immigration | 4.1 | (12) | 1.4 | (10) |
| Foreign policy | 3.3 | (13) | – | (17.5) |
| Education | 2.4 | (14) | 1.4 | (10) |
| Other issues | 1.7 | (16) | 1.0 | (13) |
| Taxes | 0.8 | (18) | – | (17.5) |
| Crime | – | (20) | – | (17.5) |
| Gun control | – | (20) | – | (17.5) |
| Environment | – | (20) | – | (17.5) |
| *Sub-total* | 44.6 | | 21.0 | |
| Total | 100.0 | | 100.0 | |

Press releases from October 21 and October 28, 2004, explained the special report that Telemundo had on Election Day. There was no evidence of a corporate plan to create a definitive agenda.

Univisión's partnership with NALEO had a clear and specific purpose. A press release from April 13, 2004, described their relationship: "NALEO and Univisión joined forces to launch 'Voces del Pueblo,' an ongoing multimedia campaign that utilizes Univisión's influence in the Hispanic community to educate Hispanics about voting and encourage them to play a decisive role in the upcoming elections" (Understanding the Voting Power of Hispanics, 2004: 1). Scott Roskowski, vice president of sales and marketing for Univisión, commented, "this partnership enables both Univisión and NALEO to leverage both our core competencies to help stimulate voter registration and voter turnout" (Understanding the Voting Power of Hispanics, 2004: 2). As a result of this collaboration, Univisión and NALEO produced public services announcements, and created a phone line (1–888- VE Y VOTA) which provided voting information.

Univisión also created a campaign that assisted politicians and media advisors in their quest to win the Latino vote and inform them about the growing Hispanic electorate. Michael D. Wortsman, president, Univisión Television Group explained, "The Hispanic Vote Tool Kit [CD-ROM] offers them [politicians and media advisors] the information necessary to successfully target the nation's largest minority group by understanding and addressing the issues they [Latinos] care about in the most effective way. Univisión is thrilled to play a role in facilitating the political community's recognition of the voting power of U.S. Hispanics" (Understanding the Voting Power of Hispanics, 2004: 1). The CD-ROM was released on April 13, 2004, and contains eight different topics: (1) the Hispanic vote opportunity, (2) the Hispanic voter profile, (3) the best way to reach the Hispanic voter, (4) political calculator, designed to customize campaign budgets, (5) Univisión's corporate information, (6) commercial and messaging, (7) market-by-market analysis, and (8) a few case studies.

The CD-ROM also contains testimonials from well known politicians and media advisors who explained the power of the Hispanic vote during the 2004 political landscape. Lionel Sosa, media advisor to President George W. Bush explains, "for the Bush campaign [Latinos] is [was] one of the top three target audiences. We know that without the Hispanic vote George W. Bush can't be re-elected" (Univisión, The Hispanic Vote, 2004). Sergio Bendixen, pollster/consultant with Bendixen & Associates, believes that Spanish television newscast airtime is the quickest way to reach Latino voters: "[T]he local news, the national news, and the morning news have [viewer] concentrations as high as 30, 40, 50% voters. When I suggested to my clients what to buy on Spanish language, I emphasize the news programming for Spanish language television heavily" (Univisión, The Hispanic Vote, 2004). Politicians themselves believe that investing in Spanish media is crucial. Fernando Ferrer, candidate for the mayor of New York City in 2001, suggested: "In 2001, [I] made the appropriate media investments and saw a dramatic turnout in Hispanic vote" (Univisión, The Hispanic Vote, 2004). Xavier Becerra, Member of Congress (D-CA): "I think that it is unfortunate that more advertisers and more elected officials don't use Spanish language media to try to communicate, because it is a phenomenal way to reach an audience that is very interested in what is going on in this country. While that audience might appreciate what you said in English, they will appreciate that you said it also in Spanish" (Univisión, The Hispanic Vote, 2004).

*Table 16.2* Comparison of media agenda and public agenda

| Issues and news topics | SLTV agenda n=196 | | Public agenda n=943 | |
| --- | --- | --- | --- | --- |
| | % of stories | (rank of issue/topic) | % of mentions | (rank of issue/topic) |
| Terrorism | 9.1 | (1) | 8.6 | (5) |
| War in Iraq | 6.3 | (2) | 20.0 | (2) |
| Economy and jobs | 5.1 | (3) | 20.2 | (1) |
| Religion/moral values | 4.0 | (4) | 10.7 | (4) |
| Health care, Medicare | 3.4 | (5.5) | 8.4 | (6) |
| Immigration | 3.4 | (5.5) | 2.9 | (8) |
| Foreign policy | 2.3 | (7.5) | ** | (13) |
| Education | 2.3 | (7.5) | 7.1 | (7) |
| "Other" issues | 2.0 | (9) | 16.6 | (3) |
| Taxes | 0.6 | (10) | 1.5 | (10) |
| Crime | * | (12) | 2.4 | (9) |
| Gun control | * | (12) | 0.8 | (11.5) |
| Environment | * | (12) | 0.8 | (11.5) |
| Total | *** 38.5 | | 100.0 | |

* Topics silent in media agenda ** Topics silent in public agenda (r =+0.254) *** This percentage is based on issue cover only, see Table 16.1

## Agenda-setting effects

The William C. Velazquez Institute's 2004 National Latino Election Day Exit Poll revealed that public opinion in the Hispanic community was focused on 12 major issues. Table 16.2 reports the size of the constituency and the rank-order for these issues. Table 16.2 also reports the consolidated issue agenda for Spanish-language television (Univisión and Telemundo combined). This TV agenda consists of 11 major issues. All but one of these issues, foreign policy, also appears on the public agenda. However, the public agenda also includes two issues, crime and gun control, that did not appear at all in the election coverage of the Spanish-language TV services. In short, there is considerable overlap between the media's issue agenda and the public's issue agenda. More precisely, the rank-order correlation (Spearman's rho) between the TV issue agenda and the public issue agenda is +.72. In the context of agenda-setting effects found in a wide variety of elections worldwide over the years, this is a very strong relationship. (Given the high correlation previously found between the issue agendas of Univisión and Telemundo (+.74), it is not surprising that the correlations with the public issue are nearly identical for the two television networks: +.72 for Univisión and +.76 for Telemundo.)

Examining the details of the issue agendas for the media and the public in table 16.2 confirms the strong association between the television news coverage and the issues regarded as most important by the public in casting their ballots. For the top four issues on the media agenda, three of these also rank among the top four for the public—the economy, Iraq, and religion and morality. The disagreement, which is not that much in the context of a 13-item agenda, is in regard to terrorism. While terrorism ranks number one on the media agenda, it ranks number five among the public. All in all, the ranks across all 13 issue categories are reasonably similar for the media and the public, and support the idea of an agenda-setting role of the news media.

## CONCLUSION

This detailed examination of Spanish-language television and Latino voters during the 2004 U.S. presidential election makes important contributions to the literature. The major contribution is an examination of the agenda-setting process among voters who consider themselves to be members of a particular ethnic group and their major ethnic media outlet. It is important to pay attention to culture during any election period because race and ethnicity do play a crucial function in political communication. Traditionally, agenda-setting studies delimit their examination area based on particular geographic location. However, agenda-setting effects can also use invisible boundaries such as culture. Ethnic voters and ethnic media have a particular set of public issues that creates a specific agenda, which is based on their system of beliefs. Here we replicated for Spanish-language television news a strong correlation between the agendas of competing news organizations (+.75), and we replicated the frequently found strong correlation between the media agenda and the issue agenda of the public (+.72). This extension of Agenda-Setting Theory into a cultural setting is an important addition to our knowledge.

## NOTES

1   This research project was supported by a Faculty Development Grant from Saint Edward's University to Professor Joanna McClendon.
2   In the early 1990s, Camejo was appointed advisor to the Hawaii Capital Stewardship Forum by the Lieutenant Governor of the islands. Camejo is also a writer. Some examples of his work include *Who killed Jim Crow: The Story of the Civil Rights Movement and it's Lessons for Today* (1977), *Racism, Revolution, Reaction, 1861–1877: The Rise and Fall of Radical Reconstruction* (1977); and *The SRI Advantage: Why Socially Responsible Investing has Outperformed Financially* (2002).

3 According to Miller and Wanta, to "ensure that a reasonable number of minorities was included in the Eugene survey, additional minority respondents were over selected" (1996: 916).

4 At that time, McAllen's population was approximately 110,000 where 91 percent were Latinos. "The response rate for working telephone numbers was approximately 72 percent. The telephone number were selected by random digit dialing and each number was attempted three times, yielding 297 completed questionnaires" (Ghanem and Wanta, 2001: 283), survey was conducted in English or Spanish based on respondents' language preference.

5 All articles published by Austin American Statement between January 1, 2002, and March 12, 2002, were content analyzed. The unit of analysis was an individual assertion in a news story. Overall, 1,198 assertions were recorded from 106 total articles published by Texas' *Capital* newspaper. The inter-coder reliability was over 80 percent. The public opinion survey was conducted over telephone interviews with randomly selected adults in the Greater Austin, Texas area from February 28, 2002 through March 11, 2002—one day before the primary elections. A total of 286 questionnaires were completed which resulted in a margin of error of plus or minus 5.9 percentages of points at the 95 percent confidence level.

6 Special thanks to Saint Edward's University students Nicolás Anaya, Jr., Cindy López, Brenda Marquez, Sarah Olim, Marcela Zavala and Jamie E. Wilson for their assistance with the coding conducted for this research.

# 17

# SUMMARY AND CONCLUSION

Recommendations for new directions for
Latino political communication research

*Federico A. Subervi-Vélez*

in collaboration with
*Stacey L. Connaughton*

This book has explored the relationships between media and Latino politics by answering three fundamental questions: What are the political
messages for or about Latinos disseminated by the mass media? How have
the major political parties used the media to attempt to gain Latino votes?
And, what evidence exists to suggest that exposure to the media influences Latino political participation?

The data and analyses presented here reveal that media-related factors
that contribute to Latino political life in the U.S. are diverse and complex. The findings also help explain the apparent incongruity between
the exuberant claim that Latinos are a major political force and the still
limited political mobilization and voting participation of Latinos, particularly in national elections.

First, analyses of the data gathered over the past 20 years document
that, during presidential election periods, the political messages for or
about Latinos disseminated by the English-language news media have
been very scarce and narrow in scope. Meanwhile, in the major Spanish-
language news media the coverage has been more extensive, yet mostly
traditional, with a major emphasis on the "horse race" news and few
examples of explicit mobilization advocacy.

Second, the Republican and Democratic Parties have certainly used
general market and Latino-oriented mass media to woo Latinos in presidential elections. And not only have paid and free media been used to
reach Latinos, covert propaganda in the form of planted "news" and
"opinion columns" have also been among the outreach tools directed at
Latinos. However, those mass media-based outreach efforts have been, for

*Figure 17.1* Courtesy of Cagle Cartoons, Inc.

the most part, inconsistent in their intensity and in the Latino communities targeted in various campaigns.

Third, exposure to the mass media seems to be a significant and positive contributing factor to Latinos' political knowledge and/or participation. During the 2004 presidential campaign, Spanish-language television in particular was considered to possibly contribute to some agenda-setting functions. But, to date, the evidence about media effects, including agenda setting, on Latinos is partial at best.

The studies presented in this book contribute to "What is known?" about mass communication and Latino politics. They advance new data and analyses that can serve as additional foundations for future research on the intersections among Latinos, media, and politics. To help guide those future efforts, the rest of this chapter offers a series of observations and recommendations that complement and expand the theoretical, contextual and methodological considerations discussed in chapter 3. These are divided into three main topics: (a) analysis of the media institutions and their content, (b) assessments of the outreach strategies of the political parties, and (c) research related to the uses and effects of the media on Latinos.

## MEDIA INSTITUTIONS AND THEIR CONTENT

Given the sustained and rapid growth of Latino-oriented media (LOM) in the United States, political communication researchers must continue to assess the potential impacts such media might have on U.S. Latino political life. Whether future studies examine content or investigate the uses and effects of these media, some fundamental issues must be kept in mind and addressed when possible. Foremost is that, just as all general market or mainstream media are not the same, nor do they provide equal amounts, quality and/or variety of political news and information, such is the case for LOM. This was mentioned in chapter 3, and is discussed more extensively by Subervi-Vélez (2006) and Subervi and Eusebio (2005), both of whom point out how Latino-oriented media are complex and diverse, with different types of ownership and structure, and they vary in the social, cultural, economic, and political functions they play.

Second, it is imperative to recognize (as observed in chapter 4) that the major continuously published Spanish-language daily newspapers have their own patterns and orientations when covering political news. For example, *El Miami Herald* and *La Opinión*, partially because of their broadsheet format, provide their readers with a greater number of political news that are much more detailed than is the case for the tabloid *El Diario-La Prensa*. Yet the latter two papers are more liberal (pro-Democratic Party) oriented than is the case for the former, or for *Diario Las Américas*, which is very much conservative (i.e., pro-Republican) in its editorial stands. Similar patterns may be evident in the newer 15 or so daily papers that have emerged within the last decade. Future studies about the political content of any or all of these daily newspapers—as well as of the hundreds of weekly papers (e.g., *Ahora Sí, La Raza, El Mensajero, La Prensa*) and even of the dozens of magazines published for and/or by Latinos across the country (e.g., *Hispanic, Latina*)—should begin by at least acknowledging and better yet assessing if and how the different types and functions of that press significantly affect (in social, not necessarily statistical terms), what is covered and how it is covered.

For example, commercial corporate and chain-owned daily newspapers such as *Hoy* (published in Chicago, and Los Angeles by the Tribune company) have different resources for, and patterns of, covering political news than is the case for the corporative independent family-owned dailies such as *Diario Las Américas* (Miami, FL) and *La Visión* (Lawrenceville, GA). If nothing else, a corporate-owned daily or weekly newspaper affiliated to a major English-language daily would have, at a minimum, the resources of the established news rooms from which stories, including those from the newswire services subscribed to, can be borrowed, translated, or even enhanced with quotations from Latino sources. In contrast, family-owned Latino-oriented newspapers must have their own staff or use the wire services, the latter of which do not necessarily produce news stories specifically about or directed to Latino audiences. The other option for these smaller newspapers (albeit one that—as discussed by Santillán and Subervi-Vélez (1991) and alluded to in chapter 12—has been used by larger established Spanish-newspapers, too) is to accept "planted" stories and opinion columns produced by the outreach (propaganda) offices of the national political parties.

Third, the corporate or family ties of these media may be influential factors regarding not only the emphasis (e.g., placement and headlines) given to political news, but also the slant of such news. This does not imply that overseers or censors from the corporate or business office explicitly call the shots of the news operations, especially regarding political stories produced by the editorial departments. Nevertheless, most media operations are run as businesses and are likely to be managed by businessmen and women. To the extent that these business-minded individuals are inclined to favor the tax policies of the Republican Party, the vantage point from which political news gets selected and published is likely to be conservative or traditional, not advocacy oriented. An exception may be if they have a personal civil rights or social justice vantage point that serves as a raison d'être, such as is the case with the publishers and editors of various grass roots weeklies (e.g., *La Politiquera* in Central Texas).

When research is subsequently conducted about the interplay between LOM ownership, the functions the media play, and the political content they publish or produce, it would not be surprising to find that, across the newsrooms, many editors and journalists might prefer—consciously or unconsciously—to tow the line of their company's superiors, especially if it is known that those corporate or editorial VIPs are major supporters of or donors to a particular political party or candidate for high office.

Our knowledge of this industry leads us to suggest that it would be of little or no surprise if future content analyses of Spanish-language newspapers reveal patterns similar to those observed with the five dailies studied in the previous pages of this book: that is, even in liberal-oriented Latino communities the daily or weekly papers might reflect more conservative-leaning political stories and/or editorials and op-ed columns.

While the above discussion has focused primarily on newspapers, these issues certainly apply to analyses of news stemming from Latino-oriented television or radio networks or from independent stations.

With respect to television, the political news and information about presidential campaigns produced and aired by networks such as Univisión and Telemundo—whose audience is primarily U.S. Latinos—is quite extensive (and not immune to political leanings, as noted in chapters 5–7). But that content is notably different from that available on Galavisión or on Azteca América Network, for which most programs are produced in Mexico for Mexican audiences and made available in select U.S. cities primarily via cable or low-power stations. Different political content, if any, is also to be expected from Univisión's broadcast partner network (Telefutura) and Telemundo's cable counterpart (Mun-2), as both operations are more entertainment oriented toward their younger, bilingual audiences. On the other hand, the upstart broadcast-based network LAT-TV (launched in Austin, Houston, Phoenix and San Antonio on April 28, 2006), might end up covering much more local political news if its pre-launch promises come to fruition.[1] Likewise, local stations—be those owned and operated by, or affiliated with, Telemundo, Univisión, or another network—might develop and produce a regular offering of local news, including political news (and even public service programs) if the financial, technical, and human resources are made available to such ends.

All this implies that just because a community has access to Spanish-language television does not mean that it will readily have at hand political news and information in general or specific to an ongoing political campaign. It also does not imply that the news produced will provide direct connections to the local Latinos, their political leadership, the main issues or concerns of local relevance. Whether or not political campaign news and information are available on the diverse Spanish-language networks and stations requires careful analysis. Most importantly, discussions about if and how exposure to those stations might contribute to political knowledge demands specific survey questions that directly query the type of exposure. There is more on this latter subject in section three of this chapter.

With respect to radio networks and stations, practically all of the issues discussed above apply. But some additional points are called for. For example, as mentioned in chapter 3, the norm of practically all Spanish-language radio stations is to have little or no news, with the exceptions noted in those pages. One is the community-based and supported Cadena Radio Bilingüe (operating mainly in California), and another is the weekly English-language nationally syndicated Latino USA, both of which very regularly offer news, interviews, and important insights about political (as well as social, cultural, and economic) affairs that directly affect Latinos. A second exception is the select stations in the Miami area where news, talk, and interviews—albeit primarily very conservative and critical of liberal Democratic Party candidates and perspectives—are regular fare. A third exception is Univisión's news and public affairs program *Tu Voz En Washington*, which is broadcast live on Sunday mornings via the network's AM stations.[2] The third exception is the independently produced news and/or commentary programs that sprinkle the airwaves (usually short, at most half-hour, and typically early morning or late night) in select stations across the country. These stations/programs are among the few that have the potential to significantly influence the political socialization and mobilization of Latinos. Other stations, popular as they may be, contribute to the cultural socialization, pluralism or retro-acculturation of Latinos but not necessarily the political socialization—that is, unless the disk jockeys engage in some political mobilization efforts, as was the case during the spring of 2006 when pro-immigration marches were promoted and encouraged more by the DJs of precisely those stations than by anyone else. But if there were to be any potential influence stemming from exposure to radio news, it would be in the respective communities where the news is aired.[3]

The geographical boundaries imposed by the range of airwaves, however, do not restrict the political role that could be played by stations that offer news and simultaneously transmit their programming via the Internet. The same applies for the Latino-oriented "radio stations" that are exclusively based on the Internet (e.g., www.crnlive.com, www.chicanoexpress.com, www.chicano-radio.com). If political information were part of the norm in any of these sites, the potential impact would no longer be subject to local audiences.

Undoubtedly, Spanish-language radio stations have profound political mobilization potential. This was clearly illustrated in spring 2006 when Latinos, following the rallying calls repeatedly aired by many (but not all) Latino-oriented stations, marched by the thousands on behalf of immigrants' rights (Navarro, 2006). Researchers have yet to study whether or not such potential is possible stemming from political campaign news.

When the potential political impact of Latino-oriented radio is assessed, the aforementioned issues merit consideration. But even if political news content is otherwise scarce on those airwaves, Latino-oriented radio nonetheless merits serious study—especially Univision's *Tu Voz En Washington* program, as it is the only live show of its kind. As mentioned elsewhere in this text, over the past 20 years, both the Democratic Party and the Republican Party have occasionally produced distinct and unique radio programs and commercial spots specifically oriented to Latinos. Some of the radio programs have been planted—that is, distributed by the political parties but then broadcast as if they were neutral news stemming from non-partisan sources. Others have been aired and have been identified publicly as partisan programs. Likewise, political spots are aired regularly and repeatedly during almost every national election and many local elections. What are the distinct characteristics of those partisan news programs and the radio spots? What effects, if any, do they have on the population? The first question has yet to receive more than just passing attention (Santillán and Subervi, 1991); the second has yet to be systematically explored on a national basis.

A final arena under this first rubric focuses on the Latino-oriented web sites created by the political parties or their supporters. Two studies

(Barbarena, 2005; Len-Rios, 2002) have explored the content characteristics of those sites. We predict that in the next few years, Democrats, Republicans, and any independent candidate or party will greatly develop and enhance Latino-oriented political campaign web sites directed to Latinos. Those sites, be they for local, statewide, or national candidates or causes, will be available in Spanish, and possibly in English. Some sites or sections will be direct translations of content produced for the general audiences regardless of ethnic background. But other content, in either language, is prone to be more niche oriented—that is, with messages that appeal specifically to different subgroups of the Latino community: business owners, professionals, working-class Latinos, and those who have recently become U.S. citizens. In sum, future studies about Latino political communication should not overlook documenting and critically analyzing that content, as well as its uses and potential effects.

In essence, the field of political communication is still wide open to analyze the whole spectrum of issues and topics related to Latino-oriented media institutions and the content they produce. Moreover, let us not forget, as mentioned in chapter 3, that many Latinos do not have access to Latino-oriented media nor have the language skills necessary to consume the Spanish-language media. Thus, it is also imperative to assess if and how general market media are providing content that is specifically for Latinos and relevant to their political knowledge, and the extent to which that media content contributes to their political socialization and mobilization.

## POLITICAL PARTIES AND THEIR OUTREACH TO LATINOS

Given the evidence presented in this book, there should be no doubt that the Democratic Party, and even more so the Republican Party, have devoted considerable monetary and human resources to targeting and winning the political allegiance and votes of Latinos via the mass media. Our interviews and informal conversations with party leaders and strategists lead us to affirm that such efforts will be enhanced in future local, state, and national elections.

Here again, the field of political communication is ripe for delving into hereto practically unexplored questions and issues related to Latinos. What organizational structures are being set up at the national, state, and local levels to produce media and other outreach materials directed to Latinos? To what extent are these coordinated efforts? What will be the nature of party-sponsored Latino-oriented messages in future campaigns? Will the Democrats and Republicans make discursive moves similar to those each party has made in the past? Or will they adopt different discursive strategies? Will public relations professionals specializing in Spanish-language *and* English-language media specifically directed to Latinos be hired to facilitate the contacts between reporters and party candidates and spokespersons, or will there only be more one-way communication from the party propagandists to the media? What consequences do such moves have for Latino-oriented media?

Will the free media efforts include even more covert or stealth propaganda being passed on to Latino-oriented media (or to other media) as if it were legitimate non-partisan news and information? What are the themes, issues, images, sounds, and frames being used in the construction of both the free media messages and the paid political spots—or for that matter in any planted stories? Are emotionally loaded messages promoting the Republican Party and its candidates as ideal for Latinos to achieve the "American dream" going to continue to be that party's distinctive mark? Or will the messages focus again on selective issues, as was newly evident in the 2004 campaign (see chapter 14)? Will the Democratic Party continue to focus on issues that are presumed to appeal to Latinos, or will its Latino-oriented strategists and advertisers develop more emotional-laden sounds and images that are designed to appeal to the heart? Which, if any, of the messages will be produced as translations of content created for the general public vis-à-vis those specifically produced for the pan-Hispanic or niche Latino constituencies?

How closely or independently will the presidential and other campaign personnel work with each other or with the "independent" supporting groups in the development of the general vis-à-vis niche paid and/or free messages? Will more and new professionals be brought in, or will grass roots organizers and operatives be given stronger voices in the development of the messages that appeal to their particular constituencies? Will strategists who know the Latino community and media be given meaningful voices not only in the Latino campaigns but also in the general campaigns, or will it be the power brokers of the general campaign who will be the ultimate decision makers of what is or is not created and disseminated to woo Latinos?

Other important questions relate to the strategies each party will make to assess the pulse of the campaign and the outcome of their outreach efforts. Will the assessments be based on internal polls and focus groups, by contracting surveys and queries carried out by partisan researchers, or by way of collaborative efforts of independent non-partisan entities such as the Pew Hispanic Center?

Questions such as these are among the many that can be explored to better understand what the political parties and candidates do to, via, and with the mass media in order to win Latino voters. As we observed during the 2000 presidential campaign, one of the reasons the Republican Party received more coverage, especially on Spanish-language television,

*Figure 17.2* Courtesy of Cagle Cartoons, Inc.

is because it hired a Latina television reporter, Sonia Colín, who then became a public relations specialist dedicated to attaining the goal of increased and favorable exposure for candidate Bush and the GOP (see Colín, 2004). It was in great part thanks to her efforts that Republican candidates were prepared and made available to Latino reporters and Latino-oriented media. She was also proactive in getting press releases and other information distributed to those media on a regular basis. Altogether, she was instrumental in the increased free media afforded to the Republican Party, its candidate, and messages specifically tailored to Latino voters.

Moreover, studies that examined these questions would be revealing not only of Latino political dynamics, but also of the pulse of American politics in general. Latino and other ethnic-oriented media strategies and messages cross over and influence the rhythm and flavor of the general campaigns. Consider, for example, how many Latino entertainers—singers, actors, Mariachi and other types of bands—have been featured in political rallies and even the conventions in recent years. Even if in chapters 8–11 it was observed that general market news media offer very limited coverage of Latino-themed political news, there is nonetheless evidence of some "Latinization" of American politics, at least related to the communication and public relations efforts of the Democratic and Republican Parties.

However, what has been left mostly unexplored in the field of political communication pertains to Latinos' use of media and the effects of media on Latinos. Observations and recommendations on such matters are considered in the next section of this chapter.

## LATINOS' USE OF THE MEDIA AND MEDIA EFFECTS ON LATINOS' POLITICAL LIFE

The fact that this book has only two chapters that present data based on a survey of Latinos' use of media and the potential effects of the media on Latinos' political knowledge, attitudes and behaviors is indicative of a major gap in this field. And it is not that there have not been any public opinion type surveys of this population. The problem lies in the lack or inadequate formulation of specific and appropriate questions related to exposure to and uses of the media that would yield valid and reliable empirical evidence as to if and how the media in Spanish and/or English have significant effects—in statistical and social terms—on the political socialization, opinions, and mobilization of this population.

While the questions that could be suggested for this line of research are almost infinite, the ones listed here focus on specific recommendations that should be applied for future survey research that would assess the actual, observable role of media in Latino politics. Aside from the contextual and methodological considerations discussed in chapter 3, some additional proposals merit attention. These are divided into three categories: (a) questions to be asked in field surveys research, (b) contextual information that should be presented with the data analysis, and (c) other recommendations.

### Survey research proposals

First, when analyses are to be conducted about Latinos' use of, or exposure to, Spanish-language or English-language Latino-oriented media, survey subjects should first be queried if they, the respondents, are aware of *any Latino-oriented media* in their immediate community directed to Latinos in general, or to Hispanics of their own national origin in particular? If so, *which media* (print and broadcast) are they aware of? And, how *accessible* are those media in terms of (a) cost (be it for cable or print subscriptions, on-the-spot purchase of printed copies), (b) location to purchase them (regarding print), and (c) quality of broadcast reception (for VHF, UHF, low-power stations, or AM or FM radio waves)? What this set of questions helps to establish is whether the respondents know about and can potentially become exposed to or use LOM in their immediate environment.

Second, if Latino-oriented media are identified as present and accessible to the respondent, then questions should follow about whether or not each of those identified media are *perceived* as offering any political content. If so, it would be valuable to ask whether or not that political content includes news and information about the Latino community in general, or about the Latino community of his/her national origin in particular.[4] Depending on the respondent's answers to those queries, it would follow to ask whether or not the respondent reads the print, watches the TV, or listens to that particular political content and, if so, how regularly that is done.

Third, at this point, other traditional questions can follow. For example, do you read Spanish/English-language newspapers or magazines and, if so, how often? Do you tune into Spanish/English-language television/radio and, if so, how often? Do you pay attention to political news in print/broadcast media?[5]

Fourth, in addition to querying about exposure to media in general, and about use of it for political news and information in particular, there are at least two more crucial questions that should be asked to accurately assess the potential role of the media on Latinos: Which medium do you *rely on* (or find most dependable) for political news and information in general? And, which medium do you *rely on* (or find most dependable) for political news and information *about the Latino community or about your specific* (Mexican, Mexican American, Puerto Rican, Cuban, Cuban American, etc.) *community?*

Similarly, if the goal is to inquire about Latinos' exposure to political advertising and/or to assess whether or not that exposure had any political influence, specific questions about access, perception, and political value (i.e., for the individual as a Latino) of these are called for. The same would be true for research about the use of the Internet.

Here we must point out that, often times, questions about a respondent's main source of political news/information include as answer options not just media outlets, but also "friends," "family members" and/ or "co-workers." When a respondent states one of these, instead of identifying a mass media outlet for such purposes, there should be a follow-up question such as: What is (or what do you think is) that person's main source of information? We suspect that many, if not most respondents might state the media as their family member's/friend's/co-worker's most important source for political news/information, which would then suggest at least an indirect media effect.

When the responses to these or any other questions specifically geared to assess political use of media are compiled, tabulated and analyzed with the answers to traditional demographic and socio-economic questions, along with those about political knowledge, attitudes, and behaviors, then conclusions can more adequately be drawn about the political role of the media, be these Latino-oriented or general market media.

## Contextual information

Whether or not a field survey can ask all the questions suggested above, any analysis and report about Latinos' political life should be accompanied by contextual information related to the Latino-oriented media in the studied community. For example, findings about Latinos' registration, voting, or other forms of mobilization (or lack thereof) should at least provide the reader with some notions about the characteristics of the LOM in that community: Are there any widely circulating newspapers or not? Is it a community in which one or more of the television networks are easily available over the air or via cable? Are there any regular and extended news programs on radio? Do the LOM newspapers regularly cover political news and are local or nationally syndicated Latino writers contributing to the opinion pages? Are there any activist or advocacy Latino-oriented media or programs?

With respect to general market English-language media, it would also be important to know if these have in their news department reporters, especially Latinos, who cover the Latino community. Are there regular news items about Latino political activities, not just about crime and immigration? Most importantly, does the local press include local or nationally syndicated Latino authors or opinion leaders? If the answers to these questions are affirmative, the chances are much better that Latinos in that community will be more attentive to the media, especially to the news and opinion pages, thus increasing their chances of political socialization. The opposite, e.g., political alienation, might be the case if, on the contrary, news and opinions about or stemming from Latinos are absent.

The answers to these questions would be very revealing about the options available to that community for gaining political news and information that might be politically relevant to them. And if a complementary content analyses study of a representative sample of that media can be conducted, a much richer understanding could then be drawn about some crucial factors that contribute to or impede Latinos' political involvement in that locality.

At a minimum, national survey research should make clear distinctions between the data stemming from respondents who live in communities that have LOM vis-à-vis those who do not have such media in their community. As noted in chapter 15, the data yielded print media effects (partial as they were) when this factor was taken into consideration.

## Other recommendations

In social science studies about Latinos, it has been common to run statistical analysis that correlate Latinos' age or their years in the United States with some other variable or measures, e.g., political participation, media use in English vis-à-vis Spanish, acculturation indexes, etc. Valuable as those statistical analyses may be, it has been our experience that one of the most revealing variables is that which assesses the proportion of years spent by respondents in the U.S. Ten years of U.S. residency for a 20-year old represent half his/her life in this country, whereas for a 50-year old person that is only 20 percent of his or her life. When this combined variable is analyzed along with other data, it can be much more telling than is the case when the component variables are analyzed individually.

Finally, not all evidence about potential media effects has to be based on survey research. Systematic field observations can also be enlightening. No systematic random sample survey research is needed to affirm without hesitation that Spanish-language radio was instrumental in the spring 2006 mobilization of thousands of Latinos across the country to march in support of undocumented immigrants; or that the steady advocacy of local community newspapers has at times brought positive social change in cases of blatant social injustice such as racial discrimination or environmental pollution.

Likewise, when it comes to political mobilization, the media may have significant impact on the Latino community. And the impact may be—depending on the placement, repetition, and framing of the content—conducive to mobilization or stagnancy. How that plays out varies from community to community and is contingent on multiple other factors that interplay with the audiences' perceptions, exposure, and uses of the available media.


## CONCLUSION

The data, analyses and arguments presented in this manuscript clearly suggest that the mass media do and can play major roles in the political life of Latinos in the United States. To better understand when, where and how that happens requires new generations of research that is more detailed and focused on specific issues, contexts, and methodologies as suggested in these pages. What will also be needed are ventures into theory construction that take into consideration the complexity of the Latino population, their communities, and the full range of media available to them.

Much work remains to be done. For now we will propose that the greater the availability of Latino-oriented media that offer political content, and the more that such media as well as general market media provide a regular and steady stream of political news that are relevant and conducive to political socialization of Latinos, then the greater the mobilization and fuller participation of Latinos in U.S. politics. This, too, is a proposition left for future research.

## NOTES

1 During a pre-launch press conference on March 31, 2006, in Austin, Texas, the spokespersons for LAT-TV stated that local news produced by local freelance journalists would be broadcast regularly on the local affiliates of the network.
2 This program was launched on September 26, 2004.
3 As mentioned in chapter 3, after the Radio Única national network ceased operations, there has yet to emerge a national radio network that offers on a daily basis more than just a few minutes of political news and commentary across the country. The stations that carry the nationally syndicated weekly Latino USA air it at different days and times. Univisión's *Tu Voz en Washington* news and public affairs program on Sunday mornings, is only weekly, too.
4 Verification of the presence of LOM and their political content in the respondents' communities should obviously be made by the researcher prior to deriving conclusions about the replies to these series of questions. It is possible that respondents affirm that there are LOM and that these offer political content, when in fact such is not the case. Or respondents might state that there are no such media or that, if they exist, they do not print/air political content, when in fact the opposite is true. Responses that contradict what exists would then be a reflection of how those media are (incorrectly) perceived by the surveyed Latinos.
5 Of course, these and all the questions would be properly constructed to obtain specific and accurate responses. They should not be double-barreled as summarized here.

# BIBLIOGRAPHY

Acosta, S., & Velasquez, R. (1992). The Hispanic market's leading indicators. *Hispanic Business*, December 1992: 30–34.

Acosta-Belén, E. (1988). From settlers to newcomers: The Hispanic legacy in the United States. In E. Acosta-Belén & B. Sjostrom (eds.), *The Hispanic experience in the United States*: 81–106. New York: Praeger.

Adams-Means, C., Flores, M., & McCombs, M. E. (2005). Agenda setting: The hip hop culture and civic engagement in the 2004 presidential election: 29.

Adler, I. (1987, April 7–12). *Functions of the Latino media in Chicago: The view of the gatekeepers*. Paper presented at the annual convention of the society of applied anthropology, Oaxaca, Mexico.

Aguirre, B. (1979). Ethnic newspapers and politics: *Diario las Americas* and the Watergate affair. *Ethnic Groups*, 2: 155–165.

Albert, S., Ashforth, B. E., & Dutton, J. E. (2000). Organizational identity and identification: Charting new waters and building new bridges. *Academy of Management Review*, 25: 13–17.

Albert, S., & Whetten, D. (1985). Organizational identity. In L. L. Cummings & B. M. Staw (eds.), *Research in organizational behavior*, 7: 263–295. Greenwich, CT: JAI Press.

Allen, M. W., & Caillouet, R. H. (1994). Legitimation endeavours: Impression management strategies used by an organization in crisis. *Communication Monographs*, 41: 44–62.

Allen, R. & Chaffee, S. (1979). Mass communication and the political participation of Black Americans. In D. Nimmo (ed.), *Communication Yearbook*, 3: 507–522. New Brunswick, NJ: Transaction Books.

Almond, G., & Verba, S. (1963). *The civic culture*. Princeton, NJ: Princeton University Press.

Altschull, J. H. (1984). *Agents of power. The role of the news media in human affairs*. New York: Longman

Altschull, J. H. (1995). *Agents of power. The media and public policy*. New York: Longman.

Alvesson, M. (1990). Organization: From substance to image? *Organization Studies*, 11: 373–394.

American Political Science Association (2005, January 26). Press release. *Exit polls' claim of record-high Latino support for Bush found "suspect" by political scientists*. Washington, DC.

Americas Review, The (1989). *La Prensa* [Special issue]. The Americas Review, 17 (3–4): 121–184.

Ansolabehere, S., Behr, R., & Iyengar, S. (1993). *The media game: American politics in the television age*. New York: Macmillan.

Ansolabehere, S., & Iyengar, S. (1994). Riding the wave and claiming ownership over issues: The joint effects of advertising and news coverage on campaigns. *Public Opinion Quarterly*, 58: 335–357.

Ansolabehere, S., & Iyengar, S. (1995). *Going negative: How political advertisements shrink and polarize the electorate*. New York: Free Press.

Ansolabehere, S., & Iyengar, S. (1996). The craft of political advertising: A progress report. In D. C. Mutz, P. M. Sniderman, & R. A. Brody (eds.), *Political persuasion and attitude change*: 101–121. Ann Arbor: The University of Michigan Press.

Ansolabehere, S., Iyengar, S., & Simon, A. (1999). Replicating experiments using aggregate and survey data: The case of negative advertising and turnout. *American Political Science Review*, 88: 829–38.

Arvizu, J. R., & García, F. C. (1996). Latino voting participation: Explaining and differentiating Latino voting turnout. *Hispanic Journal of Behavioral Sciences*, 18 (2): 104–128.

Ashforth, B. E. & Mael, F. (1989). Social identity theory and the organization. *Academy of Management Review*, 14: 20–39.

Associated Press (1999, October 25). Bush courts Hispanics in ads.

Austin, E. W., & Nelson, C. L. (1993). Influences of ethnicity, family communication, and media on adolescents' socialization to U.S. politics. *Journal of Broadcasting and Electronic Media*, 37 (4): 419–435.

Avila, A. (1996). The new Hispanic congress. *Hispanic Magazine*, September 1996: 24.

Avila, A. (1997, January–February). Trading punches: Spanish-language television pounds the competition in the fight for Hispanic advertising dollars. *Hispanic Magazine*, January–February 1997: 39–44.

Ayers, B. D., Jr. (1996). The expanding Hispanic vote shakes republican strongholds. *The New Times*, November 10, 1996: A1.

Babbie, E. (1984). *The practice of social research* (4th edn). Belmont, CA: Wadsworth.

Bagdikian, B. (2004). *The new media monopoly*. Boston, MA: Beacon.

Barberena, L. (2005). Hispanic-targeted web pages of the 2004 election: How national political parties and presidential candidates utilized the Internet to foster identification with Hispanic voters. Unpublished paper, University of Texas at Austin.

Barone, M. (ed.) (2000). *Almanac of American politics 2000*. National Journal Publications.

Barrera, A. (2001). *Looking for Carrascolendas*. Austin: University of Texas Press.

Barrientos, T. (1997). Americans becoming Latin lovers. *Austin American Statesman*, March 6, 1997: E1.

Bartels, L.M. (1988). *Presidential primaries and the dynamics of public choice*. Princeton: Princeton University Press.

Bartels, L. M. (1993). Messages received: The political impact of media exposure *American Political Science Review* 87 (2): 267–285.

Bartels, L. M. (1998). Where the ducks are: Voting power in a party system. In J. G. Geer (ed.), *Politicians and Party Politics*. Baltimore: Johns Hopkins Press.

Bass, B. M., & Avolio, B. J. (1992). *Improving organizational effectiveness through transformational leadership*. Thousand Oaks, CA: Sage.

Bean, F. D., & Tienda, M. (1987). *The Hispanic population of the United States*. New York: Russell Sage Foundation.

Beck, P. A., Dalton, R. J., Greene, S., & Huckfeldt, R. (2002). The social calculus of voting: Interpersonal, media and organizational influences on presidential choices. *American Political Science Review*, 96: 57–73.

Bennett, W. L. (1992). *The governing crisis: Media, money, and marketing in American elections*. New York: St. Martin's Press.

Bennett, W. L. (2001). *The politics of illusion*. New York: Longman.

Bennett, W. L. (2002). *News: The politics of illusion* (5th edn). New York: Longman.

Bennett, W. L. & Entman, R. (eds.) (2005). *New media campaigns and the managed citizen*. Cambridge: Cambridge University Press.

Benoit, W. L. (2000). Comparing the Clinton and Dole advertising campaigns: Identification and division in 1996 presidential television spots. *Communication Research Reports*, 17: 39–48.

Benoit, W. L. (2001). The functional approach to presidential television spots: Acclaiming, attacking, defending 1952–2000. *Communication Studies*, 52: 109–126.

Benze, J. G., & Declercq, E. R. (1985). Content of television political spot ads for female candidates. *Journalism Quarterly*, 62 (2): 278–283.

Berg, C. R. (2002). *Latino images in film: Stereotypes, subversion, resistance*. Austin: University of Texas Press.

Berger, C. (1986). Social cognition and intergroup communication. In W.B. Gudykunst (ed.), *Intergroup communication*: 51–61. London: Edward Arnold Publishers.

Berry, G., & Mitchell-Kernan (eds.) (1982). *Television and the socialization of the minority child*. NY: Academic Press.

Biocca, F. (1991). The orchestration of codes and discourses: Analysis of semantic framing. In F. Biocca (ed.), *Television and political advertising*, 2: 61–89.

Bosque Pérez, R. & Colón Morera, J. J. (2006). *Puerto Rico under colonial rule: Political persecution and the quest for human rights*. New York: State University of New York Press.

Brady, H. E., & Johnston, R. (1987). What's the primary message: Horserace or issue journalism. In G.R. Orren & N.W. Polsby (eds.), *Media and momentum*. Chatham, NJ: Chatham House.

Brady, H. E., Verba, S., & Schlozman, K.L. (1995). Beyond SES: A resource model of political participation. *American Political Science Review*, 89: 271–294.

Brand, R. (1949). A general view of the regular Spanish language press in the United States. In C. Cortés (ed.), (1980). *Latinos in the United States*. New York: Arno Press. (Reprinted from *Modern Language Journal*, (1949), 33 (5): 363–370.)

Brasher, H. (2003). Capitalizing on contention: Issue agendas in U.S. Senate campaigns. *Political Communication*, 20: 453–471.

Braverman, A. (n.d.). *Enviros hit Bush en Espanol*. Retrieved September 20, 2000, from http://www.nationaljournal.com.

Brians, C. L. & Wattenberg, M. P. (1996). Campaign issue knowledge and salience: Comparing reception from TV commercials, TV news and newspapers. *American Journal of Political Science* 40 (1): 172–193.

Brischetto, R. R. (1984). *The Hispanic Electorates*. New York: Southwestern Voter Registration Education Project.

Brischetto, R. R. (1986, December 5). *Trends in ethnic voting in Texas State election: 1978–1986*. San Antonio, Texas: Southwestern Voter Registration Education Project.

Brischetto, R. R. (1987, March 19). *Chicano voting and vicious in the 1986 election*. Paper presented at the annual meeting of the Southwestern Social Science Association, Dallas, TX.

Brischetto, R. R. (1988). *The political empowerment of Texas Mexicans, 1974–1988*. San Antonio: Southwest Voter Research Institute.

Brischetto, R., & de la Garza, R. (1985). The Mexican-American electorate: Political opinions and behavior across cultures in San Antonio. *The Mexican American electorate series* (Occasional Paper No. 5). The University of Texas at Austin, Center for Mexican American Studies.

Buchanan, B. (1991). *Electing a president: The Markle commission research on Campaign '88*. Austin, TX: University of Texas Press.

Buehler, M. (1975). Political efficacy, political discontent, and voting turnout among Mexican-Americans in Michigan. Unpublished doctoral dissertation, University of Notre Dame.

Burke, K. (1969). *A rhetoric of motives*. Berkeley, CA: University of California Press (originally published in 1950).

*Burrelle's Hispanic Media Directory*. (1984). Livingston: NJ.

Calvo, M. A., & Rosenstone, S. J. (1989). *Hispanic political participation*. Latino Electorate Series. San Antonio, TX: Southwest Voter Research Institute.

Cámara-Fuertes, L. R. (2004). *The phenomenon of Puerto Rican voting*. Gainesville, FL: University Press of Florida.

Campbell, A. G., & Hero, R. E. (1996). Understanding Latino political participation: Exploring the evidence from the Latino national political survey. *Hispanic Journal of Behavioral Sciences*, 18 (2): 129–141.

Campbell, C. P. (1995). *Race, myth and the news*. Thousand Oaks, CA: Sage.

Cappella, J. N., & Jamieson, K. H. (1997). *Spiral of cynicism: The press and the public good*. Oxford: Oxford University Press.

Capus, S. (2000, September 8). Presidential debate. (Television broadcast transcript.) New York, NY: *NBC Nightly News*.

Capus, S. (2000, October 3). Presidential debate. (Television broadcast transcript.) New York, NY: *NBC Nightly News*.

Capus, S. (2000, October 11). Presidential debate. (Television broadcast transcript.) New York, NY: *NBC Nightly News*.

Capus, S. (2000, October 17). Presidential debate. (Television broadcast transcript.) New York, NY: *NBC Nightly News*.

Carter, S., Fico, F., & McCabe, J. A. (2002) Partisan and structural balance in local television news coverage. *Journalism and Mass Communication Quarterly*, 79 (1): 41–53

Castro, T. (1974). *Chicano power. The emergence of Mexican America*. New York: Saturday Review Press.

Cavanaugh, J. W. (1995). *Media effects on voters: A panel study of the 1992 presidential election*. New York: University Press of America.

Center for Integration and Improvement of Journalism (1994). *News watch: A critical look at coverage of people of color*. San Francisco, CA: San Francisco State University.

Center, P. H., & Foundation, K. F. (2004). *The 2004 national survey of Latinos: Politics and civic participation*. Washington, DC: Pew Hispanic Center and Kaiser Family Foundation

Chacón, R. (1977). The Chicano immigrant press in Los Angeles: The case of *El Heraldo de México*, 1916–1920. *Journalism History*, 4 (2): 48–50, 62–63.

Chávez, M. L. (2004). Overview. In S. A. Navarro & A. X. Mejía, (eds.), *Latino Americans and political participation: A reference handbook*, 1–56. Santa Barbara, CA: ABC-CLIO.

Cheney, G. (1983). The rhetoric of identification and the study of organizational communication. *Quarterly Journal of Speech*, 69: 143–158.

Cheney, G., & Christensen, L. T. (2001). Identity at Issue: Linkages between "internal" and "external" communication. In F. M. Jablin & L.M. Putnam (eds.), *The new handbook of organizational communication: Advances in theory, research, and methods*: 231–269. California: Thousand Oaks.

Cheney, G., & Vibbert, S. L. (1987). Corporate discourse: Public relations and issue management. In F. Jablin, L. L. Putnam., L. H. Porter., & K. H. Roberts (eds.), *Handbook of organizational communication: An interdisciplinary perspective*: 165–194. California: Sage Publications.

Colín, S. (2004). *¡Sí se pudo! El poder hispano en el futuro*. Mexico City: Librería y Ediciones Botas S.A.

Connaughton, S. L. (2002). Invitations for identification: An organizational communication analysis of the Democratic and Republican parties' attempts to court Latinos. Unpublished doctoral dissertation, University of Texas, Austin.

Connaughton, S. L. (2005). *Inviting Latino voters: Party messages and Latino party identification*. New York, NY: Routledge.

Connaughton, S. L., & Jarvis, S. E. (2004). Invitations for partisan identification: Attempts to court Latino voters through televised Latino-oriented political advertisements, 1984–2000. *Journal of Communication*, 54: 38–54.

Constantakis-Valdés, P. (1992). *Toward a theory of immigrant and ethnic media: The case of Spanish-language television*. Paper presented at the annual convention of the International Communication Association, Miami, FL.

Constantakis-Valdés, P. (1993). *Spanish-language television and the 1988 presidential elections: A case study of the dual identity of ethnic minority media*. Unpublished doctoral dissertation, The University of Texas at Austin.

Conway, M. M. (1991). Political participation in the United States. Washington, DC: *Congressional Quarterly Press*.

Cook Political Report. www.cookpolitical.com/races/report_pdfs/2004_senate_ratings_oct26.pdf (accessed August 26, 2007)

Cortés, C. (ed.). (1980). *Latinos in the United States*. New York: Arno Press.

Cortés, C. (1987). The Mexican-American press. In S. M. Miller (ed.), *The ethnic press in the United States: A historical analysis and handbook*: 247–260. New York: Greenwood Press.

Cortés, C. (2000). *The children are watching: How the media teach about diversity*. New York: Teachers College Press.

Cundy, D. T. (1986). Political commercials and candidate image: The effects can be substantial. In L. L. Kaid, D. Nimmo, & K. R. Sanders (eds.), *News perspectives* on political advertising: 210–234. Carbondale: Southern Illinois University Press.

Dahl, R. A. (1956). A Preface to Democratic Theory. Chicago, IL: University of Chicago Press.

Dahl, R. A. (1961). Who governs? Democracy and power in an American city. New Haven, CT: Yale University Press.

Dahlgren, P., & Chakrapani, S. (1982). The third world on TV news: Western ways of seeing the other. In W. C. Adams (ed.), Television coverage of international affairs: 45–65. Norwood, NJ: Ablex.

Damore, D. F. (2004). The dynamics of issue ownership in presidential campaigns. Political Research Quarterly, 57 (3): 391–397.

Danigelis, N. D. (1978). Black political participation in the United States: Some recent evidence. American Sociological Review, 43 (5): 756–771.

Dávila, A. (2000). Mapping latinidad: Language and culture in the Spanish TV battlefront. Television & New Media 1 (1): 75–94.

Dávila, A. (2001). Latinos, Inc.: The marketing and making of a people. Berkeley, CA: University of California Press.

Davis, D. K. (1990). News and politics. In D. L. Swanson., & D. Nimmo (eds.), New directions in political communication: 147–184. Newbury Park, CA: Sage.

Debenport, E., & Dahl, D. (1992, October 28). Clinton heats up Tampa crowd. St. Petersburg Times: A1

DeFleur, M. L., & Ball-Rokeach, S. J. (1989). Theories of mass communication (5th edn). White Plains, N.Y: Longman.

de la Garza, R. O. (1987). Ignored voices: Public opinion polls and the Latino Community. Austin: The University of Texas at Austin, Center for Mexican American Studies.

de la Garza, R. O. (1992). From rhetoric to reality: Latinos and the 1988 election in review. In R. O. de la Garza & L. DeSipio (eds.), From rhetoric to reality: Latinos and the 1988 elections: 171–180. Boulder, CO: Westview Press.

de la Garza, R. O., Bean, F. D., Bonjean, C. M., Romo, R., & Alvarez, R. (eds.) (1985). The Mexican American experience: An interdisciplinary anthology. Austin, TX: University of Texas Press.

de la Garza, R. O., Brischetto, R. R., Hernandez, A., & Vaughan, D. (1982). The Mexican American electorate: A demographic profile. The Mexican American electorate series (Occasional Paper No. 1). Austin: The University of Texas at Austin, Center for Mexican American Studies.

de la Garza, R. O., Brischetto, R. R., & Vaughan, D. (1983). The Mexican-American electorate: Information sources and policy orientations. The Mexican American electorate series (Occasional Paper No. 2). Austin: The University of Texas at Austin, Center for Mexican American Studies.

de la Garza, R. O., Brischetto, R. R., & Weaver, J. (1984). The Mexican American electorate: An explanation of their opinions and behaviors. The Mexican American electorate series (Occasional Paper No. 4). Austin: The University of Texas at Austin, Center for Mexican American Studies.

de la Garza, R. O., & DeSipio, L. (eds.) (1992). From rhetoric to reality: Latinos and the 1988 elections. Boulder, CO: Westview Press.

de la Garza, R. O., & DeSipio, L. (eds.) (1999). Awash in the mainstream: Latino politics in the 1992 elections. Boulder, CO: Westview Press.

384

de la Garza, R. O., & DeSipio, L. (eds.) (2005). *Muted voices: Latinos and the 2000 elections.* Boulder, CO: Rowman & Littlefield.

de la Garza, R. O., DeSipio, L., García, F, C., García, J. A., & Falcón, A. (eds.) (1992). *Latino voices: Mexican, Puerto Rican, and Cuban perspectives on American politics.* Boulder, CO: Westview Press.

de la Garza, R. O., Menchaca, M., & DeSipio, L. (1994). *Barrio ballots: Latino politics in the 1990 elections.* Boulder, CO: Westview Press.

de la Isla, J. (2003). *The rise of Hispanic political power.* Santa Maria: CA: Archer Books.

Delener, N., & Neelankavil, J. (1990). Informational sources and media usage: A comparison between Asian and Hispanic subcultures. *Journal of Advertising Research*, June–July 1990: 45–52.

del Olmo, F. (1971). Voices for the Chicano movimiento. *The Quill*, October 1971: 8–11.

Delpit, L. (1993). *Other people's children: Cultural conflict in the classroom.* New York City: The New Press.

del Valle, E. (edn.) (2005). *Hispanic marketing and public relations: Understanding and targeting America's largest minority.* Boca Raton, FL: Poyeen Publishing

Denton, R. E. (1994). *The 1992 presidential campaign: A communication perspective.* Westport, CT: Praeger.

DeSipio, L. (1993). *Counting on the Latino vote: Latinos as a new electorate.* Unpublished doctoral dissertation, The University of Texas at Austin.

DeSipio, L. (1996). *Counting on the Latino Vote: Latinos as a new electorate.* Charlottesville: University of Virginia Press.

DeSipio, L. (2003). *Latino viewing choices: Latino bilingual television viewers and the language choices they make.* Claremont, CA: Tomás Rivera Policy Institute.

DeSipio, L., de la Garza, R.O., & Setzler, M. (1999). Awash in the mainstream: Latinos and the 1996 elections. In R.O. de la Garza, & L. DeSipio (eds.), *Awash in the mainstream: Latinos and the 1996 elections*: 3–45. Boulder, CO: Westview.

DeSipio, L., & Rocha, G. (1992). Latino influence on national elections: The case of 1988. In R. O. de la Garza, & L. DeSipio (eds.), *From rhetoric to reality: Latinos in the 1988 elections*: 3–22. Boulder, CO: Westview Press.

de Uriarte, M. (1996). *Crossed wires. U.S. newspaper construction of outside "others": The case of Latinos.* Unpublished doctoral dissertation, Yale University

Devlin, L. P. (1973–1974). Contrasts in presidential campaign commercials of 1972. *Journal of Broadcasting*, 18 (1): 17–26.

Devlin, L. P. (1977). Contrasts in presidential campaign commercials of 1976. *Central States Speech Journal*, 28: 238–249.

Devlin, L. P. (1986). An analysis of presidential television commercials, 1952–1984. In L. L. Kaid, D. Nimmo, & K. Sanders (eds.), *New perspectives on political advertising.* Carbondale: Southern Illinois University Press.

Devlin, L. P. (1994). Television advertising in the 1992 New Hampshire presidential primary election. *Political Communication*, 11 (1): 81–99.

Dexter, L. A. (1970). *Elite and specialized interviewing.* Evanston: IL: Northwestern University Press.

Diamond, E., & Bates, S. (1984). *The spot: The rise of political advertising on television.* Cambridge, MA: The MIT Press.

Diamond, E. & Bates, S. (1992). *The spot: The rise of political advertising on television*, (3rd edn). Cambridge, MA: The MIT Press.

DNC (2000) Media Report: Hispanic Satellite Media Tours and DNC 2000 Media Report: Radio QRS Newmedia report.

Downs, A. (1957). *An economic theory of democracy*. New York: Harper.

Durán, D. F. (1977). *The Latino communication project: An investigation into the communication patterns and organizational activities among Mexican, Cuban, and Puerto Rican residents of Chicago*. Unpublished doctoral dissertation, University of Wisconsin, Madison.

Durán, D. F. (1980). *Latino communication patterns: An investigation of media use and organizational activities among Mexican, Cuban, and Puerto Ricans in Chicago*. New York: Arno Press.

Dutton, J. E., & Dukerich, J. M. (1991). Keeping an eye on the mirror: Image and identify in organizational adaptation. *Academy of Management Journal*, 34 (3): 517–554.

Dybing, H. E. (1970). *An analysis of political communication through television*. Produced by the Robert Goodman Agency, Inc. Doctoral dissertation, Southern Illinois University.

Edmonds, K., Russell S., Edmonds, T., & Lewis, J. *Wake up everybody*. (CD-ROM), Wake up Productions, 2004.

Elsbach, K. D. (1998). The process of social identification: With what do we identify? In D. A. Whetten., & P. C. Godfrey (eds.), *Identity in organizations: Building theory through conversations*: 232–237. Thousand Oaks, CA: Sage.

Entman, R.M. (1992). Blacks in the news: Television, modern racism and cultural change. *Journalism Quarterly* 69 (2): 341–362.

Espino, R. (2003). Electoral influences on Latino representation in Congress. Paper presented at the annual convention of the Midwest Political Science Association convention, Chicago, IL.

Esser, F., & d'Angelo, P. (2003). Framing the press and the publicity process: A content analysis of meta-coverage in campaign 2000 network news. *American Behavioral Scientist*, 46: 617–641.

Estrada, L. F. (1997). The 1996 elections Latinos breakthrough. *Latino Journal*, 2, (1): 12–13, 18–19.

Farnsworth S. J., & Lichter S. R. (2003). *The nightly news nightmare: Network television's coverage of the U.S. presidential elections 1988–2000*. New York: Rowan and Littlefield.

Federal Communications Commission (2003). Report and order: In the matter of 2002 biennial regulatory review of the Commission's Broadcast Ownership Rules and other rules adopted pursuant to section 2002 of the Telecommunications Act of 1996, cross ownership of broadcast stations and newspapers, rules and policies concerning multiple ownership of radio broadcast stations in local markets, definition of radio markets, MB Docket No 02-277, MM Dockets 02-235, 01-317, 00244, July 2, 2003, para. 420.

Federal Communications Commission (2006). Review of the Commission's Broadcast Ownership Rules and other rules adopted pursuant to Section 202 of the Telecommunications Act of 1996, 18 F.C.C.R. 13620 (July 2, 2003), *affirmed in part*, 373 F.3d 372 (3d Cir. 2004), *remanded to* 21 F.C.C.R. 8834 (July 24, 2006).

Ferrante, J., & Prince, B., Jr. (2000). *The social construction of race and ethnicity in the United States*, (2nd edn). New York: Longman.

Figueroa, R. A., & Sonia H. (2000). *President's advisory commission on education excellence for Hispanic Americans*. Washington D.C.: Department of Education.

Fischer, W. C., Gerber, D. A., Guitart, J. M., & Seller, M., S. (eds.) (1997). *Identity, community, and pluralism in American life*. New York: Oxford University Press.

Fishman, J. (1966). Language loyalty in the United States. In J. Fishman, R. G. Hayden, & M. E. Warshauer (eds.), *The non-English and the ethnic group press, 1910–1960*: 51–74. London: Mouton & Co.

Fishman, J., & Casiano, H. (1969). Puerto Ricans in our press. *Modern Language Journal*, 53 (3): 157–162.

Fishman, J., Gertner, M., Lowy, E., & Milan, W. (eds.) (1985). *Ethnicity in action*. Binghamton, NY: Bilingual Press/Editorial Bilingüe.

Fitzgerald, M. (2004). Lozanos, CPK media form Latino newspaper chain. http://www.editorandpublisher.com/eandp/news/article_display.jsp?vnu_content_id=2070845.

Fitzpatrick, J. (1987). The Puerto Rican press. In S. M. Miller (ed.), *The ethnic press in the United States. A historical analysis and handbook*: 303–314. New York: Greenwood Press.

Flores, H. (2004) *The 2004 WCVI National Latino Election Day exit poll*. San Antonio, TX: William C. Velasquez Institute.

Fowler, E. F., Goldstein, K., Hale, M & Kaplan, M. (2007) Does local news measure up? *Stanford Law and Policy Review*, 18: 377.

Fox, G. (1996). *Hispanic nation. Culture, politics, and the constructing of identity*. Secaucus, NJ: Carol Publishing Group.

Fregoso, R. (1993). *The bronze screen: Chicana and Chicano film culture*. Minneapolis: University of Minnesota Press

Frymer, P. (1999). *Uneasy alliances: Race and party competition in America*. Princeton, NJ: Princeton University Press.

Gandy, O. H., Jr. (1998). *Communication and race. A structural perspective*. New York: Oxford.

Gandy, O. H., Jr., & Matabane, P. W. (1989). Television and social perceptions among African Americans and Hispanics. In M. K. Asante., & W. B. Gudykunst (eds.), *Handbook of international and intercultural communication*. Newbury Park, CA: Sage.

Gans, H. (1979). *Deciding what's news*. NY: Pantheon.

García, F. C. (ed.) (1974). *Latinos and the political system*. Notre Dame, IN: University of Notre Dame Press.

García, F. C. (ed.) (1988). *La causa política. A Chicano politics reader*. Notre Dame, IN: University of Notre Dame Press.

García, F. C. (ed.) (1997). *Pursuing power: Latinos and the political system*. Notre Dame, IN: University of Notre Dame Press.

García, F. C., de la Garza, R. O., & Torres, D. J. (1985). Introduction to part III. Political participation, organizational development, and institutional responsiveness. In R. O. de la Garza, C. M. Bean., B. R. Romo., & R. Álvarez (eds.), *The Mexican American experience. An interdisciplinary anthology*: 185–200. Austin: University of Texas Press.

García, F. C., García, J. A., de la Garza, R. O., Falcón, A., & Abeyta, C. J. (1991). *Latinos and politics. A selected research bibliography.* Austin, TX: Center for Mexican American Studies.

García, F. C., García, J. A., Falcón, A., & de la Garza, R. O. (1989). Studying Latino politics: The development of the Latino political survey. *PS: Political Science and Politics, 22* (4): 848–852.

García, F. C., Falcón, A., & de la Garza, R. O. (eds.) (1996). Ethnicity and politics: Evidence from the Latino National Political Survey. [Special issue]. *Hispanic Journal of Behavioral Sciences, 18* (2): 91–103

García, J. A. (2005). *Latino politics in America: community, culture, and interests.* New York: Rowman & Littlefield.

García Bedolla, L. (2005). *Fluid borders: Latino power, identity, and politics in Los Angeles.* Berkeley: University of California Press.

García Berumen, F. J. (2003). *Brown celluloid: Latino/a film icons and images in the Hollywood film industry.* New York: Vantage.

Garramone, G. M. (1984). Voter responses to negative political ads. *Journalism Quarterly, 61* (2): 250–259.

Garramone, G. M., Atkin, C. K., Pinkleton, B. E., & Cole, R. T. (1990). Effects of negative political advertising on the political process. *Journal of Broadcasting & Electronic Media, 34* (3): 299–311.

Gerbasi, K. (2000a, September 25). (Television broadcast transcript.) New York, NY: NBC *The Today Show.*

Gerbasi, K. (2000b, October 25). (Television broadcast transcript.) New York, NY: NBC *The Today Show.*

Gerbasi, K. (2000c, October 26). (Television broadcast transcript). New York, NY: NBC *The Today Show.*

Gerbasi, K. (2000d, November 4). (Television broadcast transcript.) New York, NY: NBC *The Today Show.*

Geron, K. (2005). *Latino political power.* Boulder, CO: Lynne Rienner Publishers, Inc.

Gershon, B. (2000a, September 4). (Television broadcast transcript.) New York, NY: ABC *World News Tonight.*

Gershon, B. (2000b, September 7). (Television broadcast transcript.) New York, NY: ABC *World News Tonight.*

Gershon, B. (2000c, October 11). (Television broadcast transcript.) New York, NY: ABC *Nightline.*

Gershon, B. (2000d, October 16). (Television broadcast transcript.) New York, NY: ABC *World News Tonight.*

Gershon, B. (2000e, October 17). (Television broadcast transcript.) New York, NY: ABC *World News Tonight.*

Ghanem, S. I., & Wanta, W. (2001). Agenda-setting and Spanish cable news. *Journal of Broadcasting & Electronic Media, 45*(2): 277–289.

Gilliam, F.D., & Iyengar, S. (2000). Prime suspects: The influence of local television news on the viewing public. *American Journal of Political Science, 44:* 560–73.

Gioia, D. A., Schultz, M., & Corley, K. G. (2000). Organizational identity, image, and adaptive instability. *Academy of Management Review, 25:* 63–81.

Gitlin, T. (ed.) (1986). *Watching television.* New York, NY: Pantheon Books.

Glaberson, W. (1995, March 3). Investor group to provide for expansion of *El Diario*. *The New York Times*: C2.

Glanton, D. (2000, November 26). Hispanics turn Florida into more of a swing state. *Chicago Tribune*: 17.

Glaser, B., & Strauss, A. (1967). *The discovery of grounded theory*. Chicago: Aldine.

Goffman, E. (1959). *The presentation of self in everyday life*. Garden City, NY: Doubleday Anchor.

Goldberg, C. (1997). Hispanic households struggle as poorest of the poor in US. *New York Times*, January 30, 1997: A1.

Goldstein, K., & Freedman, P. (2002). Campaign advertising and voter turnout: New evidence for a stimulation effect. *The Journal of Politics*, 64: 721–740.

Gómez-Quiñones, J. (1990). *Chicano politics. Reality and promise, 1940–1990*. Albuquerque: University of New Mexico Press.

Gonzáles, J. (1977). Forgotten pages: Spanish-language newspapers in the southwest. *Journalism History*, 4, (2): 50–51.

Gordon, M. (1964). *Assimilation in American life*. New York: Oxford University Press.

Graber, D. A. (1984). Media magic: Fashioning characters for the 1983 mayoral race. In M.G. Holli., & P.M. Green (eds.), *The Making of the mayor: Chicago 1983*. Grand Rapids: William B. Eerdmans Publishing.

Graber, D. A. (1989). *Mass media and American politics*. Washington DC: Congressional Quarterly Press.

Graber, D. A. (1993). *Mass media and American politics* (4th edn). Washington, DC: Congressional Quarterly Press.

Graber, D. A. (ed.) (1994). *Media power in politics* (3rd edn). Washington, DC: Congressional Quarterly Press.

Graber, D. (2000). *Mass media and American politics* (6th edn). Washington, DC: Congressional Quarterly Press.

Graber, D.A. (2001). *Processing politics: Learning from television in the Internet Age*. Chicago: University of Chicago Press.

Graber, D. (2005). *Mass media and American politics* (7th edn). Washington, DC: Congressional Quarterly Press.

Graber, D., McQuail, D., & Norris, P. (1998). *The politics of news: The news of politics*. Washington, DC: Congressional Quarterly Press.

Greenberg, B. S., & Brand, J. E. (1994). Minorities and the mass media: 1970s to 1990s. In J. Bryant, & D. Zillman (eds.), *Media effects*: 273–314. Hillsdale, NJ: Lawrence Earlbaum Associates, Inc.

Greenberg, B. S., Burgoon, M., Burgoon, J. K. & Korzenny, F. (1983a). *Mexican Americans and the mass media*. Norwood, NJ: Ablex.

Greenberg, B. S., Heeter, C., Burgoon, J. K., Burgoon, M., & Korzenny, F. (1983b). Local newspaper coverage of Mexican Americans. *Journalism Quarterly*, 60 (4): 671.

Griswold del Castillo, R. (1977). The Mexican revolution and the Spanish-language press in the borderlands. *Journalism History*, 4 (2): 42–47.

Guadalupe, P. (1998). Election results highlight Hispanic clout. *Hispanic Business*, December 1998: 28.

Gudykunst, W. B. (1994). *Bridging differences: Effective intergroup communication* (2nd edn). Thousand Oaks, CA: Sage.

Gudykunst, W. B., Ting-Toomey, S., & Chua, E. (1988). *Culture and interpersonal communication*. Newbury Park, CA: Sage.

Guernica, A. (1982). *Reaching the Hispanic market effectively*. New York: McGraw Hill.

Guerra, F. J. (1992). Conditions not met: California elections and the Latino community. In R. O. de la Garza., & L, DeSipio (eds.), *From rhetoric and reality: Latinos politics in the 1988 elections*. Boulder, CO: Westview Press.

Gutiérrez, F. F. (1977). Spanish-language media in America: Background, resources, history. *Journalism History*, 4 (2): 34–41, 65–68.

Gutiérrez, F. F. (1978). Reporting for La Raza: The history of Latino journalism in America. *Agenda*, 8, July–August 1978: 29–35.

Gutiérrez, F. F. (1983). Latinos and the media. In M. Emery., & T. C. Smythe (eds.), *Readings in mass communications*: 163–176. Dubuque, Iowa: William C. Brown Company.

Gutiérrez, F. F., & Ballesteros, E. (1979). The 1541 earthquake: Dawn of Latin American journalism. *Journalism History*, 6 (3): 79–83.

Gutiérrez, F. F., & Schement, J. R. (1979). *Spanish-language radio in the southwestern United States*. The University of Texas at Austin, Center for Mexican American Studies.

Gutiérrez, F. F., & Schement, J. R. (1981). Problems of ownership and control of Spanish-language media in the United States: National and international policy concerns. In E. McAnany, J. Schnitman, & N. Janus (eds.), *Communication and social structure: Critical studies in mass media research*: 181–203. New York: Praeger.

Guzmán, R. C. (1976). *The political socialization of the Mexican American people*. New York: Arno Press.

Hale, M., Fowler, E. F., Goldstein, K. (2007). Capturing multiple markets: A new method of analyzing local television news. *Electronic News*, November 2007.

Hallin, D. C. (1992). Sound bite news: Television coverage of elections, 1968–1988. *Journal of Communication*, 42 (2): 5–24.

Hansen, G. J., & Benoit, W. L. (2002). Presidential television advertising and public policy priorities, 1952–2000. *Communication Studies*, 53: 284–296.

Hart, R. (1999). *Seducing America: How television charms the modern voter*. Thousand Oaks: Sage Publications.

Hart, R. (2000). *Campaign talk: Why elections are good for us*. Princeton, NJ: Princeton University Press.

Hart, R. (2005). *Political keywords: Using language that uses us*. New York: Oxford University Press.

Heider, D. (2000). *White news: Why local news programs don't cover people of color*. Mahwah, NJ: L. Erlbaum Associates.

Heilemann, J. (1996). Republicans fumbled the Macarena. *Austin American Statesman*, November 27, 1996: A15.

Hellerstein, J. K. (2005). *Workplace segregation in the United States: Race, ethnicity, and skill*. Cambridge, MA: National Bureau of Economic Research.

Herman, E., & Chomsky, N. (2002). *Manufacturing consent: The political economy of mass media*. NY: Pantheon.

Hernández, A. (2001). The Latino vote in 2000, 2002 and 2004. An in-depth examination of the character of the 2000 Latino vote and an analysis of Latino electoral impact and influence in the 2002 senatorial and gubernatorial elections and the 2004 presidential election. Prepared by United States Hispanic Leadership Institute Research Department. Washington, DC.

Hero, R. E. (1987). The election of Hispanics in city government: An examination of the election of Federico Pena as mayor of Denver. *Western Political Quarterly*, 40: 93–105.

Hero, R. E. (1992). *Latinos and the U.S. political system. Two-tiered pluralism*. Philadelphia, PA: Temple University Press.

Hero, R. E., & Campbell, A. G. (1996). Understanding Latino political participation: Exploring the evidence from the Latino national political survey. *Hispanic Journal of Behavioral Sciences*, 18 (2): 129–141.

Hero, R. E., & Tolbert, C. J. (1997). Latinos and substantive representation in the U.S. House of Representatives: Direct, indirect, or nonexistent? In F. C. García (ed.), *Pursuing power Latinos and the political system*: 265–278. Notre Dame, IN: University of Notre Dame Press.

Hester, A. (1979). Newspapers and newspaper prototypes in Spanish America, 1541–1750. *Journalism History*, 6 (3): 73–78.

Hewitt, J. (2000a, September 10). (Television broadcast transcript.) New York, NY: CBS *60-Minutes*.

Hewitt, J. (2000b, October 29). (Television broadcast transcript.) New York, NY: CBS *60-Minutes*.

*Hispanic Almanac, The* (1986). Hispanic policy development project. Washington, DC.

*Hispanic Journal of Behavioral Sciences* (1996). Special edition on Latinos and politics. 18 (2).

*Hispanic Business*. (1998). A robust economy bolsters purchasing power. *Hispanic Business*, December 1998: 60.

Hofstetter, R. (1976). *Bias in the news*. Columbus, OH: Ohio State University Press.

Hofstetter, R. (1978). News bias in the 1972 campaign: A cross-media analysis. *Journalism Monographs*, 58.

Hofstetter, R. (1981). Content analysis. In D. Nimmo, & K. Sanders (eds.), *Handbook of political communication*: 529–560. Beverly Hills, CA: Sage.

Hofstetter, R., & Judge, M. J. (1974). *Content analysis of taped television stories: Coding Manual*. Making paper number 2 in the television election news coverage project. Polimetrics Laboratory Report No. 12, The Ohio State University.

Hofstetter, R., & Zukin, C. (1979). TV network news and advertising in the Nixon and McGovern campaigns. *Journalism Quarterly*, 56 (1): 106–152.

Holtz-Bacha, C., Kaid, L., & Johnston, A. (1994). Political television advertising in Western democracies: A comparison of campaign broadcast in the United States, Germany, and France. *Political Communication*, 11 (1): 67–80.

Hosti, O. R. (1969). *Content analysis for the social sciences and humanities*. Reading, MA: Addison-Wesley.

Iyengar, S. (1991). *Is anyone responsible? How television frames political issues*. Chicago, IL: University of Chicago Press.

Iyengar, S., & Kinder, D. (1987). *News that matters: Television and American opinion.* Chicago: University of Chicago Press.

Jackman, R. W. (1987). Political institutions and voter turnout in the industrial democracies. *American Political Science Review,* 81: 405–483.

Jackson, B. O., & Preston, M. B. (eds.) (1991). *Racial and ethnic politics in California.* Berkeley, CA: Institute of Governmental Studies.

Jamieson, K. H. (1992a). *Dirty politics: Deception, distraction, and democracy.* New York: Oxford University Press.

Jamieson, K. H. (1992b). *The interplay of influence: News, advertising, politics, and the mass media* (3rd edn). Belmont, CA: Wadsworth.

Jamieson, K. H. (1996). Scholarship and the discourse of election campaigns. *The Chronicle of Higher Education,* November 22, 1996: B4.

Jamieson, K. H. (2000). *Everything you think you know about politics—and why you're wrong.* New York: Basic Books.

Jamieson, K. H., & Campbell, K. K. (1997). *The interplay of influence: News, advertising, politics, and the mass media.* Belmont, CA: Wadsworth.

Jamieson, K. H., & Waldman, P. (2003). *The press effect: Politicians, journalists, and the stories that shape the political world.* NY: Oxford.

Jamieson, K. H., Waldman, P., & Sherr, S. (2000). Eliminate the negative? Categories of analysis for political advertisements. In J. A. Thurber, C. J. Nelson, & D. A. Dulio (eds.), *Crowded airwaves: Campaign advertising in elections:* 44–64. Washington, D.C: Brookings Institute.

Jarboe, J. (1980). The special case of Spanish-language television. *Washington Journalism Review,* 2 (8): 21–25.

Jeffres, L. (1999). The impact of ethnicity and ethnic media on presidential voting patterns. *Journalism & Communication Monographs,* 1: 197–262.

Jeffres, L. (2000). Ethnicity and ethnic media use. A panel study. *Communication Research,* 27 (4): 496–535.

Jennings, J., & Rivera, M. (1984). *Puerto Rican politics in urban America.* Westport, CT: Greenwood Press.

Joge, C. T. (2000). *The Latino vote in the '90s.* Washington, DC: National Council of La Raza.

Johnston, A., & Kaid, L. L. (2002). Image ads and issue ads in U.S. presidential advertising: Using videostyle to explore stylistic differences in televised political ads from 1952 to 2000. *Journal of Communication,* 52: 281–301.

Jones, S. (2000a, September 25). (Television broadcast transcript.) New York, NY: ABC Good Morning America.

Jones, S. (2000b, September 26). (Television broadcast transcript.) New York, NY: ABC Good Morning America.

Jones, S. (2000c, September 29). (Television broadcast transcript.) New York, NY: ABC Good Morning America.

Joslyn, R. A. (1980). The content of political spot ad. *Journalism Quarterly,* 57 (1): 92–98.

Joslyn, R. A. (1984). *Mass media and elections.* Menlo Park, CA: Addison-Wesley Publishing.

Joslyn, R. A. (1986). Political advertising and the meaning of elections. In L.L. Kaid, D. Nimmo., & K.R. Sanders (eds.), *New perspectives on political advertising.* Carbondale, IL: Southern Illinois University Press.

Just, M. R., Crigler, A. N., Alger, D. E., Cook, T., Kern, M., & West, D. (1996). *Crosstalk: Citizens, candidates, and the media in a presidential campaign.* Chicago: University of Chicago Press.

Just, M. R., Crigler, A. N. & Buhr, T. (1999). Voice, substance, and cynicism in presidential campaign media. *Political Communication* 16 (1): 25–44.

Just, M., Crigler, A., & Wallach, L. (1990). Thirty seconds or thirty minutes: What viewers learn from spot advertisements and candidate debates. *Journal of Communication,* 40: 120–132.

Kahlenberg, R. D. (1996, October 7). Goaline. *The New Republic,* 27.

Kahn, K.F., & Kenney, P. (1999). Do negative campaigns mobilize or suppress turnout? Clarifying the relationship between negativity and participation. *American Political Science Review* 93: 877–90.

Kaid, L. L. (1981). Political advertising. In D. Nimmo., & K. Sanders (eds.), *The Handbook of Political Communication*: 249–271. Beverly Hills, CA: Sage Publications, Inc.

Kaid, L. L. (1982). Paid television advertising and candidate name identification. *Campaigns and Elections,* Spring 1982: 34–37.

Kaid, L. L. (2004). Political advertising. In L. L. Kaid (ed.), *Handbook of political communication research*: 155–202. Mahwah, NJ: Lawrence Erlbaum Associates.

Kaid, L. L. (ed.) (2004). *Handbook of political communication research.* Mahwah, NJ: Lawrence Erlbaum Associates.

Kaid, L. L., & Davidson, D. K. (1986). Elements of videostyle: Candidate presentation through television advertising. In L. L. Kaid, D. Nimmo,, & K. Sanders (eds.), *New perspectives on political advertising.* Carbondale: Southern Illinois University Press.

Kaid, L. L., & Johnston, A. (2000). *Videostyle in presidential campaigns: Style and content of televised political advertising.* Westport, CT: Praeger.

Kaid, L. L., Nimmo, D., & Sanders, K. R. (eds.) (1986). *New perspectives on political advertising.* Carbondale: Southern Illinois University Press.

Kaid, L. L., & Sanders, K. R. (1978). Political television commercials: An experimental study of type and length. *Communication Research,* 5 (1): 57–70.

Kanellos, N. (1994). A socio-historic study of Hispanic newspapers in the United States. In F. Padilla (ed.), *Handbook of Hispanic cultures in the United States: Sociology*: 239–256. Houston, TX: Arte Público Press.

Kaplan, M., Goldstein, K., & Hale, M. (2005). *Spanish-language TV coverage of the 2004 campaigns.* Los Angeles: The Lear Center Local News Archive.

Kassarjian, H. H. (1977). Content analysis in consumer research. *Journal of Consumer Research,* 4: 8–18.

Keever, B.A.D, Martindale, C. and M. A. Weston (eds.) (1997). *U.S. News coverage of racial minorities: A sourcebook, 1934–1996.* Westport, CN, Greenwood Press.

Keller, G. D. (1985). *Chicano cinema: Research, reviews, and resources.* Binghamton, NY: Bilingual Review/Press.

Keller, G. D. (1997). *A biographical handbook of Hispanics and United States film.* Tucson, AZ: Bilingual Press.

Keller, G. D., & van Hooft, K. S. (1982). A chronology of bilingualism and bilingual education. In J. A. Fishman., & G. D. Keller (eds.), *Bilingual education for Hispanic students in the United States.* New York: Teachers College Press.

Kelly, T. (2003). *El Diario* is sold to Los Angeles equity firm. *New York Times* online, July 4, 2003. http://www.nytimes.com/2003/07/04/nyregion/04PAPE.html.

Kennamer, D. (1987). How media use during campaign affects the intent to vote. *Journalism Quarterly*, 64 (2): 291–300.

Kenski, K., & Tisinger, R. (2006). Hispanic voters in the 2000 and 2004 presidential general elections. *Presidential Studies Quarterly*, 36: 189–202.

Kern, M. (1989). *30 second politics: Political advertising in the eighties*. New York: Praeger.

Kiefer, F. (2001, May 14). Bush plans 2004 wedding with Hispanics. *Christian Science Monitor*: 3.

Kim, Y. Y. (1986). Understanding the social context of intergroup communication: A personal network approach. In W. B. Gudykunst (ed.), *Integroup communication*: 86–95. London: Edward Arnold Publishers.

Kim, Y. Y. (1988). *Communication and cross-cultural adaptation*. Philadelphia, PA: Multilingual Matters.

Kim, Y. Y. (2001). *Becoming intercultural: An integrative theory of communication and cross-cultural adaptation*. Thousand Oaks, CA: Sage.

King, E. G. (1990). Thematic coverage of the 1988 presidential primaries: A comparison of *USA Today* and the *New York Times*. *Journalism Quarterly*, 67: 83–87.

Knaggs, J. (1986). *Two party Texas*. Austin, TX: Eakin Press.

Korzenny, F., & Korzenny, B. A. (2005). *Hispanic marketing: A cultural perspective*. Miami, Fl: Elsevier Butterworth Heinemann.

Kotler, P. (1986). *Principles of marketing* (3rd edn). Englewood Cliffs, NJ: Prentice-Hall.

Kraeplin, C. & Subervi-Vélez, F.A. (2003). Latinos in the mainstream media: A case study of coverage in a major Southwestern daily. In D. Ríos & A. Mohamed (eds.), *Brown and Black communication: Latino and African conflict and convergence in mass media*: 105–122. Westport, CT: Greenwood.

Krosnick, J. A., & Brannon, L.A. (1993). The impact of the Gulf War on the ingredients of presidential evaluations: Multidimensional effects of political involvement. *American Political Science Review*, 87 (4): 963–975.

Latimer, M. K. (1983). The newspaper: How significant for Black voters in presidential elections? *Journalism Quarterly*, 60 (1): 16–47.

Latimer, M. K. (1984). Policy issues and personal images in political advertising in a state election. *Journalism Quarterly*, 61 (4): 776–784, 852.

Latimer, M. K. (1985). Political advertising for federal and state elections: Image or substance? *Journalism Quarterly*, 62 (4): 861–868.

Leal, D. L., Barreto, M. A., Lee, J., & de la Garza, R. O. (2005). The Latino vote in the 2004 election. *PS: Political Science and Politics*, 38: 41–49.

Leeds, J. (2004). Clear channel is expanding in Spanish radio. *The New York Times*, September 17, 2004: Business section.

Leighley, J. E. (2001). *Strength in numbers?: The political mobilization of racial and ethnic minorities*. Princeton: Princeton University Press.

Len-Rios, M. (2002). The Bush and Gore presidential campaign web sites: Identifying with Hispanic voters during the 2000 Iowa caucuses and New Hampshire primary. *Journalism & Mass Communication Quarterly*, 79 (4): 887–904.

Lewels, F. J. (1974). *The uses of the media by the Chicano movement: A study in minority access*. New York: Praeger.

Lewin, T. (1992). Study points to increase in tolerance of ethnicity. *New York Times*, January 8, 1992: A10.

Lewis, G. K. (1974). *Notes on the Puerto Rican revolution*. New York: Monthly Review Press.

*Library Microfilms, 40th anniversary issue: Materials on microfilm, historical collections* (no date). Sunnyvale, CA.

Lopes, T. (1995). Numbers but little clout. *Austin American Statesman*, April 16, 1995: D1, D5.

Lopez, R. W., & Enos, D. D. (1974). Spanish-language-only television in Los Angeles County. *Aztlan*, 4 (2): 283–313.

López-Escobar, E., Llamas, J. P., McCombs, M. E., & Rey Lennon, F. (1998). Two levels of agenda setting among advertising and news in the 1995 Spanish elections. *Political Communication*, 15: 225–238.

López-Godoy, R. M. (1991). Image versus issues: The appeals used to reach Hispanic voters in Texas—a content analysis of the 1982 and 1986 gubernatorial campaigns. Unpublished master's thesis, University of Texas at Austin.

Lozano, J. C. (1988). Issues and sources in Spanish-language television: A comparison of *Noticiero Univisión* and NBC evening news. *Frontera Norte*, 1: 151–174.

Lozano, J. C. (1988). Hispanic candidates and issues in the Texas press: the case of the Express-News and the San Antonio Light. Unpublished paper, Austin, TX.

Lyons, J. J. (1990). The past and future directions of federal bilingual-education policy. *Annals of the American Academy of Public Policy*, 508: 66–80.

MacCurdy, R. (1951). *A history and bibliography of Spanish language newspapers and magazines in Louisiana, 1808–1949*. Albuquerque: University of New Mexico Press.

Marbut, R. Jr. (2005). ¿Un nuevo día? Republican outreach to the Latino community in the 2000 campaign. In R. de la Garza & L. DeSipio (eds.), *Muted voices: Latinos and the 2000 elections*: 61–83. New York: Rowman & Littlefield.

Marshall, C., & Rossman, G. B. (1995). *Designing qualitative research*. Thousand Oaks, CA: Sage.

Martindale, C. (1986). *The White press and Black America*. NY: Greenwood.

Martínez, M. (1984). Hispanic Victory Initiative '84. A proposed strategy for the Reagan–Bush '84 Hispanic campaign. (Unpublished. Personal files of Subervi-Vélez.)

Mayer, V. (2003). *Producing dreams, consuming youth: Mexican Americans and mass media*. New Brunswick, NJ: Rutgers.

McCardell, W. S. (1976). *Socialization factors in El Diario-La Prensa, the Spanish-language newspaper with the largest daily circulation in the United States*. Unpublished doctoral dissertation, The University of Iowa.

McCombs, M. E. (1968). Negro use of television and newspapers for political information, 1952–1964. *Journal of Broadcasting*, 12: 261–266.

McCombs, M. E. (2004). *Setting the agenda: The mass media and public opinion*. Cambridge, UK: Polity Press.

McCombs, M. E., & Shaw, D. R. (1972). The agenda-setting function of the mass media. *Public Opinion Quarterly*, 36: 176–187.

McCracken, G. (1988). *The long interview*. Sage University paper series on qualitative research methods, 13. Beverly Hills, CA: Sage.

McKinnon, L., Kaid, L., Murphy, J., & Acree, C. (1996). Policing political ads: An analysis of five leading newspapers' responses to the 1992 political advertisements. *Journalism Quarterly*, 73 (1): 66–76.

McLeod, J., Kosicki, G., & McLeod, D. (1994). The expanding boundaries of political communication effects. In J. Bryand, & D. Zillman (eds.), *Media effects. Advanced in theory and research*: 123–162. Hillsdale, NJ: Lawrence Erlbaum Associates, Inc.

McLeod, J., Kosicki, G., & Rucinski, D. M. (1988). Political communication research: An assessment of the field. *Mass Comunication Review*, 15 (1): 8–15.

McLeod, J., & Reeves, B. (1981). On the nature of mass media effects. In G. C. Wilhoit, & H. deBock (eds.), *Mass communication review yearbook 2*: 245–282. Beverly Hills, CA: Sage.

McQuail, D. (1987). *Mass Communication theory* (2nd edn). Newbury Park, CA: Sage.

Medeiros, F. (1980). *La Opinión*, a Mexican exile newspaper: A content analysis of its first years, 1926–1929. *Agenda*, 11: 65–87.

Mendosa, R. (1991). Blaya beams it Up: Exclusive interview. *Hispanic Business*, October 1991: 16–22.

Mendosa, R. (1992). Telemundo wired for TV wars. *Hispanic Business*, December 1992: 38–52.

Merritt, S. (1984). Negative political advertising: Some empirical findings. *Journal of Advertising*, 13 (3).

Meyer, A. (1982). Adapting to environmental jolts. *Administrative Science Quarterly*, 27: 515–583.

Miles, R. H., & Cameron, K. (1982). *Coffin nails and corporate strategies*. Englewood Cliffs, NJ: Prentice Hall.

Miller, R. E., & Wanta, W. (1996). Race as a variable in agenda setting. *Journalism & Mass Communication Quarterly*, 73 (4): 913–925.

Mitchell, R. K., Agel, B. R., & Wood, D. J. (1997). Toward a theory of stakeholder identification and salience: Defining the principle of who and what really counts. *Academy of Management Review*, 22: 853–886.

Miyares, M. (1978). *Models of political participation of Hispanic-Americans*. Unpublished doctoral dissertation, Northwestern University, Evanston, Illinois.

Montejano, D. (1999). *Chicano politics and society in the late twentieth century*. Austin: University of Texas Press.

Moore, J., & Pachon, H. (1985). *Hispanics in the United States*. Englewood Cliffs, NJ: Prentice-Hall.

Mueller, C. (1973). *The politics of communication*. New York: Oxford University Press.

Mulder, R. (1979). The effects of television political ads in the 1975 Chicago mayoral election. *Journalism Quarterly*, 56 (2): 336–340.

Murphy, J. (2000a, September 23). (Television broadcast transcript.) New York, NY: CBS *Evening News*.

Murphy, J. (2000b, September 25). (Television broadcast transcript.) New York, NY: CBS *Evening News*.

Murphy, J. (2000c, October 29). (Television broadcast transcript.) New York, NY: CBS *Evening News*.

Murphy, J. & Murphy, S. (1981). *Let my people know. American Indian Journalism.* Norman: University of Oklahoma Press.

Nader for President 2004 (2004, June 21). Press release: *Nader selects Peter Miguel Camejo as vice-presidential running mate.* Washington, D.C. (www.votenader.org/media_press/index.php?cid=80).

National Council of La Raza. (2000). *The Latino agenda: issues at stake in the 2000 presidential election.* Washington DC: National Council of La Raza.

National Council of La Raza. (2004). *How did Latinos really vote in 2004?* Washington, DC: National Council of La Raza.

NALEO (1989). *The national Latino immigrant survey.* Washington DC: Author.

NALEO (2004). Press Release. *Latinos win big on election night.* November 2, 2004. Los Angeles, CA.

NALEO (2006). Press Release. *Latinos achieve new political milestones in Congress and State Houses. Latinos in states with emerging communities are writing the next chapter of Latino political history.* November 11, 2006. Los Angeles, CA.

Navarro, M. (2006). Between gags, a D.J. rallies immigrants. *New York Times*, April 30, 2006: section 9, p. 12.

Navarro, S. A., & Mejía, A. X. (eds.) (2004). *Latino Americans and political participation: A reference handbook.* Santa Barbara, CA: ABC–CLIO.

National Association of Hispanic Publications (2004). The National Association of Hispanic Publications media kit & resource book. Carlsbad, CA: WPR Publishing.

Neighbor, H. D., & Villarreal, R. E. (1991). The role of media in Latino empowerment. In R. E. Villarreal, & N. G. Hernández (eds.), *Latinos and political coalitions: Political empowerment for the 1990s*: 19–31). New York: Greenwood.

Nelson, D. (1984). *Hispanic political behavior: A comparison of Chicanos, Cubans, and Puerto Ricans.* Unpublished paper, Department of Political Science, Fordham University, New York City.

Nevaer, L. E. V. (2004). *The rise of the Hispanic market in the United States: Challenges, dilemmas, and opportunities for corporate management.* Armonk, NY: M.E. Sharpe.

Newman, B., & Perloff, R (2004). Political marketing: Theory, research, and applications. In L. L. Kaid (ed.), *Handbook of political communication research*: 17–43. Mahwah, New Jersey: Lawrence Erlbaum Associates, Publishers.

Nicolini, P. (1986). Philadelphia Puerto Rican community leaders' perceptions of Spanish-language media. *Mass Comm Review*, 13 (1): 11–17.

Nielson Media Research (n.d.). *Hispanic Audience Samples.* Retrieved on March 6, 2006, from http://www.nielsenmedia.com/nc/portal/site/Public/menuitem.9ce6d8547da552da212845c647a062a0/?vgnextoid=76e6665fe2906010Vgn VCM100000880a260aRCRD.

Nimmo, D., & Sanders, K. R. (eds.). (1981). Political advertising. The handbook of political communication. Beverly Hills, CA: Sage Publication.

Noriega, C. (ed.) (1992). *Chicanos and film: Representation and resistance.* Minneapolis: University of Minnesota Press.

Noriega, C. (2000a). *Shot in America: Television, the state, and the rise of Chicano cinema.* Minneapolis: University of Minnesota Press.

Noriega, C. (ed.) (2000b). *The future of Latino independent Media: A NALIP sourcebook*. Los Angeles: UCLA Chicano Studies Research Center Publications.

Noriega, C., & Lopez, A. (eds.) (1996). *The ethnic eye: Latino media arts*. Minneapolis: University of Minnesota Press.

Notingham, W. (2005). Q&A: Campaign donations: Lists of political contributions can reveal much about candidates. *Los Angeles Times*, November 4, 2005.

Nuiry, O. E. (1996). Ban the bandito: Madison Avenue takes more sophisticated approach to Latino stereotypes. *Hispanic Magazine*, July 1996: 26–32.

Oberfield, Z. W. (2003). Tenemos mucho en común: American party appeals to Hispanics. Unpublished seminar paper.

Oczon, A. M. (1979). Bilingual and Spanish-language newspapers in territorial New Mexico. *New Mexico Historical Review*, 44: 45–52.

O'Keefe, M. T., & Sheinkopf, K. P. (1974). The voter decides: Candidate image or campaign issue? *Journal of Broadcasting*, 18: 403–412.

Orozco, G. (2005). *Los medios de comunicación en español en Estados Unidos*. Mexico, DF: Fundación Solidaridad Mexicano-Americana.

Padilla, F. M. (1985). *Latino ethnic consciousness: The case of Mexican Americans and Puerto Ricans in Chicago*. Notre Dame, IN: University of Notre Dame Press.

Padilla, F. M. (1994a). On Hispanic identity. In F. Padilla (ed.), *Handbook of Hispanic cultures in the United States: Sociology*: 292–302. Houston, TX: Arte Público Press.

Padilla, F. (ed.) (1994b). *Handbook of Hispanic cultures in the United States: Sociology*. Houston, TX: Arte Público Press.

Parenti, M. (1986). *Inventing reality. The politics of the mass media*. New York: St. Martin's Press.

Parenti, M. (1988). *Democracy for the few* (5th edn). New York: St. Martin's Press.

Park, R. E. (1950). *Race and culture: Essays in the sociology of contemporary man*. New York: Free Press.

Parrillo, V. N. (1996). *Diversity in America*. Thousand Oaks, CA: Pine Forge Press.

Patterson, T. E. (1980). *The mass media election*. New York: Praeger.

Patterson, T. E. (1994). *Out of order*. New York: Vintage.

Patterson, T. E., & McClure, R. D. (1973). *Political advertising: Voter reaction to televised political commercials*. Princeton, N.J.: Citizens' Research Foundation.

Patterson, T. E., & McClure, R. D. (1976). *The unseeing eye: The myth of television power in national politics*. New York: G. P. Putnam's Sons.

Patton, M. Q. (1990). *Qualitative research and evaluative methods* (2nd edn). Newbury Park, CA: Sage.

Paxman, A., & Fernández, C. (2000). *El Tigre. Emilio Azcárraga y su imperio Televisa*. México, DF: Editorial Grijalbo, S.A.

Payne, J. G. (1989). Campaign '88: Mediated reality of the candidates and the race for the White House. *American Behavioral Scientist*, 32 (4).

Pease, T., Smith, E., & Subervi-Vélez, F.A. (2001). *The news and race models of excellence project. Overview: Connecting newsroom attitudes and news content*. Report to the Poynter Institute, St. Petersburg, FL.

Perlmutter, D. (ed.) (1999). *The Manship School guide to political communication*. Baton Rouge, LA: Louisiana State University Press.

Perloff, R. (1998). *Political communication: Politics, press, and public in America*. USA: Lawrence Erlbaum Associates.

Petrocik, J. R. (1996). Issue ownership in presidential elections, with a 1980 case study. *American Journal of Political Science*, 40: 825–850.

Petrocik, J. R., Benoit, W. L., & Hansen, G. J. (2003–04). Issue ownership and presidential campaigning, 1952–2000. *Political Science Quarterly*, 118 (4): 599–626.

Pfau, M., Holbert, R. L., Szabo, A., & Kaminski, K. (2002). Issue-advocacy versus candidate advertising: Effects on candidate preferences and democratic process. *Journal of Communication*, 52: 301–315.

Phillips, C. (1993). Black Entrepreneurship: Data Gap. *The Wall Street Journal*, February 19, 1993: R18.

Piatt, B. (1997). *Black and brown in America: The case for cooperation*. New York: New York University Press.

Pitt, L. (1966). *The decline of the Californios: A social history of Spanish-speaking Californians, 1848–1890*. Berkeley, CA: University of California Press.

Pitts, L. (2000a, September 18). (Television broadcast.) New York NY: CBS *The Early Show*.

Pitts, L. (2000b, October 30). (Television broadcast.) New York, NY: CBS *Morning News*.

Popkin, S. L. (1991). *The reasoning voter: Communication and persuasion in presidential campaigns*. Chicago: University of Chicago Press.

Poyo, G. E. (1984). Cuban communities in the United States: Toward an overview of the nineteenth century experience. In M. Uriarte-Gastón., & J. Cañas Martínez (eds.), *Cubans in the United States*: 44–64. Boston, MA: Center for the Study of the Cuban Community.

Pratt, M. G., & Foreman, P. O. (2000). Classifying managerial responses to multiple organizational identities. *Academy of Management Review*, 25: 18–42.

Presidential campaign activities of 1972 (1972). Executive session hearings before the select committee on Presidential campaign activities of the United States Senate. Ninety-Third congress, Second session. Watergate and related activities. Book 10. Phase II: Campaign Practices. Washington, DC: U.S. Government Printing Office.

Presidential campaign activities of 1972 (1972). Executive session hearings before the select committee on presidential campaign activities of the United States Senate. Ninety-Third Congress, Second Session. Watergate and related activities. Book 13. Phase III: Campaign Financing. Washington, DC: U.S. Government Printing Office.

Presidential campaign activities of 1972 (1972). Executive session hearings before the select committee on presidential campaign activities of the United States Senate. Ninety-Third Congress, Second Session. Watergate and related activities. Book 19. Use of incumbency—responsiveness program (additional documents). Washington, DC: US Government Printing Office.

Primeau, R. (1979). *The rhetoric of television*. New York: Longman.

Price, V., & Zaller, J. (1993). Who gets the news? Alternative measures of news reception and their implications for research. *Public Opinion Quarterly* 57: 133–164.

*Prometheus Radio Project v. Federal Communications Commission*, 373 F.3d 372 (3d Cir. 2004)

Project, H. V. (2004). *Total Spanish-language TV spending by market in the 2004 presidential election*. Washington, DC: Hispanic Voter Project.

Protess, D. & McCombs, M. (eds.) (1991). *Agenda setting: readings on media, public opinion, and policymaking.* Hillsdale, N.J.: Erlbaum.

Putnam, R. D. (2000). *Bowling alone: The collapse and revival of American community.* New York: Simon & Schuster.

Quiroga, J. (1995). *Hispanic voices: Is the press listening?* (Discussion Paper D-18). Cambridge, MA: Harvard University, Joan Shorenstein Center on the Press, Politics & Public Policy.

Quiroga, J. (1997). Hispanic voices: Is the press listening? In C. E. Rodríguez (ed.), *Latin looks: Images of Latinas and Latinos in the U.S. media:* 36–56). Boulder, CO: Westview.

Ramos, J. (2004). *The Latino wave: How Hispanics will elect the next American president* (E. E. Fitz, trans.) (2nd edn). NY: Rayo.

Ratzan, S. C. (1989). The real agenda setters. *American Behavioral Scientist,* 32 (4): 451–463.

Ray, M. L. (1982). *Advertising and communication management.* Englewood Cliffs, NJ: Prentice-Hall.

Rendón, A. B. (1974). The Chicano press. A status report on the needs and trends in Chicano journalism. Published mimeograph. Washington, DC.

Renz, B. (2006). The role of the ethnic media. In G. T. Meiss, & A. A. Tait (eds.), *Ethnic media in America: Building a system of their own* (1st edn, vol. 1). Dubuque: Kendall/Hunt.

Republican National Committee. *Hispanic Victory Initiative '84: A proposed strategy for the Reagan–Bush '84 Hispanic campaign.* (For further information about the accessibility of this document, please contact the principal author, Federico Subervi-Vélez.)

Riggins, S. H. (ed.) (1992). *Ethnic minority media. An international perspective.* Newbury Park, CA: Sage.

Ríos, D. I. (1993). *Mexican American audiences: A qualitative and quantitative study of ethnic subgroup uses for mass media.* Unpublished doctoral dissertation, The University of Texas at Austin.

Ríos, D., & Mohamed, A. N. (eds.) (2003). *Brown and black communication: Latino and African American conflict and convergence in mass media.* Westport, CT: Greenwood.

Ríos, H. (1972). Toward a true Chicano bibliography, (Pt. 2). *El Grito, A Journal of Contemporary Mexican-American Thought,* 5: 40–47.

Ríos, H., & Castillo, G. (1970). Toward a true Chicano bibliography, Mexican-American newspapers: 1848–1942. *El Grito, A Journal of Contemporary Mexican-American Thought,* 3: 17–24.

Roberts, D., & Bachen, C. (1982). Mass communications effects. *Mass Communications Review,* 3: 29–78.

Robinson, M. J. (1985). The media in campaign '84 (Pt. 2): Wingless, toothless and hopeless. In M. J. Robinson, & A. Ranney (eds.), *The mass media in campaign 84.* Washington, DC: American Enterprise Institute.

Robinson, M. J., & Sheehan, M. (1983). *Over the wire and on TV: CBS and UPI in campaign '80.* New York: Russell Sage.

Rodríguez, A. (1999). *Making Latino news: race, language, class.* Thousand Oaks, CA: Sage.

Rodríguez, C. (ed.) (1997). *Latin looks: Images of Latinas and Latinos in the U.S. media.* Boulder, CO: Westview Press.

Rodríguez, C. (2004). *Heroes, lovers, and others: The story of Latinos in Hollywood.* Washington, DC: Smithsonian Books.

Roscigno, V. J., & James, W. A. (1999). Race, cultural capital, and educational resources: Persistent inequalities and achievement returns. *Sociology of Education,* 72: 158–78.

Rose, E. D., & Fuchs, D. (1986). Reagan vs. Brown: A TV image playback. *Journal of Broadcasting,* 12 (3): 247–260.

Rosenstiel, T. (1993). *Strange bedfellows: How television and the presidential candidates changed American politics, 1992.* New York: The Hyperion.

Rosenstone, S. J., & Hansen, J. M. (1993). *Mobilization, participation, and democracy in America.* NY: Macmillan.

Roslow, P., & Nicholls, J. A. (1996). Targeting the Hispanic market: Comparative persuasion of TV commercials in Spanish and English. *Journal of Advertising Research:* 67–76.

Royce, A. P. (1982). *Ethnic identity. Strategies of diversity.* Bloomington, IN: Indiana University Press.

Rudd, R. (1986). Issues as image in political campaign commercials. *The Western Journal of Speech Communication,* 50: 102–118.

Rust, R., Bajaj, M., & Haley, G. (1984). Efficient and inefficient media for political campaign advertising. *Journal of Advertising,* 13 (3): 45–49.

Saad, L. (1998, December 31). Admiration for Hillary Clinton surges in 1998. Gallup News Service (Online). http://www.gallup.com/poll/4108/Admiration_Hillary_Clinton_Surges_1998.asp.

Sabato, L. (1991). *Feeding frenzy: How attack journalism has transformed American politics.* New York: Free Press.

Salwen, M. B., & Soruco, G. R. (1997). The Hispanic Americans. In B. A. D. Keever, C. Martindale and M. A. Weston (eds.), *U.S. News coverage of racial minorities: A sourcebook, 1934–1996:* 147–190). Westport, CN, Greenwood Press.

Sánchez Korrol, V. (1994). *From colonia to community: the history of Puerto Ricans in New York City.* Berkeley, CA: University of California Press.

Santa Ana, O. (2002). *Brown tide rising. Metaphors of Latinos in contemporary American public discourse.* Austin, TX: University of Texas Press.

Santillán, R. (1973). *Chicano politics: La raza unida.* Los Angeles, CA: Tlaquilo Publications.

Santillán, R. (1988). The Latino community in state and congressional redistricting. In F. C. García (ed.), *Latinos and the political system:* 328–348. University of Notre Dame, Indiana.

Santillán, R., & Subervi-Vélez, F. A. (1991). Latino politics in Republican Party politics in California. In B. O. Jackson & M. B. Preston (eds.), *Racial and ethnic politics in California:* 285–319. Berkeley, CA: Institute of Governmental Studies.

Schaefer, R. (1979). *Racial and ethnic groups.* Boston: Little Brown.

Schaefer, R. (2006). *Race and ethnicity in the United States* (4th edn). Upper Saddle River, N.J.: Pearson/Prentice Hall.

Schiffman, M., & Subervi-Vélez, F. A. (2002). Targeting the Latino vote in 2000.

Part I: The construction of Latinos and Latino issues. In M.J. Collier (ed.), *Transforming communication about culture: Critical new directions. International and intercultural communication annual*, vol. 24: 162–188. Thousand Oaks, CA: Sage.

Schudson, M. (1978). *Discovering the news: a social history of American newspapers.* NY: Basic Books.

Schudson, M. (1995). *The power of news.* Cambridge, MA: Harvard.

Scott, C. (1997). Identification with multiple targets in a geographically dispersed organization. *Management Communication Quarterly*, 10: 491–522.

Scott, S. G., & Lane, V. R. (2000). A stakeholder approach to organizational identity. *Academy of Management Review*, 25: 43–62.

Seder, D. (1986). Film vs. tape: Choosing a format for political television Ads. *Campaigns and Elections*, July–August, 1986: 9–12.

Segal, A. (2003). *The Hispanic priority: The Spanish-language television battle for the Hispanic vote in the 2000 U.S. presidential election.* Hispanic Voter Project, John Hopkins University, Washington DC. January 2003. http://www.jhu.edu/advanced/government/hvp.

Segal, A. (2004). *Presidential Spanish-language political television advertising set records in early primaries.* John Hopkins University's Washington Center for the Study of American Government. Washington, DC.

Severin, W. J., & Tankard, J. W. J. (2001). *Communication theories* (5th edn). New York, NY: Addison Wesley Longman.

Shearer, J. F. (1954). Periódicos españoles en los Estados Unidos. *Revista Hispánica Moderna*, 20: 45–57.

Shoemaker, P., Reese, S., & Danielson, W. (1985a). *Media in ethnic context* (published monograph). The University of Texas at Austin, Department of Journalism.

Shoemaker, P., Reese S., & Danielson, W. (1985b). Spanish-language print media use as an indicator of acculturation. *Journalism Quarterly*, 62 (4): 734–740

Shyles, L. (1983). Defining the issues of a presidential election from televised political spot advertisements. *Journal of Broadcasting*, 27 (4): 333.

Shyles, L. (1984a). Defining images of presidential candidates from televised political spot advertisements. *Political Behavior*, 6: 171–181.

Shyles, L. (1984b). The relationships of images, issues, and presentational methods in televised spot advertisements for 1980's American presidential primaries. *Journal of Broadcasting*, 28 (4): 405–421.

Shyles, L. (1986). The televised political spot advertisement: Its structure, content and role in the political system. In L. L. Kaid., D. Nimmo & K. Sanders (eds.), *New perspectives on political advertising.* Carbondale: Southern Illinois University Press.

Shyles, L. (1991). Issue content and legitimacy in 1988 televised political advertising: Hubris and synecdoche in promoting presidential candidates. In F. Biocca (ed.), *Television and political advertising: Vol 2. Signs, codes, and images*: 133–162. Hillsdale, NJ: Lawrence Erlbaum Associates.

Sigelman, L., & Bullock, D. (1991). Candidates, issues, horse races, and hoopla: presidential campaign coverage, 1888–1988. *American Politics Quarterly*, 19 (1): 5–32.

Simpson, C. (2000). (Television broadcast transcript.) September 26, 2000. New York, NY: ABC *World News Now*.

*Sinclair Broadcasting, Inc. v. FCC*, 284 F. 3rd 148 (D.C. Circ. 2002).

Smoller, F. (1998). Latino politics: Local republicans should take a road. *Los Angeles Times* (Orange County edn), May 17, 1998: B9.

Sorkin, A. R. (2001). Televisa NBC is paying $1.98 billion for Telemundo. *The New York Times*, October 12, 2001: C1.

Sorkin, A. R. & Edmonton, P. (2006). Televisa Group May Still Pursue Univisión. *The New York Times*, September 12, 2006: C4.

Soruco, G. (1996). *The Cuban exiles of southern Florida and the mass media: The struggle of culture*. Gainesville, FL: University of Florida Press.

Sosa, L. (1998). *El sueño americano: cómo los latinos pueden triunfar en Estados Unidos*. New York: Dutton.

Sosa, L. (1998). *The Americano dream: How Latinos can achieve success in business and in life*. New York: Dutton.

Sosa, L. (2006). *Think and grow rich: A Latino choice*. New York: Ballantine Books.

Southwest Voter Research Notes, vol. 1. no. 2., November 1986.

Stempel, G. H., & Windhauser, J. H. (1991). *The media in the 1984 and 1988 presidential campaigns*. Westport, CT: Greenwood.

Stevens, D., Alger, D., Allen, B., & Sullivan, J. (2006). Local news coverage in a social capital: Election 2000 on Minnesota's local news stations. *Political Communication*, 23: 61–83.

Strategy Research Corporation (1991). *U.S. Hispanic market, 1991*. Miami, FL: Author.

Stratton, P. A. (1969). *The territorial press of New Mexico, 1834–1912*. Albuquerque: University of New Mexico Press.

Strauss, A., & Corbin, J. (1990). *Basics of qualitative research: grounded theory procedures and techniques*. Newbury Park, CA: Sage.

Subervi, F., & Eusebio, H. (2005). Latino media: A cultural connection. In E. del Valle (ed.), *Hispanic Marketing and Public Relations: Understanding and targeting America's largest minority*: 285–325. Boca Raton, FL: Poyeen Publishing.

Subervi, F., & Ríos, D. (2005). Latino identity and situational Latinidad. In E. del Valle (ed.), *Hispanic marketing and public relations: Understanding and targeting America's largest minority*: 29–46. Boca Raton, FL: Poyeen Publishing.

Subervi, F. with Torres, J. & Montalvo, D. collaborators (2004). *Network Brownout 2004: The portrayal of Latinos in network television news, 2003*. National Association of Hispanic Journalists, Austin, TX, and Washington, DC.

Subervi, F. with Torres, J. & Montalvo, D. collaborators (2005). *Network Brownout 2005: The portrayal of Latinos in network television news, 2004, with a retrospect to 1995*. National Association of Hispanic Journalists, Austin, TX, and Washington, DC.

Subervi-Vélez, F. A. (1984). *Hispanics, the mass media, and politics: Assimilation vs. pluralism*. Unpublished doctoral dissertation, University of Wisconsin, Madison.

Subervi-Vélez, F. A. (1986). The mass media and ethnic assimilation and pluralism. A review and research proposal with special focus on Hispanics. *Communication Research*, 13 (1): 71–96.

Subervi-Vélez, F. A. (1988). Spanish-language daily newspapers and the 1984 elections. *Journalism Quarterly*, 65 (3): 678–685.

Subervi-Vélez, F. A. (1992). Republican and democratic mass communication strategies: Targeting the Latino vote. In R. O. de la Garza & L. DeSipio (eds.), *From rhetoric to reality: Latino politics in the 1988 elections*: 23–42. Boulder: Westview Press.

Subervi-Vélez, F. A. (2006). Los medios de comunicación latinos en Estados Unidos: Categorías y funciones. In D. González-Sasanova (ed.), *Los mexicanos de aquí y de allá: Problemas communes*: 199–216). Memoria del Segundo Foro de Reflexión Binacional. Mexico, DF: Fundación Solidaridad Mexicano Americana.

Subervi-Vélez, F. A., Báez, J., & Saenz, N. (2005). News networks. In S. Oboler & D. González (eds.), *The Encyclopedia of Latinos and Latinas in the United States*: 265–266. NY: Oxford University Press

Subervi-Vélez, F. A., & Connaughton, S. L. (1999). Targeting the Latino vote: The Democratic Party's 1996 mass communication strategy. In R. O. de la Garza & L. DeSipio (eds.), *Awash in the mainstream: Latino politics in the 1996 elections*: 47–71. Boulder: Westview Press.

Subervi-Vélez, F. A., Herrera, R., & Begay, M. (1987). Toward and understanding of the role of the mass media in Latino political life. *Social Science Quarterly*, 68 (1): 185–196.

Subervi-Vélez, F. A., Ramirez Berg, C., Constantakis-Valdés, P., Noriega, C., Ríos, D., & Wilkinson, K. (1994). Mass communication and Hispanics. In F. Padilla (ed.), *Handbook of Hispanic cultures in the United States: Sociology*: 304–357. Houston, TX: Arte Público Press.

Suro, R. (2004, April 19). *Changing channels and crisscrossing cultures: A survey of Latinos and the news media*. Washington, DC: Pew Hispanic Center (http://pewhispanic.org).

Suro, R., Fry, R., & Jeffrey, P. (2005). *Hispanics and the 2004 election: Population, electorate and voters*. Washington, DC: Pew Hispanic Center.

Takaki, R. (ed.) (1994). *From different shores. Perspectives on race and ethnicity in America* (2nd edn). New York: Oxford University Press.

Takeshita, T. (2002). Expanding attribute agenda setting into framing: An application of the problematic situation scheme, *International Communication Association*. Seoul, Korea.

Tan, A. (1981). Political participation, defense support, and perceptions of political efficacy as predictors of mass media use. *Communication Monographs*, 48 (2): 133–145.

Tan, A. (1983). Media use and political orientations of ethnic groups. *Journalism Quarterly*, 60 (1): 126–132.

Taylor, C. R., Lee, J. Y., & Stern, B. B. (1995). Portrayals of African, Hispanic, and Asian Americans in magazine advertising. *American Behavioral Scientist*, 38 (4): 608–621.

Taylor, P. (1928–1934). *Mexican Labor in the United States*, (3 vols.). Berkeley, CA: University of California Press.

Telemundo (2004, January 6). (Press release.) *Maria Celeste Arraras en debate presidencial junto a Lester Holt de MSNBC*. Miami, FL. www.nbcumv.com/telemundo/release_detail.nbc/telemundo-sp200401060000000-mariacelestearrarasen.html.

Telemundo (2004, January 15.) (Press release.) *El debate presidencial co-presentado por Maria Celeste Arraras aumento los ratings de la television por cable.* Miami, FL. www.nbcumv.com/telemundo/release_detail.nbc/telemundo-sp20040115095858-eldebatepresidencialco.html.

Telemundo (2004, October 13). (Press release.) *Telemundo continues its commitment to the U.S. Hispanic community by airing the final presidential debate live and without commercial interruption.* Miami, FL. http://www.nbcumv.com/telemundo/release_detail.en.nbc/telemundo-2004101363129-telemundocontinues.html)

Telemundo (2004, October 20). (Press release.) *Aviso a los medios: Pedro Sevcec entrevista al Presidente Bush.* Miami, FL. www.nbcumv.com/telemundo/release_detail.nbc/telemundo-20041020000000-avisoalosmedios.html.

Telemundo (2004, October 21). (Press release.) *Telemundo anuncia su cobertura para las elecciones presidenciales Decision 2004.* Miami, FL. www.nbcumv.com/telemundo/release_detail.nbc/telemundo-20041021000000-telemundoanunciasu.html

Telemundo (2004, October 28). (Press release.) *Telemundo continúa ofreciendo la mejor y más completa cobertura en español de las elecciones presidenciales.* Miami, FL. www.nbcumv.com/telemundo/release_detail.nbc/telemundo-20041028000000-telemundocontinuao.html.

Tichenor, P. J., Donohue, G. A., & Olien, C. N. (1980). *Community conflict and the press.* Beverly Hills, CA: Sage.

Tienda, M., & Mitchell, F. (2006). *Multiple origins, common destinies: Hispanics and the American future.* Washington, DC: National Academies Press.

Tomás Rivera Center, The. (1996). *The Latino vote at mid-decade.* Claremont, CA: Author.

Torres, L. M. (1997). *Puerto Rican discourse: A sociolinguistic study of a New York suburb.* Mahwah, NJ: Lawrence Earlbaum Associates.

Treadwill, D. F., & Harrison, T. M. (1994). Conceptualizing and assessing organizational image: Model images, commitment, and communication. *Communication Monographs*, 61: 63–85.

Tucker, D. E. (1959). Broadcasting in the 1956 Oregon senatorial campaign. *Journal of Broadcasting*, 3: 225–243.

Turk, J. V., Richstad J., Bryson R. L. Jr., & Johnson S. M. (1989). Hispanic Americans in the news in two Southwestern cities. *Journalism Quarterly*, 66 (1): 107–115.

U.S. Census Bureau (1991). *The Hispanic population in the United States: March 1991.* Washington, DC: U.S. Government Printing Office.

U.S. Census Bureau (1995). Hispanic-Latinos: Diverse people in a multicultural society. Washington, DC: U.S. Government Printing Office.

U.S. Census Bureau (1997). *National population projections.* http://www.census.gov/population/www/projections/natproj.html.

U.S. Census Bureau (2005). *National population projections.* http://www.census.gov/population/www/projections/natproj.html.

U.S. Kerner Commission (1968). *Report of the National Advisory Commission on Civil Disorders.* Washington, DC: U.S. Government Printing Office.

Univisión. *The Hispanic Vote: The tool kit.* (2004) [CD-ROM Univisión].

Univisión (2004, April 13). [Press release] *Understanding the voting power of*

*Hispanics* Miami, FL. http://www.univision.net/corp/es/pr/Los_Angeles_ 13042004-3.html.

Univisión (2005, February 17). [Press release] *Univisión network rivals ABC, CBS, and NBC in quantity and focus of campaign coverage* Los Angeles, CA. http:://pewhispanic.org/newsroom/releases/release.php?RealiaseID=19.

Valdés, M. I. (2000). *Marketing to American Latinos: A guide to the in-culture approach. Part I & Part II.* Ithaca, NY: Paramount Market Publishers.

Valdés, M. I., & Seoane, M. H. (1996). *Hispanic market handbook.* Detroit, MI: Gale Research Inc.

Valdés y Tapia, D. (1976). *Hispanos and American politics.* New York: Arno Press.

Valentino, N. A. (1999). Crime news and the priming of racial attitudes during evaluations of the President. *Public Opinion Quarterly,* 60(4): 515–41.

Vargas, L., & de Pyssler, B. (1999). U.S. Latino newspapers as health communication resources: A content analysis. *The Howard Journal of Communications,* 10 (3): 189–205.

Varo, C. (1973). *Radiografía de un pueblo asediado.* Río Piedras, Puerto Rico: Ediciones Puerto.

Veciana-Suárez, A. (1987). *Hispanic media, USA.* Washington, DC: The Media Institute.

Veciana-Suárez, A. (1990). *Hispanic media: Impact and influence.* Washington, DC: The Media Institute.

Verba, S., & Nie, N. H. (1972). *Participation in America.* New York: Harper & Row.

Vidal, D. (1980). The strange case of Reverend Moon and his new paper in New York. *Washington Journalism Review,* November 1980: 28–29.

Vigil, M. (1978). *Chicano politics.* Washington, DC: University Press of America.

Vigil, M. (1987). *Hispanics in American politics. In search for political power.* Washington, DC: University Press of America.

Vigil, M. (1988). Hispanics gain seats in the 98th Congress after reapportionment. In F. C. García (ed.), *La causa política. A Chicano politics reader:* 275–290). Notre Dame, IN: University of Notre Dame Press.

Vigil, M. (1997). Hispanics in the 103rd congress: The 1990 census, reapportionment, redistricting, and the 1992 elections. In F. C. García (ed.), *Pursuing power Latinos and the political system:* 234–264. Notre Dame, IN: University of Notre Dame Press.

Villareal, R. E., Hernández, N. G., & Neighbor, H. D. (1988). *Latino empowerment. Progress, problems, and prospects.* New York: Greenwood.

Villescas, J. (2002). *Framing the Latino vote: Content analysis of ABC, CBS, NBC, and CNN news coverage of Latino issues during the 2000 presidential campaign.* Unpublished master's thesis, University of Texas at Austin.

Vitucci, J. (1999). Hispanic purchasing power remains strong. *Hispanic Business,* December 1999: 72.

Wagner, H. R. (1937). New Mexico Spanish press. *New Mexico Historical Review,* 12: 1–40.

Wagner, J. (1983). Media do make a Difference: The differential impact of mass media in the 1976 presidential race. *American Journal of Political Science,* 27 (3): 407

Waisath, J. P. (2002). The agenda-setting effects of Hispanic candidates in the

2002 primary election for Texas governor. University of Texas at Austin, Austin, TX.

Weaver, D. (Ed.) (1981). *Media agenda-setting in a presidential election: issues, images, and interest*. New York. Praeger.

Weber, D. (1973). *Foreigners in their native land: Historical roots of the Mexican Americans*. Albuquerque: University of New Mexico Press.

Welch, S., & Hibbing, J. R. (1988). Hispanic representation in the U.S. Congress. In F. C. García (ed.), *La causa política. A Chicano politics reader*: 291–299. Notre Dame, IN: University of Notre Dame Press.

Weyr, T. (1988). *Hispanic U.S.A. Breaking the melting pot*. New York: Harper & Row.

West, D. M. (1997). *Air wars: Television advertising in election campaigns, 1952–1992*, (2nd edn). Washington, D. C.: Congressional Quarterly.

Whisler, K., & Nuiry, O. (1999). *The 1999 national Hispanic media directory*. Arkansas City, AR: Gilliland Printing, Inc.

White House 2000. (2000). Bush says campaign could very well end in NH. January 14, 2000. Retrieved from http://hotlineblog.nationaljournal.com/

Williams, S. (2005). Market slump or long-term trend? *Hispanic Business*. December 2005: 22–24.

Wilson, C. C., Jr., & Gutiérrez, F. F. (1985). *Minorities and media. Diversity and the end of mass communication*. Newbury Park, CA: Sage.

Wilson, C. C., Jr., & Gutiérrez, F. F. (1995). *Race, multiculturalism, and the media: The rise of class communication in multicultural America*. Thousand Oaks, CA: Sage.

Wilson, C. C., Jr., Gutiérrez, F. F., & Chao, L. (2003). *Race, sexism, and the media: From mass to class communication*. Thousand Oaks, CA: Sage.

Winter, J. P., & Eyal, C. H. (1981). Agenda setting for the civil right issue. *The Public Opinion Quarterly*, 45(3): 376–383. www.algore.com (available during the 2000 campaign) www.bush2000.com (available during the 2000 campaign) www.hispanictrends.com.

York, A. (n.d). Viva Iowa. Retrieved on October 25, 1999 from http://www.salon.com/news/feature/1999/10/25/bush.

York, A. (n.d.). Drop the Chalupa, Al Gore. Retrieved on November 19, 1999 from http://www.salon.com/news/feature/1999/11/19/gop/index.html

Zate, M. (1996, December). Media buyers raise the stakes: Top 50 advertisers invest $332 million to reach Hispanic consumers, TV spending skyrockets. *Hispanic Business*, December 1996: 46–47.

Zmud, J. (1992). *Ethnic identity, language, and mass communication: An empirical investigation of assimilation among United States Hispanics*. Unpublished doctoral dissertation. University of Southern California.

# INDEX

Page numbers in *italics* indicate figures and tables.